Global Tourism

SOCIETY FOR ECONOMIC
ANTHROPOLOGY (SEA) MONOGRAPHS

Lisa Cliggett, University of Kentucky
General Editor, Society for Economic Anthropology

Monographs for the Society for Economic Anthropology contain original essays that explore the connections between economics and social life. Each year's volume focuses on a different theme in economic anthropology. Earlier volumes were published with the University Press of America, Inc. (#1–15, 17) and Rowman & Littlefield Publishers, Inc. (#16). The monographs are now published jointly by AltaMira Press and the Society for Economic Anthropology (https://seawiki.wikidot.com).

No. 18   Jean Ensminger, ed., *Theory in Economic Anthropology*
No. 19   Jeffrey H. Cohen and Norbert Dannhaeuser, eds., *Economic Development: An Anthropological Approach*
No. 20   Gracia Clark, ed., *Gender at Work in Economic Life*
No. 21   Cynthia Werner and Duran Bell, eds., *Values and Valuables: From the Sacred to the Symbolic*
No. 22   Lillian Trager, ed., *Migration and Economy: Global and Local Dynamics*
No. 23   E. Paul Durrenberger and Judith Martí, eds., *Labor in Cross-Cultural Perspective*
No. 24   Richard Wilk, ed., *Fast Food/Slow Food*
No. 25   Lisa Cliggett and Christopher A. Pool, eds., *Economies and the Transformation of Landscape*
No. 26   Katherine E. Browne and B. Lynne Milgram, eds., *Economics and Morality: Anthropological Approaches*
No. 27   Eric C. Jones and Arthur D. Murphy, eds., *The Political Economy of Hazards and Disasters*
No. 28   Robert C. Marshall, ed., *Cooperation in Economy and Society*
No. 29   Walter E. Little and Patricia A. McAnany, eds., *Textile Economies: Power and Value from the Local to the Transnational*
No. 30   Sarah Lyon and E. Christian Wells, eds., *Global Tourism: Cultural Heritage and Economic Encounters*

To find more books in this series, go to www.altamirapress.com/series.

Global Tourism

Cultural Heritage
and Economic Encounters

Edited by Sarah Lyon
and E. Christian Wells

A division of
ROWMAN & LITTLEFIELD PUBLISHERS, INC.
Lanham • New York • Toronto • Plymouth, UK

Published by AltaMira Press
A division of Rowman & Littlefield Publishers, Inc.
A wholly owned subsidary of The Rowman & Littlefield Publishing Group, Inc.
4501 Forbes Boulevard, Suite 200, Lanham, Maryland 20706
http://www.altamirapress.com

10 Thornbury Road, Plymouth PL6 7PP, United Kingdom

British Library Cataloguing in Publication Information Available

Library of Congress Cataloging-in-Publication Data
Global tourism : cultural heritage and economic encounters / edited by Sarah
Lyon and E. Christian Wells.
     p. cm. — (Society for economic anthropology (SEA) monographs no.30)
   Includes index.
   ISBN 978-0-7591-2091-4 (cloth : alk. paper) — ISBN 978-0-7591-2093-8
(electronic)
   1. Heritage tourism. 2. Culture and globalization. 3. Economic anthropology.
I. Lyon, Sarah II. Wells, E. Christian.
   G156.5.H47G56 2012
   910—dc23   2011048746

Printed in the United States of America

Contents

List of Figures

1

✛

Ethnographies of Global Tourism

Cultural Heritage, Economic Encounters, and the Redefinition of Impact

Sarah Lyon and E. Christian Wells

Global tourism is perhaps the largest-scale movement of goods, services, and people in human history. Consequently, it has been (and continues to be) a significant catalyst for economic development and sociopolitical change (Stronza 2001). According to the United Nations World Tourism Organization (2010), international tourist arrivals in 2009 totaled 880 million and generated U.S. $852 billion in receipts, representing 6 percent of worldwide exports and 30 percent of worldwide services exports. Moreover, international arrivals are projected to top U.S. $1.6 billion annually by the year 2020 (UNWTO 2001). The worldwide economic growth of this industry significantly outpaces gross domestic product (GDP) growth. While the United States, France, and Spain consistently lead in arrivals and receipts, China represents the fastest-growing sector over the past decade. Although these figures are impressive, they represent a decline of roughly 4 percent from 2008, indicating that international tourism demand depends strongly on global economic conditions in generating markets.

While tourism increasingly accounts for ever-greater segments of national economies, the consequences of this growth for intercultural interaction are diverse and uncertain. The proliferation of tourists also challenges classic theoretical descriptions of just what an economy is.

What are the commodities being consumed? What is the division of labor between producers and consumers in creating the value of tourist exchanges? How do culture, power, and history shape these interactions? What are the prospects for sustainable tourism? How do tourists and stakeholders around the world shape cultural heritage? These critical questions inspired this volume, in which the contributors explore the connections among economy, sustainability, heritage, and identity that tourism and related processes make explicit.

The goal of this volume is to move beyond the limits of geographical discussions, case studies, and best-practice examples—investigations that have been recently deemed "stale, tired, repetitive and lifeless" (Franklin and Crang 2001:5), with "limited additional scientific value" (Oppermann 2000:145; see also Franklin 2007; Hall, Williams, and Lew 2004; Xiao and Smith 2007). Within anthropology, Castañeda (1996) forcefully argues that such studies assume that "locals" are objects lacking agency and obscure the key forces shaping social reality. Furthermore, as Stronza (2001) points out, much of the existing research is bifurcated between a focus on the origins of tourism centering on tourists and a focus on the impacts of tourism analyzing locals.

As a result of increased global interconnectedness, the differences between everyday spaces and tourism places have increasingly become blurred. Tourists, objects, and information compose tourismscapes in a nonlinear and two-sided way: tourists and images travel from generating markets (which are also destinations in their own right) to destination regions (which also generate flows) and back (Franklin 2003; Van der Duim 2007). In recent years, more nuanced theoretical understandings of tourism have emerged within anthropology and beyond. For example, Burns (2004) argues for a systems approach to tourism, emphasizing its interconnectedness with political, economic, social, and natural environments. Similarly, Babb (2010, 2004) conceptualizes tourism as a set of cultural practices under constant negotiation that may illuminate broader social and historical processes.

The contributions in this volume ethnographically explore with rich detail the global flows and translocal processes characterizing contemporary tourism. Each of the chapters explores different dimensions of tourism mobilities, such as the unfettered financial flows made possible by the conditions of late capitalism, transnational circuits that blur the increasingly arbitrary distinction between tourists and migrants, concerns over the environmental by-products of tourism (such as carbon emissions), and the experience of immobility in an increasingly globalized and interconnected world. The volume is organized according to three overarching themes: exploring dimensions of cultural heritage, the complex nature of economic encounters in touristic spheres, and the multifaceted impacts of tourism on both hosts and guests. While based on ethnographic and archaeological research conducted in distinct locations, the contributors' conclusions and theoretical arguments reach far beyond the limits of isolated case studies. Together they contribute to a new synthesis for the anthropology of tourism while simultaneously demonstrating how emerging theories of the economics of tourism and cultural heritage can lead to the rethinking of traditionally nontouristic domains—from spirituality to reproduction.

GLOBAL FLOWS AND "TOURISMSCAPES": RETHINKING THE ECONOMICS OF TOURISM AND HERITAGE

Research on tourism has moved far beyond the collective representations of international tourism, which Crick (2002:16) refers to as the "four Ss"—sun, sex, sea, and sand—that once characterized scholarship on tourism in the social sciences. Franklin and Crang (2001) argue that tourism can no longer be viewed as a specialist consumer product or a mode of consumption. Rather, "Tourism has broken away from its beginning as a relatively minor and ephemeral ritual of modern life to become a significant modality through which transnational modern life is organized" (Franklin and Crang 2001:7). As a result, tourism can no longer be bounded as a discrete activity, tidily contained in specific locations and delineated periods of time. Tourism encompasses more than simple leisure activity—it is also a global business consumed at a local level and a condition of postmodernism shaping the world we live in. This version of life and culture, which Urry (2001) describes as a "shift from solid, fixed modernity" to a much more fluid and hyper "liquid modernity" characterized by bodies on the move and traveling cultures, emphasizes the idea that the "flows and scapes" (Appadurai 1996) of tourism cannot be disaggregated from globalization as a complex social phenomenon (Burns and Novelli 2008).

The contributions to this volume reflect an emerging mobility paradigm in tourism and cultural heritage studies. As Sheller and Urry write (2006:214):

> A clear distinction is often drawn between places and those travelling to such places. Places are seen as pushing or pulling people to visit. Places are presumed to be relatively fixed, given, and separate from those visiting. The new mobility paradigm argues against this ontology of distinct "places" and "people." Rather, there is a complex relationality of places and persons connected through performances.

A focus on tourism mobilities moves us away from the preoccupation with the tourist and travels to distant lands and recognizes instead the interconnected movements of a range of individuals, including leisure shoppers, second-home owners, entrepreneurial migrants, business travelers, students, and a host of other people voluntarily on the move (Gale 2008). This more nuanced approach to tourism is reflected in many of the chapters in the present volume. For example, Speier's contribution (chapter 11) explores the motivations and experiences of reproductive "tourists" whose quest for parenthood, rather than simple leisure, brings them to the Czech Republic in search of donor eggs and a comfortable, culturally rich environment in which to relax after their in vitro fertilization (IVF) treatments.

Importantly, the concept of tourism mobilities presupposes its opposite—immobility. In a globalizing world that celebrates the free flow of capital, ideas, products, and bodies, it is easy to be seduced by the notion that everyone and everything is on the move. However, anthropological attention to the details of lived experiences in diverse locales clearly demonstrates that the very processes that have enhanced the mobility of some people have merely served to highlight and reinforce the immobility of others (Gale 2008; Hannam et al. 2006). In arguing for a focus on tourism mobilities rather than static examinations of tourists and destinations, this volume also explicitly engages with critiques of mobile forms of subjectivity, such as Ahmed's (2002:462) argument that the "idealization of movement, or transformation of movement into a fetish, depends upon the exclusion of others who are already positioned as *not free in the same way*" (original emphasis) and Skeggs's (2004:49) related assertion that "mobility and control over mobility both reflect and reinforce power. Mobility is a resource to which not everyone has an equal relationship." For example, Maxwell's research (chapter 6) on the indigenous vendors who live on the Inca Trail and their interactions with the stream of hikers who pass by their front doors each season eloquently describes the experience of being fixed in space, surrounded by flows of wealthier, more mobile others. However, as she demonstrates, the experience of immobility is not necessarily equated with lack of agency, as the trail residents turn heritage tourism on its head by socially constructing hikers themselves as a resource.

Importantly, the tourism mobilities paradigm promotes an examination of the interrelationships between tourism and migration (Hall and Williams 2002). For example, Coles and Timothy (2004) observe that diasporas precipitate a number of different modes of travel and tourism inspired by the collision between migration histories (their "routes"), their attachment to the "home" country (their "roots"), and their experiences of and in the host country (their "routine") (see also Hall and Tucker 2004).

In this volume, these complex and overlapping links between tourism and migration are explored in Delaney and Rivera's contribution (chapter 8), which illustrates the ways in which Tongan migrants participate in ongoing forms of generalized reciprocity with their family members who remain on the island of Tonga. Returning Tongans, who regularly send remittances home, are rewarded by their island friends and relatives with the opportunity to "become Tongan again," to claim their place in Tongan society, and to reinvigorate their sense of identity as Tongans through their travels. Relatedly, in his examination of tourism development, cultural heritage, and bureaucratic conflict at two destinations in China, Shepherd's contribution to the volume (chapter 4) illustrates the complex negotiations of identity and state development goals that exist in a country where two distinct stakeholder groups have recently become mobile: the marginalized peasant class and affluent urban residents with the disposable income and leisure time to tour. Shepherd demonstrates that what links these two forms of spatial movement is not simply economic development but also the development of a modern, "civilized" sensibility that the government believes will be fostered through domestic tourism.

Finally, a focus on tourism mobilities entails a concern for the by-products of tourism, such as greenhouse gas emissions from jet aircraft and motor vehicles as well as threats to biosecurity arising from certain tourist flows (Gale 2008). The ways in which tourists and stakeholders in tourism-based economies conceptualize and attempt to mitigate these by-products have only recently become the subject of social scientific attention. Therefore, Isenhour's research (chapter 10) on middle-class Swedish consumers' attempts to lower or justify their carbon emissions from international travel (and consequently their personal ecological footprint) represents a significant contribution. Isenhour finds that, for environmentally conscious Swedish residents, international travel is one of the most difficult things to relinquish because it is intimately tied to social status and cultural capital in a society that celebrates an egalitarian ethos.

Another, more frequently noted, by-product of tourism relates to the diverse and complex consequences of cultural commodification, a topic that several of the chapters in this volume explicitly engage. As anthropologists have noted, commodifying the cross-cultural experience in the tourism setting problematizes the divide between what is thought possible to buy and sell as a quantitative, monetary value is placed on culture, which is believed to have qualitative value (Bunten 2008). As Appadurai (1986:380) points out, the development of mass international tourism during the course of the twentieth century has contributed to the disaggregation of traditional trade systems, gift systems, and markets "bringing about the commoditization of an ever wider range of things and activities." As the chapters by Salazar (chapter 2) and Figueroa and colleagues (chapter 3) demonstrate, the translocal politics of heritage management and promotion can have unintended by-products, including conflicts between externally represented cultural values and locally imagined meanings and identities. Similarly, the chapters by Medina (chapter 12) and Luque and colleagues (chapter 13) illustrate the profound impacts of environmental commodification as ecotourism initiatives shape stakeholder identities in highly specific ways. Finally, contributions by Huberman (chapter 5), Greene (chapter 9), and others explore the processes (and by-products) of self-commodification in the tourism and heritage industries. Together, their studies support Bunten's (2008) claim that self-commodification is a dual process: both an economic response to the global expansion of the service sector and a politically motivated expression of identity.

While each of the contributions to this volume is rooted in place-specific, case-study research, considered together they speak to the power of tourismscapes to influence both daily life around the world *and* translocal flows of capital, culture, and ideas. The concept of tourismscapes represents a broadening of Appadurai's (1996) theory of the global cultural flows shaping the contemporary social imaginary. Tourismscapes are actor-networks consisting of relations between people and things within and across different societies and regions. The main constituents of tourismscapes include people, those using tourism services and the people and organizations providing them, and an array of networked objects (media, machines, and technologies) that structure, define, and configure interaction. Tourismscapes do not endure by themselves—they need constant performance, maintenance, and repair (Van der Duim 2007). As the chapters in this volume demonstrate, understanding travel and heritage in a global world through the lens of tourismscapes contributes to an understanding of power as a phenomenon that can be grasped only relationally, rather than as a "thing" that can be possessed by people (Cheong and Miller 2000; Clegg 2003; Van der Duim 2007).

PART I: CULTURAL HERITAGE

Interrogating the promise and potential of heritage sites for tourism, the contributions to the volume's first section on "Cultural Heritage" follow three main themes: contested values and economies, struggles with notions of authenticity and indigeneity, and the role of state support and intervention. It is estimated that between 35 and 40 percent of tourism today represents cultural tourism or heritage tourism (UNWTO 2006). As an alternative to mass tourism, cultural and heritage tourism offer opportunities for place-based engagement that frames contexts for interaction with the "lived space" and "everyday life" (Lefebvre 1974) of other peoples as well as sites and objects of global historical significance. One of the major engines for growth in this sector has been the United Nations Educational Scientific and Cultural Organization (UNESCO), which, since 1972, has designated (and financially underwritten) World Heritage Sites—properties that UNESCO sees as having "outstanding universal value." As of 2010, there were 911 properties on the list, a number that continues to increase each year. Such sites include cultural (704), natural (180), and mixed (27) properties spanning 151 nation-states across the globe.

While many recent studies from the commerce sector of cultural heritage sites, such as those on the UNESCO list, tout the economic benefits to local communities as well as the preservation and celebration of heritage and identity (e.g., Hall et al. 2005; Wahab and Pigram 1997), some researchers question these assumptions and provide convincing case studies to the contrary (e.g., Jamal and Robinson 2009; Richards 2007; Silverman and Ruggles 2007; Smith and Robinson 2006). The contributors to this volume's first section find that values, heritage, indigeneity, and economy are contested issues that often do not always result in economic development benefitting local communities or the protection or preservation of cultural heritage. For example, in chapter 2, "Shifting Values and Meanings of Heritage: From Cultural Appropriation to Tourism Interpretation and Back," Noel B. Salazar considers the shifting meanings and values of heritage in central Java by exploring heritage policymaking and management around the Prambanan complex, a UNESCO World Heritage Site and one of the largest Hindu temple compounds in Southeast Asia. Focusing on the changeable discursive tools used by tour guides, he argues that "pluriversality" and a product of interaction characterize the significance of heritage in the tourism industry. Heritage appropriation and interpretation, he maintains, is entangled in webs of cultures and economies, variably recognized and appreciated by stakeholders at multiple levels.

Cultural tourists seeking "authenticity" (Jamal and Hill 2002:103) or "extra-authenticity" (Boniface and Fowler 1993:7) in the touristic experience are sometimes faced by the invented traditions of artificial and contrived attractions (Rojek 1997; Tresidder 1999), often developed at the expense of local traditions and meanings (Smith 2007:104). In chapter 3, "Mayanizing Tourism on Roatán Island, Honduras: Archaeological Perspectives on Heritage, Development, and Indigeneity," Alejandro J. Figueroa, Whitney A. Goodwin, and E. Christian Wells combine archaeological data and ethnographic insights to explore a highly contested tourism economy in their discussion of how places on Roatán Island, Honduras, have become increasingly "Mayanized" over the past decade. As tour operators and developers continue to invent an idealized Maya past for the island, non-Maya archaeological remains and cultural patrimony are constantly being threatened and destroyed. Figueroa and colleagues argue that, while heritage tourism provides economic opportunities for some, it intentionally or coincidentally devaluates contributions made by less familiar groups.

Finally, state support or intervention in tourism economies seeking to serve multiple stakeholders in equitable ways is a challenging enterprise (Timothy and Nyaupane 2009; Walle 2010). There is an undeniable relationship between cultural heritage tourism and national identity (Palmer 1999). As Soper states, "In the production of tourism, the use of historic symbols, signs, and topics form a discourse that characterizes a nation and can play an active role in nation building" (Soper 2008:55). In this way, cultural heritage tourism can be co-opted to build national identity, a process that often occurs despite local opposition or at least with minimal local involvement (Ardren 2004). Robert Shepherd's contribution, "Shaping Heritage to Serve Development: Bureaucratic Conflict and Local Agency at Two Chinese Heritage Sites" (chapter 4), explores how the Chinese state is using heritage tourism as a tool for economic development and national identity in one of the fastest-growing tourism economies in the world. Shepherd demonstrates how local residents struggle to adapt to this shifting cultural, political, and economic terrain. Focusing on the Buddhist temple complex of Mount Wutai and the state-designated site of "Shangri-la," he shows how the overlapping and often conflicting interests and responsibilities of different government sectors have created extraordinary challenges for communities attempting to derive revenue from heritage tourism.

Together, these three chapters powerfully demonstrate the unintended consequences of heritage-related economic development and commodification. However, they also show that processes of national identity building related to the tourism industry are not necessarily uncontested at the community level. In some cases, these processes are accompanied by a reappropriation of cultural patrimony by local populations (Cyphers and Morales-Cano 2006) and self-conscious cultural (re)formulation (Adams 1997).

PART II: ECONOMIC ENCOUNTERS IN TOURISTIC SPHERES

The chapters in the second section of the volume provide critical insights into the processes of both self- and cultural commodification that result from tourism mobilities. For anthropology, tourism has proven to be an ideal context for studying issues of political economy, social change, natural resource management, and cultural identity. And yet there has been very little development of theory specific to touristic encounters.

As Gmelch (2003) points out, what makes the work of tourism distinctive from many other forms of employment is the frequent interaction workers and entrepreneurs have with guests. Workers, who are most often from modest educational and social backgrounds and possess few financial assets, intermingle with guests from distant lands and cultures who have widely different lifestyles and levels of income. The encounters between host and guest are mostly transitory, nonrepetitive, and asymmetrical (Cohen 1984). However, as the contributors to this section, "Economic Encounters in Touristic Spheres," point out, this kind and degree of interaction does not mean that such encounters are not meaningful for all involved.

The chapters in this section represent an important contribution to our collective understanding of the role of small-scale tourism entrepreneurs, or brokers, in this sprawling, global industry. The category of private-sector tourism broker denotes those who derive a living through involvement in tourism production; these include hotel and restaurant owners, employees, vendors, and guides who provide tourists with goods and services (Cheong and Miller 2000). In light of the recent heightened focus on smaller-scale and low-density tourism development, which is thought to more evenly disperse benefits within host communities and avoid the problems associated with foreign exchange leakages, the lack of scholarly research on the ties between tourism development and small businesses and entrepreneurship is remarkable (Dahles 2000; Koh 2000). Therefore, the chapters in this section fill a critical gap in the existing research. They demonstrate the ways in which small-scale tourism entrepreneurs, whether child guides in India or spiritual leaders in Guinea-Bissau, are actively involved in the ordering of this global industry (Ateljevic and Doorne 2005).

Tourism researchers have long observed that the travel experience plunges tourists into a liminal state. For example, Boissevain (1996) contends that one of the thrills of being abroad is temporarily permitted illicit behavior, made possible by the anonymity that visitors enjoy in foreign lands. Crick (2002) maintains that when on holiday the tourist's world is inverted from what it is at home—from work to play, morality to promiscuity, saving to spending, structure to freedom, and responsibility to self-indulgence. Similarly, Graburn (2010) argues that tourism is akin to a secular ritual—that the nonordinariness, excitement, and relaxation from the normal duties of life allow people on holiday to symbolically recreate and thus renew themselves for the return to their working lives. However, in chapter 5, "Of Sales Pitches and Speech Genres: Peddling Personality on the Riverfront of Banaras," Jenny Huberman critically questions these assumptions through an exploration of the lengths that foreign tourists will go to forge lasting connections with the street children they encounter. Her contribution explores the way value is produced and consumed in the informal tourist economy. Drawing from theoretical work on speech genres by Bakhtin (1986), she argues that children's varying abilities to animate the classic sales pitch play a structuring role in the affective dimensions of commercial exchange and the objects of touristic consumption. Using a wide repertoire of tactics, the children sometimes successfully encourage visitors to share their substantial financial resources with them and their families long after the tourist's trip has ended. In the process, the children engage in self-commodification, a set of beliefs and practices in which an individual chooses to construct a marketable identity product while striving to avoid alienating himself or herself (Bunten 2008).

In chapter 6, "Tourism as Transaction: Commerce and Heritage on the Inca Trail," Keely Maxwell focuses on the fleeting, ephemeral nature of seasonal tourist markets. Her research demonstrates that vending space on the Inca Trail to Machu Picchu is contoured by the trail's linearity, undirectionality, and temporality. Tourists are a captive but fleeting audience for the sellers who line the trail, and hiker movement is akin to a salmon run—a one-way current with daily and seasonal ebbs and flows. Maxwell explores how moral and monetary economies intersect in this trail-vending industry. Following a "host" agency approach to tourism, she challenges locally entrenched notions that heritage tourism contaminates local cultures and economies. Bunten (2008) argues that what is missing from the scholarly dialogue concerning the commodification of people and identity within the tourism context is a discussion of how "hosts" come to exercise, experience, and reflect on their activities—this is an important gap that Maxwell's research fills.

While host agency is often depicted in primarily commercial terms (Franklin 2007), it is also critical to highlight its cultural and even religious dimensions. In chapter 7, "Spiritual Spaces, Marginal Places: The Commodification of a Nalú Sacred Grove," Brandon D. Lundy explores cultural tourism among the Nalú in southwestern Guinea-Bissau and the ways in which the sacred grove of Kassumba is being commodified as it is transformed from a site of traditional religion into an arena of performance aimed at providing an "authentic" experience for the touristic gaze. Lundy's findings pose a challenge to Urry's (2002) influential theory of the "tourist gaze," which serves as a mirror to ultimately transform the people being gazed on while simultaneously inducing pleasurable experiences for tourists that, "by comparison with the everyday, are out of the ordinary" (Urry 2002:2). Lundy argues that the touristic encounter does not necessarily alter the host's subjectivity and culture if the original religious space was designed for just such a meeting.

Finally, the contributions by Patricia L. Delaney and Paul A. Rivera and by Katrina T. Greene explore the critical intersection of tourism mobilities, economic encounters, and broader cultural and political processes. In "Becoming Tongan Again: Generalized Reciprocity Meets Tourism in Tonga" (chapter 8), Delaney and Rivera consider how out-migration, remittances, and the return of "tourists" to the Kingdom of Tonga in the South Pacific represent a system of generalized reciprocity in which returning Tongans are rewarded with social and cultural opportunities to reactivate their Tongan identity. Within this system, gifts are used as levers to maximize one's prestige rather than household consumption. In this way, Delaney and Rivera show how the (re)production of Tongan culture is dependent, to some extent, on Tongan tourists.

Similarly, Katrina Greene's contribution, "Women, Entrepreneurship, and Empowerment: Black-Owned Township Tourism in Cape Town, South Africa" (chapter 9), explores women's roles in the development of black-owned township tourism in Cape Town, South Africa, highlighting the complex economic impacts of "pro-poor tourism." Greene's research focuses on how women entrepreneurs create bed-and-breakfast establishments to empower themselves and address issues of poverty and unemployment in their local communities. She argues that the gender status of women reinforces their efforts because of women's culturally defined roles as caretakers of the home. Thus, her chapter makes an important contribution to our understanding of the ways in which gender shapes forms of tourism entrepreneurship.

PART III: REDEFINING TOURISM'S "IMPACT"

Tourism was once represented as an easy option for economic development because it relied largely on natural resources already in place, for example, sand, sun, and friendly people, and therefore required no vast capital outlays for infrastructure (Crick 2002). However, empirical research on the "impact" of tourism on both travelers and destinations problematizes this simplistic assessment. The chapters in the volume's final section, "Redefining Tourism's 'Impact,'" provide a heightened focus on touristic experience within the context of both individual lives and wider forces and also more comprehensive examinations of local participation in tourism-based economies. The contributions are particularly attuned to gender and class dynamics as well as the contested claims to community membership that so often shape access to the economic resources that participation in tourism markets might provide. Collectively, the chapters contribute to an emergent theoretical approach within the anthropology of tourism, which recognizes that far from an exceptional experience, tourism is an integral part of an individual's life course and, consequently, intimately linked to the very social, cultural, and political milieu that produce tourism and the desire to travel in the first place. Increasingly, social scientists note that it is critical to pay as much attention to where tourists are coming from, including their cultural background, as to where they are going (Salazar 2004), for there is "a necessary relationship between the two spheres of life—work and home vs. leisure and travel" (Graburn 1983:1). The contributions in this section demonstrate that changes in tourist styles are not random but rather are connected to class competition, prestige hierarchies, and the succession of changing lifestyles (Graburn 1983).

In response to impact studies demonstrating the negative consequences of international tourism on resident populations, social scientists have called for the development of more responsible and inclusive modes of tourism development rooted in community collaboration and participatory decision-making (e.g., Bramwell and Lane 2000; Bramwell and Sharman 1999; Burns 2004; Cottrell et al. 2007; de Araujo and Bramwell 1999; Mowforth and Munt 2003; Selin and Chavez 1995; Teo 2002; Timothy 2007). However, anthropologists note that terms such as *local*, *community*, and *participation* are highly problematic (Joseph 2002; Li 1999; Stonich 2000; Tsing et al. 2005). For example, the term *community*, commonly used in tourism impact studies, invokes a false sense of tradition, homogeneity, and consensus, and evades definition (Richards and Hall 2000). Anthropologists raise similar concerns about the term *local*, as it is often difficult to determine what the qualifications are for inclusion in this category. Furthermore, despite the renewed focus on host involvement in tourism development, many questions remain in terms of why and under what conditions residents may choose, or be driven, to become involved in tourism, and the extent to which hosts act as decision-makers in shaping the kinds of tourism that take place in their own communities (Stronza 2001). Several of the chapters in this section of the volume answer these complex questions in detail.

In chapter 10, "Sacrificing Cultural Capital for Sustainability: Identity, Class, and the Swedish Staycation," Cindy Isenhour examines how and why environmentally minded Swedes, increasingly concerned with the ecological impacts of air travel on climate change, are turning to "staycations" as a new form of tourism. Isenhour argues that staying put has socioeconomic as well as environmental implications for these would-be global travelers. She finds that staycations among the Swedes threaten the accumulation of cultural capital that global tourism affords, which promises to restructure how Swedes differentiate themselves without breaching cultural taboos that discourage more explicit displays of difference and privilege.

Amy Speier examines the surge in medical tourism in the Czech Republic in chapter 11, "Reproductive Tourism: Health Care Crisis Reifies Global

Stratified Reproduction." Focusing on the owners and clients of one reproductive travel agency, she explores the political and economic reasons why Americans travel to the country for more affordable or less regulated reproductive care. Criticizing the commodification of fertility treatment in the United States, these "reproductive travelers" seek out the Czech Republic, where egg donation is legislatively mandated to be voluntary, gratuitous, and anonymous. Drawing on gift exchange theory, Speier questions the altruistic nature of egg donation in this and other contexts.

Macleod and Carrier (2010) argue that the definition of ecotourism is so elastic that it may be close to meaningless. The result is a label that is easily appropriated by interested parties. In chapter 12, "The Uses of Ecotourism: Articulating Conservation and Development Agendas in Belize," Laurie Kroshus Medina expertly demonstrates this discursive flexibility in her exploration of how different governmental and nongovernmental groups in Belize have strategically deployed particular definitions of ecotourism to advance particular agendas. She also examines the extent to which members of three rural communities in southern Belize participated in ecotourism under different conceptions of what ecotourism means. Medina finds that ecotourism serves as a means to diverse ends: conservationists sought the creation of protected areas, the government sought economic expansion and foreign exchange, and rural communities sought cash incomes and social justice.

Similarly, in chapter 13, "Who Owns Ecotourism? The Ecoturismo Seri Case," Diana Luque and colleagues (Beatriz Camarena, Patricia L. Salido, Moisés Rivera, Eduwiges Gomez, María Cabral, and Rubén Lechuga) present a related argument in the discussion of a community ecotourism project initiated by the Comcáac (Seri), an indigenous group residing along the central coast of the Sonoran Desert in northwest Mexico. The project, called Ecoturismo Seri, sought to capitalize on the region's biocultural diversity (for example, its "environmental services") to attract Mexican national tourists to this economically marginalized part of the country. Luque and colleagues detail the complex entanglements that ensued between different stakeholders in the community over ownership of ecotourism and the natural and cultural resources it seeks to exploit.

In cultural tourism, the focus is on differences in lifeways—costume, diet, rituals, language, handicrafts, housing, and other features. It forms an integral part of what Comaroff and Comaroff (2010) label the "identity economy," in which the sale of culture has replaced the sale of labor. They argue that ethno-commerce may open up unprecedented opportunities for creating value of various kinds: "Chambers (2000:102), among others, shows that any number of minority populations, north and south, have enhanced their autonomy, their political presence, and their material circumstances by adroitly managing their tourist potential—and all that it has come to connote" (Comaroff and Comaroff 2010:24). Cultural tourism is a highly competitive industry and often relies on gendered images of women. Therefore, while it is critical to explore the gendered dimensions of tourist market participation, this is especially true when examining cultural tourism and the artisan markets that cater to foreign visitors. In chapter 14, "The Effects of Tourism and Western Consumption on the Gendered Production and Distribution of Bogolan: Development Initiatives and Malian Women as Agents for Change," Sarah Lockridge considers the effects of tourism and consumption on the gendered production and distribution of Malian *bogolan*, a textile characterized by complex black-and-white patterns made with mud. The commoditization of this cloth has caused major shifts in the traditional production and distribution of the textile, creating a new group of urban producers and distributers composed of both women and men. Borrowing from Marxist feminist theory, Lockridge investigates the marginalization of Malian women's traditional socioeconomic status once their craft products are integrated into tourist and international markets as well as social action taken to combat their subordination.

Collectively the chapters in this section address important questions about the contested nature of community identity, the ownership of natural and cultural resources, and the ways in which ambiguous terms, such as ecotourism, can be used by powerful figures to shape access to markets and the financial rewards they bring. The contributors show that, far from being isolated, local concerns—critical issues directly related to translocal flows of people, capital, and ideas—contribute to a nuanced understanding of the power relations constituting tourismscapes.

CONCLUSION

The contributions to this volume represent a mix of traditional and novel approaches to the anthropological study of tourism that examine the social, cultural, political, economic, environmental, religious, and gendered dimensions of cultural convergence, divergence, and hybridization. They document in ethnographic detail the complex processes associated with the commodification of culture and the self, the quest for "authentic" experiences, and the invention of tradition. The chapters forge new directions in examining the sustainability, resilience, degradation, and adaptation that communities are experiencing worldwide. In an era of grand challenges to the human condition, the study of tourism mobilities helps us make sense of the ever-changing nature of translocal power relations and the multifaceted links between global North and South. As global tourism continues to expand in the coming years, anthropologists will surely continue to be engaged in studying tourism in all its many forms. Hopefully, we will also keep pace with finding new ways to apply our research results.

REFERENCES

Adams, Kathleen M. 1997. Ethnic Tourism and the Renegotiation of Tradition in Tana Toraja. *Ethnology* 36(4):309–20.

Ahmed, Sara. 2002. This Other and Other Others. *Economy and Society* 31(1):558–72.

Appadurai, Arjun. 1986. *The Social Life of Things*. Cambridge: University of Cambridge Press.

———. 1996. *Modernity at Large: Cultural Dimensions of Globalization*. Minneapolis: University of Minnesota Press.

Ardren, Traci. 2004. Where Are the Maya in Ancient Maya Archaeological Tourism? Advertising and the Appropriation of Culture. In *Marketing Heritage: Archaeology and the Consumption of the Past*, eds. Y. Rowan and U. Baram, pp. 103–12. Walnut Creek, CA: AltaMira Press.

Ateljevic, Irena, and Stephen Doorne. 2005. Dialectics of Authentication: Performing "Exotic Otherness" in a Backpacker Enclave of Dali, China. *Tourism and Cultural Change* 3(1):1–27.

Babb, Florence E. 2004. Recycled Sandalistas: From Revolution to Resorts in the New Nicaragua. *American Anthropologist* 106(3):541–55.

———. 2010. *The Tourism Encounter: Fashioning Latin American Nations and Histories*. Palo Alto, CA: Stanford University Press.

Bakhtin, Mikhail M. 1986. *Speech Genres and Other Late Essays*. Austin: University of Texas Press.

Boissevain, Jeremy. 1996. "But We Live Here!" Perspectives on Cultural Tourism in Malta. In *Sustainable Tourism in Islands and Small States: Case Studies*, eds. L. Briguglio, R. Butler, D. Harrison, and W. Filho, pp. 220–40. London: Pintar.

Boniface, Priscilla, and Peter J. Fowler. 1993. *Heritage and Tourism in "The Global Village."* London: Routledge.

Bramwell, Bill, and Bernard Lane. 2000. *Tourism Collaboration and Partnerships: Politics, Practice and Sustainability*. Clevedon, UK: Channel View.

Bramwell, Bill, and Angela Sharman. 1999. Collaboration in Local Tourism Policymaking. *Annals of Tourism Research* 26(2):392–415.

Bunten, Alexis Celeste. 2008. Sharing Culture or Selling Out: Developing the Commodified Persona in the Heritage Industry. *American Ethnologist* 35(3):380–95.

Burns, Georgette Leah. 2004. Anthropology and Tourism: Past Contributions and Future Theoretical Challenges. *Anthropological Forum* 14(1):5–22.

Burns, Peter M., and Marina Novelli. 2008. Introduction. In *Tourism and Mobilities: Local-Global Connections*, eds. P. M. Burns and M. Novelli, pp. xvii–xxvi. Wallingford, UK: CABI Press.

Castañeda, Quetzil E. 1996. *In the Museum of Maya Culture: Touring Chichén Itzá*. Minneapolis: University of Minnesota Press.

Chambers, Erve. 2000. *Native Tours: The Anthropology of Travel and Tourism*. Prospect Heights, IL: Waveland Press.

Cheong, So-Min, and Marc L. Miller. 2000. Power and Tourism: A Foucauldian Observation. *Annals of Tourism Research* 27(2):371–90.

Clegg, Stewart. 2003. From Frameworks of Power. In *Power: A Reader*, ed. M. Haugaard, pp. 249–73. Manchester, UK: University of Manchester Press.

Cohen, Erik. 1984. Pilgrimage and Tourism: Convergence and Divergence. In *Sacred Journeys: The Anthropology of Pilgrimage*, ed. E. A. Morinis, pp. 47–61. Westport, CT: Greenwood Press.

Coles, Timothy E., and Dallen J. Timothy, eds. 2004. *Tourism, Diasporas and Space*. London: Routledge.

Comaroff, John L., and Jean Comaroff. 2010. *Ethnicity, Inc*. Chicago: University of Chicago Press.

Cottrell, Stuart P., Jerry J. Vaske, Fujun Shen, and Paul Ritter. 2007. Resident Perceptions of Sustainable Tourism in Chongdugou, China. *Society and Natural Resources* 20(6):511–25.

Crick, Malcolm. 2002. Representations of International Tourism in the Social Sciences: Sun, Sex, Sights, Savings and Servility. In *The Sociology of Tourism: Theoretical and Empirical Investigations*, eds. Y. Apostolopoulos, S. Leivadi, and A. Yiannakis, pp. 15–50. London: Routledge.

Cyphers, Ann, and Lucero Morales-Cano. 2006. Community Museums in the San Lorenzo Tenochtitlán Region, Mexico. In *Archaeological Site Museums in Latin America*, ed. H. Silverman, pp. 30–46. Gainesville: University Press of Florida.

Dahles, Heidi. 2000. Tourism, Small Enterprises and Community Development. In *Tourism and Sustainable Community Development*, eds. G. Richards and D. Hall, pp. 154–69. London: Routledge.

de Araujo, Lindemberg Medeiros, and Bill Bramwell. 2002. Partnership and Regional Tourism in Brazil. *Annals of Tourism Research* 29(4):1138–64.

Franklin, Adrian. 2003. *Tourism: An Introduction*. Thousand Oaks, CA: Sage.

———. 2007. The Problem with Tourism Theory. In *The Critical Turn in Tourism Studies: Innovative Research Methodologies*, eds. I. Ateljevic, A. Pritchard, and N. Morgan, pp. 131–48. Oxford: Elsevier.

Franklin, Adrian, and Mike Crang. 2001. The Trouble with Tourism and Travel Theory? *Tourist Studies* 1(1):5–22.

Gale, Tim. 2008. The End of Tourism, or Endings in Tourism? In *Tourism and Mobilities: Local-Global Connections*, eds. P. M. Burns and M. Novelli, pp. 1–14. Wallingford, UK: CABI Press.

Gmelch, George. 2003. *Behind the Smiles: The Working Lives of Caribbean Tourism*. Bloomington: Indiana University Press.

Graburn, Nelson H. H. 1983. The Anthropology of Tourism. *Annals of Tourism Research* 10(1):9–33.

———. 2010. Tourism: The Sacred Journey. In *Hosts and Guests: The Anthropology of Tourism*, ed. V. Smith, pp. 21–36. Philadelphia: University of Pennsylvania Press.

Hall, Colin Michael, and Hazel Tucker. 2004. *Tourism and Postcolonialism: Contested Discourses, Identities and Representations*. London: Routledge.

Hall, Colin Michael, and Allan M. Williams, eds. 2002. *Tourism and Migration: New Relationships between Production and Consumption*. Dordecht, Netherlands: Kluwer.

Hall, Colin Michael, Allan M. Williams, and Alan A. Lew. 2004. Tourism: Conceptualizations, Institutions and Issues. In *A Companion to Tourism*, eds. A. Lew, C. M. Hall, and A. Williams, pp. 3–21. Malden, MA: Blackwell.

Hall, Derek R., Irene Kirkpatrick, and Morag Mitchell. 2005. *Rural Tourism and Sustainable Business*. Clevedon, UK: Channel View.

Hannam, Kevin, Mimi Sheller, and John Urry. 2006. Mobilities, Immobilities and Moorings. *Mobilities* 1(1):1–22.

Jamal, Tazim, and Stephen Hill. 2002. The Home and the World: (Post)Touristic Spaces of (In)Authenticity? In *The Tourist as a Metaphor of the Social World*, ed. G. M. S. Dann, pp. 77–107. Wallingford, UK: CABI Press.

Jamal, Tazim, and Mike Robinson. 2009. *The SAGE Handbook of Tourism Studies*. Thousand Oaks, CA: Sage.

Joseph, Miranda. 2002. *Beyond the Romance of Community*. Minneapolis: University of Minnesota Press.

Koh, Khoon Y. 2000. Understanding Community Tourism Entrepreneurism: Some Evidence from Texas. In *Tourism and Sustainable Community Development*, eds. G. Richards and D. Hall, pp. 205–17. London: Routledge.

Lefebvre, Henri. 1974. *The Production of Space*. London: Wiley-Blackwell.

Li, Tanya Murray. 1999. Compromising Power: Development, Culture, and Rule in Indonesia. *Cultural Anthropology* 14(3):295–322.

Macleod, Donald V. L., and James Carrier. 2010. Tourism, Power and Culture: Insights from Anthropology. In *Tourism, Power and Culture: Anthropological Insights*, eds. D. V. L. Macleod and J. Carrier, pp. 3–25. Clevedon, UK: Channel View.

Mowforth, Martin, and Ian Munt. 2003. *Tourism and Sustainability: Development, Globalization and New Tourism in the Third World*. London: Routledge.

Oppermann, Martin. 2000. Tourism Destination Loyalty. *Journal of Travel Research* 39(1):78–84.

Palmer, Catherine. 1999. Tourism and the Symbols of Identity. *Tourism Management* 20(3):313–21.

Richards, Greg, ed. 2007. *Cultural Tourism: Global and Local Perspectives*. Binghamton, NY: Hayworth Press.

Richards, Greg, and Derek Hall. 2000. The Community: A Sustainable Concept in Tourism Development? In *Tourism and Sustainable Community Development*, eds. G. Richards and D. Hall, pp. 1–13. London: Routledge.

Rojek, C. 1997. Indexing, Dragging and the Social Construction of Tourist Sites. In *Ways of Escape: Modern Transformations of Leisure and Travel*, eds. C. Rojek and J. Urry, pp. 52–74. London: Routledge.

Salazar, Noel B. 2004. Developmental Tourists vs. Development Tourism: A Case Study. In *Tourist Behaviour: A Psychological Perspective*, ed. A. Raj, pp. 85–107. New Delhi, India: Kanishka.

Selin, Steve, and Debbie Chavez. 1995. Developing an Evolutionary Tourism Partnership Model. *Annals of Tourism Research* 22(4):844–56.

Sheller, Mimi, and John Urry. 2006. The New Mobilities Paradigm. *Environment and Planning A* 38(2):207–26.

Silverman, Helaine, and D. Fairchild Ruggles. 2007. *Cultural Heritage and Human Rights*. New York: Springer.

Sarah Lyon and E. Christian Wells

uc t on

Skeggs, Beverley. 2004. *Class, Self, and Culture*. London: Routledge.
Smith, Laurajane, ed. 2007. *Cultural Heritage: Critical Concepts in Media and Cultural Studies*. London: Routledge.
Smith, Melanie K., and Mike Robinson. 2006. *Cultural Tourism in a Changing World: Politics, Participation and (Re)Presentation*. Clevedon, UK: Channel View.
Soper, Anne K. 2008. Mauritian Landscapes of Culture, Identity, and Tourism. In *Landscape, Tourism, and Meaning*, eds. Anne K. Soper, Charles E. Greer, and Daniel C. Knudsen, pp. 51–64. London: Ashgate.
Stonich, Susan C. 2000. *The Other Side of Paradise: Tourism, Conservation, and Development in the Bay Islands*. New York: Cognizant Communication Corporation.
Stronza, Amanda. 2001. Anthropology of Tourism: Forging New Ground for Ecotourism and Other Alternatives. *Annual Review of Anthropology* 30:261–83.
Teo, Peggy. 2002. Striking a Balance for Sustainable Tourism: Implications of the Discourse on Globalisation. *Journal of Sustainable Tourism* 10(6):459–74.
Timothy, Dallen J. 2007. Empowerment and Stakeholder Participation in Tourism Destination Communities. In *Tourism, Power and Space*, eds. A. Church and T. Coles, pp. 199–216. London: Routledge.
Timothy, Dallen J., and Gyan P. Nyaupane. 2009. *Cultural Heritage and Tourism in the Developing World: A Regional Perspective*. London: Routledge.
Tresidder, Richard. 1999. Tourism and Sacred Landscapes. In *Leisure/Tourism Geographies: Practices and Geographical Knowledge*, ed. D. Crouch, pp. 137–48. London: Routledge.
Tsing, Anna Lowenhaupt, J. Peter Brosius, and Charles Zerner. 2005. Introduction: Raising Questions about Communities and Conservation. In *Communities and Conservation: Histories and Politics of Community-Based Natural Resource Management*, eds. J. P. Brosius, C. Zerner, A. L. Tsing, pp. 1–34. Walnut Creek, CA: AltaMira Press.
United Nations World Tourism Organization. 2001. *Tourism 2020 Vision*. Madrid: World Tourism Organization, United Nations.
———. 2006. *Cultural Tourism and Local Communities*. Madrid: World Tourism Organization, United Nations.
———. 2010. *World Tourism Barometer* 8(2):1–64. Madrid: World Tourism Organization, United Nations.
Urry, John. 2001. Transports of Delight. *Leisure Studies* 20(4):237–45.
———. 2002. *The Tourist Gaze*. Thousand Oaks, CA: Sage.
Van der Duim, René. 2007. Tourismscapes: An Actor-Network Perspective. *Annals of Tourism Research* 34(4):961–76.
Wahab, Salah, and John J. Pigram, eds. 1997. *Tourism, Development and Growth: The Challenge of Sustainability*. London: Routledge.
Walle, Alf H. 2010. *The Equitable Cultural Tourism Handbook*. Charlotte, NC: Information Age.
Xiao, Honggen, and Stephen L. J. Smith. 2007. Knowledge Impact: An Appraisal of Tourism Scholarship. *Annals of Tourism Research* 35(1):62–83.

I

CULTURAL HERITAGE

2

✛

Shifting Values and Meanings of Heritage

From Cultural Appropriation to Tourism Interpretation and Back

Noel B. Salazar

This chapter explores how translocal processes of heritage policymaking and management influence its values and meanings—both in times of stability and of turmoil—but also how "foreign" elements are incorporated and strategically (mis)used by local service providers in the heritage products told and sold to tourists.[1] The case study from Central Java, Indonesia, provides unique insights because the current socioeconomic conditions have intensified existing conflicts over heritage appropriation and interpretation on local, national, regional, and global levels (cf. Salazar 2010b). An in-depth analysis of the empirical findings leads to a broader reflection on the dynamic interplay between the externally imaged (represented) and locally imagined value and meaning of world heritage in Indonesia and beyond. The ethnographic data illustrate that the significance of heritage—be it natural or cultural, tangible or intangible—is characterized by ever-changing pluriversality. However, before delving into the crux of the matter, it is essential to sketch the wider context.

Java is the fifth largest and most populated island of the Indonesian archipelago. The Javanese are Indonesia's largest ethnic group and play a dominant role in the country's economic and political life. The central region of the island comprises two provinces: Central Java and the much smaller Yogyakarta Special Province. The earliest signs of habitation in this fertile volcanic area are prehistoric. From the seventh century, the region was dominated by Hindu and Buddhist kingdoms, giving rise to the eighth-century Buddhist shrine of Borobudur, the ninth-century Hindu temple complex of Prambanan, and many other sanctuaries and palaces. Islam, coming mainly via India, gained ground in the inner areas of the island during the sixteenth century. The Dutch began to colonize the archipelago in the early seventeenth century. The British established a brief presence on Java under Sir Thomas Stamford Raffles (1811–1816), but the Dutch retained control until Indonesia's independence 130 years later. When the Dutch reoccupied Jakarta after the short Japanese occupation of Java during World War II (1946–1949), the city of Yogyakarta functioned as the stronghold of the independence movement by becoming the provisional capital of the newly declared Republic of Indonesia. In return for this unfailing support, the first Indonesian central government passed a law in 1950 granting Yogyakarta the status of Special Province.

Economically, Central Java is marked by small-scale enterprises, cottage industries, and self-employed people in a large, informal sector. Because of the absence of any substantial industrial infrastructure, Central Java's prosperity greatly depends on its ability to capitalize on its tangible as well as intangible cultural heritage. Much of the existing manufacturing is related to tourism, one of the area's major sources of income. The three Indonesian cultural sites on UNESCO's World Heritage List—the Prambanan Temple Compounds (1991), the Borobudur Temple Compounds (1991), and Sangiran Early Man Site (1996)—are all located in Central Java.[2] Four others—the Yogyakarta Palace Complex, the Ratu Boko Temple Complex, the Sukuh Hindu Temple, and the Great Mosque of Demak—have since 1995 been on UNESCO's tentative list (figure 2.1). The most common tour package includes visits to Borobudur, the Yogyakarta Palace, and Prambanan. When time permits, tourists also have a chance to experience Central Java's rich, intangible cultural heritage, including performing arts (traditional court dances, Ramayana Ballet, shadow puppet plays, and gamelan orchestra performances), traditional craftsmanship (wood carving, batik design, the silverware from Kotagede, and the pottery from Kasongan), and the occasional ritual or festive events (such as the annual Sekaten and Labuhan festivals).

Organized tourism first developed under Dutch colonial rule at the beginning of the twentieth century. After independence, the new Indonesian government continued to promote international tourism. The opening of the luxurious Ambarrukmo Palace Hotel in 1966—built with funds provided by war reparations from Japan on land owned by the family of Yogyakarta's sultan—marks the beginning of mass tourism in the region. Since then, the provincial city of Yogyakarta has become a major gateway

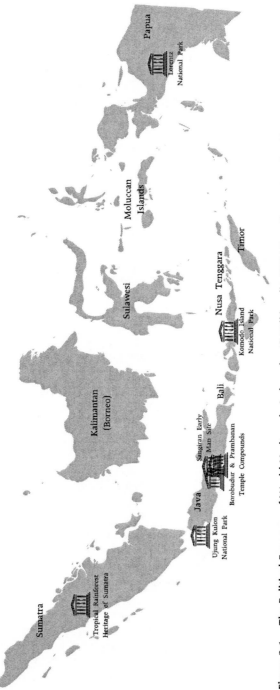

Figure 2.1. The Political Economy of World Heritage in Indonesia. (© Wikimedia GNU Free Documentation License)

to Central and East Java, both for international and domestic visitors. By the mid-1990s, tourism had become one of Indonesia's most important sources of foreign revenue and Yogyakarta the second-most visited destination (after Bali). A whole range of natural and human-made disasters, however, led to a decline in growth rates in the late 1990s (Salazar 2010a). Before 1997, Yogyakarta received 10 percent (three hundred thousand) of Indonesia's foreign visitors (three million). In 2005, the number of international tourists in the area was down to 115,000, merely 2.5 percent of Indonesia's total of five million tourists, and the region received a similar small fraction of the 4.5 million U.S. dollars in national receipts (UNWTO 2006). The situation has improved little since then. Challenges facing Indonesian tourism in general (with the exception of Bali) include the low volume of tourists, the harsh competition with neighboring regions and countries offering similar products, and an international image of Indonesia that is a political instead of a promotional asset. Some of the shortfall in foreign tourists in Central Java has been met by a rise in domestic tourism. Nevertheless, many local service providers cannot survive from tourism alone anymore and need other income-generating activities, especially during the low season. These conditions clearly influence people's relation to the area's cultural heritage.

WHOSE CULTURAL HERITAGE?

Heritage is valued because it has instrumental, symbolic, and other functions (Salazar 2005). However, the vague descriptions above illustrate how *value* is an elusive concept that usually presents itself indirectly and imprecisely (de la Torre 2002).[3] Value, as a model for human "meaning-making" (Graeber 2001), suggests usefulness and benefits, and this in two interrelated domains. On the one hand, sociocultural values are attached to heritage because it holds meaning for people or social groups due to its age, beauty, artistry, or association with a significant person or event or (otherwise) contributes to sociocultural affiliation and identification. Such values are produced through complex processes, learning, and maturing of (increasingly global) awareness. On the other hand, heritage also has economic value, referring to the degree to which it is desired (Hansen et al. 1998; Kim et al. 2007; Tuan and Navrud 2007). The use or market value of cultural heritage is the goods and services that flow from it that are tradeable and priceable in existing markets. However, the nonuse or nonmarket values described above—those for which no markets exist—also contribute to the total economic value of heritage (Sinclair and Stabler 1997:193).[4] As Sahlins (1976) argued a long time ago, one can only understand economic value as the product of meaningful distinctions. To grasp why people want to buy things or services (for example, access to and interpretation of cultural heritage sites), we have to understand the place that thing or service has in a larger web of meaning. I will illustrate this below by presenting and analyzing some ethnographic findings regarding the dynamics of heritage appropriation (value related) and interpretation (meaning related) at one particular site. The data show that economic value does not always prevail over socioeconomic value, even when the economic conditions are precarious.

As Dahles (2001:20) points out in her study on the politics of cultural tourism in Indonesia, "The cultural heritage of the Yogyakarta area has shaped the (international) images of Indonesia, as government propaganda has used architectural structures like the temples and the sultan's palace and expressions of art like the Ramayana dance to promote Indonesian tourism world-wide." This kind of image building particularly happened during Major General Suharto's New Order era (1966–1998), when the central government (led by Javanese) strongly favored Central Java in their (re)invention of Indonesia, promoting it as the cultural heart of the nation. The current planning and development of heritage tourism in the area is in the hands of many stakeholders at various levels: city (Yogyakarta City Department of Tourism, Arts and Culture) and regency (Magelang, Sleman, and Klaten Tourism Offices), provincial (Central Java and Yogyakarta Provincial Tourism Offices), Java (Jawa Promo), national (Ministry of Culture and Tourism), regional (ASEAN Committee on Trade and Tourism and APEC Tourism Working Group), and global (UNWTO and UNESCO) levels. Because policymakers at these different echelons have a diversity of interests, decisions taken at one level are often contested at another.

UNESCO has a long-standing history of involvement in Central Java's heritage. In 1972, it launched a U.S. $25 million safeguarding campaign to restore Borobudur, often listed as one of the seven (forgotten) wonders of the world. Concurrent with the elevation of Borobudur and Prambanan to World Heritage Sites in 1991, UNESCO (1992) collaborated with the United Nations Development Programme (UNDP) and the former Indonesian directorate general of tourism in the ambitious 1991 to 1994 Cultural Tourism Development Central Java–Yogyakarta project. This led, among other things, to increased cooperation between the provinces of Central Java and Yogyakarta in the planning and promotion of heritage tourism. Since the May 2006 earthquake, UNESCO has been actively involved in the rehabilitation of the damaged Prambanan temple complex. Other important global players in the area's heritage management include the nongovernmental International Council on Monuments and Sites (ICOMOS, with an Indonesian secretariat in Bandung) and the nonprofit World Monuments Fund. All this foreign involvement in Central

Java's cultural heritage indicates that it is considered as highly valuable. According to intergovernmental organizations such as UNESCO, certain sites even have "outstanding universal value." The 1972 *Convention concerning the Protection of the World Cultural and Natural Heritage* specifies that such value can be historical, aesthetic, scientific, ethnological, or anthropological (UNESCO 1972:2). The *Operational Guidelines for the Implementation of the World Heritage Convention* (UNESCO 2008:14) further explain that "outstanding universal value means cultural and/or natural significance which is so exceptional as to transcend national boundaries and to be of common importance for present and future generations of all humanity" (art. 49).[5]

Having begun as a system of identifying, protecting, and preserving heritage that represents and belongs to all humankind, UNESCO's World Heritage List has become an accreditation scheme for heritage sites, used either to serve the purposes of tourism (as a major source of revenue) or as nation building (Salazar 2011). This illustrates how transnational processes are always subject to national and local economic considerations and political agendas. It is no coincidence that sites such as Sangiran (prehistoric), Prambanan (Hindu), and Borobudur (Buddhist) appear on UNESCO's list of World Heritage Sites, whereas Sukuh Temple or the Sultan's Palace are not (yet) included. After all, the central government in Jakarta proposes sites to UNESCO (see Di Giovine [2008] about the process of UNESCO recognition). It is in their strategic interest to nominate politically "neutral" monuments. Sukuh Temple, for instance, is a beautiful Hindu temple tucked away in the highlands of Central Java. It is unique, not only in overall design but also in decoration: it is the only known erotic temple on Java, with statues and reliefs of erected male members abounding. Given the moral sensibilities of the majority Muslim population (and the increasing power of fundamentalists), Sukuh is not a site the Indonesian government would want to promote. The Sultan's Palace, however, is Muslim (or, at least, partly), but a place where current politics are being played out, instead of a "dead" heritage site.[6] This serves as a reminder that, ultimately, a World Heritage Site is the product of agency on the national level.

PRAMBANAN

The Prambanan complex, named after the surrounding village, is one of the largest Hindu temple compounds in Southeast Asia. It was built around AD 850, but one century later the Hindu court and most of the population moved to East Java, and the 224 temples were abandoned. The structures themselves collapsed during an earthquake in the sixteenth century. The earliest written report of the ruins is by Cornelis A. Long, an officer of the Dutch East India Company who made an excursion to Prambanan in 1733 and found damaged statues among the piles of stone blocks. Despite the fact that the ruins were the earliest reported in the region (Borobudur was rediscovered only in 1814, after a survey expedition by Raffles) and were relatively easily accessible and, therefore, often visited by Europeans, the site was only cleaned in 1885. The restoration of the main temple was the subject of long discussions. Reconstruction work started in 1918 and continued from 1937 until 1953.

The Prambanan Temple Compounds were recommended by the International Council on Monuments and Sites (ICOMOS) as world heritage in 1991, on the basis of criteria I ("The site is an outstanding example of Siva art in Indonesia, and the region") and IV ("The site is an outstanding religious complex, characteristic of Siva expression of the 10th century"). This international recognition made many Indonesians (re)appropriate and revalorize the site, an outcome that has been noted elsewhere: "If foreigners point out to indigenous people that their piles of old stones are actually cultural treasures and that they are willing to pay to conserve them, the indigenous people change their perception of those stones and may even begin to value them. Get a cultural good listed on the UNESCO world heritage list, and people will value that good more" (Klamer 2003:201). In the case of Prambanan, this led to a rapid development of the site. The park surrounding the temples and the related infrastructure (ticket booths, interpretative services, and parking lots) are administered by PT Taman Wisata, a state-owned enterprise that also manages the sites of Borobudur and Ratu Boko. Souvenir stands, food stalls, and other tourism-related structures outside the main grounds fall under the control of the Provincial Tourism Office of the province in which they are located (Prambanan is located right on the border between Central Java and Yogyakarta). The actual monuments, however, resort under the responsibility of the National Archaeology Department of Indonesia (and, with the ongoing process of regional autonomy, increasingly the provincial archaeology departments of Central Java and Yogyakarta). Because of this fragmented distribution of authority, funding and conservation duties are unbalanced, leading to multiple problems in the management of the site. The Prambanan case nicely illustrates how the sociocultural and economic values attributed to heritage are, in fact, political, in that they are part of power struggles and exertions that determine the fate of heritage. Values occupy center stage when it comes to the decisions, the politics, and the management of heritage.

FROM A PILE OF STONES TO WORLD HERITAGE

Not only values but also meanings attached to heritage play an important role. This becomes clear in closely analyzing the practices of heritage interpretation. Visitors have three ways of touring the temple complex: (1) on their own; (2) with their own tour guide or tour leader (most often from Yogyakarta, Bali, or abroad); or (3) with an on-site tour guide. Depending on which of the three options they take, visitors can have potentially very divergent experiences of the site. The majority of on-site tour guides (only ten men) live in Prambanan village. After a short course and exam (organized by the Provincial Tourism Office), they obtain their guiding certificate and become members of the small Prambanan branch of the Yogyakarta Chapter of the Indonesian Tourist Guide Association (with over four hundred members). Most are autodidacts with a genuine interest in local heritage and culture, which their self-studies of history, archaeology, or anthropology and their ability to perform traditional arts (for example, classical Javanese dance or music) illustrate (Salazar 2010a). Since Prambanan is located in what is now a predominantly Muslim area, the temples are only rarely used for Hindu rituals. Many Indonesians would thus disagree with the ICOMOS description of Prambanan as a "religious complex" but rather see it as a "heritage monument." Since the bombing of Borobudur by Muslim fundamentalists in 1985, this is also the official stance of the Indonesian government. Furthermore, in order to accommodate the religious needs of the many Muslims working at and visiting Prambanan, a *musholla* (small building where Muslims perform their religious duties) was built right next to the entry gate. Foreign tourists may find it odd that while visiting the Hindu temple complex around prayer time they can hear the Islamic call to prayer far into the compound.

Thanks to sustained efforts by the central government in Jakarta to create and disseminate image campaigns of nation building, Prambanan has become a cultural icon of Indonesia. As a result, every year thousands of domestic tourists visit the temples, not primarily to learn more about Hindu religious heritage but to personally witness the beauty of this great Indonesian monument (and to have a good time). The Javanese have an added reason to visit the site. Apart from a general appreciation of the monumental architecture—quickly captured in overpopulated snapshots—they particularly come to see the north chamber of the central Shiva shrine. According to local beliefs and oral history, the statue in that room does not represent the Hindu goddess Durga but *Loro Jonggrang* (Javanese for "slender virgin"). Legend has it that she was a Javanese princess who agreed to marry a man she did not love if he could build her a temple ornamented with one thousand statues, between the setting and rising of the sun. When the man was about to fulfill her demand, she tried to trick him. He was so furious that he petrified her and she became the last (and most beautiful) of the thousand statues. At the time I was doing research, there were two signboards at the entrance of the main complex: an older "Candi Prambanan, World Heritage List number 642" and a newer "Candi Rara Jonggrang" (figure 2.2). This is a clear visual marker of the conflicting meanings of the site.

The on-site guides often stop at the signs to point out that the "correct" name of the main site is Rara Jonggrang Temple, and they love to explain why the Loro Jonggrang statue is so important. They have learned about this story through widely circulating oral histories. One explains the folkloristic beliefs surrounding the shrine of Durga:

> If women want to look prettier, you have to touch the face [of the statue] and then [touch] your own face, three times. After the visit, one becomes really pretty. But it only works for women. For you and you and you [pointing to the men in the party], you can touch, but only here [touching the breasts of the statue], it brings good luck [laughing]. If you touch the face, afterwards you walk like this [imitates a stereotypical gay gait] . . . The face of Jonggrang is very black because every day girls and women come to touch it. The breasts of Jonggrang are also black because I often come up here. Twice a day! [Everybody laughing]

Foreign visitors are also informed about these local interpretations of the site. What is more, when guiding for international tourists, local guides also criticize traditional Javanese beliefs and cultural practices. Interpreting elements of Javanese culture for foreign tourists:

> The Javanese only come to visit the statue of Jonggrang and then, finished! . . . Can you see the birds here? [pointing to a wall relief] It's the cockatoo here. The cockatoo is a symbol for both Hindus and Buddhists. The same like you have the white dove in Christianity, the symbol of peace. But we have parrots, because parrots always say yes.

Figure 2.2. The Multiple Meanings of Cultural Heritage. (Photo by Noel B. Salazar)

In the first comment, the guide belittles his fellow Javanese for their perceived lack of appreciation of "high culture," here translated as interest in the cultural history of the temples. There is some self-interest of the guide involved in this commentary because the described situation often implies that the Javanese do not want the service of a guide when visiting the site. On the metadiscursive level, the guide is transmitting yet another message. By taking distance from the Javanese commoner, he is positioning himself on the side of the tourists, as a person with a broad cosmopolitan interest in cultures and religions. The second comment contains an implicit criticism of Javanese culture. Parrots are known for their ability to mimic sounds or speech. The guide suggests Javanese in general are uncritically parroting one another, and they are certainly not contradicting the traditional holders of power (Anderson 1972). This is an illustration of how tour-guide discourse sometimes works as a hidden transcript, expressing socioeconomic and political dissatisfaction without directly confronting or challenging the authorities. This type of subtle agency is extremely popular on Java, where people continue adhering to traditional ideas of deference and hierarchy. It is interesting to note that the later comment also illustrates that local guides, the majority of whom are Muslim, have not only studied the cultural history of Hinduism (and Buddhism) but also seem familiar with elements of Christianity, allowing them to create shared frames of religious reference with their predominantly European clientele.

The on-site guides at Prambanan are very well aware that the heritage site in which they operate has value that goes far beyond the local or national. This awareness greatly informs the way in which the site is interpreted for visitors. As briefly mentioned before, the temple complex has a clearly visible signboard indicating its privileged status as a UNESCO "world heritage."[7] With international tourists, guides will often stop at the sign for a photo opportunity, while using the information on the sign to reinforce their own tales. Bruner (2005:169–88) calls this strategy "dialogic narration" because the guide's narrative is not just indexically referencing what is actually written—for instance, that the Prambanan Temple Complex is a UNESCO World Heritage Site—but also takes account of all the stories tourists have heard, read, or seen about other World Heritage Sites as well. Explicit comparisons with those other monuments are used to put the local site on an equal level of global value. The structure of the temple complex in Prambanan is explained thusly:

> For example, also in Cambodia, in Angkor Wat, there are five pillars . . .
> Prambanan temple is the largest Hindu temple in the world outside of India.
> It resembles the temples in South India.

This kind of supralocal legitimacy, stressing the global value of the place visited, gives the guiding narrative more weight. At the same time, it gives local guides a chance to show off their own cosmopolitan knowledge (figure 2.3).

Using simile and metaphor, guides repeatedly compare their explanatory narratives with cultural elements that foreign tourists can easily recognize, a technique used to mollify the effects of strangeness associated with a trip abroad (Dann 1996:171–74). Of course, the strategy only works if the tourists share the same frame of reference. Some examples illustrate the common use of references to global (popular) culture.

Interrupting the narration of the Ramayana story before taking the visitors to the neighboring temple where the depicted story on the wall reliefs continues, the guide states:

Lakshmana [Rama's brother] takes his Swiss knife, ouch no, his Javanese knife, called keris, to make a magic circle to protect Sita . . . Rama and Lakshmana leave for the forest, Sita stays alone in the magic circle . . . to be continued next week! [tourists laughing]

Figure 2.3. Enhancing the Value of Heritage by Cosmopolitan Comparison. (Photo by Noel B. Salazar)

He continues the Ramayana tale:

> Hanuman [king of apelike humanoids] tells Rama: Don't worry, be happy!

At the last Ramayana wall relief in the Shiva temple at Prambanan, the guide states:

> So, that's the end of the Ramayana story. Now if you go to the theatre this evening, you can follow the story. Even if you sleep well [during the performance], you'll be able to follow. [laughing]

Pointing to a particular geometric pattern on a wall relief panel, the guide says:

> A mandala, but don't be confused with Mandela.

After the lighthearted comparison between the relatively unknown Javanese *keris*—a sacred, double-bladed heirloom dagger—and the globally renowned Swiss army knife, the guide started mimicking the genre of a soap opera: briefly summarizing the latest developments in the story and stopping the narration at a dramatic moment. The guide used the time needed to walk to the second temple to promote the nightly performance at the Ramayana Ballet Open Theatre (local advertising time), making the interdiscursive comparison even more striking. The whole tour was a prime example of intertextual narrative performance. The tour guide, formerly a Ramayana Ballet dancer, not only narrated but also enacted (in a very dancelike fashion) parts of the Ramayana story, changing voice pitch when talking about different characters. In addition, he imitated the chants of a Brahman priest while explaining the Hindu rituals taking place in the temple. This illustrates the important intangible cultural heritage aspect in the visitor experience of heritage sites.

The second comment immediately struck my attention because it was uttered during a French-language tour and involved code switching (French to English). The guide quickly added the French translation (*"ne vous inquietez pas"*), but it is obvious he was referring to the legendary Bobby McFerrin song that is widely used in films, advertising, and popular culture. The next stretch of guiding narrative contains an implicit recognition that the Ramayana Ballet performance in the open-air theatre next door is long and can be boring, especially for tourists who lack the cultural cues to grasp the subtleties of the show and who are tired at the end of a long day. The reference to Mandela is a nice pun, although somewhat outdated and out of context—by 2006, South Africa's former president Nelson Mandela had greatly retreated from public life due to his age and health issues. It should rather be seen as a way the guide is checking whether his clients are as cosmopolitan as he is (or imagines himself to be).

Issues of positionality are also at stake with Asian visitors. Their presence poses many challenges for local guides (Salazar 2008). Interestingly, this is not because tourism of Asian origin is a newer phenomenon. Actually, Asian tourists (especially Japanese) arrived in the region as early as Western visitors did. Rather, local guides have been trained mainly to serve Western clients.[8] Through trial and error, they learn that for Asian tourists it matters more to be treated well as guests than to be told extensive contextual narratives about a site. The guide is expected to be a good organizer and entertainer of the group, more than an information giver or culture broker for the individual tourists. To make matters even more complex, having close contact with a *bule* ("white" person) is considered as status enhancing (and thus valuable) in Indonesia. In the personal imagination of many guides, Westerners act as their gateway into an imagined better world, a Promised Land they know from television programs, advertisements, and movies (Salazar 2010a). The privileged interaction with Westerners nourishes their dreams of escape from their harsh local life. Asian tourists are perceived as sociocultural proxies, people who have (materially) "made it" in their lives and are able to travel abroad. Many Asians devotedly embrace their role of *nouveau riche* by being much more demanding toward service personnel (cf. Cochrane 2008). This (and, importantly, the different tipping culture) explains why the on-site guides at Prambanan generally prefer guiding for Westerners.

WHEN TRAGEDY STRIKES . . .
AND THE VALUE OF HERITAGE CHANGES

During the last decade, Central Java's tourism has suffered from a series of unfortunate events in Indonesia and the wider region (Salazar 2010a). However, 2006 dealt a fatal blow to the already ailing service sector. Between May and July of that year, the area endured numerous natural disasters. Mount Merapi, one of the most active volcanoes in the world, erupted multiple times. While few people died, many were evacuated and everybody had to cope psychologically with the almost constant threat of a major eruption. A similar story can be told about the tsunami that hit the southern shores on July 17. The damage and casualties were minor, but the memory of the 2004 tsunami in Aceh was still fresh in everybody's mind, and people, in panic and fear, overreacted. On May 27, people had a valid reason to be afraid. On that infamous day, a major earthquake of 5.9 on the scale of Richter struck, killing around six thousand people and leaving an estimated 1.5 million Javanese homeless. Tourists massively cancelled their trips to Java, and the local service industry was crippled because tourist workers had died, were injured, or had lost their houses. The entire situation exposed the fragility of the local tourism sector but also brought to light the resilience of its workers. Prambanan was among those heritage sites hit by the quake, along with the Royal Graveyard of Imogiri and parts of the Sultan's Palace. Although the Prambanan main temples appeared to be structurally intact, internal damage was significant. Large pieces of debris, including carvings, lay scattered on the ground. The parking lot of the site became a temporary shelter for villagers who had lost their houses. The main area was closed to the public until damage could be fully assessed. For a year and a half, the immediate surroundings remained off limits for safety reasons.

The calamities did not spare the local guides. Some lost their relatives, others their houses; most were deprived of their main source of income. The disasters also disclosed some of the politics of local tourism. The low position guides occupy in the tourism hierarchy became particularly clear in the case of Prambanan. Although UNESCO rapidly sent experts to assess the damage, it took a long time before the people working at the site were informed about the recovery plans.[9] After the assessment, a newly built viewing platform (very similar to the ones erected after September 11, 2001, around Ground Zero in New York) allowed tourists to see the main temples from a safe distance, without being allowed to enter them. PT Taman Wisata, the state-owned enterprise managing the park, decided not to lower the entrance fees (U.S. $10 for foreigners). Anticipating tourist complaints, many local tour operators decided to suspend trips to Prambanan. The few tourists who still visited the temple complex did not want the service of a local guide (approximately U.S. $5 extra) because they knew that they could not get near the main temples anyway. This left the Prambanan guides in a very precarious situation. Some of the security guards in charge of protecting the site offered foreign tourists the opportunity to enter the damaged main complex anyway, in exchange for sizeable amounts of cash. The on-site guides knew about these practices but preferred to keep quiet.

The series of disasters became the feeding ground for new narratives and imaginaries. Visually confronted with the damage the quake caused, tourists obviously asked for more information about it. In Prambanan, the on-site guides replaced the flashy "Take a guide with you for a better visit" sign at the ticket booth with a more sober message: "Announcement: Please consider taking a guide. U help also the victims of the catastrophic earthquake. Thank for your attention. Head of the Prambanan Guide Association." This new message gave guides a chance to complain about the little aid the central government was giving to the affected families—U.S. $9 per month for "living costs." While walking around the closed main compound, guides did not always mention to tourists that the rubble they saw had not been caused by the earthquake but was simply the ruins of smaller temples that had never been restored. In addition, the large photographic panel "Prambanan Temple before & after the 'gempa,'" on display inside the temple park, made the imagined impact of the recent quake all the more dramatic (figure 2.4).

Interestingly, at a time when the economic value of Prambanan was dramatically affected, local tour guides felt the strong emotional need to change their usual interpretative narratives, hereby revealing the importance of some deeper cultural meanings attached to the site instead of merely recounting the facts and figures that they had learned through intense study when they were studying to become a professional guide (Salazar 2010a). The adversity precipitated a spontaneous revitalization of old Javanese myths and mystical beliefs. Inspired by folk disaster theories, guides had a good excuse to entertain their clients with endless tales about the legendary queen of the South Sea and her troubled relations with the current sultan of Yogyakarta.[10] This kind of narrative widely circulates every time a disaster strikes in the area (Schlehe 1996). According to these stories, the earthquake was the result of an escalating conflict between the queen of the South Sea and the sultan. The mythical queen appeared to be angry because the sultan did not want to take her as his second wife (polygamy used to be common in the sultanate). A related hypothesis pointed to the quake as the queen's protest against the proposed national antipornography legislation (which would prohibit some age-old Javanese rituals). In the stories, Mbah Marijan, the eighty-year-old spiritual gatekeeper of Mount Merapi, arose as a new hero and protector of Javanese tradition because he openly challenged the authority of

Figure 2.4. Capitalizing on Disaster. (Photo by Noel B. Salazar)

the sultan regarding the evacuation of the villagers living on the mountain's slopes.

Little did the heritage visitors hearing these tales know that they also served as a criticism in disguise against the sultan and his political agenda of rapid regional modernization. Over the last decade, the sultan (who is simultaneously the governor of the province) has endorsed the construction of shopping malls. He claims the malls, which he and his entourage co-own, will stimulate regional economic growth. Traditionalists, however, argue the malls obstruct the spiritual line between the sea and the volcano. They claim the sultan is destroying Yogyakarta's heritage while his divine mandate is to protect the cradle of Javanese culture. Both the northern and southern powers are showing their disagreement, and the sultan does not have enough spiritual authority to negotiate a truce. Guides were very careful, though, in how they framed their own opinions. The calamities facilitated critical commentaries as well as allowing the business-as-usual narratives and practices to take on new dimensions. Guides often preferred not to tell their clients what losses they themselves had suffered. They instead used humor to entertain the tourists, and also to obtain some relief from the accumulated stress. This is commentary while passing by a pile of bricks: "Brick makers, now, they have a good business [laughing]. Ya, after the earthquake!" In this case, the tourists had no clue that their guide had also lost her house and some of her relatives in the quake. Even in these difficult circumstances, it is rare for Javanese guides to draw the attention to their own economic situation.

In the weeks following the earthquake, the guides blamed UNESCO for keeping the main temples closed to the public (preventing them from earning their living). This translated in their narratives containing much fewer references to the organization. Through initiatives such as the 2008 Prambanan Camp for World Heritage Volunteers, the negative perception of UNESCO in Prambanan was somewhat adjusted. This project, in collaboration with the archaeology department and the Provincial Tourism Office of Central Java, enabled international volunteers to assist the experts with the restoration of the temple and to increase the heritage awareness of local youth.

DISCUSSION

Much of the theorizing on heritage appropriation and interpretation has relied upon inherited or borrowed (Euro-American) conceptions and assumptions about what should be valued and meaningful. As this chapter has illustrated, instead of one universally accepted value or meaning, the significance of heritage—be it natural or cultural, tangible or intangible—

is characterized by pluriversality. Heritage appropriation and interpretation are always enmeshed in complex webs of economics and culture, variously cherished and expressed by shareholders at different levels (Porter and Salazar 2005; Salazar and Porter 2004). Studies of heritage tourism such as the one at hand make it clear that heritage value is not fixed but always a product of interaction. Regarding interpretation, the tales that visitors will hear depend upon the guide, the way both tourists and guide position one another, and the broader context in which the guided tour is taking place. This can lead to multilayered heritage narratives but also to "heritage dissonance," or the mismatch between heritage and people caused by the selectivity with which heritage is marked and used in tourism—notably, to reflect back to visitors their own heritage rather than to reflect the heritage perceptions of local residents (Tunbridge and Ashworth 1996). While the externally imaged (represented) and locally imagined value and use of world heritage can be divergent, it is also important to recognize that, even at the local level, not everyone necessarily speaks with one voice. The Prambanan case illustrates that the feelings of vulnerability and insecurity caused by the recent series of disasters made many people return to traditional Javanese interpretations of their life world, including heritage. This was not only an internal process but it also became visible in tour-guide narratives, despite the possible economic repercussions this might have. Given the precarious economic situation, it is remarkable that the sociocultural value of the site became somehow more important than its economic value (at least for the guides).

There are a variety of meanings, uses, and functions ascribed to heritage. Traditionally, values were articulated by expert analyses of heritage as a work of art or a record of the past. Only recently has the heritage field begun to embrace such factors as economics, cultural change, public policy, and social issues. The advantage of an ethnographic approach in this aperture is that it can focus on the way values function in everyday life and in particular on the deliberations in which they are formed and expressed. The study of Central Java's cultural history shows how outsiders have set the agenda since the time heritage became an issue of importance: Dutch and British colonials, the central government in Jakarta, and UNESCO and other international organizations. Such growing extralocal interdependence is irreversible but variously received. Guides interpreting for foreign tourists use the global recognition by UNESCO strategically, but local guides clearly sensed and criticized the organization's "distance" in the period after the earthquake. This study reminds us that the instrumental value of heritage is susceptible to rapid change, while the cultural meaning it has seems to change much slower. Despite the fact that Central Java is constantly undergoing economic and social transformations, the Sultan's Palace and its revered inhabitants still symbolize the power of traditional Javanese life. As far as Prambanan is concerned, the continuing efforts by the Indonesian authorities toward the structural rehabilitation of the complex, in cooperation with UNESCO's World Heritage Centre, ICOMOS, and other international partners, have led in 2009 to the reopening of all damaged temples to the public. Meanwhile, the letters on the "Candi Rara Jonggrang" signboard were replaced with "Candi Prambanan," and the struggle over heritage appropriation and interpretation continues.

NOTES

1. The material presented here is based on research supported by the National Science Foundation under Grant No. BCS-0514129 and additional funding from the School of Arts and Sciences, University of Pennsylvania (for full details, see Salazar 2010a). The fourteen months of fieldwork in Indonesia (July–August 2003, January–December 2006) were conducted under the auspices of the Indonesian Institute of Sciences and were kindly sponsored by Gadjah Mada University. The methodology used, distinctively (though not uniquely) anthropological, involved mixed methods, including direct observation and free-flowing interviews with informants and key actors in the field of heritage management and interpretation (Salazar 2010c). I also gathered ancillary data such as secondary sources, audio-visual data, news media information, documents, archives, and so forth. In addition, I used exhaustive notes and personal diary entries to record all my findings. My two local research assistants were instrumental not only in data collection but also in critical analysis.

2. The World Heritage List includes 936 sites forming part of the cultural and natural heritage that UNESCO considers as having outstanding universal value. The first twelve sites were inscribed in 1978. As of 2011, the list includes 725 cultural, 183 natural, and 28 mixed sites in 153 countries.

3. I am referring here to value as a characteristic or (attributed) quality, not in the common ethical sense of morals, principles, or other ideas of what is ultimately good, proper, or desirable in human life that serve as a guide to (individual and collective) action.

4. The terminology used here is not to be confused with the Marxian framework of use value (consumption) versus exchange value (trade) (cf. Graeber 2001). Economists have been debating for a very long time how values can be objectively measured. Such exercises become problematic when attempting to quantify the economic value of cultural goods and services, in levels exceeding their monetary benefits (Navrud and Ready 2002; Noonan 2003; Snowball 2008). The difficulty in measuring values is that they are contingent and socially constructed, not objectively given or intrinsic—an anthropological perspective opposed to the normative, art historical view, which a priori privileges artistic and historical values over others.

5. Article 77 of the *Operational Guidelines* (UNESCO 2008:20) outlines six possible criteria that define "outstanding universal value" for cultural heritage:

(1) represent a masterpiece of human creative genius; (2) exhibit an important interchange of human values, over a span of time or within a cultural area of the world, on developments in architecture or technology, monumental arts, town planning, or landscape design; (3) bear a unique or at least exceptional testimony to a cultural tradition or to a civilization that is living or which has disappeared; (4) be an outstanding example of a type of building, architectural or technological ensemble, or landscape that illustrates (a) significant stage(s) in human history; (5) be an outstanding example of a traditional human settlement, land use, or sea use that is representative of a culture (or cultures), or human interaction with the environment, especially when it has become vulnerable under the impact of irreversible change; and (6) be directly or tangibly associated with events or living traditions, with ideas, or with beliefs, with artistic and literary works of outstanding universal significance.

6. The current sultan, Hamengku Buwono X, was elected as governor of Yogyakarta in 1998. In 2008, his tenure was extended by three years in a bid to prevent a vacuum of power in the province. The sultan also considered contending in the 2009 presidential race, but his candidacy did not gain enough national support.

7. The placing of signs is actually part of UNESCO's *Operational Guidelines for the Implementation of the World Heritage Convention*. Article 268 of that policy document states, "Properties inscribed on the World Heritage List should be marked with the emblem jointly with the UNESCO logo, which should, however, be placed in such a way that they do not visually impair the property in question" (UNESCO 2008:69).

8. As part of the Cultural Tourism Development Central Java–Yogyakarta project in the 1990s, an Italian consultant wrote general job descriptions for guides and tour managers and helped create the first national occupational skill standards, including the design of national tourism training standards and programs. He also organized a three-month upgrading course for already licensed guides.

9. Although local people perceived it differently, UNESCO's Emergency Assessment Mission in June 2006 consisted of only one international expert (an Italian professor in the field of structural engineering), while the other participants were Indonesian experts and representatives from the UNESCO office in Jakarta. An international meeting was organized in March 2007, bringing together Indian, Indonesian, Italian, and Japanese experts from various fields (including archaeology, architecture, civil engineering, geodetic engineering, geology, and history), representatives from UNESCO, ICOMOS Australia, and the Global Heritage Fund, and government representatives from China, India, Italy, Japan, and the Kingdom of Saudi Arabia.

10. As is common throughout Southeast Asia, also in Java perturbations in the natural realm have long been interpreted as presaging disruptions in the social and political realm (Anderson 1972). The construction of shrines in Central Java is based on an idealized mountain-sea polarity. Both Hindu and Buddhist temples, which are considered as the meeting points between gods and humans, were built on a spiritual line between Mount Merapi and the South Sea (Dumarçay 1986:88–91). The old fault from Merapi to Bantul, which was reactivated during the May 2006 earthquake, lies parallel to the sacred north-south axis in Javanese

cosmology. Javanese Muslims traditionally combine their Islamic faith with belief in this Javanese spirit world (Geertz 1960).

REFERENCES

Anderson, Benedict R. 1972. The Idea of Power in Javanese Culture. In *Culture and Politics in Indonesia*, ed. C. Holt, pp. 1–69. Ithaca, NY: Cornell University Press.

Bruner, Edward M. 2005. *Culture on Tour: Ethnographies of Travel*. Chicago: University of Chicago Press.

Cochrane, Janet, ed. 2008. *Asian Tourism: Growth and Change*. Amsterdam: Elsevier.

Dahles, Heidi. 2001. *Tourism, Heritage and National Culture in Java: Dilemmas of a Local Community*. Richmond, VA: Curzon Press.

Dann, Graham M. S. 1996. *The Language of Tourism: A Sociolinguistic Perspective*. Wallingford, UK: CABI.

de la Torre, Marta, ed. 2002. *Assessing the Values of Cultural Heritage*. Los Angeles: Getty Conservation Institute.

Di Giovine, Michael A. 2008. *The Heritage-Scape: UNESCO, World Heritage, and Tourism*. Lanham, MD: Lexington Books.

Dumarçay, Jacques. 1986. *The Temples of Java*. Translated by M. Smithies. Singapore: Oxford University Press.

Geertz, Clifford. 1960. *The Religion of Java*. Glencoe, IL: Free Press.

Graeber, David. 2001. *Toward an Anthropological Theory of Value: The False Coin of Our Own Dreams*. New York: Palgrave.

Hansen, Trine Bille, Henrik Christoffersen, and Stephen Wanhill. 1998. The Economic Evaluation of Cultural and Heritage Projects: Conflicting Methodologies. *Tourism, Culture & Communication* 1(1):27–48.

Kim, Samuel Seongseop, Kevin K. F. Wong, and Min Cho. 2007. Assessing the Economic Value of a World Heritage Site and Willingness-to-Pay Determinants: A Case of Changdeok Palace. *Tourism Management* 28(1):317–22.

Klamer, Arjo. 2003. A Pragmatic View on Values in Economics. *Journal of Economic Methodology* 10(2):191–212.

Navrud, Ståle, and Richard C. Ready, eds. 2002. *Valuing Cultural Heritage: Applying Environmental Valuation Techniques to Historic Buildings, Monuments and Artifacts*. Cheltenham, UK: Edward Elgar.

Noonan, Douglas S. 2003. Contingent Valuation and Cultural Resources: A Meta-Analytic Review of the Literature. *Journal of Cultural Economics* 27 (3, 4):159–76.

Porter, Benjamin W., and Noel B. Salazar, eds. 2005. Heritage Tourism, Conflict, and the Public Interest. Special issue of *International Journal of Heritage Studies* 11(5).

Sahlins, Marshall D. 1976. *Culture and Practical Reason*. Chicago: University of Chicago Press.

Salazar, Noel B. 2005. Tourism and Glocalization: "Local" Tour Guiding. *Annals of Tourism Research* 32(3):628–46.

———. 2008. "Enough Stories!" Asian Tourism Redefining the Roles of Asian Tour Guides. *Civilisations* 57(1, 2):207–22.

———. 2010a. *Envisioning Eden: Mobilizing Imaginaries in Tourism and Beyond*. Oxford: Berghahn.

———. 2010b. The Globalisation of Heritage through Tourism: Balancing Standardisation and Differentiation. In *Heritage and Globalization*, eds. S. Labadi and C. Long, pp. 130–47. London: Routledge.

———. 2010c. From Local to Global (and Back): Towards Glocal Ethnographies of Cultural Tourism. In *Cultural Tourism Research Methods*, eds. G. Richards and W. Munsters, pp. 188–98. Wallingford, UK: CABI.

———. 2011. Imagineering Cultural Heritage for Local-to-Global Audiences. In *The Heritage Theatre*, eds. A. van Stipriaan, P. van Ulzen, and M. Halbertsma, pp. 49–72. Newcastle upon Tyne: Cambridge Scholars Publishing.

Salazar, Noel B., and Benjamin W. Porter, eds. 2004 Heritage and Tourism, PIA and Global Interests. Theme issue, *Anthropology in Action* 11(2/3).

Schlehe, Judith. 1996. Reinterpretations of Mystical Traditions: Explanations of a Volcanic Eruption in Java. *Anthropos* 91(4, 6):391–409.

Sinclair, Thea M., and Mike Stabler. 1997. *The Economics of Tourism*. London: Routledge.

Snowball, Jeanette D. 2008. *Measuring the Value of Culture: Methods and Examples in Cultural Economics*. Berlin: Springer Verlag.

Tuan, Tran Huu, and Ståle Navrud. 2007. Valuing Cultural Heritage in Developing Countries: Comparing and Pooling Contingent Valuation and Choice Modelling Estimates. *Environmental and Resource Economics* 38(1):51–69.

Tunbridge, John E., and Gregory J. Ashworth. 1996. *Dissonant Heritage: The Management of the Past as a Resource in Conflict*. Chichester: J. Wiley.

UNESCO. 1972. *Convention concerning the Protection of the World Cultural and Natural Heritage*. Paris: UNESCO.

———. 1992. *Cultural Tourism Development Central Java–Yogyakarta: Final Report*. Yogyakarta: UNESCO/UNDP/Directorate General of Tourism.

———. 2008. *The Operational Guidelines for the Implementation of the World Heritage Convention*. Paris: UNESCO World Heritage Centre.

UNWTO. 2006. *Tourism Highlights*. Madrid: United Nations World Tourism Organization.

3

+

Mayanizing Tourism on Roatán Island, Honduras

Archaeological Perspectives on Heritage, Development, and Indigeneity

Alejandro J. Figueroa, Whitney A. Goodwin, and E. Christian Wells

Historian Darío Euraque (1998, 2004, 2010:49) has used the term *Mayanization* to characterize the past century of tourism and development in Honduras in which many tour operators and business owners have capitalized on the geographic proximity of their well-known neighbors, the Classic Maya, to name (and claim as "Maya") everything from handicrafts to entire buildings. The island of Roatán (figure 3.1) off the north coast of Honduras has become increasingly "Mayanized" over the last few years as heritage tourism has amplified dramatically in the wake of new development opportunities for the island's residents. The proliferation of Maya names for hotels, restaurants, and the like and the recent construction of an outdoor interpretive center with reproductions of famous Maya monuments from the mainland have opened up new conversations and conflicts about heritage and indigeneity on the island. As various stakeholders assert competing claims to being "indigenous," few people agree on what the term means. And shifting meanings have become strategically relevant on the island as different groups vie for revenue from the expanding tourism industry.

Our recent research on the island has collected archaeological, historical, and ethnographic data, which we are using to contextualize these dialogues and to understand their trajectory. Since the pre-Hispanic oc-

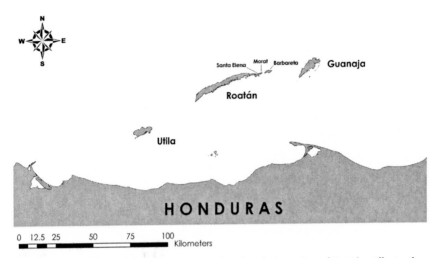

Figure 3.1.   The Bay Islands of Honduras, Showing the Location of Roatán. (Illustration by Alejandro J. Figueroa)

cupants of the island were likely multilingual (Chibchan, Tolatecan, Misumalpan, and Mayan), and the centuries that followed brought Spanish, Dutch, and English settlers as well as the establishment of the Garínagu (Garífuna) of mixed West African and Carib/Arawak descent, many island residents have multiple claims to multiple identities. Over time, these complex arrangements of culture, power, and history have rendered notions and assertions to "first occupancy" problematic for understanding contemporary struggles for social and political-economic rights and the entanglement of agendas that has ensued. The island's unique genealogy and the resulting controversy over indigeneity have also resulted in the large-scale destruction—in the name of development—of significant archaeological and historical remains that are central to these struggles. Our research documents some of these complexities and seeks to understand the long-term consequences of heritage tourism on cultural patrimony in Honduras.

HERITAGE TOURISM ON ROATÁN ISLAND

On Roatán, the largest of the Bay Islands (covering about 480 km^2), a trip to the local museum housing artifacts and describing the practices of the pre-Hispanic inhabitants of the island—last updated in the 1990s and occupying a space of about 250 m^2—will cost you a single U.S. dollar. To spend a day on the newly constructed, resort-owned, multi-million-dollar interpretive center, minizoo, and replica of the World Heritage Maya site of Copán, occupying the entirety (11.5 acres) of the cleverly named "Maya Key," will run you about thirty U.S. dollars. The discrepancy in price between these two venues reflects, in part, the value that islanders and tourists place on the information presented. But who decides what is presented in these places? And equally as important, who profits from the (re)presentation?

Archaeology is no stranger to being co-opted in the name of touristic objectives. The importance of heritage and history to the tourism industry is not novel, nor is it an issue unique to this area (e.g., Breglia 2006; Brunner 2005; Burns 2004; Iseminger 1997; Kincaid 1988; Lea 2000; Lowenthal 1996; McKercher and du Cros 2002; Merriman 2004; Potter 1997). Multiple and contested presentations of an idealized indigenous past have often stemmed from the misuse or mischaracterization of archaeological findings (Cronin and O'Connor 2003; Lowenthal 1985; Urry 2002; Zimmerman 2003). Heritage tourism on the island of Roatán has mainly focused on presenting the Maya, despite the lack of any physical evidence supporting their presence in antiquity. Indeed, on Roatán and throughout the mainland, the Maya past has become canonized, and the "official" discourse has become Maya centered and not multiethnic (Joyce 2003, 2008). While these efforts attract visitors and the resources that flow to and from them, it intentionally or coincidentally devalues contributions made by less familiar groups.

In many cases, these misrepresentations stem from larger issues surrounding nationalist agendas and the appropriation of symbols and histories. In Honduras, Euraque (1998, 2004, 2010) has outlined the development of what he has termed the "Mayanization" of Honduran tourism and business (see also Joyce 2003:85–86). Because Maya archaeological sites are viewed as "signs of status vis-à-vis neighboring states and international communities" (Joyce 2003:81–82), businesses in Honduras that range from banks to street vendors have capitalized on the fame of the Maya by deploying symbols and terms from the Maya site of Copán, located in the southwestern tip of the country. With the recent boom in tourism on the Bay Islands, home to the second-largest coral reef system in the world, different individuals and groups are competing to find the most effective ways to capture the attention of visitors and secure their space in the ever-expanding tourism market. To better understand this struggle and the economic complexities surrounding it, questions concerning the future of tourism on the island, which are inseparable from those regarding representation and identity, must be contextualized historically.

The cultural affiliations of the pre-Hispanic Bay Islanders have been hotly debated for many years and are still very much contested today, mainly due to a lack of sustained research on the islands (Wells 2008). It has been suggested that the islanders were Pech, Maya, or Tolupan, but because islands have typically been ports of trade and commerce with constant movement of peoples and things, boundaries are understood in very different ways among island communities, and we should not expect to see clear or static expressions of affiliations (Goodwin 2011). Just as with the Roatán islanders of today, pre-Hispanic islanders were probably multiethnic and multilingual, and the complications that this presents for archaeological research and interpretation cannot be ignored.

ORIGINS OF PRESENT-DAY CULTURAL HETEROGENEITY ON ROATÁN

In addition to questions about the identity and cultural affiliations of the pre-Hispanic islanders, present-day issues of power and representation are further complicated by the various groups that have arrived to the island over the last half millennium, the presence of probable descendants of the displaced "original" island inhabitants surviving today on mainland Honduras, and the confused and often conflicting historical accounts of the fate of these native island inhabitants (Conzemius 1928; Davidson 1974; Newson 1986). European presence in the Bay Islands began with French buccaneer incursions and attacks on Spanish convoys, forts, and settlements during the first half of the sixteenth century (Davidson 1974:42). This harassment increased later on in the century with the arrival of Dutch and English buccaneers, whose disruptions forced the Spanish to evacuate all Bay Islanders to mainland Honduras and Guatemala in the mid-seventeeth century in an attempt to cut off the provision and support of freebooters, which was done at the expense of provisioning Spanish ships (Davidson 1974:43). Spanish and English conflicts continued to escalate well into the eighteenth century, culminating with the founding of the first English military settlement on Roatán, named New Port Royal, in 1742, which was subsequently abandoned in 1749 following the signing of the Treaty of Aix-la-Chapelle (Davidson 1974:58).

The next wave of migrants to Roatán was that of the Garínagu or Garífuna, an Afro-Caribbean group born of the mixture of West African and Carib/Arawak peoples from the western Caribbean island of Saint Vincent. In 1791, the English deported to Roatán approximately two thousand Garífuna as punishment for their uprising on Saint Vincent (Davidson 1974:65; Gonzalez 1988:39). Historic and ethnographic evidence suggest that many of these first Garífuna soon abandoned Roatán because of unfavorable living conditions there, and they settled throughout the Atlantic coasts of Belize, Guatemala, Honduras, and Nicaragua (Davidson 1974:67; Gonzalez 1988:48–49). Today, the original Garífuna town, Punta Gorda, still exists on Roatán, though its occupants have extended to neighboring communities.

Following these abrupt population movements, the slow but continuous contemporary settlement of the island began in the first half of the nineteenth century, initially by migrant slaves and slave owners from the Cayman Islands, referred to as the Anglo-Antilleans, and later by other Afro-Antilleans and by Protestant missionaries and colonists from Belize (Davidson 1974:84, 86). Despite the signing of the Wyke-Cruz Treaty in 1859, which returned sovereignty of the Bay Islands to Honduras, Hispanicized Ladinos from the mainland did not make their way to the islands until the 1950s and 1960s, following the boom of the banana and fishing industries on the island (Davidson 1974; Stonich 1998, 2000). Though many of these Ladinos first occupied the already established settlements on the southern coast of the island, a large group founded the villages of Corozal and Juticalpa, the first, and even today the only, inland settlements on Roatán (Davidson 1974). Although the majority of the islanders currently live along the coast, they are constantly being displaced by the tourism industry, which is founded on the appeal of the island's beaches and reefs.

THE DEVELOPMENT AND EXPANSION OF TOURISM IN THE BAY ISLANDS

Tourism is by no means a new activity in the Bay Islands. What is new is the pace at which it has grown and expanded in the past twenty years, including new strategies of construction and development being implemented over the past decade (Currin 2002). For example, the Honduran Institute of Tourism (IHT 2007:46, 2010:12) reports that, during the period from 2000 to 2008, the number of foreign overnight visitors to Roatán more than doubled (from 21,145 to 45,633), nearly matching the island's resident population of approximately sixty thousand. That the number of hotel rooms has not risen significantly during this period (from 953 in 2001 to 1,073 in 2008; IHT 2001, 2010) suggests that there is unmet demand or, more likely, that the influx of visitors is linked to the burgeoning cruise line industry that brings day visitors to port. In 2010, 171 cruise ships visited the island, brining approximately nine hundred thousand visitors (IHT 2010).

Even though the appeal of the Bay Islands has drawn visitors and enthusiasts since historical times, it was the continuous passing of national legislation, growing foreign and local elite interests, and the assistance of international funding agencies, including the International Monetary

Fund (IMF) and Inter-American Development Bank (IDB), that has contributed to an almost uninterrupted growth of the tourism industry on Roatán. In 1965, the Bay Islands were chosen as one of five areas of Honduras to be developed intensely for tourism (Ritchie et al. 1965:120). Initial efforts to develop the islands following this ruling failed, and it was not until the decline of military dictatorships in the 1980s and the subsequent economic crisis that the Honduran government decided to implement more strenuous legislation, including the creation of "tourism zones" and "tourism free zones" (IHT 1993) as well as the Law of Tourism Incentives (IHT 1998). Such legislation provided several incentives for local and foreign investors to participate in Honduras's open tourism economy, which focused particularly on the Bay Islands (Stonich 1998:26, 2000:64–66; Stonich et al. 1998). As a direct consequence of this legislation, the main Roatán highway was constructed, an international runway was added to Roatán's airport, and several new resorts and hotels were established (Stonich 2000:66). In the early 1990s, "El Mundo Maya" was created as a joint attempt by the governments of Belize, El Salvador, Guatemala, Honduras, and Mexico to promote tourism throughout Central America. Outside of Copán, the two areas promoted as part of the Honduran portion of the tour were Roatán and La Mosquitia, neither of which have any demonstrable connection to the Maya, past or present (Stonich 2000:9–10).

A third, and much more recent, wave of legislation has been brought about by the National Strategy for Sustainable Tourism (ENTS), created by the Ministry of Tourism (SETUR) and the Honduran Institute of Tourism (IHT), and backed by the IDB. The Bay Islands, and especially Roatán, have been designated as primary short-term priorities by the ENTS, which has aided in the construction of two new cruise ship terminals on the island that encompass twenty acres of waterfront property and can accommodate up to eight thousand passengers daily (Carnival News 2010; IHT 2005:89). What is most surprising about the growth rate of Roatán's tourism industry is its resilience, particularly in the face of the ongoing global economic crisis and the ousting of now-former president Manuel Zelaya during a military coup in July of 2009.

TOURISM, REPRESENTATION, AND POWER ON ROATÁN

According to a survey conducted by Susan Stonich (2000), the majority of Roatán's inhabitants favors tourism and are overwhelmingly employed in the tourism industry. However, most islanders are growing increasingly skeptical of the tangible benefits of tourism development and the uneven distribution of wealth that it produces. Many are also reluctant to follow newly imposed restrictions to their land-use and subsistence practices, recognizing the pattern of displacement wherein island inhabitants are being stripped of access to beachfront property and associated resources by development corporations and local governments (Stonich 2000:142). It has often been shown that when this situation arises, resentment of the actions of local elites who control much of the industry is redirected toward the tourists themselves (for example, Currin 2002:73–76). As Erve Chambers (2000:22–23) notes, "Relatively little attention has been paid to the emic categorizations that are made by the members of communities that receive tourists . . . local populations that receive tourists are all too often left to play a passive role in the process." Moving beyond the essentializing discourse of a guest/host dichotomy, the anthropological study of tourism encompasses more than simply tourists and local populations, even in cases where the local population might be homogenous or easily defined. Chambers (2000:30) suggests that most of the tourism industry is fueled and shaped by mediators, which range from government officials to travel agents.

It is clear that those who have benefited the most from the tourism industry are those who were initially wealthy enough to have the resources needed to invest in these enterprises or to become mediators themselves (e.g., Place 1991). An example of these "emerging mediators" is the current mayor of the island, who owns and operates both Anthony's Key Resort, which houses the local museum of "indigenous" (pre-Hispanic) material culture, and the exclusive Maya Key Private Island Resort (the location of the Copán reconstruction). Local elite such as this influence the direction of tourism development on the island with businesses backed by multinational investors, associations with powerful government officials, and even strong connections to influential nongovernmental organizations.

Often working in the higher-paid positions within larger businesses are the English-speaking Bay Islanders, a heterogeneous group made up of the previously mentioned Anglo- and Afro-Antilleans with further social, economic, and even spatial distinctions and stratifications found within. Hindered by their lack of knowledge of English, the primary language of the majority of island tourists, the mainlanders (Ladinos or "Spanyards," as they are called by "native" islanders) also lack the local social networks needed to serve as a system of support during the off-season periods when work is scarce. This degree of social stratification is supported by Stonich's (2000:141) anthropometric study of children of different ethnic groups in several communities on the island, which found that only Ladino children were consistently undernourished.

Given the context outlined above, the Garífuna are a unique minority on the island, who boast the longest continuous habitation of the island since the depopulation of pre-Hispanic communities during the early colonial period. The story of the Garífuna is a salient example of the complexities surrounding indigenous tourism and the commodification of culture. In a struggle to gain and control the rights to their cultural performances, currently being commodified by more experienced and business-savvy outsiders, the dangers and powers associated with heritage tourism are clear. Not only are they fighting for the right to reap the economic benefits of these performances but also they are struggling to regain control of the presentation of their heritage as a way to reinforce their identity as a group and their authority over the creation of that identity (Kirtsoglou and Theodossopoulos 2004). Chambers (2000) recognizes that, because tourism has become a tool for economic development, competition for control over both tangible and intangible heritage is fierce within and among communities. Tourism becomes synonymous with representation because a certain image must be created and marketed. In many cases, that image is strong enough to change the community's perception of itself, and therefore those in charge of that representation often have even greater power than it may seem initially.

In the case of Roatán, while some of the earliest accounts of the island may mention the pre-Hispanic islanders, their story is otherwise unknown and their voice silenced, despite possible living descendant communities. As archaeologists, we seek to bring their narrative to life through research that may uncover histories unwritten by the winners of the past, those with the power to write. Being involved in writing the history of the islands, we cannot forget that power is not a property of the past. There is power in the interpreting, displaying, and the writing that we do today. If we seek balance among the stakeholders in today's Roatán as we situate ourselves into the traditions of the past, we cannot forget the political and social contexts of the present.

PREVIOUS ARCHAEOLOGICAL
RESEARCH IN THE BAY ISLANDS

Although archaeological research on the island has been recent and sporadic, historical documents from the time of the earliest interactions between contact-period islanders and Europeans have continued to shape perceptions of the islanders' identity. In 1502, Ferdinand, the son of Christopher Columbus, recorded an important encounter between islanders and his father's crew, including information about their physical appearance and the biophysical environment of the island. This account also provided details about the connections that the islanders had with the Maya when, by chance, a trading party arrived on the island by canoe with goods presumably from the area of present-day Belize and Yucatan (Columbus 1959).

Accounts from numerous visitors to the islands in the mid-nineteenth century describe "curious" and "uncivilized" artifacts being taken out of mounds or found in the collections of local inhabitants (Mitchell 1850; Squier 1858; Young 1847). During the 1930s, several short visits and explorations were carried out by major scientific institutions, including the Museum of the American Indian (then known as the Heye Foundation; Houlson 1934; Mitchell-Hedges 1954), the American Museum of Natural History (reported in Strong 1935), the Smithsonian Institution's Bureau of American Ethnology (Strong 1934, 1935), and the University of Cambridge's Royal Geographic Society (Feachem 1940; Feachem and Braunholtz 1938). The first scientific excavations on the islands did not take place until 1950 at the eighty-acre site on the island of Utila (Epstein 1957, 1959). From this research, Jeremiah Epstein (1957) first categorized the ceramic materials and defined the Selín Horizon (ca. AD 600–900) and the Cocal Horizon (ca. AD 900–1520), the classification system that is still in use today for Bay Islands pottery (see Dennett 2007, 2008; Healy 1993).

This research was followed in the 1970s with formal archaeological surveys of the islands (Davidson 1974; Epstein 1975, 1977, 1978; Epstein and Véliz 1977; Goodwin et al. 1979; Hasemann 1975, 1977; Healy 1978; Véliz et al. 1976, 1977). The most recent period of archaeological investigation includes Christopher Begley's (1992, 1999a, 1999b) excavations at the site of Difficulty Hill on Roatán and Plan Grande on the island of Guanaja, which led to the creation of a new typology for Roatán pottery. The latest archaeological work carried out on Roatán has been salvage archaeology, conducted by technical and administrative personnel of the Honduran Institute of Anthropology and History (IHAH) in response to, or to prevent, site destruction from construction and development activities (Cruz Castillo 1999; Cruz Castillo et al. 2000).

Most of the preliminary evidence collected through these short-term investigations and analyses of looted collections is primarily rooted in comparisons of ceramic material and suggests the strongest connection with the Pech (Paya) of northeastern Honduras (Davidson 1974:19–20; Wells 2008), a contemporary indigenous group believed to be the descendants of pre-Hispanic occupants of the area who migrated from South America over three thousand years ago (Aguilar 2006; Conzemius 1927; Cuddy 2007:34–35; Griffin et al. 2009; Holt 1986; Lanza et al. 1992; Stone 1939). A recent analysis conducted by Carrie Dennett (2007, 2008) of the data collected in 1975 at the site of Río Claro in the Department of Colón, in northeast mainland Honduras, expands on Begley's (1999b) typology for Roatán ceramics and provides some interesting insights and observations regarding cultural affiliations and social and economic exchange in antiquity (Healy 1993).

The University of South Florida's (USF) contribution to this debate began in 2003, when 157 whole pottery vessels and a number of associated artifacts from Roatán were "rediscovered" in the collections of the department of anthropology (Wells 2008). A local Tampa family originally from Roatán had donated the materials to the university in the 1990s. After conducting an analysis of these materials, José Moreno Cortés and Christian Wells (2006) concluded that this collection consisted of objects very similar to those used in ceremonies conducted by Pech peoples today.

TOWARD A NEW FORM OF
ARCHAEOLOGY IN THE BAY ISLANDS

In 2008, nearly fifty years after they were removed from Honduras, the pottery in the USF collection was returned to the IHAH. In preparation for the repatriation, we began to investigate the provenance of the collection on Roatán. After speaking with the family who donated the material, we determined that the artifacts are associated with the pre-Hispanic site of El Antigual. In August of 2008, Project Roatán was initiated by USF in conjunction with the IHAH as an initial means of developing a long-term cultural heritage project in collaboration with local communities.

The archaeological ruins of El Antigual are located at roughly N16°22′57″, W86°24′23″, placing the settlement near the center of the island. The site spreads across two small hilltops and the saddle that connects them, covering about three thousand square meters of sometimes steep and uneven terrain. From either hilltop, one can clearly see both coasts of the island and a clear view of the mainland of Honduras. Epstein (1975:39–40), who observed "plain pottery and one 'monkey' lug similar to that found on the handles of San Marcos ware," last formally recorded the site. After his visit, Epstein (1975:40) concluded that "the hilltop seems to have served as an offertory or burial area since it is too small to have contained a single family unit. It is possible that a small population lived further down the slope. There seems little here that is left to excavate."

The site has no observable architecture, although much of it is under overgrown brush and so it is presently impossible to determine if there are mounds. Numerous artifacts—as isolated finds and in concentrations indicative of activity areas—were observed throughout the entire site. Artifacts include mostly plainware and decorated (incised) pottery similar to the Dorina variety of pottery, documented by Healy (1993:209–12) and others (Epstein 1957; Stone 1939; Strong 1935). The ceramics, along with the discovery of a green obsidian blade segment, strongly suggest that the latest occupation of the site dates to the Postclassic period (Cocal phase), ca. AD 1000 to 1530 (Véliz et al. 1976:11).

The site is well preserved, save for two major disturbances: the construction of two massive cell phone towers by the state telephone company Hondutel, one on each of the hilltops. The towers' cement foundations, which measure approximately one hundred square meters, appear to completely obliterate significant portions of the site and reveal a clearly discernible A–B–C soil horizon, which extends downward for approximately 0.2 meters and ends in limey shale bedrock. The observed cultural materials, mostly in the B horizon, include ceramic, chert, quartzite, and shell.

During the summer of 2009, USF carried out the first field season of Project Roatán, which included the excavation of sections of the summit and the southern slope of the site and an intensive pedestrian survey of the immediate vicinity of the site (Wells et al. 2009). Excavations did not reveal any evidence of formal architecture on the hilltop; however, the recovery of small pieces of burned daub, patterns in soil composition and compaction on the southern slope of this area, and findings by previous projects conducted elsewhere on the island (Cruz Castillo et al. 2000) suggest that further excavation might reveal that at least some portion of the site was artificially terraced in the past. Concentrated and spatially discrete refuse deposits suggest that certain areas at the summit were swept or kept clean, perhaps following ritual activities. Comparison with historically known or contemporary practices of land use, architectural features, or ritual practices may provide further insights into these findings. Interestingly, artifacts collected during excavation did not include the full range of materials observed during a preliminary site visit in 2008, indicating that surface materials do not necessarily represent the full range of subsurface deposits. This discrepancy has important implications for the planning of future large-scale excavations on the island as well as historical reconstructions based on surface collections alone (Klassen 2010).

The survey component of the project had two major goals: first, to understand the extension and spatial and temporal relationships of El Antigual and its presumed contemporaries; and second, to evaluate how archaeological sites, particularly those situated on hilltops, have been affected by direct and indirect human actions in the form of recent economic development and urban growth (Figueroa 2011). The first season of the project covered an area of approximately seven square kilometers and identified ten archaeological sites, all of which consist of prehistoric ceramic scatters, with one site having a historic (mid-nineteenth century) component. General and diagnostic surface collections were made at each of these sites, and impact assessment data were collected through a standardized form, which is being entered into a geospatial database for analysis.

THE LAW OF THE LAND ON ROATÁN

Despite the accelerated expansion of the tourism industry on Roatán, most of it still remains anchored in the western end of the island, though this scenario is rapidly changing. Tourism, along with parallel and consequent development activities, has continually resulted in the deterioration of the landscape of Roatán (Stonich 1998). The clearing of vegetation for agricultural and construction purposes, the misplacement of water delivery and sewage systems, and the lack of geological and geomechanical studies, among other factors, have contributed to increased levels of deforestation and erosion as well as the virtual destruction of all permanent water streams across the island (Vega et al. 1993).

A preliminary analysis of the data obtained during our survey has revealed patterns of human impact and site management directly related to an increase and change in development activities on the eastern portion of the island. Of the archaeological sites identified and evaluated, those located near modern populations and other infrastructure—including the main island highway, a resort hotel, and a luxury seaside village—were the most affected. We experienced the pace of development on Roatán firsthand, when a section of the largest site identified through survey (PR06) was razed in order to make room for an access road to a complex of newly built luxury condominiums. In the face of such uncontrolled growth and expansion, pessimism makes us wonder if archaeology in the Bay Islands, particularly on Roatán, is destined to become responsive and reactive.

SHIFTING DEVELOPMENT'S MOMENTUM

Tourism, as discussed here, primarily controlled by elites, is what Chambers (2000:53) describes as "a relatively safe kind of cultural politics because it is shaped in great part by assumptions of what outsiders desire." This is an issue with important consequences for archaeology especially. If the developers of tourist attractions that we spoke with continue to argue that "the Maya is what sells" because "that is what the tourists want," then they are denying any responsibility for shaping and fueling that desire. Central to the commodification and bounding of heritage, marketability, and "the Bay Islands Brand Promise" are significant issues when it comes to the tangible aspects of heritage management. In most cases, even in formal and informal educational settings, such as museums, only the finest, most complete, or most "impressive" (to Euro-American eyes) artifacts are chosen for display. What does the island have to offer if large and majestic monuments cannot be presented, or if indigenous crafts are unknown or cannot be commoditized? How can the preservation of the past become an important issue for islanders if the economic benefits of such an enterprise cannot be demonstrated or even begin to ensure the even distribution of such benefits? Why should they trade one model for another if it will make little, if any, difference in their everyday lives and the result is not remotely connected to their personal or group histories?

Another factor urging us to address the issue of the misrepresentation of the cultural heterogeneity of the Bay Islands is the rate at which archaeological sites and landscapes are being destroyed by urban growth and development (Figueroa 2011). Uncontrolled and unrestricted development reflects the value given to Roatán's prehistoric and historic cultural heritage by the entities and elites in charge of defining the island's history and identity. However, as Stonich and colleagues (1998:282) have observed regarding environmental conservation, without the support of these local and foreign elites, there is little chance of success in any endeavor that aims to change the way tourism is built and operated in the Bay Islands. This observation is a harsh reminder that economic benefits are at the heart of tourism development, given the impossibility of measuring and anticipating social and cultural variables (Chambers 2000:32). Because of this practical reality, and keeping in mind the risk of turning archaeological interpretations into an "adjudication of land claims" (Joyce 2008:65), future archaeological research on the island must be driven by a truly multivocal approach, one that is the result of the participation of a variety of people with different perspectives examining the same phenomena.

To conclude, we believe that the value of archaeology for tourism on Roatán is its ability to highlight the multicultural history of Roatán as an asset of the island that has potential value for many different stakeholders. Beyond providing "authenticity" of what is "indigenous," archaeological information has the power to create sustainable and potentially profitable tourism alternatives that could be available to many different groups. If the history of the island is already being written by those currently in power (and practically at the same rate that the material markers of that past are being destroyed), then archaeology has an important, immediate, and multifaceted role to play in the future of representation on the Bay Islands. Archaeology's contribution lies not just in the preservation of heritage for future generations but also in the recognition that the discipline needs to go beyond the labels of "applied," "community," or "public" archaeology. Archaeology on Roatán needs to be performed from a holistic anthropological perspective that encompasses all of the characteristics that comprise those dimensions—economics, tourism, politics, identity—that anthropology seeks to understand. Moreover, one of the goals of archaeology on Roatán should be to empower local communities with the ability to interpret national (pre)history in their own terms. From this perspective, heritage, while historically contingent and emerging, is ultimately about the future, an active part of meaning making for living communities.

REFERENCES

Aguilar, Juan Carlos Vargas. 2006. *Etno-Demografía de la Etnia Pech, Honduras*. San José, Costa Rica: Centro Centroamericano de Población de la Universidad de Costa Rica.

Begley, Christopher T. 1992. *Informe Preliminar sobre las Excavaciones en Difficulty Hill, Isla de Roatán, Honduras*. Tegucigalpa, Honduras: Instituto Hondureño de Antropología e Historia.

———. 1999a. *Investigación de Plan Grande, Guanaja, Islas de la Bahía, Honduras: Ideología y Vida Cotidiana en la Frontera de Mesoamérica*. Tegucigalpa, Honduras: Instituto Hondureño de Antropología e Historia.

———. 1999b. *Elite Power Strategies and External Connections in Ancient Eastern Honduras*. PhD dissertation, Department of Anthropology, University of Chicago.

Breglia, Lisa. 2006. *Monumental Ambivalence: The Politics of Heritage*. Austin: University of Texas Press.

Brunner, Edward M. 2005. *Culture on Tour*. Chicago: University of Chicago Press.

Burns, Georgette Leah. 2004. Anthropology and Tourism: Past Contributions and Future Theoretical Challenges. *Anthropological Forum* 14(1):5–22.

Carnival News. 2010. Grand Opening Ceremonies Held for $62 Million Mahogany Bay Cruise Center. http://carnival-news.com/2010/02/11/grand -opening-ceremonies-held-for-62-million-mahogany-bay-cruise-center, accessed November 14, 2011.

Chambers, Erve. 2000. *Native Tours: The Anthropology of Travel and Tourism*. Prospect Heights, IL: Waveland Press.

Columbus, Fernando. 1959. *The Life of Admiral Christopher Columbus, by His Son Ferdinand*. New Brunswick, NJ: Rutgers University Press.

Conzemius, Eduard. 1927. Los Indios Payas de Honduras: Estudio Geográfico, Histórico, Etnográfico y Lingüístico. *Journal de la Societé des Americanistes de Paris* 19(1):245–302.

———. 1928. On the Aborigines of the Bay Islands (Honduras). *Atti del XXII Congresso Internazionale degli Americanisti* 2(1):57–68.

Cronin, Michael, and Barbara O'Connor, eds. 2003. *Irish Tourism: Image, Culture, and Identity*. Clevedon, UK: Channel View.

Cruz Castillo, Oscar Neill. 1999. *Informe de Inspección a los Sitios Arqueológicos de Plan Grande y Marble Hill, Guanaja, Islas de la Bahía, Honduras*. Tegucigalpa, Honduras: Instituto Hondureño de Antropología e Historia.

Cruz Castillo, Oscar Neill, and Idelfonso Orellana. 2000. *Informe Final de las Excavaciones Arqueológicas en Charlie Brown, Roatán, Islas de la Bahía*. Tegucigalpa, Honduras: Instituto Hondureño de Antropología e Historia.

Cuddy, Thomas W. 2007. *Political Identity and Archaeology in Northeast Honduras.* Boulder: University Press of Colorado.

Currin, Frances H. 2002. *Transformation of Paradise: Geographical Perspectives on Tourism Development on a Small Caribbean Island (Utila, Honduras).* MA thesis, Department of Geography and Anthropology, Louisiana State University, Baton Rouge.

Davidson, William V. 1974. *Historical Geography of the Bay Islands, Honduras: Anglo-Hispanic Conflict in the Western Caribbean.* Birmingham, NY: Southern University Press.

————. 1991. Geographical Perspectives on Spanish-Pech (Paya) Indian Relationships in Sixteenth Century Northeast Honduras. *Columbian Consequences* 3(1):205–26.

Dennett, Carrie L. 2007. *The Río Claro Site (A.D. 1000–1530), Northeast Honduras: A Ceramic Classification and Examination of External Connections.* MA thesis, Department of Anthropology, Trent University.

————. 2008. A Modal Analysis of Vessel Appendages from Río Claro (AD 1000–1530), Northeast Honduras. *La Tinaja* 19(2):12–16.

Epstein, Jeremiah F. 1957. *Late Ceramic Horizons in Northeastern Honduras.* PhD dissertation, Department of Anthropology, University of Pennsylvania.

————. 1959. Dating the Ulua Polychrome Complex. *American Antiquity* 25(1):125–29.

————. 1975. *Reconocimiento Arqueológico de las Islas de la Bahía: R1 a R33.* Tegucigalpa, Honduras: Instituto Hondureño de Antropología e Historia.

————. 1977. *Islas de la Bahía: Reconocimiento Arqueológico.* Tegucigalpa, Honduras: Instituto Hondureño de Antropología e Historia.

————. 1978. Problemas en el Estudio de la Prehistoria de las Islas de la Bahía. *Yaxkin* 2(3):149–58.

Epstein, Jeremiah F., and Vito Véliz. 1977. Reconocimiento arqueológico de la Isla de Roatán, Honduras. *Yaxkin* 2(1):28–39.

Euraque, Darío A. 1998. Antropólogos, Arqueólogos, Imperialismo y la Mayanización de Honduras: 1890–1940. *Yaxkin* 17(1):85–103.

————. 2004. *Conversaciones Históricas con el Mestizaje y Su Identidad Nacional en Honduras.* San Pedro Sula, Honduras: Centro Editorial.

————. 2010. *El Golpe de Estado del 28 de Junio de 2009, el Patrimonio Cultural y la Identidad Nacional de Honduras.* San Pedro Sula, Honduras: Centro Editorial.

Feachem, Richard W. 1940. The Bay Islands, Gulf of Honduras. *Geographical Journal* 96 (3):181–89.

Feachem, Richard W., and Hermann J. Braunholtz. 1938. Exhibition of Antiquities and Photographs. *Man* 38(1):73–74.

Figueroa, Alejandro J. 2011. *The Clash of Heritage and Development on the Island of Roatán, Honduras.* MA thesis, Department of Anthropology, University of South Florida, Tampa.

Gonzalez, Nancie L. 1988. *Sojourners of the Caribbean: Ethnogenesis and Ethnohistory of the Garifuna.* Urbana: University of Illinois Press.

Goodwin, R. Christopher, Cyd Heymann, and Glen T. Hanson. 1979. Archaeological Sampling on Utila, Bay Islands, Honduras. *Journal of the Virgin Islands Archaeological Society* 7(1):3–26.

Goodwin, Whitney A. 2011. *Archaeology and Indigeneity, Past and Present: A View from the Island of Roatán, Honduras*. MA thesis, Department of Anthropology, University of South Florida, Tampa.

Griffin, Wendy, Hernán Martínez Escobar, and Juana Carolina Hernández Torres. 2009. *Los Pech de Honduras: Una Etnia que Vive*. Tegucigalpa, Honduras: Instituto Hondureño de Antropología e Historia.

Hasemann, George E. 1975. *Survey Report of Utila Island*. Tegucigalpa, Honduras: Instituto Hondureño de Antropología e Historia.

———. 1977. Reconocimiento Arqueológico de Utila. *Yaxkin* 2(1):41–76.

Healy, Paul F. 1978. La Arqueología del Noreste de Honduras: Informe Preliminar de la Investigación de 1975 y 1976. *Yaxkin* 2(3):159–73.

———. 1993. Northeastern Honduras. In *Pottery of Prehistoric Honduras: Regional Classification and Analysis*, eds. J. S. Henderson and M. Beaudry-Corbett, pp. 194–213. Los Angeles, CA: Cotsen Institute of Archaeology.

Holt, Dennis. 1986. *The Development of the Paya Sound System*. PhD dissertation, Department of Anthropology, University of California, Los Angeles.

Houlson, Jane Harvey. 1934. *Blue Blaze: Danger and Delight in Strange Islands in Honduras*. Indianapolis, IN: Bobbs-Merrill.

Instituto Hondureño de Turismo (IHT). 1993. *Decree Number 98-93*. Tegucigalpa, Honduras: Instituto Hondureño de Turismo.

———. 1998. *Decree Number 314-98*. Tegucigalpa, Honduras: Instituto Hondureño de Turismo.

———. 2001. *Boletín Estadístico de Turismo Numero 11*. Tegucigalpa, Honduras: Instituto Hondureño de Turismo.

———. 2005. *Estrategia Nacional de Turismo Sostenible. Informe Final, Fase II: Prospectiva y Planificación: Modelo Turístico Futuro de Honduras (MTF 2021)*. Tegucigalpa, Honduras: Instituto Hondureño de Turismo.

———. 2007. *Statistics Bulletin: The Importance of Tourism in its National Economy, 2000–2006*. Tegucigalpa, Honduras: Instituto Hondureño de Turismo.

———. 2010. *Boletín de Estadísticas Turísticas, 2005–2009*. Tegucigalpa, Honduras: Instituto Hondureño de Turismo.

Iseminger, William R. 1997. Public Archaeology at Cahokia. In *Presenting Archaeology to the Public: Digging for Truths*, ed. J. H. Jameson, pp. 147–55. Walnut Creek, CA: AltaMira Press.

Joyce, Rosemary. 2003. Archaeology and Nation Building: A View from Central America. In *The Politics of Archaeology in a Global Context*, ed. S. Kane, pp. 79–100. Boston: Archaeological Institute of America.

———. 2008. Critical Histories of Archaeological Practice: Latin American and North American Interpretations in a Honduran Context. In *Evaluating Multiple Narratives: Beyond Nationalist, Colonialist, Imperialist Archaeologies*, eds. J. Habu, C. Fawcett, and J. M. Matsunaga, pp. 56–68. New York: Springer.

Kincaid, Jamaica. 1988. *A Small Place*. New York: Farrar, Straus and Giroux.

Kirtsoglou, Elisabeth, and Dimitrios Theodossopoulos. 2004. "They Are Taking Our Culture Away": Tourism and Culture Commodification in the Garifuna Community of Roatán. *Critique of Anthropology* 24(2):135–57.

Klassen, Sarah. 2010. *El Antigual: A Test of Surface Collection Methods*. BA Thesis, Department of Anthropology, Dartmouth College, Hanover, New Hampshire.

Lanza, Rigoberto de Jesús, Marcio Tulio Escobar, Mauren Denise Carías Moncada, and Rosa Carminda Castellanos. 1992. *Los Pech (Payas): Una Cultura Olvidada.* Tegucigalpa, Honduras: Editorial Guaymuras.

Lea, Joanne. 2000. Teaching the Past in Museums. In *The Archaeology Education Handbook: Sharing the Past with Kids*, eds. K. Smardz and S. J. Smith, pp. 315–25. Walnut Creek, CA: AltaMira Press.

Lowenthal, David. 1985. *The Past Is a Foreign Culture.* Cambridge: Cambridge University Press.

———. 1996. *Possessed by the Past.* New York: The Free Press.

McKercher, Bob, and Hilary du Cros. 2002. *Cultural Tourism: The Partnership between Tourism and Cultural Heritage Management.* New York: Routledge.

Merriman, Nick. 2004. Involving the Public in Museum Archaeology. In *Public Archaeology*, ed. N. Merriman, pp. 85–108. New York: Routledge.

Mitchell, Robert C. 1850. A Statistical Account and Description of the Island of Roatán. *Colburn's United Service Journal and Navy and Military Magazine*, August.

Mitchell-Hedges, Frederick A. 1954. *Danger My Ally.* London: Elek Books.

Moreno Cortés, José E., and E. Christian Wells. 2006. *Explaining Standardization without Explaining It Away: Inferring Production Scale from Ancient Pech Pottery of Roatán Island, Honduras.* Paper presented at the 105th Annual Meeting of the American Anthropological Association, San Jose, California.

Nance, James V. 1970. *Resources for Tourism on the Island of Roatán, Republic of Honduras.* MA thesis, Department of Geography, University of Colorado, Boulder.

Newson, Linda. 1986. *The Cost of Conquest: Indian Decline in Honduras under Spanish Rule.* Boulder, CO: Westview Press.

Place, Susan E. 1991. Nature Tourism and Rural Development in Tortuguero, Costa Rica. *Annals of Tourism Research* 18:186–201.

Potter, Parker B. Jr. 1997. The Archaeological Site as an Interpretive Environment. In *Presenting Archaeology to the Public: Digging for Truths*, ed. J. H. Jameson Jr., pp. 35–42. Walnut Creek, CA: AltaMira Press.

Ritchie, L., W. Fothergill, R. Oliver, and M. Wulfing. 1965. *A Regional Study of Tourists Development in Central America.* Tegucigalpa, Honduras: Central Bank for Economic Integration.

Squier, Ephraim George. 1858. *The States of Central America.* New York: Harper and Brothers.

Stone, Doris Z. 1939. A Delimitation of the Paya Area in Honduras and Certain Stylistic Resemblances Found in Costa Rica and Honduras. In *Vigesimoseptimo Congreso Internacional de Americanistas: Actas de la Primera Sesion, Celebrada en la Ciudad de México en 1939*, ed. SEP INAH, pp. 226–30. Mexico City: Secretaría de Educación Pública, Instituto Nacional de Antropología e Historia.

Stonich, Susan C. 1998. Political Ecology of Tourism. *Annals of Tourism Research* 25(1):25–54.

———. 2000. *The Other Side of Paradise: Tourism, Conservation, and Development in the Bay Islands.* Elmsford, NY: Cognizant Communications.

Stonich, Susan C., Jerrel H. Sorensen, and Gus W. Salbador. 1998. Water, Power, and Environmental Health in Tourism Development: The Bay Islands, Honduras. In *Water, Culture, and Power: Local Struggles in a Global Context*, eds. J. M. Donahue and B. Rose Johnston, pp. 263–84. Washington, DC: Island Press.

Strong, William Duncan. 1934. An Archaeological Cruise among the Bay Islands of Honduras. In *Explorations and Field-Work of the Smithsonian Institution in 1933*, ed. Smithsonian Institution, pp. 49–53. Washington, DC: Smithsonian Institution.

———. 1935. *Archaeological Investigations in the Bay Islands, Spanish Honduras*. Washington, DC: Smithsonian Institution.

Urry, John. 2002. *The Tourist Gaze*. Thousand Oaks, CA: Sage.

Vega, A., W. Alevizon, R. Dodd, R. Bolauos, E. Villeda, C. Cerrato, and V. Castro. 1993. *Watersheds, Wildlands, and Wildlife of the Bay Islands, Honduras: A Conservation Strategy*. Gainesville, FL: Tropical Research and Development.

Véliz, Vito, Gordon R. Willey, and Paul F. Healy. 1976. Una Clasificación Preliminar Descriptiva de Cerámica de la Isla de Roatán, Honduras. *Revista de la Universidad* 6(11):19–29.

———. 1977. Clasificación Descriptiva Preliminar de Cerámica de Roatán. *Yaxkin* 2(1):7–18.

Wells, E. Christian. 2008. La Arqueología y el Futuro del Pasado en las Islas de la Bahía. *Yaxkin* 24(1):66–81.

Wells, E. Christian, Alejandro J. Figueroa, and Whitney A. Goodwin. 2009. *Proyecto Roatán: Informe Preliminar, Primera Temporada*. Report submitted to the Instituto Hondureño de Antropología e Historia, Tegucigalpa, Honduras.

Young, Thomas. 1847. *Narrative of a Residence on the Mosquito Shore, with an Account of Truxillo, and the Adjacent Islands of Bonacca and Roatán, and a Vocabulary of the Mosquitian Language*. London, England: Smith, Elder, and Co.

Zimmerman, Larry J. 2003. *Presenting the Past*. Walnut Creek, CA: AltaMira Press.

4

+

Shaping Heritage to Serve Development

Bureaucratic Conflict and Local Agency at Two Chinese Heritage Sites

Robert Shepherd

Just decades removed from the Great Proletarian Cultural Revolution (1966–1976), during which Maoist Red Guards sought to destroy all aspects of both tangible and intangible cultural heritage, the Chinese Communist Party has become an influential supporter of cultural heritage preservation. To this end, the Chinese government has worked closely with UNESCO authorities to achieve World Heritage status for major cultural heritage sites while actively encouraging the development of a domestic tourism industry focused in large part on heritage sites. This chapter examines this state use of tourism as an economic development tool, how these policies impact cultural heritage and environmental policies, and the role local community actors hold in this process.

To provide context to this analysis I focus on two heritage sites, the Buddhist temple complex of Wutai Shan (Mount Wutai), located in Shanxi Province approximately three hundred miles southwest of Beijing, and the state-designated site of "Shangri-la," the Tibetan frontier town of Zhongdian (Tibetan Gyalthang), located 270 miles north of Kunming, capital of Yunnan Province. Wutai Shan in recent years has become a popular domestic tourist destination and, as of June 2009, an official site on the World Heritage list. The ongoing development of this heritage site

has included the displacement of several thousand residents, the rework-
ing of local geography, and what from a distance appears to be the commodification of a previously sacred space. Zhongdian, in contrast, was a
relatively minor town on the Tibetan frontier until 2001, when Chinese officials declared it the site of the fictitious Shangri-la in James Hilton's 1933
novel, *Lost Horizon*. In the past decade the local government has funded
the construction of a Tibetan "old town" and assiduously promoted the
region as a tourist destination for Han Chinese. This research is based on
field visits to Wutai Shan during the summers of 2008, 2009, and 2010 and
to Zhongdian in 2008, and on interviews with visitors, local merchants,
and guides and archival research.

My research offers two broad findings. First, because different parts
of "the state" have different interests and responsibilities in Wutai Shan
and Zhongdian, including forest management, the preservation of temple
sites, the regulation of religious practices, and tourism development, how
tourism, heritage policies, and economic development interact remains
a contested governmental question. Second, while these issues appear
to leave little room for local citizen interests, there is little concern about
cultural commercialization among residents at either site. Instead, people
struggle to achieve tangible material gains from the state-directed promotion of heritage and tourism.

PROMOTING THE PAST

The Chinese government invests significant resources in culture, heritage,
and nature projects. Between 1980 and 2000, the number of museums
in China increased from 365 to 1,353 (Denton 2005:566). China had just
nineteen nature reserves in 1965 and a handful of national parks; by 2000
there were over one thousand nature reserves and 187 national parks
(Weller 2006:77). In terms of heritage, China as of 2010 had thirty-eight
UNESCO-designated World Heritage Sites, fifty-six additional sites
awaiting UNESCO approval, and thousands of other heritage-related
sites classified as "key cultural relics protection units" (*Zhongdian Wenwu
Baohu Danwei*). These include built heritage sites such as the Forbidden
City and Temple of Heaven in Beijing, natural sites such as the Wolong
Panda Reserve and Jiuzhaigou Valley in Sichuan Province, and cultural
sites situated in "nature," such as historic mountain temple complexes,
including Emei Shan in Sichuan, Tai Shan in Shandong, and Wutai Shan
in Shanxi Provinces.

While this renewed focus on cultural preservation and nature conservation has been lauded by international organizations such as UNESCO,
politics plays a crucial role in this process. Just as an official Chinese

state discourse of multiculturalism serves to neutralize political claims of cultural differences (Gladney 2004), heritage projects aim to encapsulate all manners of a generalized past as elements of an apolitical and generic "Chinese" heritage (Hevia 2001:222). The Maoist intent during the Cultural Revolution to erase the past has been replaced by a campaign that seeks to shape material culture into a leisure commodity (Hevia 2001:236), one that, however, clearly carries political intentions. In other words, the erasure not of the past but of historically *specific* contexts of particular *aspects* of the past guides the heritage industry in China.

This process in turn has been made possible by a strategic retreat by the Party-State in its control of citizen movement. Before economic reforms began in 1979, all citizens were tied economically and socially to either agricultural collectives or state enterprises, and any sort of travel required official permission. This control was possible because all transportation and hotel services were state owned and access required official documentation. However, economic reform policies have spurred a demand for cheap labor in production zones along the east coast. At the same time, the elimination of agricultural collectives and the creation of a lease-holding land system have created a large surplus labor pool in the countryside. The net result has been the emergence for the first time in Chinese history of a significant migrant labor class that today numbers approximately 150 million and an increasingly mobile professional and managerial class of entrepreneurs and white-collar workers (Lee 2007).

While tourism as a development policy was initially aimed at foreign tourist arrivals, these policies began to shift in the early 1990s toward domestic tourism after the Tiananmen Square violence of 1989 curtailed international arrivals. In 1998 tourism was officially defined as a "key growth area" of the national economy, in part to encourage domestic consumer demand during the Asian financial crisis of 1998 and 1999 (Nyíri 2009:153). According to official statistics, 1.6 billion domestic tourist trips were made in 2007, which generated just over U.S. $100 billion (CNTO 2007). The size and scope of this sector now overshadows international tourism arrivals, which as of 2009 numbered approximately 130 million. However, the vast majority of foreign tourists are ethnic Chinese residents of Hong Kong, Taiwan, and Macau. In 2009, the actual number of non-Chinese arrivals totaled 21.93 million, of which almost 50 percent (10.2 million) were citizens of Japan, Russia, or the Republic of Korea. Approximately 7.1 million visitors were from the European Community and North America (CNTO 2008, 2009). However, just 10.13 million of total foreign visitors indicated that tourism was their primary purpose, while just 3.9 million Europeans and North Americans did so. As these statistics illustrate, the tourism industry in China is overwhelmingly domestic and regional, and the impact, whether economic or cultural, of arrivals from traditional "Western" countries is minimal.

In summary, China today is a country in which two groups have become mobile: a marginalized peasant class of factory hands, construction workers, nannies, street vendors, and other marginal occupations that increasingly affluent urban residents no longer want to do, and an emerging urban consumer class with the disposable income and leisure time to tour. What links these two forms of spatial movement is not just economic development but also the development of a modern sensibility, which in Chinese is referred to as a "civilized" (*wenming*) consciousness. Just as rural migrant workers are perceived to serve national economic development goals, they are also tasked by the party with bringing an increased level of "civilization" (*wenming de chengdu*) back with them to their rural communities. In like manner, domestic tourism is supposed to raise the levels of civility of both tourists and local residents of toured sites (Nyíri 2009:154).

State-encouraged tourism at heritage sites thus has several objectives. At the local level (the primary source of funding for heritage projects), economic growth, job creation, and control over new forms of wealth creation are certainly goals. But just as important from the national perspective is the promotion of a new class of consumers, citizen-subjects trained to be modern in an appropriate (consumer) manner.

CONSTRUCTING A WORLD HERITAGE SITE

As early as the Han dynasty in AD 200 the Wutai area served as a Daoist mountain retreat. In the fifth century the rulers of the northern Wei dynasty began construction of a series of temples dedicated to the Bodhisatva Manjusri (*Wenshi Shuli*), and by the ninth century Wutai Shan had become a major Buddhist pilgrimage site for much of East Asia (Gimello 1992). Tibetan Buddhism was introduced to the area in the thirteenth century by the Mongolian Yuan dynasty, and during the Qing dynasty (1644–1911) became very influential. In 1659 Tibetan Buddhists gained control of the major religious sites in the valley, and in 1705 Emperor Kangxi decreed that ten Mahayana monasteries be converted to Tibetan Buddhism (Kohle 2008:78). As Kohle argues, this reflects the key role Tibetan Buddhism held not just during the Qing dynasty but also in both the (Chinese) Ming dynasty and (Mongolian) Yuan dynasty, as a symbol of legitimacy and also as a source of heavenly protection.

After the 1949 establishment of the People's Republic, government authorities initially protected monasteries at Wutai as national historical sites. During the collapse of state authority in the Cultural Revolution

(1966–1976), local residents by their own account prevented marauding Red Guards from looting and destroying most of the buildings. Nevertheless, religious practice was banned and all temples and monasteries closed. Only in the last two decades has a measure of religious freedom returned. Although this continues to be monitored and managed by state authorities, there are currently forty-seven monasteries functioning, with more than 1,500 monks and five hundred nuns in residence, making this the largest concentration of religious devotees in China outside of the Tibet Autonomous Region.[1]

Wutai Shan was named a national scenic spot (*jingdian*) by the State Council in 1982 and designated a national forest preserve in 1992. In 2004 nearly 1.8 million people visited the valley; a year later, arrivals had risen to 2.5 million. Local government officials, seeking to capitalize on the renewed popularity of Wutai, submitted a master plan that would turn the valley into a national park and World Heritage Site. They also imposed a gateway fee to the entire valley. This admission fee was set at 90 Yuan (approximately U.S. $13) in 2004, which later increased to 168 Yuan (U.S. $23) in 2007.

Wutai Shan was added to China's tentative list of UNESCO Heritage Sites in 2001.[2] In the original application, the State Administration of Cultural Heritage (part of the Ministry of Culture) cited the area's Buddhist heritage, its unique environmental features, and its strategic importance during the Anti-Japanese War as reasons for inclusion on the World Heritage list.[3] This application was upgraded to a formal nomination in March 2008, this time as an exclusively cultural site consisting of thirteen temples and a "core zone" of Taihuai town. References to the anti-Japanese struggle were replaced by a statement that the built pagodas, temples, and other architectural forms "catalogue the way in which Buddhist architecture developed and influenced palace building in China for over a millennium" (UNESCO 2009b). The application also asserted that Wutai is an example of the "seamless blend of the Chinese and Tibetan cultures" and serves as "an important bridge for cultural exchanges between the Han, Tibetan, Mongolian people and people of other ethnic origins." This claim portrays a unified territory of like-minded citizens in which ethnic and other differences are submerged beneath a shared "culture." In the spring of 2009 Wutai Shan was formally approved as a World Heritage Cultural Site.

The preservation of the Taihuai core zone of Wutai has included the eviction of a significant number of local residents, who will be relocated to Jingangku Township, a satellite community twenty-three kilometers away outside the park boundaries. Just how many people are impacted depends on the source, ranging from 583 (the official total) to more than five thousand (the total some residents assert). Whatever the actual number, this resettlement project has caused considerable problems for these residents. First, while compensation was paid for the loss of homes and businesses, this averaged just 400 Yuan per square meter (U.S. $60), according to local residents. Second, while the new housing at Jingangku is relatively spacious (averaging eighty to two hundred square meters), the increased size and cost (1,200 Yuan per square meter) has made purchasing this difficult for some. In addition, as of June 2010, the new complex remained empty because of a payment dispute between the developer and the district government. Finally, most residents work in service industries in and around temples and monasteries in Taihuai, running shops, cafes, and restaurants, selling souvenirs, or driving taxis. The master plan will eliminate most local businesses, a new shuttle bus service has curtailed the use of taxis, and souvenir sellers have been restricted to a few sites. The largest of these, in a parking lot at the base of Dailuo Terrace, has over one hundred vendors, most of whom sell the same objects and so must compete with each other for potential customers. In addition, to sell at this market requires an annual license that costs 5,000 Yuan (approximately U.S. $750). Because of the seasonal nature of visitors, vendors must make most of their sales between May and October.

Local residents have responded to their displacement with tactics that mirror other popular protests in China (cf. Lee 2007). Anger has focused on local officials, not the central government, and complaints have been articulated in a language of morality and fairness.

Shortly after demolition work started in early 2008, residents sent a delegation to Beijing with a petition. This letter begins by noting that people lived at Wutai before Buddhism arrived. It then notes that local residents have served Buddhist pilgrims for hundreds of years and were also the main labor force for temple construction. Finally, it reminds its audience of the Cultural Revolution years:

> During the Cultural Revolution, when external rebel forces came to Wutai mountain to smash, beat and loot, the Red Guards carried three huge barrels of petrol to set fire to the temples, and it was the masses of Wutai mountain who risked their lives to battle the Red Guards, driving them out and therefore allowing Wutai mountain to escape the disaster of fire, enabling it to have the valuable resources it needs to apply for World Heritage today. (Anonymous 2008)

In other words, residents assert rights based on longevity, service to Buddhism, and as defenders of this heritage site against revolutionary extremists. Yet they argue that they stand to gain no benefits from Wutai's new popularity. Moving them to a satellite town far from the temple sites is, in their words, "ungrateful and devoid of reason and emotion," as well as contrary to the "scientific development" promoted by the central government. The petition closes by posing the central question for heritage proponents:

> The ultimate goal for applying for World Heritage site is to accelerate social development, and to improve the living standards of people. Does the application for World Heritage status mean turning the site into a depopulated wasteland? Do successful World Heritage applications all over the world depend on damaging the interests of local residents?

In this petition residents offer their interpretation of the history of Wutai as well as their opinion of its ongoing preservation. Absent is any concern with the authenticity of the site or a desire to maintain the sacredness of it in the face of tourism. Instead, the petition asks a clear question: Why should they suffer in this preservation process?

For their part, UNESCO authorities deal with the political realities and economic effects of heritage and tourism projects in China by emphasizing a biocentric process of preserving and conserving natural and cultural sites separated from contemporary social action (Li and Sofield 2009:160). For example, the UNESCO summary recommendation report on Wutai Shan briefly notes that the movement of residents had provoked local demonstrations, yet asserts "most of the people are willing to cooperate" (UNESCO 2009a:6). It then notes that "unauthorized construction" continues and should be better controlled (UNESCO 2009a:6). Finally, the report states that by 2020 Jingangku Township will host parking, service, and tourist facilities, thus suggesting that in the long term local residents will benefit from this heritage project.

What this report fails to note is the ongoing construction of large hotel complexes close to Taihuai, which have a significant comparative advantage over local facilities in terms of location, amenities, and, most importantly, relationships with state travel agencies, bureaucracies, and institutions. This in turn points to another factor absent from this report—that different parts of "the State" have different interests in this site.

First, the forest preserve that encompasses much of the valley falls under the purview of the State Forestry Administration, formerly the Ministry of Forestry until 1998 when it was placed under the direct authority of the State Council, the highest governing body in the People's Republic of China (PRC). The preservation of temple sites is the responsibility of the State Administration of Cultural Heritage, which is subordinate to the Ministry of Culture. Religious practices are regulated by the State Administration for Religious Affairs, while the State Ethnic Affairs Commission oversees the affairs of ethnic minorities. Finally, the National Tourism Administration is tasked with promoting the Wutai area as a tourist destination. These vertical ties clash at times not only with each other but also with a different set of state actors emanating from the

Shanxi provincial government down to local county authorities, who are responsible for funding most of the infrastructure costs. From the local government perspective, the transformation of the Wutai Valley into a vast heritage park and tourist attraction is the best means of achieving economic modernization.

Not to be overlooked is the evolving demographics of visitor arrivals. While a generation ago most visitors were either European and American tourists or practicing Buddhists from the surrounding Asian region, today the vast majority are Chinese citizens. These include religious devotees from Inner Mongolia and Tibetan areas, state enterprise and government employees on state-funded vacations disguised as "field inspections" (*kaocha*), and, most interestingly, significant numbers of regular Han Chinese who visit to *baifo*, literally to pay homage to Buddha—a practice that was politically unthinkable for most a generation ago.

LOST HORIZONS FOUND

In one of the more unusual examples of life imitating art, local authorities in Zhongdian County, capital of the Diqing Tibetan Autonomous Prefecture of northwestern Yunnan Province, announced in 2001 that the State Council in Beijing had approved its petition to change the county's name to "Shangri-la."

In 1996, local authorities invited local historians and anthropologists to study whether the region could claim to be the "authentic" site of Hilton's (fictional) Shangri-la. Not surprisingly, conference participants decided this was, in fact, true (Li 1999). Shortly thereafter, major infrastructure projects were announced for Jiantang, the county seat (usually referred to by Chinese residents as "Zhongdian" but historically named Gyalthang), including an airport, a cultural center, a Tibetan "ancient town" (*gu cheng*) complete with a town square, a golden-painted *chorten* (Buddhist stupa) and an enormous prayer-wheel, and several starred hotels, as well as major improvements to the area's most important Tibetan Buddhist monastery, Songtseling (in Chinese, Songzimin). Local policies aimed at tapping into the large pool of tourist arrivals at Lijiang, a Naxi-minority town and UNESCO World Heritage Site located four hours south. Lijiang is one of China's top tourist attractions, recording 5.3 million visitors in 2007, 92 percent of whom were domestic tourists (Xinhua 2008). By 2007 tax revenue from tourism in Shangri-la County exceeded the revenues lost from a ban on logging, and as of 2007 tourist arrivals had reached 2.9 million.

Contesting the symbolism of "Shangri-la" is one more example of the ongoing conflict between the Tibetan exile movement and the Chinese state. However, in this case it is a struggle over literally a nonplace. Chi-

nese authorities have seized on the ideal of Shangri-la and now seek to
locate this in a particular place, literally renamed Shangri-la, located not
in Tibet but in a border zone historically populated by not just Tibetans
but also Han Chinese and minority groups such as Bai, Lisu, and Naxi.
Indeed, the Diqing Tibetan Autonomous Prefecture, consisting of Zhongdian, Diqin, and Weixi Lisu Counties, is one of the most ethnically diverse
areas in all of China. According to 2000 census figures, 33.1 percent of the
Prefecture's 353,000 residents were Tibetan, 27.8 percent Lisu (a Tibetan-
related group), 16 percent Han Chinese, and the remainder a variety of
other official minorities, including Bali, Yi, Naxi, Hui, and Miao (Hillman
2003:175). This Shangri-la thus serves as a shining example of the state-
imagined demographics of modern China, a diverse array of minority
peoples living in harmony with each other while being guided toward
modernity by the benevolent and already-modern Han (Gladney 2004).

To judge by foreign news accounts of the remaking of Gyalthang/
Zhongdian into Shangri-la, the project has been a failure because it lacks
authenticity. Not only is this Shangri-la a transparent marketing ploy by
state authorities but the region is also not actually part of Tibet. It is thus
portrayed as a cynical attempt to cash in on a Western obsession with
Tibet-as-Shangri-la. Two facts complicate this narrative. First, the remaking of the region into Shangri-la has proven, at least in the short term,
to be a significant tourism draw, mainly for Chinese citizens. In 2000,
94 percent of approximately one million visitors were Chinese (Hillman
2003:176), and, as already noted, by 2007, the number of arrivals had
reached 2.9 million. Secondly, a local government decision to promote
tourism was a direct result of a central government decision to ban all
logging in the region (the mainstay of the local economy) after devastat-
ing 1998 floods in the Yangzi River basin were blamed on large-scale
deforestation in northwestern Yunnan (Hillman 2003:176). The shift to a
tourism-driven economy has boosted environmental protection efforts in
the region. But to what extent has it benefitted local residents?

Paradoxes abound in Shangri-la. In front of Songtseling Monastery
dozens of Tibetans and Hui Muslims sell jade jewelry, small brass statues of Buddha, and other Tibetan-themed objects, most of which are
imported from Nepal. The carpenters responsible for the careful creation
of the Tibetan "ancient town" are mainly of the Bai nationality. The
"Mandela Square" at the center of the Tibetan quarter is advertised in
travel brochures as built in "Tibetan style" (*zangzu fengge*) to "traditional
standards" (*chuantong biaozhun*), although most of the businesses in the
square are Han-, Hui-, and Naxi-run tourist restaurants and cafes. And
in the new quarter of Zhongdian, faux Tibetan buildings house a cultural center, entertainment complex, and government buildings. Indeed,
the built space between the (Tibetan) "new old town" and the (former)

Chinese "new town" that dates to the 1950s is rapidly being transformed by faux-Tibetan stone facade buildings, creating a "new new town." Sichuan Han migrants drive taxis, run restaurants, and fill the service jobs in stores, while Naxi and Bai people work in the hotels. Almost no Tibetans fill any of these jobs.

While the number of tourist arrivals is high, the average stay is not. According to local travel agents, most Han Chinese tourists take a two-day tour from Lijiang. On the first day they stop at Hutiao (Tiger Leaping) Gorge, midway between Lijiang and Shangri-la, before spending the evening at a Zhongdian hotel. On their second day they visit Songtseling Monastery and nearby Bitahai Lake before returning to Lijiang. Relatively few appear to spend much time in the newly constructed Tibetan quarter of town. Indeed, several Chinese tourists in Lijiang who had taken one of these trips told me they did not even know Gyalthang/Zhongdian has a Tibetan quarter.

What motivates these tourists to visit Shangri-la? Unlike the state enterprise groups and Buddhist practitioners that fill Wutai Shan's hotels, the tourists who visit this region reflect the urban consumerism of post-Mao China. They are people who can afford to vacation in Northern Yunnan and dress up in fashionable outdoor clothes, even if they never do anything more strenuous than sit on a tour bus and get off occasionally for nature shots. Indeed, Lijiang and Gyalthang/Zhongdian each have numerous outdoor shops aimed not at foreigners but at this new class of Han tourist. And these shops all stock the same gear—hiking pants, pullovers, and jackets, hiking boots, backpacks, day packs, and fanny packs.

If Gyalthang/Zhongdian has thrived as the supposedly real Shangri-la, people in the region do not agree on just what "Shangri-la" means or even where it is located. The official Chinese name, *xianggelila*, translates as "fragrant place that attracts." Yet there are shops and hotels in town that advertise their location as *Xiangbala*, "fragrance that grasps and pulls." The latter makes sense from a Tibetan perspective because it alludes to "Shambala," a mythical kingdom located to the west of Tibet. In the same way, *xianggelila* makes sense in Chinese because it alludes to a paradise first described by the fourth-century poet Tao Yuanming as *shiwai taoyuan* ("other-worldly peach garden"), populated by people who had fled the chaos and destruction of the first Qin emperor, Qin Shi Huangdi (Kolas 2008:110–11).

At the local state bookstore in the county seat, a Han Chinese clerk explained that Shangri-la was another name for Zhongdian. "An Englishman wrote about it," she said. At Songtsamlin Monastery a monk said it meant "beautiful place" (*meilide defang*), but he insisted Shangri-la was actually two hours north, not in Zhongdian. A waitress in a café in town explained that Shangri-la and Zhongdian were the same: "Zhongdian became Shangri-la a few years ago because the government decided it was very beautiful (*mei-li*)." So what did the name mean, I asked? "It is from a book," she said. What kind of book? "I don't know, I haven't read it," she responded. A man from Beijing sitting at the next table said the name didn't mean anything, an odd answer to offer in a language in which every place name means something. "But it must mean something," I said to him. "Zhongdian means something. Lijiang means something. So what does Shangri-la mean?" He shrugged and repeated, "It's just a name, like Washington. Or Disney."

NATURE, CULTURE, AND "THE ENVIRONMENT"

In Europe and North America, discussions about the environment tend to focus on whether humans should exploit, preserve, or manage natural resources. Each of these perspectives assumes a nature/culture divide, which implies a sort of zero-sum game: natural resources, and by implication a space called "nature," is finite, and thus can and will be used up, or at a minimum spoiled, unless humans act as stewards. As a consequence of this, most people accept with little debate not just the need for nature preserves and parks but also, and more importantly, the ideal form for these—places that have as little permanent human presence as possible. We thus go "back" to nature when we visit, say, Yosemite or the Grand Canyon (though what we find in these places are many people like us, seeking something called "nature").

It is useful to recall just how recent is the transformation of "nature" in the popular Euro-American consciousness into something to be admired and protected rather than feared (Weller 2006). The roots of what Milton would refer to as the "aesthetics of the infinite" are found in late-seventeenth- and early-eighteenth-century advances in navigation and measurements, precursors to advances in biology and related fields that culminated in Darwin's theory of evolution (Nicolson 1959:273). If in the seventeenth century mountains served to both awe and frighten, by the nineteenth century they were expected to offer subliminal experiences that demonstrated the infinity of both nature and God (Nicolson 1959:279–82). The Romantic pastoral view of peasants at home *in* nature that strongly influenced European and North American intellectuals in the eighteenth century soon gave way in the mid-nineteenth century to the jarring dislocations of industrialization. As an outgrowth of this, the transformation of urban life by what James Scott (1998) has termed "high modernism," with its emphasis on visual order, uniformity, and material reality, further stimulated a desire, especially among, paradoxically, those classes (European and North American elites) who benefited the most

from these transformations, to seek spaces outside of modernity as a re-
action to modernity (Weller 2006:6). In the United States this culminated
in the efforts of the American naturalist John Muir, founder of the Sierra
Club, and his supporters for a federally controlled natural park system
that would set aside and protect wilderness land for the enjoyment of all
citizens (Weller 2006:54).

While a "nature" cleansed of a permanent human presence might seem
second nature to many Americans, this environmental perspective is far
from universal. *Nature* in Chinese (*zi ran*) conveys a sense of "all reality becoming" as part of the five elements (fire, water, earth, wood, and
metal) (Li and Sofield 2009:159). This term does not carry any sense of
an essential quality or of an otherworldly force that directs reality, both
of which are core meanings of the English word *nature* (Weller 2006:21).
Thus, to state in Chinese that a product is "all natural" or that an event
was an "act of nature" is much more difficult, simply because humans in
the Chinese perspective are part of nature as well. Weller (2006) offers the
useful term *anthropocosmic resonance* to describe the relationship of people
to the world around them. This (ideally) harmonious mutual dependence
coexists with an obligation to harness *qi*, the energy force that emanates
everywhere, as a means of both self and society's improvement (Weller
2006:23–29). "Nature" from this perspective is characterized by the perva-
siveness of *qi*, the lack of any division between humans and the physical
world and the obligation for humans to use the physical world to benefit
themselves and others.

Of course, as Weller and others note, this anthropocosmic view can
serve as the basis for not just a social order that uses the physical world
but also one that seeks to subjugate nature. In this sense the modernization movement in China did not begin with Mao but with late nineteenth-
century Qing efforts to build a modern regime, much like what was
occurring in Japan at the time. The resulting exploitation of nature was
enthusiastically supported by Qing reformers and Chinese Nationalists as
well as the Communist Party after it gained power in 1949. This approach,
which culminated with Mao's war on nature during the Cultural Revolution, was just as much an outgrowth of a Confucian emphasis on controlling nature as it was a rejection of Confucianism. What Mao rejected
was not Confucian views of nature per se but the Confucian emphasis on
using nature within an overarching structure of harmony. Confucian utility and harmony (*tian ren heyi*) were replaced by Maoist utopianism and
conquest—*ren ding shengtian* (Shapiro 2001:7).

A striking aspect about Wutai Shan is an ongoing temple construction program. From a Euro-American perspective, this "making up" of
a heritage site is a simulacrum, at best a Colonial Williamsburg, at worst
an Epcot Center. What links these, the historically accurate recreation and

the kitschy fake, is the assumption that neither is real. This is premised on several foundational assumptions about what constitutes realness, the most important of which is a faith that an original or unique object or quality exists that can be used to measure similar objects or practices.

This reliance on an original versus copy paradigm that privileges age, uniqueness, or both does not necessarily travel well in the context of either Buddhism or Chinese aesthetic norms. Buddhism, for example, is profoundly utilitarian when it comes to material culture (Lopez 1998:154). *Thangka* paintings and images get touched up and repainted, temples rebuilt and ritually renewed, and statues of the Buddha refinished or replaced. From this perspective, not only is reality, material or otherwise, an illusion but also it is extremely fluid (Kieschnick 2003:4). This deemphasizing of material reality in the religious sphere intersects with a long tradition of travel in China that emphasizes a personal affirmation of canonical representations (Nyíri 2006:71–72). These representations evoke not a personal response to a scene but instead an experience tied mimetically to already existing responses. In other words, when many Chinese travel, they do not go in search of a pristine space called "nature" that is worthy of a visit because it is empty of a human presence but rather in search of already marked spaces worthy of a visit precisely because other humans have acted upon these in the past *and* visit them in the present. Chinese routes through nature, such as trails and paths at sacred mountains like Wutai Shan, are structured around a variety of literary, religious, and anthropomorphic signposts. Chinese characters inscribed on rocks and boulders, scenes and sights linked to snatches of classical poetry, and named hills, rocks, and trees are as important on these routes as are pavilions and temples. Thus, rather than appearing to be pristine and "natural," an authentic Chinese sacred site paradoxically looks crowded and developed, at least from a Euro-American aesthetic perspective (Li and Sofield 2009:162–63). "Nature" and "culture" from this perspective are not separate realms: "culture" is as natural as "nature." This, then, is a worldview at once anthropocentric *and* anthropomorphic. Humans exist as superior beings in a world filled with humanlike things (Li and Sofield 2009:159). Visits to natural sites are not unnatural or spoiled when signs of human culture are encountered but are instead confirmed as both valid and credible.

SACRED SITES AND TOURISM

In 2006 the Yunnan People's Publishing House released both English- and Chinese-language editions of James Hilton's *Lost Horizon*. This illustrates how, despite the colonial overtones of its plotline—a lamasery filled with foreigners who live forever while being served by Tibetan peasants who act suspiciously like feudal serfs—*Lost Horizon* has become a marketing tool in an official campaign to delineate the "real" Shangri-la. According to one report, local authorities mandated that a copy of this book be placed in each hotel room in Gyalthang/Zhongdian (Zhang and Gao 2008:2).

The transformation of an obscure frontier town in northwestern Yunnan Province into the purported site of a fictional utopia filled paradoxically with foreigners and aimed at domestic Chinese tourists seems a perfect example of how mass tourism destroys local ways of meaning. As in the case of Chinese tourism in Lhasa, such a narrative lends itself to the Euro-American fear of both the destruction of Tibetan culture at the hands of Han Chinese tourists and the ruination of Tibet's natural environment. Indeed, it is relatively easy to emphasize the commodification of Tibetan culture in this new Shangri-la. Yet the fact that the consumers of this elaborate cultural production are overwhelmingly Han Chinese raises important questions about the marketing of culture and identity. Tibet and an Orientalized image of Tibetan Buddhism have become market commodities not just in Gyalthang/Zhongdian but also throughout urban China, reflected in advertisements, films, music, and art that frame Tibet as a land of purity, simplicity, cleanliness, and special powers (Kapstein 2005:258). This illustrates how, as Louisa Schein (2000) has noted, domestic Orientalized images of minority peoples are increasingly produced by a range of actors in contemporary China, not simply by "the state." For example, Tibetans now sell jewelry, clothing, and prayer beads not just in front of international hotels filled with foreigners in cities such as Beijing and Guangzhou but also in front of university gates and at metro stops, which indicates that the audience and market for these objects are no longer only Americans and Europeans in search of "their" Shangri-la.

This raises an important question: In the hypermarket realities of contemporary China, is the marketing of Tibetan culture evidence of its commodification and all this term implies, including the erasure of the "real"? Or might the emergence of a market for "Tibet" as a consumer object among Han Chinese indicate a shift in popular Chinese attitudes about the nature of Tibet?

Ethnic tourism in Shangri-la, like religious tourism at Wutai Shan, does not follow a neat and orderly state-directed script. Instead, at places such as Zhongdian and Wutai Shan, state-desired narratives of identity clash with local perceptions of self and with a jumble of images produced and consumed by a range of visitors.

This in turn leads to the question of pilgrimage. To what extent are visitors to sites such as Wutai Shan and Shangri-la pilgrims, and if so, what are they in search of? At Wutai Shan, the reemergence of Buddhism among Han Chinese is the primary motivation for visiting this sacred valley. The resacralization of this site (not by state fiat or with UNESCO endorsement) might well lead to new tensions, as visitors increasingly come to worship rather than simply tour (the motivation desired by local authorities) or appreciate a World Heritage Site (the motivation desired by UNESCO authorities). In other words, while UNESCO seeks to protect this site from tourism and local authorities seek to promote it for tourism, an increasing number of visitors view it as a religious destination—neither ancient heritage site nor tourist attraction, but a sacred space made sacred by the presence of the Buddha of wisdom, Manjusri. This is in contrast to Shangri-la, where many visitors appear to be on a pilgrimage of a different sort, one that aims at experiencing modernity through a tour on its borderlands.

What also marks these sites as different is the role of minority and class identities in the marketing of culture. Urban Han tourists do not seek encounters with peasants when they tour; they seek such encounters with minority peasants. The local residents in and around Wutai Shan are Han Chinese, while the majority of residents in and around Gyalthang/Zhongdian are Tibetan and Lisu. At the latter site, the development goal appears to be to replicate the success of tourism at the World Heritage Site of Lijiang and the backpacker haven and now popular Chinese tourist destination of Dali (both located within six hours of Gyalthang/Zhongdian). At Lijiang and Dali, both the site and residents are tourist destinations because they are promoted and marketed by both local authorities and local residents as different from everyday Han Chinese life. Of course, while Han Chinese tourists in these places visit minority cultural shows of singing and dancing, they also visit cafes, bars, and restaurants such as the Café de Jack in Dali or the Compass Café in Shangri-la. These ostensibly "Western" establishments are actually global places that promote a pseudo-East in their décor. Their rustic wood furniture, paper lamps, *Ohm* symbols, and *thankha* paintings on the walls, reggae music, and standard menus of pizza, pasta, burgers, and fried rice link them not with their locale but with other pseudo-East cafes in places such as the Thamel district of Kathmandu, Kosan Road in Bangkok, and Kuta Beach in Bali. This pseudo-East essentializes and differentiates, exoticizes and empowers, yet in this case does something more: it sets off a predominantly Han cliental from a local Other, one that nevertheless cannot be situated as not-yet modern, precisely because Naxi residents of the area have achieved so much material success from tourism.

Tibetans in a place like Shangri-la, in contrast, are assumed to have a "culture" that sets them apart from their Han Chinese audience while lacking in the "civilization" (*wenming*) required by modern citizen-subjects. As tourism arrivals in the area increase, the most pressing local issue is not how to protect the purity of cultural practices from the supposed destructive effects of market action but how to benefit from the interaction between outside expectations and desires and local ways of meaning, especially given the fact that mass tourism has been promoted as the replacement for the formerly lucrative logging industry, shut down in the 1990s by central authorities. Yet in the local economy the limits to the tourism industry as a development tool are quite clear. While jobs have been created, most of those are low-skilled service jobs. Moreover, most of these service jobs require Mandarin Chinese skills. The net result is a tourism industry that has benefited many Yunnan citizens, but not many local residents. Instead, the sector is filled with Naxi, Bai, Hui, and Han transplants from Dali and Lijiang.

In this case, this development paradox is similar to the identity politics of Tibetan exile communities in Kathmandu, Nepal, and Dharamsala, India. However, where these cases differ is in audience perceptions of "Tibetan-ness." While Tibetans at a site such as Shangri-la must grapple with both state *and* popular Han Chinese assumptions about the efficacies of minorities becoming "civilized," Tibetans in exile have quite the opposite problem: how to use the language of their Western liberal humanist admirers as a means of increasing their international standing (Frechette 2002:101–3). In other words, how to benefit from a (Euro-American) tourist fascination with one's supposed nonmodernity versus how to benefit from a (Han Chinese) tourist presumption of one's need for modernity.

For residents of Wutai Shan, ethnicity plays no role; being Han Chinese peasants, their culture is a rural life marked by both the state and urban Chinese society as "backward" and lacking in "civilization" (*wenming*). Far from being a marketable commodity, this "culture" is targeted for disappearance through the process of tourism promotion.

CONCLUSION: WHO HAS A STAKE?

Through its World Heritage list, UNESCO portrays a new type of imagined world community, one which simultaneously transcends the nation-state through, paradoxically, the cooperation of nation-states (Turtinen 2006:4). It does so through a particular "grammar" of global heritage that aims to define the rules and boundaries for a truly universal set of unique practices, places, and objects (Turtinen 2006:7). Yet international heritage conventions are agreements between nation-states, not with local communities. Moreover, nominations for World Heritage status can only be made through central governments. The role of state authorities in the promotion and definition of heritage sites is usually viewed by both

UNESCO-affiliated groups and outside preservationist advocates as a net good, thus ignoring the political questions of why certain state authorities seek World Heritage status for particular sites and what impact these projects have on local communities.

While retelling the past through intangible means and tangible sites is a socially constructed endeavor, this is a practice that often privileges "good myths over bad facts" (Gable and Handler 1996:576). A case in point is the UNESCO narrative of Wutai Shan's relationship with state authorities in the twentieth century. According to this story, "Mount Wutai declined through social instability" during the last years of the Qing dynasty and the Republican period (1911–1949), but, "since 1949 and the founding of the People's Republic of China, efforts have been directed at reviving and protecting the buildings" (UNESCO 2009a:4). This story completely erases the chaos of the Cultural Revolution and the paradoxes that followed, such as local workers and peasants defending religious sites from marauding urban Red Guards intent on destroying material aspects of "old culture." This also illustrates how "the past" is not preserved by heritage projects—instead, some aspects are, while others are, if not erased, then not mentioned. Sites, no matter if they are "cultural," or "natural," or some combination of these, always have contested histories.

Both Wutai Shan and Gyalthang/Zhongdian have been promoted by state tourism authorities as "religious-cultural tourism" (*zongjiao wenhua luyou*) destinations. The bureaucratic focus at these sites is on managing the consumption of Buddhism (by pilgrims, monks, and tourists), not on banning its practice (Kang 2009:243), and thus similar to a state desire to manage and not erase Tibetan quotidian cultural practices in strategic cities such as Lhasa. However, different aspects of the national state have different interests at these sites, ranging from temple preservation and environmental conservation to tourism promotion. Not only do these interests sometimes clash with each other but also with how provincial and local authorities choose to act. Finally, local interests as well are quite diverse: while Buddhist practitioners and monks seek to use tourist visits as a way to raise funds to support temples and monasteries, other local residents might seek only to make a living off tourism.

Nevertheless, local residents, as at other heritage destinations in China, use history, festival activities, and official state discourse to not contest the commodification of these sites but to seek economic benefits. Indeed, this issue is what links the Han Chinese residents of the Wutai Valley with the Tibetan and Lisu residents in and around "Shangri-la": tourism as a commodification project is not a major concern; gaining a better material life is.

NOTES

1. Religious practice falls under the domain of the State Religious Affairs Council and national associations that oversee the five official faiths—Daoism, Buddhism, Islam, Catholicism, and Protestant Christianity. For example, Catholic institutions must belong to the Chinese Patriotic Catholic Association, while Buddhist temples and monasteries are affiliated by state decree with the Chinese Buddhist Association. A key policy shift took place in 1982 when the State Council issued "Document 19," which provided citizens with the right to believe in any of the five officially tolerated religions, limited private funding, and explicitly linked all religious institutions to the state. In 1991 "Document 6" reasserted tolerance for religious orthodoxy but warned against heterodoxy, such as nonsanctioned Muslims, pro–Dalai Lama Tibetans, Vatican-tied Catholics, and charismatic Christian groups.

2. UNESCO follows a four-stage process in evaluating heritage sites. In the first stage, national authorities add a site to its tentative list, an inventory of sites to be proposed during the next decade. Within this time span, sites are then formally nominated to the World Heritage Council. Nominated sites are then examined and evaluated by either the International Council on Monuments and Sites (ICOMOS) or the World Conservation Union (IUCN). The World Heritage Committee, an intergovernmental body, makes final decisions on sites' inclusion.

3. According to the original application, Mount Wutai was once the headquarters of the communist Eighth Route Army. It hosts a house where Mao Zedong, Zhou Enlai, and other CCP leaders once stayed.

REFERENCES

Anonymous. 2008. Moving Residents Betrays History. *Manchester Guardian*, March 13, 2008. www.guardian.co.uk/world/2008/mar/13/china?commentpage=1, accessed November 21, 2011.

China National Tourism Office (CNTO). 2007. Major Statistics of Domestic Tourism 2007. http://74.125.93.132/search?q=cache:http://www.cnta.gov.cn /html/2008-6/2008-6-2-21-29-3-319.html, accessed November 21, 2011.

———. 2008. Major Statistics of Chinese Tourism, January–December 2008. www .cnta.gov.cn/html/2009-2/2009-2-18-9-34-95871.html, accessed November 21, 2011.

———. 2009. Foreign Visitor Arrivals by Purpose, January–December 2009. http:// cnto.org/chinastats_2009ArrivalsByPurpose.asp, accessed November 21, 2011.

Denton, Kirk. 2005. Museums, Memorial Sites and Exhibitionary Culture in the People's Republic of China. *China Quarterly* 183 (September):565–86.

Frechette, Ann. 2002. *Tibetans in Nepal: The Dynamics of International Assistance among a Community in Exile*. New York: Berghahn Books.

Gable, Eric, and Richard Handler. 1996. After Authenticity at an American Heritage Site. *American Anthropologist* 98(3):568–78.

Gimello, Robert. 1992. Chang Shang-Ying on Wutai Shan. In *Pilgrims and Sacred Sites in China*, eds. Susan Naquin and Chun Fang-Yu, pp. 89–149. Berkeley: University of California Press.

Gladney, Dru. 2004. *Dislocating China: Muslims, Minorities, and Other Subaltern Subjects*. Chicago: University of Chicago Press.

Hevia, James. 2001. World Heritage, National Culture, and the Restoration of Chengde. *Positions* 9(1):219–43.

Hillman, Ben. 2003. Paradise under Construction: Minorities, Myths, and Modernity in Northwest Yunnan. *Asian Ethnicity* 4(2):175–88.

Hilton, James. 1933. *Lost Horizon*. New York: William Marrow and Company.

———. 2006. *Lost Horizon*. Kunming, Yunnan, China: Yunnan People's Publishing House.

Kang, Xiaofei. 2009. Two Temples, Three Religions and a Tourist Attraction: Contesting Sacred Space on China's Ethnic Frontier. *Modern China* 35(3):227–55.

Kapstein, Mathew. 2005. Thorn in the Dragon's Side. In *Governing China's Multiethnic Frontiers*, ed. Morris Rossabi, pp. 230–69. Seattle: University of Washington Press.

Kieschnick, John. 2003. *The Impact of Buddhism on Chinese Material Culture*. Princeton: Princeton University Press.

Kohle, Natalie. 2008. Why Did the Kangxi Emperor Go to Wutaishan? Patronage, Pilgrimmage, and the Place of Tibetan Buddhism at the Early Qing Court. *Late Imperial China* 29(1):73–119.

Kolas, Ashild. 2008. *Tourism and Tibetan Culture in Transition: A Place Called Shangri-la*. London: Routledge.

Lee, Ching Kwan. 2007. *Against the Law: Labor Protests in China's Sunbelt and Rustbelt*. Berkeley: University of California Press.

Li, Fung Mei, and Trevor Sofield. 2009. Huangshan (Yellow Mountain), China: The Meaning of Harmonious Relationships. In *Tourism in China: Destinations, Cultures, and Communities*, eds. Chris Ryan and Gu Huimin, pp. 157–67. London: Routledge.

Li, Ming. 1999. *New Edition of Diqing History*. Kunming, China: Yunnan People's Press.

Lopez, Donald. 1998. *Prisoners of Shangri-La: Tibetan Buddhism and the West*. Chicago: University of Chicago Press.

Nicolson, Marjorie. 1959. *Mountain Gloom and Mountain Glory*. New York: W.W. Norton.

Nyíri, Pál. 2006. *Scenic Spots: Tourism, the State, and Cultural Authority*. Seattle: University of Washington Press.

———. 2009. Between Encouragement and Control: Tourism, Modernity and Discipline in China. In *Asia on Tour: Exploring the Rise of Asian Tourism*, eds. Tim Winter, Peggy Teo, and T. C. Chang, pp. 153–69. London: Routledge.

Schein, Louisa. 2000. *Minority Rules: Miao and the Feminine in China's Cultural Politics*. Durham: Duke University Press.

Scott, James. 1998. *Seeing Like a State: How Certain Schemes to Improve the Human Condition Have Failed*. New Haven, CT: Yale University Press.

Shapiro, Judith. 2001. *Mao's War against Nature: Politics and the Environment in Revolutionary China*. London: Cambridge University Press.

Turtinen, Jan. 2006. *Globalizing Heritage: On UNESCO and the Transnational Construction of World Heritage*. Stockholm Center for Organizational Research, Rapportserie 12.

UNESCO. 2003. Convention for the Safeguarding of Intangible Cultural Heritage. www.unesco.org/culture/ich/index.php?pg=00006, accessed November 21, 2011.

———. 2009a. World Heritage Evaluation Report 2009, Mount Wutai (No 1279). http://whc.unesco.org/archive/advisory_body_evaluation/1279.pdf, accessed November 21, 2011.

———. 2009b. World Heritage List: Mount Wutai. http://whc.unesco.org/en /list/1279, accessed November 28, 2011.

Weller, Robert. 2006. *Discovering Nature: Globalization and Environmental Culture in China and Taiwan*. London: Cambridge University Press.

Xinhua News Agency. 2008. A Rich Past, a Bright Future, June 10. http://news .xinhuanet.com/english/2008-06/10/content_8337636.htm#, accessed November 21, 2011.

Zhang, Qiu, and Gao Bo. 2008. The *Effect of Cognitive Spatial and Temporal Distance on the Creation of Tourist Space*. Paper presented at the Twenty-Sixth EuroCHRIE Conference, Dubai, UAE, October 11–14. http://pc.parnu.ee/~htooman/EuroChrie/Welcome%20to%20EuroCHRIE%20Dubai%202008/papers/The%20 Effect%20of%20Cognitive%20Spatial%20and%20Temporal%20Distance%20 on%20the%20Creation%20of%20Tourist%20Space.pdf, accessed November 28, 2011.

II

ECONOMIC ENCOUNTERS
IN TOURISTIC SPHERES

5

✛

Of Sales Pitches and Speech Genres

Peddling Personality on the Riverfront of Banaras

Jenny Huberman

"'You buy postcard? You buy postcard?' I must have had fifty kids ask me this today, I can't take it anymore!"

Itai, Israeli tourist, age twenty-five

"This one's a natural! He totally stands out from the rest, with that personality he could get you to buy just about anything!"

Brian, American tourist, age twenty-three[1]

A long the riverfront, in the city of Banaras, India, Western tourists often encounter children who sell postcards, souvenirs, and floating candles, or who offer their services as guides. In some cases, the children's solicitations leave tourists feeling aggravated, fatigued, and disinclined to purchase anything. In others, however, they inspire amusement and delight. Tourists praise the children for their "witty" and "winning" personalities and quite eagerly enter into business transactions with them. Some tourists even go so far as to purchase gifts for these children. How are we to understand these two very different yet very common reactions? Why are some of these children so successful at peddling their goods and services, whereas others commonly fail?

In this chapter I use these questions as a departure point for exploring the way value is produced and consumed within this informal tourist economy. Drawing first upon Mikhail Bakhtin's (1986) essay on speech genres, I argue that the children's varying abilities to "master," "manipulate," and "reanimate" the sales pitch play a pivotal role in their collective ability to endear themselves and their products to Western tourists. I then use this discussion to raise some further questions about the affective dimensions of commercial exchange and the object of touristic consumption.

CHILDREN ON THE RIVERFRONT

Located in the northern state of Uttar Pradesh, and steeped along the banks of the Ganga River, Banaras has long been a popular destination among foreign travelers. In the mid-sixteenth and seventeenth centuries the town attracted merchants and explorers who were variously awe-struck and revolted by the religious spectacles they witnessed (Eck 1993). By the end of the eighteenth century and throughout the nineteenth, when the city was officially under British rule, Banaras, and its riverfront in particular, came to be regarded as one of the "must see" destinations on "the standard traveler/tourist route" (Cohn 1996:6). For instance, in his *Handbook for European Travelers*, W. S. Caine chronicled the "scoffing globetrotters from Europe and America" who would "spend their days" "streaming up and down the ghats" and then "retire" in the evening to the safety and comfort of their hotels located in the British enclave of the Cantonment Area (Caine 1890:302). This pattern of residence continued well into the twentieth century. However, by the mid-1960s and 1970s, the counterculture movement brought a new wave of "hippie" and "shoe-string" travelers to the city. Many of these visitors preferred to rent houseboats on the riverfront rather than reside in the city's upscale hotels. In the 1980s, as a second wave of low-budget travelers began backpacking their way through India, the area surrounding the riverfront became much more actively developed for this tourist clientele and by the mid-1990s, these visitors could choose from a plentiful array of inexpensive riverfront lodging as well as shops and restaurants that were specifically designed to cater to their foreign tastes and desires.

The development of the foreign tourism industry in Banaras has precipitated changes in the physical, social, and economic organization of the city. My research has focused on the children who live near the riverfront and who have entered the informal tourist economy. In 2000, I went to Banaras to begin studying the children who work as unlicensed peddlers and guides near the city's "Main Ghat," Dasashwamedh.[2]

Like the riverfront itself, Dasashwamedh Ghat has long been a popular destination among foreign tourists. In part, this is because it sits directly below one of the city's most popular shopping bazaars and continues to be one of the only ghats accessible by road. Many tourists come to Dasashwamedh to arrange boat rides along the river or to enjoy a scenic view while sipping sodas or tea at the ghat's multiple drink stands. They also come to watch the pageantry of the evening puja. Since the late 1990s, the nightly *arthi* at Dasashwamedh has become another "must-see attraction" for foreign tourists, and in the process, an increasing number of neighborhood children have emerged on the ghat to do business with these visitors. My research has specifically focused on analyzing the encounters that take place among these children and tourists.

On an average day during the tourist season, there are usually between twenty and thirty children peddling their goods and services on and around the Main Ghat.[3] Most of the girls and boys who do this work are between the ages of seven and fourteen, come from the *Mallah* or boatman caste, and live in the immediate neighborhood. They peddle postcards, souvenirs, tea, and the small, floating candles (*diyas*) that are sold to both pilgrims and tourists as offerings to the goddess Ganga Ma. In many cases, boys also engage in the more lucrative enterprise of guiding and commission work, which involves taking tourists around the city and escorting them to various shops and restaurants in the bazaar. Although this work is unpredictable and sporadic, during the tourist season, which is at its peak from October to late March, these boys are often able to earn considerably more than their parents or senior kinsmen, most of whom work as hired boatmen or laborers and earn between U.S. \$30 to U.S. \$40 per month. In many cases, the girls' earnings, which can range anywhere from ten cents to U.S. \$2 per day, also provide a significant supplement to the family income.

When it comes to selling their goods and services to foreign tourists, there are, of course many elements that influence whether or not these children are successful. For instance, elsewhere, I have examined the various rules that affect the children's potential to earn, and I have argued that this informal economy is simultaneously a moral economy, embedded in traditional social relations and shared understandings of everyone's "right to earn" (*kamāney ka haq*) (Huberman 2006, 2011). However, as is perhaps the case with selling in general, much hinges on the sales pitch. What, then, is a sales pitch?

THE SALES PITCHES AS SPEECH GENRE

To borrow Bakhtin's (1986) terminology, we can conceptualize the sales pitch as a "speech genre." According to Bakhtin, "Each sphere in which language is used develops its own relatively stable types of utterances." These speech genres "reflect the specific conditions and goals" of each area of human activity through "their thematic content, style and compositional structure." Bakhtin (1986:60) noted that over time, as a particular sphere of activity develops, so does the "repertoire of genres" accompanying it. For instance, within the sphere of selling, sales pitches may "differentiate" and become "more complex." A standard and unambiguous proposition such as "Would you like a postcard?" may give way to a much more nuanced approach involving small chat, banter, jokes, or, eventually even a highly sophisticated advertising campaign. However, whether simple or complex, Bakhtin argued that speech genres provide organizing frames that guide our verbal interactions with others—lending them a certain degree of stability and predictability. Thus, as he pointed out, even in our most intimate encounters, or in our most strident efforts to express our individuality, we often end up sounding "generic."

Although Bakhtin was profoundly interested in the generic nature of human speech, he also recognized that people can play with speech genres and come to master them in ways that enhance their abilities to express their individual feelings and intentions. One of the ways speakers achieve such mastery is by being attuned to the "apperceptive background" of the listener, or in Bakhtin's language "the addressee." As Bakhtin writes, it requires taking account of "the addressee's perception of my speech: the extent to which he is familiar with the situation, whether he has special knowledge of the given cultural area of communication, his views and convictions, his prejudices (from my viewpoint), his sympathies and antipathies—because all this will determine his active responsive understanding of my utterance" (Bakhtin 1986:96). Finally, Bakhtin argued that in taking account of the apperceptive background of the addressee, the savvy speaker then accordingly modifies the genre and style in which he or she choose to express himself or herself.

Following Bakhtin, I now want to consider how the children's earning potential in this informal tourist economy is influenced by their respective abilities to master and manipulate speech genres and anticipate the "sympathies and antipathies" of their customers. As will be seen, not all of the children who work on the riverfront are equally attuned to the perceptions and feelings of their foreign customers, and their choice of sales pitch often reflects this. Some children never venture beyond the very brief and routine "You want postcard?" appeal, whereas others develop far more sophisticated sales pitches that enable them to let their individual personalities shine through.

PERSISTENCE AND PESTERING

During the time of my fieldwork, Priya, age eight, was one of the most successful and yet, from the perspective of many Western tourists, one of the most "annoying" and "irritating" peddlers at Dasashwamedh. Her success selling postcards, therefore, had far less to do with her ability to endear herself to foreign tourists than it did with her ability to wear them down through a repetitive, monotone onslaught of "You buy postcard? You buy postcard?" Often, Priya coupled this with tugging at tourists' clothes or hands or trying to physically position herself in such a way that the tourists virtually had to step over or around her if they wanted to move on. For instance, one day, she was trying to sell postcards to a German couple who were walking along the ghats. After a few minutes of positioning herself between them and pulling on the woman's skirt, the man bent over, swiftly lifted Priya high into the air, and then placed her down on the other side of them. Priya looked shocked when her feet struck the ground, and she immediately glanced over at her father, who was selling peanuts on the ghat, to see what he was going to do. He seemed nonplussed, and he motioned her with his hand to move on and pursue another tourist who was walking her way.

Although some tourists told me that they complied with Priya's persistent appeals because they "sympathized" with her plight and recognized that she herself was being continually "prompted" by her father to pursue customers, most of the tourists I observed and spoke with said that they ultimately "surrendered" to Priya's solicitations just "to make her go away" or to put an end to her "relentless pestering." This was also the case with Rakhi, age six, who sold diyas. Rakhi was also regarded as a notorious "nuisance" by many of the tourists I observed and interviewed. For instance, Sara was a Canadian tourist in her late twenties who had been doing volunteer work in Nepal. She was taking a three-week vacation in Banaras, and during her stay in the city she had become friendly with several of the children who worked on the ghats. One afternoon, Sara and I were having tea on the ghats when she pointed to Rakhi and began to tell me about their encounter from the previous evening. As she said, "I was watching the puja and I had already bought several diyas from the other kids and I just wanted to be left alone, but that one, with the curly hair, she wouldn't go away. She has one of those whiny, beggarlike voices, and it was really irritating me. So finally, I gave her some money and took a candle and then I stormed off."

Laurien is a middle-aged American tourist who also experienced Rakhi's sales techniques at the evening puja. In our interview, she described their encounter as well as some of her more general thoughts about the children who sell on the ghats:

> It doesn't bother me that they're selling stuff, I think it's just part of what goes on, it's just part of what is here. There's just, there's a point of twist to me, and I know for me what that point is, and it's very subjective, it's the point where I'm uncomfortable . . . I have a point from my perceptions, for my comfort level they're going too far and then I wonder what is it in this little tiny girl that doesn't . . . I look her right in the eye and I say, "I really don't want a candle, I'm talking to my friend." And then she won't stop. You know what I mean? It's just, [emphatically] it's a human thing! That could be a thirty-year-old person that I would be dealing with and I would be thinking the same thing. But I think, what's driving this five-year-old to be so . . . so heavy? You know? That's the question.

Finally, Kirsten, a twenty-one-year-old tourist from Germany, also spoke about the irritating persistence of the children on the ghats. My interview with Kirsten took an explosive turn when I mentioned that Western tourists often find the children on the ghats "charming and cute." As soon as the words were spoken, Kirsten turned her eyes up from the cup of milky tea that she had been staring into and looked at me with an incredulous expression. Her face flushed red under a heavy tangle of blond dreadlocks that were beginning to quiver with rage, and she replied:

> Uggh! I think that these kids on the ghats are some of the worst kids that I've met in India! They don't even treat you like you are human! They can't jump out of their roles! . . . The kids will follow you around; they won't leave you alone! I just expect to be treated like a human but they can't do this . . . [voice becoming calmer] I feel sorry for them because I know there is probably a lot of love inside them . . . but they are ruined. They have to work but still.

For Sara, Kirsten, and Laurien, these children had clearly not mastered the genre of selling. Rather, they seemed to be completely dominated and corrupted by it; the pressure to sell had imbued them with a mechanical, robotic quality that made it seemingly impossible for the children to interpret human cues or feelings. And yet, at the same time, other tourists insist that the children's relentless persistence is itself a highly intuitive and even "clever sales strategy" that is purposively intended to stir up their "antipathies." As Steven, an Australian tourist, remarked, "These kids know that if they aggravate us enough, and keep asking, we will eventually break down and buy their stuff just so they will go away. It's psychological warfare out here!" Interestingly, the children almost never suggest that aggravating tourists is part of a conscious sales strategy, but by watching tourists "break down" night after night, they do, I think, come to realize that it is a potentially effective one.

HUMOR AND JOKES

"How many people have asked you to see their shop since you came to Banaras, one thousand? Well, I'm one thousand and one."

Dipesh, ten-year-old peddler and guide

Dipesh's opening sales pitch was extremely successful at disarming tourists. Though it did not always end up securing him a customer or sale, it usually made tourists laugh, smile, and even praise him for his witty sense of humor and "natural talents as a little business man." As one tourist described Dipesh, "He is not just another broken record repeating the same line, 'You come to my silk shop.' We've heard that over and over again! This kid is funny, he's different." Indeed, when I asked Dipesh about his selling strategy, he told me, "I always think to myself, what can I say to customers to make myself different? Or, what can I say to woo these customers so they will want to come with me?"

Like Dipesh, Anita (age seven) was also more inclined to use humor and jokes as a way of softening up and persuading potential customers. Anita was well liked by tourists and her peers for her bubbly and optimistic personality, and she was particularly adept at making tourists laugh and then getting them to part with their money. Often, she would forgo the standard "You want diya?" approach; instead, she would place a diya in front of a tourist and then walk away, leaving the tourist looking bewildered. A few minutes later, she would return, and waving her finger in the air, she would reprimand the tourist for "stealing" the candle from her. On another occasion, I saw Anita put her entire basket of diyas in a tourist's lap and say, "If you not buy from me, then you sell for me." The tourist burst out laughing, began walking around with the basket soliciting his fellow travelers, and ended up making a number of sales on Anita's behalf.

Indeed, one of the advantages that Anita had over some of the other children who were selling on the ghats is that she seemed profoundly aware that many of these tourists want to play. They want to have fun, friendly, and personable exchanges that provide them with a break from what they often describe as the stressful and "dehumanizing" experience of being a foreign tourist in India. Anita's approach was also effective because she had a talent for creating parodies that actually highlighted and inverted some of the tensions that routinely pervade exchanges between tourists and locals. She turned the reluctant foreign buyer into the seller, the suspicious tourist who is afraid of getting ripped off into the thief. In so doing, she was able to transform these routine and potentially aggravating commercial transactions into amusing, and sometimes even dramatic, spectacles that could attract the attention of other tourists and locals on the ghats.

MAKING FRIENDSHIP

"First we make friendship, then we do business."

Mohan, twelve-year-old peddler and guide

Anita's approach to selling was very effective. By using humor and clever gimmicks she was able to set herself apart from her competition and endear herself to foreign tourists, thereby increasing her sales. However, another effective strategy, particularly among the boys who engage in guiding and commission work, involves "making friendship." For the boys, "these friendships" are first initiated through conversations on the ghats. When the boys approach a potential customer, they rarely begin with a direct business proposition or an immediate offer to guide the tourist around the city. Instead, they engage in small chat. As Pramod explained to me one day, "You never just ask a tourist to come see your shop, you have to talk to him first." However, many of the tourists I interviewed found the boys' "small talk" extremely generic. In fact, when I would ask tourists to tell me about how they were approached by children on the ghats, they often ended up mimicking and mocking the children. In a staccato voice, with their heads tilting from side to side, they would begin reciting the "standard" list of questions they were subjected to: "What is your name? What is your father's name? Where do you come from? What do you do? You come see my shop?" Thus, merely engaging in small chat is not enough for the boys to succeed at making a friendship. The boys have to be able, as Bakhtin puts it, to "reaccentuate" the genre in such a way as to allow their individual charms and personalities to shine through.

For example, when Dipesh approached a potential customer, he not only used humor to make himself stand out but also looked for specific conversation pieces that he could use as devices to engage tourists. One morning, we were sitting on the ghats when an Australian man with a walking stick paused in front of us to wipe some mud off his shoe. Dipesh jumped up like a firecracker and exclaimed, "Hey, nice stick! What do you use it for? Can I hold it?" The man was amused and handed the stick to Dipesh so that he could examine it. Then, once Dipesh had the stick in hand, Dipesh told the man to sit down: "It doesn't look nice if you are standing up and I am talking to you." The man complied, and they took a seat on the steps below me. Then Dipesh started in with the "standard" line of questioning, but, as always, he added his own personal twist.

"What is your name?" The man replied, "George." "Where are you from, George?" He replied, "Australia." "Oh," Dipesh said, "I have many friends in Australia. Sydney, Melbourne, Perth, Brisbane. I can show you the letters they send me. They all say I am a good boy." George nodded his head, and again looked very amused. "I am from Sydney," George said. "What do you do there?" Dipesh asked. "I was in the navy." Dipesh looked at him curiously: "What is the meaning of navy?" George started laughing and, quite happily, explained his former profession. The conversation and questions proceeded like this for about fifteen minutes before Dipesh asked George what sights he had seen in the city: "Have you seen Monkey Temple? Have you seen Golden Temple?" George shook his head. Dipesh exclaimed, "Oh, you haven't seen anything yet! I can show you, you come with me. I show you. No money, just for friendship. Okay?" George seemed genuinely flattered and thanked Dipesh for the "kind" offer, but he also told him that, unfortunately, he was leaving the city in a couple of hours and had to go back to his guesthouse to pack. Upon hearing this, Dipesh again shot up like a firecracker, said good-bye, and headed off to look for another customer.

RECIPROCITY AND INTIMACY

"If you ask for something you will never get it, and yet without asking you will get pearls."

Jaggu, ten-year-old peddler and guide,
explaining why he never asks tourists for money

"The connection between material flow and social relations is reciprocal. . . . If friends make gifts, gifts make friends."

Marshall Sahlins (1972:186)

Dipesh did not succeed in snagging the customer on that particular morning, though, having watched their interaction, I would say that he successfully "wooed" him. I had little doubt that George would have accompanied Dipesh on the tour if he had had the time. Nevertheless, the example is instructive, for it demonstrates how these children manipulate speech genres in their efforts to earn money from foreign tourists. It also suggests that much of their success is predicated upon their abilities to attune themselves to tourists' desires to have unique and personal encounters rather than just generic commercial transactions. Indeed, in addition to manipulating speech genres, another way these children try to change the terms of their relationships with tourists from commerce to "friendship" is by establishing and cultivating relations of reciprocity that involve the giving of material gifts and assistance as well as emotional support.

Like Dipesh, most of the boys who work as guides and commission agents offer to show tourists around the city free of charge. It is feasible for them to do so because unbeknownst to many tourists, they earn most of their money from the commissions they receive from business proprietors in the bazaar. However, this decision to initially forgo a guiding fee goes beyond the issue of feasibility and, I argue, is part of a more pervasive strategy for increasing profitability. The boys often rely upon "generalized" and "balanced reciprocity" as key mechanisms for maximizing their earnings from foreign tourists (Sahlins 1972).[4] For instance, when I interviewed Pramod and asked him to describe his earning strategy, he explained, "I take them [tourists] around a bit and don't charge them any money. I say, 'No, I won't take any money.' Initially I won't take money because I know that later on I will be able to earn more from them. The trick is to get money out of them by making them happy." Kailash, an eleven-year-old guide and commission agent, provides another example. My exchange with him was as follows:

> *KS:* I make sure to remove the idea from the tourist's mind that I am following him in the quest of earning some money. I will forge a friendship with him, and only after forging a friendship with him will I try to bring him into business and try to get some money out of him. And then he will give money happily.
>
> *JH:* So what is necessary for making a friendship?
>
> *KS:* In order to make a friendship first you have to make the tourist happy, ask him questions, find out what he likes, and after that you have to make sure that you don't talk about business at all with him. You have to tell him about whatever he asks you. You will have to get some information out of him, and you, too, will have to give him some information in return so that you can be friends.

In repressing the material side of these transactions and downplaying expectations of an immediate return both Pramod and Kailash drew upon forms of reciprocity that have historically characterized a wide range of social relations within Indian society.[5] However, in terms of the present discussion, what I find noteworthy is not just that these boys are able to appropriate traditional transactional models in their pursuit of profit. Rather, it is the emphasis they both place on emotions. For Pramod and Kailash, the path to profit requires more than just imbuing tourists with a sense of duty, or an obligation to eventually make a return and thereby uphold their end of the social contract. It requires being able to produce a *surplus of positive feelings* within these visitors that will ultimately translate into greater financial rewards. As Pramod stated, the trick to getting money out of tourists is "to make them happy," and the happier you make them, the more they are likely to give.

This is significant, I argue, because it has consequences for the way we conceptualize both the nature of this informal economy and the kind of work these children are engaged in. As Marshall Sahlins and many others have proposed, people do not ubiquitously share the modern, Western preoccupation with sentimentality. In many other sociohistorical contexts, the concept of "friendship," just like the concept of family, does not entail an emotional connection between the transacting subjects: it does not require that people be attuned to each other's feelings. Elsewhere, friendships can be forged and maintained as an enactment of larger social ties, duties, and obligations.[6]

Indeed, anthropologists have suggested that the premium placed on emotional intimacy may itself be reflective of a particularly Western understanding of the self that emphasizes the interiority and authenticity of human feelings. Arjun Appadurai, for instance, makes this point in his discussion of praise in Hindu India. He argues that we need to conceptualize praise as a culturally stylized emotional discourse and practice that works to create material and emotional bonds between transactors *without* presupposing communication between their "internal" states. According to Appadurai, the topography of self that underscores this form of emotional appeal is little concerned with the authenticity of feelings and more concerned with the effects produced by these highly stylized public performances. "Praise," he writes, "is not a matter of *direct* communication between the inner emotional states of the parties involved but [a matter] of a publicly understood *code* for the negotiation of expectations and obligations" (Appadurai 1990:101–102).

Appadurai's discussion also suggests that the children's "first friendship then business" strategy resonates with a broader set of transactional logics and practices within Hindu culture. However, there are some important differences that need to be considered as well. First, the children who work with foreign tourists cannot count on the fact that these visitors share a "publicly understood code for the negotiation of expectations and obligations." Nor can they assume that these tourists, most of whom are one-time visitors, will be bound to them by the kinds of long-term exchange relations that define and sustain friendships in many parts of the world. While some children do successfully establish long-term friendships with tourists by continuing to send letters and gifts, for the most part, their relationships are short lived. Moreover, the children are keenly aware that tourists have the power to walk away from the relationship if it starts to feel burdensome or, as Kailash emphasized, is not to their "liking." Consequently, to win and keep them as customers and friends, these youngsters have to be attuned to the tourists' desires and feelings. And, as I have already suggested, the children who are most skilled at doing this frequently see the greatest financial returns.

The broader implication of this, I argue, is that these children are, to varying degrees, engaged in a *particular kind* of emotional labor (Hoschild 1983). I emphasize "particular kind" because what I am trying to describe here both resonates with and diverges from the concept of emotional labor as it was initially laid out by Arlie Hoschild in her ethnographic study of flight attendants. In her now-classic text, *The Managed Heart: The Commercialization of Human Feeling*, Hoschild defines emotional labor as a form of labor that "requires one to induce or suppress feeling in order to sustain the outward countenance that produces the proper state of mind in others." She proposes that this kind of labor "calls for a coordination of mind and feelings, and it sometimes draws on a source of self that we honor as deep and integral to our individuality" (Hoschild 1983:7) Finally, she emphasizes that in contrast to "emotion work" or "emotion management," which have "use value" and may be done in private, emotional labor is a public activity that is "sold for a wage and therefore has an exchange value" (Hoschild 1983:7).

Like Hoschild's airline attendants, the children on the ghats are also concerned with managing the experiences and emotions of their customers and sustaining a "countenance" that will help them produce the "proper" state of mind in others. Moreover, although they are not wage workers (and this in itself is an important difference), they clearly realize that their ability to maintain such a countenance often translates into financial returns. However, in contrast to Hoschild's informants, these children do not seem overly concerned or bothered by having to manage their feelings. I would not argue that they come to feel "alienated" from their emotional lives or view managing their emotions as a violation against some "integral" part of the self. In this regard, Appadurai is correct to emphasize the way such concepts may be premised upon a particularly Western topography of the self. However, as I have already suggested, in contrast to Appadurai I argue that these children have developed an appreciation and sensitivity for the "internal states" of their customers. The children themselves may not be emotionally invested in these relations or concerned with "the authenticity" of the feelings involved, but many of them realize that this is an important issue for the customers they pursue. Thus, the children's business dealings with tourists are not just forged through rationalized commodity exchange or relations of material reciprocity that impose a sense of obligation. They are also animated by the children's abilities to create emotionally charged, intimate experiences for these visitors that provoke feelings of happiness as well as gratitude, sympathy, and sometimes, even guilt.

HOME IS WHERE THE HEART IS

January 31, 2000
Namaste! My dear beloved friends,
Just a quick note to say I'm thinking of you all and hope that you are doing well and staying warm. Enclosed are some sweaters and things for all the kids. I am sending a separate letter with photos. I hope you get this package. And I hope things fit. We loved being with you in Banaras and thank you from open hearts. I think of you everyday, keep you in my prayers and miss seeing your bright smiles and beautiful hearts. In *truth* we are one though, "same-same"! Much love to you, Sharmila, and big hugs for all the children. I love you,
Om Shanti Shanti Shanti!
Sophia and David

Often, the children help create these intimate experiences for tourists by bringing them home. For instance, Sophia and David, a middle-aged couple from France, had spent a week in the city. During their stay they ended up befriending Sharmila and her daughters, whom they had initially encountered selling postcards and diyas on the ghats. Though their time together was brief, as the letter above suggests, it left a deep and lasting impression on the couple. In their subsequent letter "with photos," Sophia and David again thanked the children for inviting them to their home, and they graciously complimented Sharmila for preparing such a "delicious" dinner. When I asked Sharmila about Sophia and David's visit, she had nothing but praise for them as well: "They are very kind people. They understand my situation. My daughters have made many foreign friends who have helped us. Some of them still send money for Malika; they say it is to help pay for her marriage."

These kind of intimate "backstage" experiences often translate into gifts or financial assistance from tourists. However, they do so not just because they satisfy a desire for authenticity, as MacCannell (1976) has famously argued, but also because they evoke powerful feelings such as sympathy and guilt. Like many of the other families I knew, Sharmila and her daughters shared a single-room dwelling that was considered "shockingly small" by most of the Western tourists who visited. For instance, after Sara, the Canadian traveler visiting from Nepal, had paid a visit to their home, she remarked, "When I saw where they live I couldn't believe it, I felt so bad when I got back to my room at the guesthouse and realized it was twice as big! They really don't have anything!" For the children of course, small living quarters are normal, not shocking, and inviting tourists home is more an act of strategic hospitality than a calculated attempt to make tourists feel guilty by highlighting the disparities in their standards of living. However, for many tourists, the visit home is as unsettling as it is endearing, and it does frequently emerge as a decisive factor in tourists' decisions to give money to these children. Malika, I suspected, was aware of this. In recounting her earlier experiences working with foreign tourists, she said, "I never asked anything from my tourist friends even though I had many. I never said to any of them, 'I want this and you must get this for me.' There were many such friends who came to my home and saw how we lived and they said to me on their own, 'Malika, I want to give you something and please don't refuse.'" Like Jaggu, therefore, Malika had also learned that the greatest gifts and rewards often come without asking.

THE PRODUCTION OF VALUE, THE OBJECT OF CONSUMPTION, AND THE TOURISTIC TURN INWARD

What do these examples reveal about the way value is produced within this informal tourist economy? How do they speak to a more general set of questions regarding the affective dimensions of commercial exchange? Finally, what do these examples suggest about the mode and object of touristic consumption? Is this desire for more personal and intimate encounters just another manifestation of tourists' quests for authenticity, or is it perhaps indicative of something else? In the remainder of this chapter I consider these questions and explore some of their implications.

Clearly, within this informal economy the pursuit of profit is intimately linked to the production of particular kinds of feelings. As I have argued, those children who enjoy the greatest commercial success are often the ones who are able to endear themselves to Western tourists by actively playing upon their "sympathies and antipathies." These findings should come as no surprise to those anthropologists and sociologists who have emphasized the ways that market transactions and economic values are informed by cultural meanings, sentiments, and desires (Baudrillard 1981; Foster 2007; Frank 2002; Hoschild 1983; Zelizer 1985, 2005). However, the examples discussed above also speak to more recent attempts to foreground the role that performance plays in the production of value. As sociologist Dan Cook (2008:7) has emphasized, "*How* exchanges are conducted in markets are as relevant to the 'value' of something as what is being bought and sold."[7] In this chapter, I have suggested that Bakhtin's work on speech genres provides a particularly fruitful way to address the question of "how" and to highlight and integrate both the affective and performative dimensions of these transactions. Moreover, the examples above not only beg the question of *how* but also the question of *what* exactly is being bought and sold in this informal economy. Is it just about postcards and souvenirs?

Certainly, for some tourists it is just about postcards and souvenirs, whereas for others, these items may be purchased as a means to appease "annoying" sales kids and "make them go away." However, in many cases, I argue that these transactions reveal tourists' desires for more affectively charged, intimate experiences. Moreover, I will venture that this recurring desire for more personal and intimate encounters is not something that is just limited to tourists in Banaras. Indeed, I want to suggest that it signals a more pervasive change—the emergence of what I call *the touristic turn inward*. I take this notion of "the turn inward" from Richard Sennett. In both *The Fall of Public Man* and *The Corrosion of Character*, Sennett uses this phrase to describe a profound reorientation in the psychic and social lives of modern subjects. According to Sennett, this reorientation can, in large part, be attributed to the rise and permutations of modern capitalism that increasingly demand flexibility and make long-term commitments to others much more difficult to sustain. As he argues, "Western societies are moving from something like an other-directed condition to an inner-directed condition" (Sennett 1977:5). According to Sennett (1977:259), we now live in an "intimate society":

> The reigning belief today is that closeness between persons is a moral good. The reigning aspiration today is to develop individual personality through experiences of closeness and warmth with others. The reigning myth today is that the evils of society can all be understood as evils of impersonality, alienation, and coldness. The sum of these three is an ideology of intimacy: social relationships of all kinds are real, believable, and authentic the closer they approach the inner psychological concerns of each person.

Some have argued that Sennett's thesis provides an overly critical and dour view of life in late capitalist society—for, as he sees it, our very desires for intimacy are continually frustrated by our narcissistic personality disorders that entail an inability to separate the self from the Other.[8] However, I find this notion of the turn inward compelling, and I think it can be usefully appropriated. I want to use the concept of the touristic turn inward to reference a more general shift in both the modality and object of tourist consumption, in which gazing is displaced by more interactive forms of appropriation and in which the consumption of places is not only enhanced by the production and consumption of personal relationships but also, in some cases, displaced by them. For instance, tourists in Banaras often claim that they can only have an authentic experience of a tourist destination if they establish "personal connections" with local people. In this regard, therefore, the personal relationship facilitates a more compelling experience of place. However, in other cases, these relationships become significant to tourists, not because they signify an encounter with an exotic or authentic Other or place, but rather because they satisfy tourists' psychological desires and needs for recognition—they make tourists feel as though they are unique and special people rather than generic walking dollar signs.

Obviously, more research needs to be done before it can be reasonably argued that the touristic turn inward is anything more than a specific finding based on my fieldwork in Banaras or that it is something particular to a very small market of travelers. However, if we do want to entertain the possibility that it might have relevance elsewhere, then I would like to conclude by briefly clarifying how it differs from previous forms of travel and consumption that have been discussed in the tourism literature. And I would like to at least pose the question: How might we account for its emergence? Is the touristic turn inward reflective of some of the larger socioeconomic transformations that have shaped life in late capitalist society and that have been noted by Sennett, as well as other sociologists?

The work on tourist typologies has made it immanently clear that not all tourists are driven by the desire to encounter culturally exotic or authentic Others (Cohen 1979; Feifer 1985; Hamilton-Smith 1987; Urry 1990; Wickens 2002). Feifer, for instance, argues that the post-tourists' travel experiences are much more oriented around a set of playful dispositions and an acceptance of, if not delight in, the staged and fabricated nature of tourist attractions. Moreover, the idea that the tourist's journey through space often entails an inner psychological journey as well and a quest for self-discovery has also been widely remarked upon (Cohen 1979; Galani-Moutafi 1999; Graburn 1989; Noy 2004). Finally, as Urry (1990) has pointed out, the desire for intensely emotional experiences and connections has a long history within the romantic tradition of travel and thus cannot be portrayed as merely a recent development. Taking all of this into account, therefore, it would seem that the tourists discussed in this chapter (and their consumptive practices and desires) could be adequately described and understood by referencing the existent literature on tourist typologies and trends. However, to do so would also leave two important differences unattended to.

First, while the tourists I have discussed are frequently driven by a quest for self-discovery, the discovery they long for is not just the product of an inner psychological transformation that is facilitated by their physical journey through space or their ability to *gaze* into the lives of the Other, as some scholars have noted. Rather, it is predicated upon receiving recognition from these Others and being made to *feel* that they are human beings and not just opportunities for profit. In other words, I suggest that these tourists' desires for personal connections and recognition emerge as responses to the structural machinations of the tourism industry and its perpetual tendency to commodify places as well as relationships between hosts and guests. In this regard, it may be appropriate to view the touristic turn inward as the latest manifestation of what MacCannell (1976) described many years ago as "the dialectic of authenticity." However, in this manifestation, people as opposed to places, and the tourist's self as opposed to the Other's, become the site around which the compelling travel experience is pursued and produced.[9]

Second, while Urry (1990:46) has argued that romanticism gave rise to an unprecedented yearning for highly individual and emotionally engaging travel experiences, and while he proposes that "the romantic gaze" has been one of the main "mechanisms" that has helped "spread tourism on a global scale" as it "seeks ever-new objects of the gaze," there are again important differences that make it difficult to simply transpose the comparison onto the tourists discussed here. In Urry's description of romantic or scenic tourism, the landscape is still the central object of the tourist gaze, and the gaze is still the primary mode of appropriation. Certainly, tourists in Banaras yearn for individual and emotionally charged travel experiences, but again, many of the tourists I encountered in my fieldwork pursued these ends not by gazing at landscapes but rather by trying to develop personal connections with the children who work on the riverfront. If this is indeed common among tourists elsewhere, then it seems appropriate to ask: What does this shift from places to people, and from gazing to interacting, reflect about the current status and nature of the travel industry today as well as the everyday lives and lacks of twenty-first-century leisure-class subjects?

A tentative answer to these questions may be sought in Urry's preliminary observations on the transformation from modern mass tourism to the emergence of more individuated, flexible forms of travel that have accompanied the rise of post-Fordist or "disorganized capitalism" and in his discussion of "the internationalization of the tourist gaze." As Urry observes, travel trends within the era of post-Fordist capitalism have increasingly come to reject forms of mass tourism in favor of an increase in "diversity of preferences . . . the proliferation of alternative sights and attractions . . . and forms of refreshment which are individually tailored to the consumer" (Urry 1995:151), and clearly the examples presented in this chapter seem to reflect such a reorientation. Moreover, according to Urry (1990:39), the internationalization of contemporary tourism has led to a situation in which "every potential object of the tourist gaze has to compete internationally and this has led to substantial changes in what is extraordinary and what is internationally ordinary."

I suggest that one of the ways travelers render international tourist destinations more extraordinary is precisely by going beyond gazing and by establishing more intimate relationships with local people who not only imbue the attractions with additional significance but also make the visitors themselves feel like they are more than ordinary tourists. In other words, perhaps the internationalization and democratization of *the gaze* is, in a sense, sowing the seeds of its own destruction and thus paradoxically displacing the gaze as the primary mode through which tourists want to consume places and experiences. Finally, if, as Urry has argued, analysts can glean insights about the everyday structure, organization, and lack of "normal" society by studying what and how tourists want to consume on their vacations, then what might be inferred from the examples discussed here? Do these desires for personal connections, recognition, and affectively charged interactions suggest that even with the era of "post-Fordism," "postmodernity," and "post-tourism," we still find more modernist longings and attempts to overcome the sense of alienation and disarticulation that plagues everyday modern/postmodern life? Or, alternatively, as Sennett suggests, might these tourist quests reveal, not an alienated and culturally disenchanted twenty-first-century leisure-class subject, but rather a more narcissistic one, for whom the ultimate object of desire and consumption is increasingly the self? Is it possible that some people travel halfway around the world, not necessarily to see others, but to have others see and recognize them?

NOTES

1. All the quotations used in this chapter come from fieldwork I conducted in the city of Banaras between January 2000 and October 2001. I have used pseudonyms for all of my informants and interviewees.

2. I conducted fieldwork in the city of Banaras for twenty months between January 2000 and October 2001. However, from the fall of 1997 through the spring of 1998, I also spent nine months in the city studying Hindi at the American Institute of Indian Studies. The methods I used during my fieldwork primarily involved observation, participant-observation, and formal and informal interviews with these children, tourists, and residents in the neighborhood. Much of my time was spent on the riverfront observing interactions between tourists and children. Sometimes I accompanied children and tourists on their sightseeing excursions as well. I also collected letters that tourists wrote to these children.

3. Children can be found peddling goods and services to foreign tourists along other parts of the riverfront as well. However, I decided to focus on Dasashwamedh, as it is one of the central tourist hubs.

4. As Marshall Sahlins has noted, unlike the highly calibrated and symmetrical give and take of balanced reciprocity, which variously animates relations in trade,

friendship, and even good dinner conversation, generalized reciprocity refers to a realm of "more personal transactions" where "assistance is freely given"(Sahlins 1972:191) and "goods move in one way . . . for a long period of time." For many middle-class Americans, the paradigmatic example here would be the relationship between a parent and child. When it comes to generalized reciprocity, Sahlins observes that "the expectation of a direct material return is unseemly" and "the material side of the transaction is repressed by the social" (Sahlins 1972:193–94). As Sahlins points out, therefore, generalized reciprocity can provide a key mechanism for creating and maintaining social relations and obligations. Indeed, he argues that in many precapitalist societies this was regarded as the most important function of exchange. However, he also notes that once these social relations and debts are established, they may also be used as means to pursue other ends, such as political power, or, as I will argue here, even profit.

5. For instance, such forms of reciprocity commonly underscore relations between patrons and clients, parents and children, and politicians or "big men" and their followers.

6. For similar discussions, see Anthony Giddens (1991) and Marcel Hénaff (2010).

7. The emphasis on performance has also animated the work of an increasing number of tourism scholars who have sought to understand how tourist places and experiences are continually produced and reconstituted through embodied performances (see, for instance, Baerenholdt et al. 2004; Coleman and Crang 2002; Edensor 1998, 2001).

8. For instance, while Giddens also argues that modern subjects have developed a preoccupation with intimacy and what he calls "pure relationships," he challenges the idea that this can be simply cast as a form of pathological narcissism. See Giddens 1991, 1992.

9. Recently, within studies of tourism there has been an increasing interest in moving beyond on the "gaze" and exploring the multisensory modes of touristic practice and appropriation that shape tourist experiences. For one such example, see Coleman and Crang 2002.

REFERENCES

Appadurai, Arjun. 1990. Topographies of the Self: Praise and Emotion in Hindu India. In *Language and the Politics of Emotion*, eds. Catherine Lutz and Lila Abu-Lughod, p. 92–112. Cambridge: Cambridge University Press.

Baerenholdt, Jorgen, Michael Haldrup, Jonas Larsen, and John Urry. 2004. *Performing Tourist Places*. Aldershot, UK: Ashgate Press.

Bakhtin, Mikhail. 1986. *Speech Genres and Other Late Essays*. Austin: University of Texas Press.

Baudrillard, Jean. 1981. *For a Critique of the Political Economy of the Sign*. St. Louis: Telos Press.

Caine, W. S. 1890. *Picturesque India: A Handbook for European Travelers*. London: George Routledge and Sons Limited.

Cohen, Erik. 1979. A Phenomenology of Tourist Types. *Sociology* 13:179–201.

Cohn, Bernard. 1996. *Colonialism and Its Forms of Knowledge*. Princeton, NJ: Princeton University Press.

Coleman, Simon, and Mike Crang, eds. 2002. *Tourism: Between Place and Performance*. New York: Berghahn Books.

Cook, Daniel. 2008. Introduction: Dramaturgies of Value in Market Places. In *Lived Experiences of Public Consumption: Encounters with Value in Marketplaces on Five Continents*, ed. Daniel Cook, pp. 1–10. New York: Palgrave Macmillan.

Eck, Diana. 1993. *Banaras: City of Light*. New York: Penguin Books.

Edensor, Tim. 1998. *Tourists at the Taj: Performance and Meaning at a Symbolic Site*. London: Routledge.

———. 2001. Performing Tourism, Staging Tourism: (Re)producing Tourist Space and Practice. *Tourist Studies* 1:59–82.

Feifer, Maxine. 1985. *Going Places*. London: Macmillan.

Foster, Robert. 2007. The Work of the New Economy: Consumers, Brands, and Value Creation. *Cultural Anthropology* 22(4):707–31.

Frank, Katherine. 2002. *G-Strings and Sympathy: Strip Club Regulars and Male Desire*. Durham, NC: Duke University Press.

Galani-Moutafi, Vasiliki. 1999. The Self and the Other: Traveler, Ethnographer, Tourist. *Annals of Tourism Research* 27(1):203–24.

Giddens, Anthony. 1991. *Modernity and Self-Identity: Self and Society in the Late Modern Age*. Stanford, CA: Stanford University Press.

———. 1992. *The Transformation of Intimacy: Sexuality, Love and Eroticism in Modern Societies*. Stanford, CA: Stanford University Press.

Graburn, Nelson. 1989. Tourism: The Sacred Journey. In *Hosts and Guests: The Anthropology of Tourism*, ed. Valene Smith, pp. 21–36. Philadelphia: University of Pennsylvania Press.

Hamilton-Smith, Elery. 1987. Four Kinds of Tourism? *Annals of Tourism Research* 14(3):332–44.

Hénaff, Marcel. 2010. *The Price of Truth: Gift, Money and Philosophy*. Jean-Louis Morhange, trans. Stanford, CA: Stanford University Press.

Hoschild, Arlie. 1983. *The Managed Heart: Commercialization of Human Feeling*. Berkeley: University of California Press.

Huberman, Jenny. 2006. *Working and Playing Banaras: A Study of Tourist Encounters, Sentimental Journeys and the Business of Visitation*. PhD dissertation, Department of Anthropology, University of Chicago.

———. 2011. Tourism in India: The Moral Economy of Gender in Banaras. In *A Companion to the Anthropology of India*, ed. Isabelle Clark-Deces, pp. 169–85. Malden, MA: Wiley/Blackwell.

MacCannell, Dean. 1976. *The Tourist: A New Theory of the Leisure Class*. Berkeley: University of California Press.

Noy, Chaim. 2004. This Trip Has Really Changed Me: Backpackers' Narratives of Self-Change. *Annals of Tourism Research* 31(1):78–102.

Sahlins, Marshall. 1972. *Stone Age Economics*. New York: Aldine de Gruyter.

Sennett, Richard. 1977. *The Fall of Public Man*. New York: Knopf.

Urry, John. 1990. *The Tourist Gaze: Leisure and Travel in Contemporary Societies*. London: Sage.

———. 1995. *Consuming Places*. New York: Routledge.

Wickens, Eugenia. 2002. The Sacred and the Profane: A Tourist Typology. *Annals of Tourism Research* 29(3):834–51.

Zelizer, Viviana. 1985. *Pricing the Priceless Child: The Changing Social Value of Children*. Princeton, NJ: Princeton University Press.

———. 2005. *The Purchase of Intimacy*. Princeton, NJ: Princeton University Press.

6

+

Tourism as Transaction

Commerce and Heritage
on the Inca Trail

Keely Maxwell

Each year, fifty-two thousand tourists hike the Inca Trail to Machu Picchu, accompanied by an entourage of seventy-seven thousand guides, cooks, and porters. The Inca Trail is part of the Machu Picchu Historic Sanctuary, a protected area designated a World Heritage Site for outstanding natural and cultural patrimony. The tourism industry and state agencies represent the trail as a trek through natural and cultural heritage. The "tourist gaze" of visitors (cf. Urry 1990:1–3) is directed toward archaeological sites and mountain passes. The first day's walk does not take hikers along an Inca road through the wilderness, however. They trudge along a wide dirt trail lined by houses and agricultural fields, women selling glasses of *chicha* (corn beer), and kiosks with soda and candy bars on display. For protected area officials, villagers are not part of the natural or cultural heritage but are so focused on earning money they are losing their dignity and indigeneity. Anthropological literature on tourism often is concerned with the negative impacts wrought upon local communities and environments (Honey 2008; Stronza 2001). This approach illuminates some of the problems with tourism. By portraying locals as impacted by a powerful industry, though, it can fail to capture the spectrum of ways in which locals engage with tourism. In this chapter, I eschew the impacts approach to heritage tourism. To provide better insight into local agency and economy, I examine how Inca Trail villagers conceive and enact tourism.

The very definition of tourism as "temporary travel for the purpose of experiencing a change" (Gmelch 2004:5) privileges the perspective of the visitor. Academic analyses of tourism also depict it as a consumptive activity (Judd 2006:324–27), one that involves social relations between hosts and guests (Smith 1989:1–17). Many of my informants, however, defined tourism as "when we sell things to people"—people outside the social realm of hosts and guests. Tourism thus is not defined by travel, but by transaction. Anthropologists theorize that tourism's transformative power stems from how it commodifies people and places, turning them into objects for consumption (Bruner 2001; Ness 2005; Silverman 2002). On the Inca Trail, tourists consume beautiful vistas and Inca stonework. For villagers, hikers become a communal resource. Tourism is not solely an external force that impacts villagers. It is also a resource from which they may be able to extract a few crumbs, given a combination of luck and stratagem.

An emerging anthropology of Latin America tourism explores "host" agency. It challenges characterizations of tourism impacts, and shows how local efforts to secure access to tourism resources are part of larger struggles over property rights, forms of economy, and indigeneity. Textile vendors from Otavalo, Ecuador, for example, must combat the notion that producing goods for tourists demeans "authentic" culture, a problem Inca Trail residents face as well (Meisch 2002:98–99). Meisch (2002:20) shows that this trade is not a new and corrupting economy, but rather has deep historical roots. Zorn (2004:136–43) documents both positive and negative socioeconomic changes that have taken place on Taquile Island, Peru, since tourists started arriving in 1976. Islanders have had to fight with state officials and tourism operators over boat access to the island (Zorn 2004:132–36). Struggles over access to tourism resources occur throughout Latin America. In Guatemala and Mexico, Maya vendors use a variety of strategies to maintain rights to sell souvenirs in World Heritage Sites. They draw upon local histories of property rights to show that Chichén Itzá is not just national patrimony (Castañeda 2009:293). They highlight the deep roots of Maya heritage in Antigua as a counterpoint to official representations of World Heritage that exclude the Maya (Little 2009:233). Babb (2010) shows how tourism is part of a broader refashioning of heritage and nation in postconflict countries. It also involves gender and racial identity politics at a local scale (Babb 2010:171–73). These works dissect how tourism is embedded in political conflicts over property rights, heritage, and identity, an approach I take elsewhere (Maxwell and Ypeij 2009). In this chapter, I shed light on how rural Andeans incorporate tourism into extant economic activity and resource allocation. I add to the literature of how "hosts" engage with tourism by conducting a spatialized analysis of tourism transactions. I argue that trail-vending politics produce new moralities of exchange space. I demonstrate how moral and monetary economies intersect to create new forms and spaces of exchange and income allocation.

Trail residents socially construct hikers as a resource. Here, I follow Ferry and Limbert, who show how social and political processes turn "objects, substances, people, and ideas" into "resources," which are "named, managed, and allocated" (2008:4). Foreign tourists are consumers of trail heritage and of beer in campsites. Flows of hikers become a communal resource accessible to trail residents. Peruvian trekking employees are consumers of trail refreshments while maintaining the social role of guests. Tourism transactions derive from Andean moral economic principles of sharing access to communal resources and reciprocal economic exchanges. They also lead to intense competition among vendors. While heritage tourism is not fundamentally transforming indigenous identity and economic systems, trail residents do try to buffer their local economy from the vagaries of the Peruvian travel industry.

The Inca Trail provides an excellent case study of local engagement with global heritage tourism. Trail vending is undertaken primarily by women, providing insight into gendered economic practices heretofore studied primarily in urban Andean marketplaces (Babb 1989; Gordon 2009; Seligmann 2004; Weismantel 2001). The linear nature of the trail accentuates spatial patterns of tourism transactions. I contribute to economic anthropology by examining moralities of tourism exchange space. This concept builds on Parry and Bloch (1989), who demonstrate how moralities are attached to forms of exchange. Here, I show how moralities are attached to *spaces* of exchange. Steering further away from the impacts approach to tourism, I show how heritage tourism is, in a sense, a no-impact phenomenon. Vendors earn money to "educate our children," as they say, but young adults wind up back on the trail doing the same work as their parents. Tourism's market and moral economies reproduce social hierarchies and fail to allow villagers to extricate themselves from broader socioeconomic inequities.

METHODOLOGY

I conducted fieldwork in the Machu Picchu Historic Sanctuary for eighteen months in 2000 and 2001, with several return visits. Data on time dedicated to tourism work come from a time-allocation study of three households. I visited each house once a month over the course of a year and recorded activity once an hour for a total of 5,848 observations. I coded behaviors and analyzed labor patterns by age and gender. I used ethnographic methods of interviews and participant-observation to collect data on campsites, refreshment pricing, tourism income, history of tourism activity, and vending practices. A survey of eighty-seven households in three peasant communities in the sanctuary provided additional quantitative data on demographics, education, income, and tourism work. I used numbers published by the National Cultural Institute on entries to Machu Picchu and the Inca Trail.

THE INCA TRAIL

The backbone of the Inca Empire was a 22,500-kilometer-long network of Inca highways. Today, most of the world knows only of *the* Inca Trail, or Camino Inca: a forty-kilometer path that starts at kilometer 82 on the Urubamba River and heads through the mountains to the archaeological site of Machu Picchu (figure 6.1). The trail was popularized as a backpacking destination in the 1970s and within a few years had achieved international acclaim, attracting five thousand hikers annually. Tour companies sprang up to lead guided treks. Trail visitation increased exponentially in the mid-1990s as Peru's popularity as a tourist destination grew after the containment of Shining Path and military violence, economic chaos, and a cholera outbreak. By 1998, over fifty-three thousand tourists were hiking the trail annually. The majority now traveled with trekking companies, not as independent backpackers.

Inca Trail management involves complicated institutional relations. The Machu Picchu Historic Sanctuary was created in 1981. Two years later, it was designated a UNESCO World Heritage Site for outstanding natural and cultural heritage, one of few sites that merit World Heritage status for both types of patrimony. UNESCO's role in heritage management is limited to occasional site visits and reports. Its reports cite overuse and environmental degradation of the Inca Trail as a top threat to World Heritage. UNESCO frequently threatens to put Machu Picchu on its list of heritage sites in danger as a warning that Peru must improve sanctuary management. Two agencies, the Natural Resources Institute and the National Cultural Institute, divide sanctuary management along the lines of natural and cultural heritage. They split responsibilities for, and revenue from, the Inca Trail. The two agencies disagree over many aspects of sanctuary management but promulgate similar discourses about heritage and tourism. They agree that heritage space is compatible with tourism. They acknowledge that trekking has caused environmental impacts on the trail but believe that with appropriate management, impacts can be minimized. Official rhetoric excises trail villagers from World Heritage.

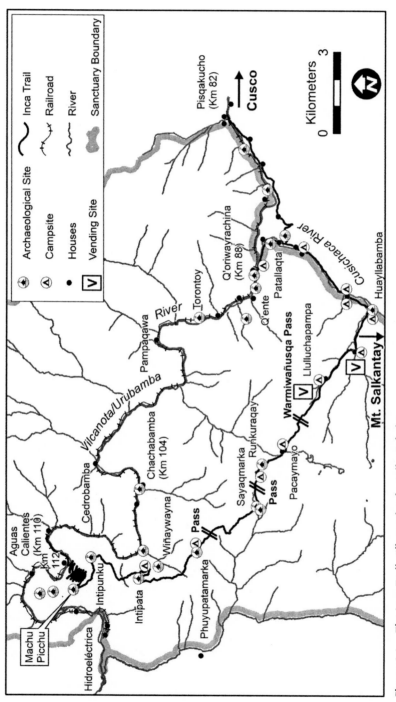

Figure 6.1. The Inca Trail. (Illustration by Mike Rahnis)

They express concern that petty commerce causes villagers to lose their culture and threatens heritage space.

The Inca Trail passes through four peasant communities, each of which has its own territory and slate of elected officials. Fifty to three hundred residents live in each community. State and local conflicts over villager rights to sell on the trail are bound up in land tenure controversies. Villagers argue that their right to sell originates with their locality and peasant community membership. Sanctuary officials claim villagers are recent invaders without residency or selling rights. Trailside residents grow maize on subsistence plots. Fields are in rest during the trail's high season of June to August, so tourism doesn't interfere significantly with farming labor. Agricultural activities are supported by reciprocal exchanges in which individuals offer (and demand) mutual aid. The advent of tourism did not make villagers newcomers to cash earnings. Men previously undertook seasonal or multiyear migrations to work on tropical plantations. Young women worked in domestic jobs in urban areas. Some residents were involved with regional trade of agricultural goods. Working in tourism became a logical extension of extant cash-earning strategies, not a radically new entrée into the market economy.

Men and young adult males (aged eleven to twenty-three) spend 19 percent of their time working in tourism; women spend 11 percent and young adult females spend 7 percent of their time in tourism work. There are three principal ways male trail residents earn tourism-related cash. A few women work in these jobs, but it is not common. Sanctuary agencies hire locals as park rangers, site wardens, trail wardens, and archaeological restoration workers. Pass porters carry tourist backpacks from the first night's campsite up to Warmiwañusca Pass (see figure 6.1). They earn up to U.S. $10 per pack in the high season. Trekking porters and cooks work for tour operators and earn U.S. $5 to 10 a day, depending on tips. They carry food and camping gear for four-day trail treks. Over 3,500 men from around the region compete for work as trekking porters.

The cash-earning strategy I discuss in this chapter is selling trailside refreshments. Hikers buy soda and candy. Porters purchase corn beer and meals. Selling refreshments is women's work, reflecting how female vendors are more common than male in Peruvian marketplaces (Babb 1989:91–95; Seligmann 2004:32; Weismantel 2001:46). Marketplace divisions of labor follow household divisions of labor, in which women are responsible for managing money and allocating harvest for food, seed, or sale (Mayer 2002:11–12). Inca Trail vendors are no exception to this gendered pattern of labor. Women do not sell every day but calculate whether it is worth it given the weather, number of hikers, and other household tasks. If a woman cannot go sell she may send a daughter in her stead, perhaps even a young son, but never her husband or older sons. Some residents have constructed kiosks that serve as small grocery stores. Tourists purchase batteries and snacks. Villagers, park rangers, and trekking employees buy food staples. Men do sell goods in kiosks, as storekeeping is an acceptable male task.

SELLING SODA: CONSUMERS AS COMMUNAL RESOURCE

Women did not start selling on a regular basis until the early 1990s, when outside goods became more readily available and hiking numbers increased. Doña Flavia, one of the first women to sell, describes her venture into trail selling as part of an ongoing entrepreneurship:

> Before, I sold potato and other tubers. I bought them in the high grasslands and took them to Quillabamba [a lowland city]. I sold them there. The rest of [the women] weren't alert. They sat in the sun all day. They were dirty. They didn't know how to sell. I went to Quillabamba and came back the next day to sell fruit here—bananas, citrus. I left my nursing children behind. Tourists always bought fruit from me. We lived in the same spot but my house was further back from the trail. Tourists looked for me to buy fruit. There was a woman from Cusco on the train who said, "Why don't you sell sodas to tourists, I'll supply them for you." Because of that, one night I went to the one campsite in the village. There was just one campsite. Later, I sent my children to all the campsites. One day I went to [Warmiwañusca] Pass with a horse carrying food, flavored drinks for the guides and porters, bottled soda and D'onofrio [a Peruvian chocolate] for the tourists. I earned 400 soles in a day. The other women just carried backpacks to the pass. The trail warden told me: "You'll see, they'll watch you, and they'll copy you one day." Afterwards, one day, another woman asked me if she could sell. Yes, I told her, I'm not envious.

Doña Flavia clearly indicates her agency in deciding to sell to tourists. Having a sponsor to supply start-up goods allowed her to enter the market. Her claim of not being "envious" reflects village moral economy principles of not being greedy, superior, or jealous. Since Flavia's first sale to hikers, tourism transactions have developed into a new type of work: "*Hacemos turismo*" [We do tourism], people told me. Women sell soda, beer, water, and candy to tourists. They sell in campsites, from their yards, and in groups along the trail. They sell corn beer and meals to porters from their yards. Women switch products and selling locations over time depending on labor availability, social relations, and income needs. Approaching tourism from a local perspective, the question is not how tourism is impacting local culture, but rather how distinct forms and spaces of exchange emerge.

Vending space is contoured by the trail's linearity and temporality. Tourists are a captive but fleeting audience for sellers who line the trail. Hiker movement is akin to a salmon run, a one-way current with daily and seasonal ebbs and flows. Trekking groups are consumers of campsites and hikers consumers of soda. They are also, for villagers, a socially constructed communal resource. Women study consumer behavior to improve sales. They experiment with whether hikers prefer animal crackers to candy. They also study resource stocks and movement, asking guides how many hikers will pass by that day. Much village gossip involves speculating about the tourism high season or observing whose campsites are occupied. Trail vendors invoke a variety of strategies to hook hikers' attention and capture part of the daily current. They call out, "Last water for three days," knowing few tourists are aware of the next selling spot uphill. Villagers build covered benches to draw tourists into their yards, where display cases tempt them with candy bars and soda. Sometimes, though, women just put themselves out there, a rock in the middle of the salmon stream. They sit all afternoon with a bucket of cold drinks and don't speak to hikers until asked how much a soda costs. These distinct strategies reflect how locals are aware that resource flows are fickle by nature. One can invest money and effort hawking goods but not get a single nibble. Villagers try to maximize access to this resource flow but explicitly describe success as a result of luck, not just hard work. Out with a group of vendors one time, I asked how much they could expect to make that day: "*Según la suerte ganamos*" [It depends on luck], they shrugged, eyeing passersby trudging up the trail.

Moral and market principles shape village politics over access to tourist flows. I follow Browne and Milgram (2009) and Parry and Bloch (1989) in problematizing boundaries between moral and market practices. Morality in Andean economies is linked to particular social goals, not general values of moral behavior (Larson and León 1995). Vendor motivations include minimizing risk, maximizing income, avoiding conflict, and heeding resource-sharing norms. Campsite management illustrates such principles in action. Nineteen families operate campsites used the first night on the trail. Camping is normally free due to concerns that sanctuary officials will hassle villagers for charging to visit national patrimony. Owners earn money by selling beer, water, and soda to thirsty campers. Each morning and evening, women and children bring out buckets of cold drinks to sell. Three campsites are considered community property (for example, the schoolyard), shared by several families who sell in rotation. Competition over attracting groups to sites is steep. Site owners give free drinks to trekking guides. They upgrade sites by constructing covered dining tables. Management of community and private campsites adheres to moral economic principles. Owners of less popular sites decry that owners of popular sites are "taking more than their share." Taking too much of a communal resource violates local norms of not being envious or greedy. Families that sell at community campsites prevent other people from showing up to sell. They even have tried to exclude some who already participate in rotations, arguing, "Her husband works as a trail warden" or "She sells chicha." Their logic is that these people are already benefiting from tourism, so they shouldn't "take more than their share" of campsites as well. Tourism transactions involve both competition and cooperation.

Norms and practices have evolved to implement moralities of tourism exchange. In one place, women spatially allocate selling rights by dividing into two groups that work in two distinct spots, as shown in figure 6.1. Around six thirty each morning, a string of women carrying bulging sacks walks briskly up the trail. One group stops a half-hour's walk from the village center; the other group continues on for another hour. Short tables made of piled stones mark the selling spots. The women set out bottled water, soda, and candy bars on display. One woman per site sells plates of hot food to porters. The women sit behind their tables and await hikers straggling uphill. Tourists may purchase a drink at U.S. $1 a bottle or U.S. $1.15 for a candy bar. Porters stop to eat a U.S. $0.85 meal. There is little bargaining with tourists. Vendors have a high price floor due to the cost of getting goods from town to trail. After a few hours, the flow slows to a trickle. The women pack their bags and head home. Their earnings are slim, perhaps U.S. $5 a day in the high season and as little as U.S. $1 a day during the rainy season. The two sites have advantages and disadvantages that vary seasonally, so the women rotate sites each week. Vending spots are allocated via cooperative social norms that reduce risk and even out variability in sales and commuting times. Vending spot allocation in urban marketplaces also follows moral exchange principles (Larson and León 1995:247). Rural tourism enterprises elsewhere in Peru rotate access to tourists. On Taquile Island, village restaurants take turns serving tour groups (Zorn 2004:134). Women alternate trips into the Pisaq market and archaeological site to pose in traditional dress for tourist cameras (Simon 2009:135). These cases differ in that on the trail, earnings parity among group members is another principle at work.

Hikers do not notice the transaction that takes place after they pay for their soda. If it is Vendor A's turn to make a sale but Vendor B sells a soda to a tourist, then Vendor B gives Vendor A the cash and Vendor A replaces Vendor B's soda. Rotating sales is a means of maximizing earnings parity and minimizing group problems. Establishing and maintaining this morality of exchange space is not without controversy. In one case, Doña Flavia charged that Doña Dulcinea, another vendor, wouldn't share a prime selling spot. Dulcinea maintained the site was hers since her house was the closest. Flavia argued that Dulcinea was "taking more than her share," the same charge leveled against owners of too-popular campsites. After taking the case all the way to the local magistrate, Dulcinea had to share her site. She still did not rotate sales with the groups. Rotating sales and selling spots reduces conflict but does not eliminate it. "There are always little problems among the women," said one man whose wife sold from her yard instead. Women who sell from their yards avoid group problems but don't benefit from mutual aid and socialization. Yard vending has a flexible schedule and no commute. Sellers catch the afternoon flow of tourists going from the trailhead to campsites, a spatially distinct market than that of the group vendors who sell to hikers going from campsites to the pass.

Vending agreements are renegotiated with changes to products and sites. In one case, a seller started putting out popcorn and animal crackers, not candy bars. When she first switched products, competitors complained she was being "greedy," as she was capturing hikers who otherwise might have bought from them. Yet they also watched carefully. When the new products caught on, they followed suit. Innovation violates rules of communal resource access until imitation establishes a new norm. Urban market vendors in Peru mix competition and cooperation (Babb 1989:158–64; Seligmann 2004:32, 38). Trail sellers face the added twist of hikers being a communal resource, requiring another layer of negotiation over exchange space.

CHICHA: DISTINCT MORALITY OF EXCHANGE SPACE

The spatial and social dynamics of chicha selling have evolved in a different direction than that of soda selling. Trekking employees who purchase chicha are consumers and guests, not a communal resource. Because of this difference, vendor competition is not tempered by norms of sharing resource access. Sellers also have less of a vested interest in cooperation because chicha is produced and sold in private spaces. When chicha vendors first started selling, they did rotate the days they sold. Today, however, a few trailside *chicherías* (corn beer bars) in house yards dominate sales. One reason why is the temporality of chicha production. It takes a week to make, so women produce large batches at a time. They then must sell it quickly due to its rapidly increasing potency, making sales rotation impractical. The unidirectional flow of porters provides a spatial deterrent to cooperation. Vendors don't communicate up-and-down trail about which days they intend to sell. Each woman plans chicha production on her own. Trekking employees know which houses are likely sources of corn beer and plan rest stops accordingly. They take a leisurely half hour to drink, gossip, and joke in Quechua with sellers. Chicha vending space is contoured by the trail's linearity and temporality, but in distinct ways than soda and candy selling because of its different commodities and customers.

INTERSECTIONS AND DIVISIONS
OF MORAL AND MARKET ECONOMIES

Heritage tourism has not caused villagers to "lose their culture." It has led to new combinations of moral and market economies as villagers integrate economic activities and allocate income. They try to protect their local economy from the uncertainty of the Peruvian tourism industry. One way they do so is by creating dual price structures. In one instance, a hungry tourist asked a vendor how much a plate of food cost. The price for porters is three soles (U.S. $0.85). As the seller opened her mouth to reply, her fellow vendors hissed in Quechua, "Tell him four soles, four!" Chicherías charge the same price as outside the trail corridor. They haven't upped the price to see what the market can bear because the moral economy has the upper hand. Porters are consumers, but they are also guests. Tourists, on the other hand, are outside the social realm and presumed to be wealthy enough to afford overpriced goods.

Another way villagers mediate market and moral economies is by maintaining day labor wages for local jobs at a lower rate than for tourism work. Pass porters typically earn around U.S. $5.70 a day and can make nearly twice that in the high season. The daily wage for house construction, on the other hand, is U.S. $1.40, along with plenty of lunch, chicha, and alcohol. Since men could earn more by portering, one might expect that remuneration would increase across the board. However, villagers continue to hire each other for a much lower wage. Rural Andeans create noncompeting labor markets to buffer against the "impact of the monetary sector" (Mayer 2002:140). Trail villagers are aware that their ability to earn cash could change at any moment—as it did after 9/11 when tourism trickled to a near halt. Had rural villagers raised wages to meet the standard set by portering, they would have found themselves facing an overvaluation of wage labor. Earning cash supplements the local economy; it does not supplant it.

A moral economy of sharing access to tourism resources does not mean egalitarian distribution of tourism income. Villagers can find day laborers to build houses for U.S. $1.40 a day, even during the high season. A look at *who* does this work is illuminating. Workers are kin badgered into helping out based on principles of reciprocal exchange, construction specialists, or lower-class villagers. The people hiring them are those community members who have managed to earn the most from tourism. Tourism money exacerbates existing social stratification. In theory, any community member could take advantage of tourist flows. There is no active leveling of opportunities to ensure everyone receives equal benefits, however. People with access to initial capital, as Flavia had, were better able to take advantage of tourism. People who started out in lower socioeconomic classes now work as day laborers in house construction or grinding corn for chicha vendors. They have been unable to profit from the trail due to a variety of factors (for example, alcoholism, single head of household). Tourism largely maintains local social hierarchies.

Local and tourism transactions take on fluid social forms. Monetary transactions are embedded in kinship networks and ritual exchanges. People assume dual identities as vendor and host, consumer and guest. One day, I visited Doña Marcela's kiosk as she was preparing spaghetti for breakfast. Doña Celestina stopped by to make some purchases. Since it was mealtime, Marcela offered both of us a plate of spaghetti, an offering made from host to guest. After we finished our meal, she sold Celestina soap and eggs, a cash transaction involving seller and buyer. The tourism economy also depends on social networks and reciprocal exchanges to succeed. Campsite owners ask trekking guides and company owners to be a child's *padrino* (godparent). Ritual kinship creates a lifelong obligation on the part of the padrino—and, the family hopes, increases the likelihood that trekking groups will frequent their campsite. Refreshment vendors use their stock to earn cash and also fulfill social obligations. Reciprocity is a demanding beast that requires constant attention and nurturing of social networks. While villagers try to buffer their local economy from the tourism economy, doing so is not the same as maintaining a discrete barrier between moral and market economies. There is continuous interplay between moral and market practices in tourism and local transactions.

EDUCATING OUR CHILDREN AND NO-IMPACT TOURISM

The annual onslaught of tens of thousands of hikers and trekking employees has altered village life. Despite these changes, tourism is a no-impact phenomenon in that it has not allowed for socioeconomic mobility within or outside village boundaries. When I asked refreshment vendors why they worked in tourism, the inevitable answer was *"para educar a nuestros hijos"* [to educate our children]. Village elementary schools graduate sixth graders who lack functional literacy. Parents with tourism income rent rooms or build houses in nearby urban centers to enroll their children in school there. Men and women across the Andes invest cash earnings in their children's education (Babb 1989:153; Hamilton 1998:59; Seligmann 1989:205; Simon 2009:133). "Educating our children" is a phrase that is at once politically strategic and economically ambiguous. It is a politically strategic discourse used in struggles with sanctuary institutions over villager rights to sell goods in a heritage site. Villagers do not use indigenous heritage-based arguments to support their right to sell as in Chichén Itzá and Antigua. Instead, they ground their claims in contemporary realities: Who are sanctuary officials to deny their children an education? This strategy tries to shift the debate away from rhetoric that trail commerce is incompatible with World Heritage and that villagers are "losing their culture" because they are too focused on earning money.

"Educating our children" is economically ambiguous in that it doesn't often result in socioeconomic advancement. Parents hope education will maximize opportunities for their children but do not have a clear vision of what that could entail. The ability to educate one's children has become a mark of social status. Lower-class families are among the few who still send children to village schools. Education also creates social difference within families. Women rely upon daughters for help with household tasks. This burden is not distributed equally among female offspring, however. Often, one girl is taken out of school to do daily chores.

On the bright side, more youth than ever are completing elementary school and attending secondary school. Most young adults under the age of twenty-five have attended at least three years of secondary school. In comparison, most adults aged twenty-five to thirty-five only completed elementary school. A few, mostly male, attended one or two years of secondary school. Most women over thirty-five studied two to four years of elementary school, and men four to six years. Teenagers in secondary school spend most of their time in town and express little desire to reside in the countryside as adults. As young adults, though, many do just that. Students who come from rural elementary schools start off secondary school behind their urban peers and often have to repeat grades. Discouraged, many fail to complete their schooling. Young men are lured back to the trail by the prospect of earning easy money by portering. Young women still get married and have babies at an early age. They then join vending groups or sell from yards like their mothers. "Educating our children" is a valuable goal, but it alone cannot leverage tourism entrepreneurship into systemic development.

CONCLUSION

Impact approaches to tourism highlight its power to cause negative impacts as people and places become commodities for consumption. Study of

Inca Trail vending shows how heritage tourism involves contested spatial practices, forms of economy, and systems of meaning. This chapter illustrates how Inca Trail villagers conceive and enact tourism through spatial and economic practices. It contributes to the literature on local engagement with tourism by providing insight into how locals integrate tourism into economic activity and resource allocation. I invert the impacts approach to show that trail hikers become communal resources. Moralities of exchange space determine local access to flows of tourists and porters. The different norms applied to chicha and soda sales show how tourism transactions have evolved in distinct directions. Selling space for products with local provenance sold to other indigenous Peruvians is governed by market competition. Selling space for global brands sold to foreign tourists is governed by competition tempered with cooperation. One reason for this difference is that porters are considered to be consumers and guests, whereas tourists are consumers and a communal resource.

Heritage tourism has not radically transformed rural Andean economy and culture. As Doña Flavia's story shows, tourism vending is but the latest stage in rural trade. Moralities of tourism exchange space are new but stem from the existing economic practices of reciprocity and entrepreneurship. Moral and monetary economies interweave in both tourism and local transactions. Villagers try to buffer their local economy from the uneven cash flows of heritage tourism. The dual pricing for goods and wage labor that results is tinted with moral and monetary principles. Low wages paid to day laborers protect the community from the uncertain tourism industry. They also maintain social inequities. Meanwhile, tourism transactions depend on ritual kinship and reciprocal exchanges as much as they do on market competition and innovation. Ultimately, what makes tourism a no-impact force is that it does little to allow villagers to change their position in socioeconomic hierarchies. "Educating our children" is an economic investment and political rhetoric but results in little upward mobility on the ground. Insights into local tourism engagement as well as impacts can help generate policies and practices to enhance positive outcomes of heritage tourism.

REFERENCES

Babb, Florence. 1989. *Between Field and Cooking Pot: The Political Economy of Market-women in Peru.* Austin: University of Texas Press.
———. 2010. *The Tourism Encounter: Fashioning Latin American Nations and Histories.* Stanford: Stanford University Press.
Browne, Katherine, and B. Lynne Milgram, eds. 2009. *Economics and Morality: Anthropological Approaches.* Lanham, MD: AltaMira Press.

Bruner, Edward. 2001. The Maasai and the Lion King: Authenticity, Nationalism, and Globalization in African Tourism. *American Ethnologist* 28(4):881–908.

Castañeda, Quetzil. 2009. Heritage and Indigeneity: Transformations in the Politics of Tourism. In *Cultural Tourism in Latin America: The Politics of Space and Imagery*, eds. Michiel Baud and Annelou Ypeij, pp. 263–95. Leiden: Brill.

Ferry, Elizabeth, and Mandana Limbert. 2008. Introduction. In *Timely Assets: The Politics of Resources and Their Temporalities*, eds. Elizabeth Ferry and Mandana Limbert, pp. 3–24. Santa Fe: School for Advanced Research Press.

Gmelch, Sharon Bohn. 2004. Why Tourism Matters. In *Tourists and Tourism, A Reader*, ed. Sharon Bohn Gmelch, pp. 3–24. Long Grove: Waveland Press.

Gordon, Katherine. 2009. Marketplace Vendors, Decision-Making, and the Household in Bolivia. *Research in Economic Anthropology* 29:123–46.

Hamilton, Sarah. 1998. *The Two-Headed Household: Gender and Rural Development in the Ecuadorian Andes*. Pittsburgh: University of Pittsburgh Press.

Honey, Martha. 2008. *Ecotourism and Sustainable Development: Who Owns Paradise?* Washington, DC: Island Press.

Judd, Dennis. 2006. Commentary: Tracing the Commodity Chain of Global Tourism. *Tourism Geographies* 8(4):323–36.

Larson, Brooke, and Rosario León. 1995. Markets, Power, and the Politics of Exchange in Tapacarí, c. 1780 and 1980. In *Ethnicity, Markets, and Migration in the Andes: At the Crossroads of History and Anthropology*, eds. Brooke Larson and Olivia Harris, pp. 224–55. Durham, NC: Duke University Press.

Little, Walter. 2009. Contesting Heritage in Guatemala. In *Cultural Tourism in Latin America: The Politics of Space and Imagery*, eds. Michiel Baud and Annelou Ypeij, pp. 217–44. Leiden: Brill.

Maxwell, Keely, and Annelou Ypeij. 2009. Caught between Nature and Culture: Making a Living within the World Heritage Site of Machu Picchu, Peru. In *Cultural Tourism in Latin America: The Politics of Space and Imagery*, eds. Michiel Baud and Annelou Ypeij, pp. 177–96. Leiden: Brill.

Mayer, Enrique. 2002. *The Articulated Peasant: Household Economies in the Andes*. Boulder: Westview Press.

Meisch, Lynn. 2002. *Andean Entrepreneurs: Otavalo Merchants and Musicians in the Global Arena*. Austin: University of Texas Press.

Ness, Sally Ann. 2005. Tourism–Terrorism: The Landscaping of Consumption and the Darker Side of Place. *American Ethnologist* 32(1):118–40.

Parry, Jonathan, and Maurice Bloch. 1989. *Money and the Morality of Exchange*. Cambridge: Cambridge University Press.

Seligmann, Linda. 1989. To Be in Between: The Cholas as Market Women. *Comparative Studies in Society and History* 31(4):694–721.

———. 2004. *Peruvian Street Lives: Culture, Power, and Economy among Market Women of Cuzco*. Urbana: University of Illinois Press.

Silverman, Helaine. 2002. Touring Ancient Times: The Present and Presented Past in Contemporary Peru. *American Anthropologist* 104(3):881–902.

Simon, Beatrice. 2009. Sacamefotos and Tejedoras: Frontstage Performance and Backstage Meaning in a Peruvian Context. In *Cultural Tourism in Latin America: The Politics of Space and Imagery*, eds. Michiel Baud and Annelou Ypeij, pp. 117–40. Leiden: Brill.

Smith, Valene. 1989. Introduction. In *Hosts and Guests: The Anthropology of Tourism*, ed. Valene Smith, pp. 1–17. Philadelphia: University of Pennsylvania Press.

Stronza, Amanda. 2001. Anthropology of Tourism: Forging New Ground for Ecotourism and Other Alternatives. *Annual Review of Anthropology* 30:261–83.

Urry, John. 1990. *The Tourist Gaze: Leisure and Travel in Contemporary Societies*. London: Sage.

Weismantel, Mary. 2001. *Cholas and Pishtacos. Stories of Race and Sex in the Andes*. Chicago: University of Chicago Press.

Zorn, Elayne. 2004. *Weaving a Future: Tourism, Cloth and Culture on an Andean Island*. Iowa City: University of Iowa Press.

7

✝

Spiritual Spaces, Marginal Places

The Commodification of a Nalú Sacred Grove

Brandon D. Lundy

I first encountered the *baloba* (sacred grove)[1] of Kassumba on my very first day in the community. I arrived with my faculty advisor, who visited this area in southwestern Guinea-Bissau on a previous trip. He suggested the village as a fascinating research setting. As we walked along a footpath through the sandy terrain of intermittent palm groves and fruit trees toward our campsite on the beach along the Cacine River, with its meandering inlets and flood plains, we stumbled upon a clearing containing a small hut that held a number of strange artifacts. Recognizing that we stood in the middle of a sacred grove, we quickly exited. If found trespassing in a Nalú sacred site, we could have been fined, or worse.

I later collected a story about how an outsider removed a sacred object from one of these sacred Nalú groves. The thief was now unwelcome in the area; if he returned, the secret society would enact swift and severe retribution. At the same time, the Nalú confided that the spirits would bring about this man's demise on their own behalf if he did not return the object to its proper locale.

Both the Nalú and *ospri* (outsiders)[2] called upon these spirits. One day in particular, fifteen people arrived to *pidi* (make special requests to the *irán*, or local spirits). Two men from Senegal "*pidi*-ed" for employment; Nyima, a recently married woman who had been living in Kassumba

121

with family, asked for success in business as she prepared to move with her new husband to Dakar; and a mother and daughter from the capital of Bissau attended this spiritual site to help alleviate the girl's headaches. In the latter case, the Nalú medium instructed the girl that she had inadvertently taken palm fruit from an *irán* who was now tormenting her. She would have to make an offering of palm oil to this spirit to alleviate the headaches.

Revisiting this and similar scenes in my field notes, I began to think about these encounters and intersections between *ospri* and the local Nalú (*fidju di tera*, literally, "children-of-the-land" or "first-settlers")[3] of southwestern Guinea-Bissau. I scoured the anthropology of tourism literature (Gmelch 2010) looking for similar examples of spiritual tourism, with minimal success. Instead, the extant theories and case studies I found dealt with a wide array of tangential issues, including perspectives on "the origins of tourism" from sending cultures, discussions of "tourism's impact" on local cultures (Stronza 2001), and theories about the encounters themselves (Smith 1989).

For the purposes of this chapter, I propose a revised explanatory approach to tourism that blends spiritual or religious tourism (Bax 1992; Geary 2008; Lewis 2008) with "ethnotourism." Ethnotourism, or cultural tourism, is centered on an indigenous group of people and their culture, which makes it participatory in nature (Robinson and Boniface 1999; Sharpley and Sundaram 2005). It is important to note, however, that as ethnotourists participate in the way of life of a host culture, they inevitably alter the experience through the encounter itself.

My approach diverges from "traditional" ethnotourism studies, however, in several key areas. First, I argue that the touristic encounter does not necessarily change the host if the original cultural space was designed for just such a meeting. Second, the intent of the ethnotourist in this specific case, while seeking an authentic cultural experience, is not interested in the profane or mundane daily routines of the people. They are instead hoping for a sacred engagement similar to forms of spiritual, religious, or pilgrimage tourism. In other words, the visitors are interested in tapping into the hosts' unique contracts with the local spiritual inhabitants as the area's first settlers. These pilgrims are seeking enlightenment that can only be attained in a particular place, through the participation of a particular people.

Amanda Stronza (2001:261) emphasizes the value of researching such an encounter when she writes, "The truth is that tourism can be an ideal context for studying issues of political economy, social change and development, natural resource management, and cultural identity and expression." In this chapter, I argue that the Nalú sacred grove of Kassumba is on the cusp of commodification as it is transformed from a site of traditional religion into an arena of performance aimed at accommodating and displaying "authentic" experience for the touristic gaze. As argued below, however, this transformation from the spiritual to the economic is complicated and may never fully develop since it is contingent upon religious identity, political stability, and economic and environmental implications.

AN ALTERNATIVE ANTHROPOLOGY OF TOURISM

In search of a definition of the "tourism concept," I quickly confronted its amorphous nature. For example, anthropological reviews of the concept invoke leisure, traveling (Nash 1981:462), and *voluntary* visits to places "away from home for the purpose of experiencing change" (Smith 1989:2). As these reviews emphasize, the anthropological study of tourism is finally a recognized, valid, and valuable undertaking in the discipline as a microcosm of both specific and universal cultural encounters (Nash 1996).

Dennison Nash (1981:462) helps to clarify the concept of tourism by considering the dynamic "touristic process" involving the flow of travelers from a sending culture to a receiving or host society. Others suggest that "tourism can serve as a unifying force in modern societies, bringing people together to define collectively the places, events, and symbols that are deemed important and somehow meaningful" (Stronza 2001:265; see also MacCannell 1976). As a processual enterprise, tourism envelops the ethnographer in limitless avenues of inquiry, including the motivations for travel; expressions of contact, change, and reinvention; representations of authenticity; global integration; commodification; power relationships between visitors and hosts; and even explorations into the difficulties of labeling, such as when the visitor-host dichotomy becomes blurred as in the recent idea of the "stay-cation" or the example of Nyima above (see Stronza 2001).

Globalization is also playing an increasing role in tourism as a catalyst for opening marginal places[4] and, as explored below, even sacred spaces.[5] Tourism, thought to be a cultural universal, is highly flexible in place and time (Bax 1992; Bruner 1996, 2001; Crick 1989; Lewis 2008; Wallace 2005). Comprehensively considered, tourism is the "largest scale movement of goods, services, and people that humanity has perhaps ever seen" (Greenwood 1989:171). The World Tourism Organization (UNWTO) estimates that even with a 4 percent decline in the number of international tourists in 2009, 880 million tourists generated $946 billion in export earnings (2010). From this global perspective, one can start to view tourism as either an asymmetrical encounter where local hosts are exploited and forced into neocolonial relationships (Crick 1989; Nash 1989) or as an ideal strategy for localized development through eco-, participatory, or alternative tourism (Crick 1989; Schwartz 1997; Stronza 2001:269, 274–75).

Alternative tourisms are "forms of tourism that are consistent with natural, social, and community values, and which allow both hosts and guests to enjoy positive and worthwhile interaction and shared experiences" (Eadington and Smith 1992:3; see also Stronza 2001:274). Some studies of alternative tourisms go even further by considering the economics of the encounter, or what has been referred to in the literature as the "commodification of culture" in which cultural traits or complexes (insider's knowledge, beliefs, etc.) such as the services provided at the Nalú sacred grove are transformed into a product with measurable (monetarily speaking) demand (Cohen 1988). These researchers are starting to consider: Do cultural items or rituals lose localized meaning once they start to be evaluated in terms of their exchange value? Or, upon commodification, is cultural identity lost? From this perspective, agency, or the host population's ability to empower their "self-representation" (Cohen 1988), is reconsidered during the dynamic host-guest interface.

In the remainder of the chapter, I consider the Nalú hosts of Kassumba, who, according to the traditions, are *obligatorily hospitable*, giving over food, time, and even their beds to guests. These tourists make offerings to the local spirits of the sacred grove through their hosts in return for spiritual mediation. If these guests' prayers are realized in the future, they are obligated to return and make another, more substantial offering to the granting spiritual agency and their Nalú counterparts.

Upon first inspection, encounters at the sacred grove seem to be a standard service exchange—in other words, payment for services rendered. In 2007, the cost to visit the Nalú sacred grove was one bundle of tobacco, one bottle of spirits, and 200 XOF (about U.S. $0.40). However, I suggest that there is more to this relationship than simple economics, travel, or leisure. During a focus group with eight Nalú males of Kassumba, I was told that "the three sacred spaces of Kassumba are the most important for all the Nalú throughout the world. Wars are started and ended here. Others [non-Nalú] recognize its power and visit as well. As children of the land, it is our responsibility to guide these visitors in their journey since our ancestors were the first to develop relationships with the spirits located here. Only Nalú of Kassumba can fulfill this role" (Notes from April 13, 2007). This type of tourism more closely relates to Valene Smith's (1989:2) definition quoted earlier as a voluntary visit to "a place away from home for the purpose of experiencing a change." What types of changes are these visitors expecting? What mechanisms are in place to help them achieve these changes? How are the hosts suffering and/ or benefiting from these exchanges? Are these costs-benefits affecting the everyday lives of the receiving culture? How are external religio-cultural pressures such as Susu- and Islamization affecting the practices at the sacred grove? These are just a few of the questions that I explore throughout the remainder of this chapter. Specifically, is the Nalú sacred grove being commoditized, or were the ethnographic observations made in 2007 and again in 2010 simply representative of "business as usual"?

METHODOLOGY

In 2007, I conducted eight months of ethnographic research in the semi-isolated village of Kassumba located along the Cacine River in southwestern Guinea-Bissau (figure 7.1). I returned for one month in 2010. The village consists of six neighborhoods. In 2007, two were inhabited by 134 Islamic Nalú, while the four remaining neighborhoods supported 542 spiritist Balanta who began arriving in 1939. My research, focusing on livelihood, globalization, and cultural identity, unexpectedly brought me into regular contact with the Nalú traditional religion.

For the Nalú, an ethnic group numbering less than twenty-five thousand worldwide and territorially spread throughout the mangrove littoral between Guinea-Bissau and Guinea Conakry, their traditional religion is something to be respected and feared. At the same time, their customs and language are under tremendous pressure as a result of (1) Islamic conversion begun in the nineteenth century stemming from both the rise of powerful Islamic empires and a push to educate their children,[6] as well as (2) sociolinguistic assimilation, often referred to as Susu-ization (Curtis and Sarro 1997; Fields-Black 2008:7–8; Hanquez Passavant 2000:385), due to their proximity to the larger Susu ethnic group, whose language today serves as a regional *lingua franca*. I eventually came to appreciate the Nalú's precarious position as they balance their customs with a shifting worldview. Through hundreds of conversations and more than three visits per month to the *baloba* alongside residents and *ospri* alike, I eventually began to understand how this site plays an important role in the community as a (1) spiritual center, (2) contested sacred space, and (3) commoditized site for tourism.

SPIRITUAL CENTER

From my first encounter with the *baloba* and subsequent stories collected regarding its quid pro quo nature, I learned that spiritual dealings in Kassumba remain in the hands of several local secret societies divided by both gender and age. The contemporary Nalú of Kassumba still tell stories of their earliest ancestors roaming the landscape. Leadership for

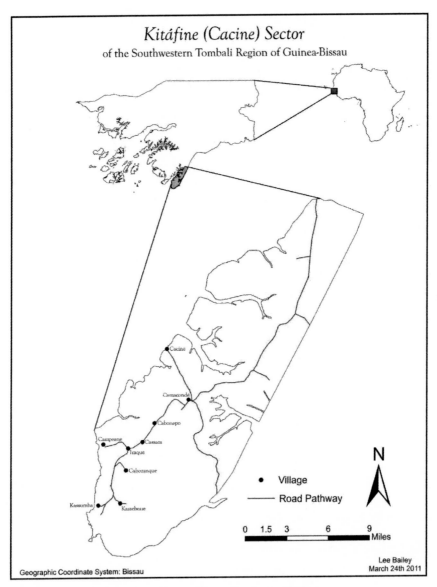

Figure 7.1.   Southern Guinea-Bissau. (Illustration by Lee Bailey)

the Nalú's ancestors entailed communal adjudication by the initiated males of a community. Nalú men referred to their seat of power as the *Mbara*, or sacred place deep in the grove. These kinsmen would sit around a large, clay pot of fresh palm or honey wine, drinking and discussing the concerns of the village. During this early period, social control for the Nalú was a matter of spiritual appeasement. The *irán* of the *Mbara* provided support for their kinsmen in exchange for reciprocal offerings of wine and food. These stories reminded me of the contemporary *baloba*, or sacred space, where the Nalú still practice their traditional religion.

Today, the Nalú's *baloba* remains well respected throughout the region (Bérenger-Féraud 1973 [1879]:316–17). Many of the more than thirty-three different ethnic groups still describe Nalú spirits as the second most powerful in all of Guinea-Bissau, just behind the Bijagos of the Bissagos Archipelago.[7] Outsiders flock to the sites of Nalú traditional religion to gain favor with their powerful spirits. In fact, Kassumba residents were still waiting for the then president, João Bernardo "Nino" Vieira, to fulfill his promise to their *baloba* by making an offering to the spirits for helping him gain the presidency in 1980 and then again in 2005.[8] I suspect that in some circles, Nino Vieira's 2009 assassination might even be thought of as retribution for his failure to fulfill his contractual debt to the many powerful spirits of the country who had aided in protecting him over the many years of his leadership.

Most likely, outsiders continue to believe strongly in these local spirits because rumors still circulate that the Nalú apical ancestor is thought to be a nature spirit, making its offspring particularly good mediums. The Nalú villages also reside close to water, believed to be home to the most powerful spirits. In addition, the Nalú were late to convert to Islam, which means that their traditional beliefs continued largely unchanged through the nineteenth century.

Politically, the Nalú continue to be detached from national politics, instead opting for isolation and self-reliance. First-comer families, as the first to establish relationships with the *irán* in a particular locale, maintain control over the land generation after generation as long as they remain in good standing with the local spirits (Temudo 2008:256).[9]

Economically, the Nalú participate in many of the same activities as other ethnic groups in the area, such as palm oil and rice production, cultivating cashews, and fishing (Fields 1999:87). I would loosely add the services provided at the local *baloba* to this list of economic activities for the Nalú, since one visit cost approximately U.S. $1.60 per person, which was then distributed among the local guide and two to five operator-mediums (figure 7.2). If a request was fulfilled by the spirits, the cost of the second offering to give thanks increased to an animal sacrifice (usually a goat), rice, palm oil, and money totaling approximately U.S.

Figure 7.2.   Sharing Out the Offerings to the Spirits. (Photo by Brandon D. Lundy)

$50, which was then divided among the community, operators, and visitors attending the sacred grove on that day. Although an insignificant percentage of the community's yearly income (less than 1 percent), the average Kassumba resident earned U.S. $1.40 per day making these offerings quite substantial for the affiliated community members during periods of high visitation. For example, I documented an average of fifteen visitors per month to the Kassumba sacred grove, or about U.S. $168 worth of offerings in eight months along with approximately U.S. $200 worth of return visits to give thanks for successful requests.

CONTESTED SACRED SPACE

The Nalú of Kassumba maintain contact with their ancestors at the *baloba* located in the sacred grove named *Kasunkal*, where two types of *irán* reside, nature and ancestral. *Ntakmon* is a "nature" *irán* from the ocean; three others are "ancestor" *irán* of the founding lineages of Kassumba—Kakubu (Kamara), Kabonka (Keita), and Kaklunk (Keita/Sylla)—each represented by both a sacred wooden object[10] located in a shrine on the men's side (figure 7.3) and as three large clay pots filled with medicinal waters enclosed at the foot of a palm tree on the female side.

On the women's side is where requests are first voiced for the benefit of *Ntakmon*, who possesses the head *baloberu*, or oracle. The person making the request is ritually bathed from one of three large, clay pots containing medicinal and powerful water after returning from the men's side of the *baloba*, where they have reiterated their appeal into a palm branch, which is then added to a large, upright bundle of other palms. This practice is similar to other African religious rituals popularly known as fetishes throughout West Africa. The supplicant's feet are then bathed over the active family *irán* (only one mask is used or active at a time until the wood is worn out, then the next mask in line is substituted while a new one is made to replace the other taking its place at the end of the line) using medicinal water taken from the shrine housing the masks and poured out from *konfurbedju* shells or other natural receptacles gathered from the ocean. But what makes the Nalú sacred grove of Kassumba special is the number of people from throughout West Africa that are willing to travel there in search of "change."

I was told by my Balanta consultants whose families have lived in close proximity to the Nalú for almost a century that they continue to be a diffident people whose villages remain close knit and semi-isolated. A majority of marriages are endogamous, and they continue to retain a profound knowledge of the grove. Because of the Nalú's perceived closeness to nature, local Balanta were often seen visiting the *Kasunkal* to discover

Figure 7.3. *Pedra* or "Rocks," Representing the Three Founding Lineages of Kassumba. (Photo by Brandon D. Lundy)

acts of witchcraft associated with deaths within their own communities as well as asking for protection during long fishing trips in the open ocean, even though they had their own traditional religion with associated beliefs, rituals, spirits, and religious specialists.

Their Balanta neighbors are not the only ones who view the Nalú as powerful diviners because of their direct connection with nature spirits. Nalú are believed to have the ability to directly communicate with *irán* because "it is in their blood." For this reason, many outsiders seek their *baloba*. During my fieldwork, I documented both male and female tourists from Kassumba, neighboring villages, the capital of Bissau, Guinea Conakry, Senegal, the Gambia, Sierra Leone, and as far away as France. Nalú themselves expressed the fact that any Nalú in the village had the ability to speak with, hear, or make requests from the *irán* of the *Kasunkal*, which demonstrates their distinctiveness from those they serve. Only those trained individuals who have demonstrated responsibility in their lives, however, are allowed to make requests from the family spirits of the *baloba* on behalf of *ospri*. Any direct descendant of the village, though, is able to accompany visiting *ospri* to the *baloba* and act as their translators.

These guides often receive small payments at the end of a session when serving in this capacity.

Making requests is viewed as potentially dangerous in the wrong hands, and those without responsibility may try to harm others for personal gain. In addition, anyone belonging to the village where a *baloba* is located (for example, *fidju di tera*, children of the land) cannot make personal requests there. The family spirits protect the village but will not directly intervene in locals' lives for personal gain. I was told by a friend that he could ask for success and riches on my behalf, but he could not do the same for himself. The *irán* will listen to *ospri* requests for good health, pregnancy, good fortune, employment, locating loved ones, and many other petitions. On one occasion, I was present when a young man was asking for his cell phone to be returned after being stolen at a local dance. Upon hearing that a *pidi* had been made at the *Kasunkal*, the perpetrator came forward out of fear. The thief not only returned the cell phone but both men also returned to the *baloba* together to make offerings of a goat, rice, and palm oil.

The Nalú, then, are located in a liminal position in society as mediators between the natural and spiritual worlds. They guard their secrets as *fidju di tera* and continue to perpetuate this identity with some economic and political benefits, including food, alcohol, tobacco, money, and respect even in the face of their own shifting religious system toward Islam. The Nalú are struggling to rectify Islam with their traditional belief system. Many Nalú elders feel that the Nalú are distinct from the Fula, Mandinka, and Beafada, who had each converted to Islam much earlier. Even my most fervent Muslim informants wanted the *baloba* to continue, although they no longer participated in the rituals held there.

COMMODIFICATION OF THE SACRED GROVE

Flexible livelihood strategies[11] allow people such as the Nalú to adjust to specific historical, environmental, political, cultural, and economic conditions. These supportive adaptations occur at various rates and levels (Madge 1995:109).[12] The aggregate of these sociocultural conditions influencing the life of an individual, community, and culture as well as the reactions to them is what ultimately helps fashion cultural identity[13] and lifeways. The inherent and necessary dynamic flexibility of these adaptive strategies, however, does not necessarily imply cultural change or global exploitation. Therefore, in the following section I discuss whether the observations made at the Kassumba sacred grove are suggestive of an ongoing process of commodification.

I use Michael Taussig's (1980:12) definition of commodification as production becoming "the aim of man and wealth the aim of production; instead of tools and the productive mechanism in general liberating man from the slavery of toil, man has become the slave of tools and the instituted processes of production." Therefore, I believe that if the Nalú of Kassumba are performing at the sacred grove for economic (as opposed to spiritual) reasons, then they have *become the slave of tools and the instituted process of production*. Otherwise, we may simply refer to the economic undertones of this spiritual touristic engagement as a livelihood strategy, one that has been going on for generations.

To illustrate, the Nalú described their ancestors as fisherpersons and palm wine collectors. Therefore, as mentioned, palm wine played a significant role in lubricating the local judicial system of the *Mbara* before the Islamization of the twentieth century, when the consumption of alcohol became frowned upon. Libations were used among the Nalú as a token of respect for their ancestors and other revered spirits. The Nalú supplicants would often spill a small quantity of wine onto the ground at the start of important ceremonies. The Nalú of Kassumba continue this tradition in the *baloba*, where *ospri* are expected to bring alcoholic offerings for the spirits, most of which end up in the hands of the ritual operators. Palm wine is still an acceptable offering at the *baloba*, although more abundant cashew wine and *cana* (distilled cashew wine) or foreign liquors such as Pastis from Guinea Conakry or sugarcane rum from Cape Verde are valued substitutes.

It is believed that the presence of *ospri*, me included, lends validity to the *Kasunkal* of Kassumba by picturing it as a place out of time, preserved in the ethnographic present. It is not, however, static, changing both physically and, quite possibly, ritually. The question that this chapter continues to ask is: Has a qualitative shift taken place through the commodification of the rituals performed at the *baloba*? It is easy to document that the sacred grove shifted locations over the years as a matter of necessity since the Cacine River continues to erode the shoreline. What is not so easy to gauge is the community's shifting attitudes toward this sacred space over the years. My only recourse is to describe the site as it is performed today and look for any inconsistencies that may be present in people's attitudes suggesting ongoing cultural shifts.

Today, palms and other vegetation that are forbidden to be harvested protect the *Kasunkal*. There are two main access points, either along the beach or, during high tide, through a small path worn along the back of the grove. Upon arrival at the *baloba*, everyone removes their shoes and is divided into three areas according to sex and residency status. Males go to the left side, women to the right, and *ospri* go to a special waiting area on the women's side. The women's part of this sacred space has a number of worn, wooden benches made from discarded pieces of canoe, several calabashes and plastic offering containers, a separate area for cooking, and a gated enclosure at the foot of an oil palm tree containing the three large, clay pots holding medicinal water. Similar to other sacred groves (Journet 1987, 1993), only a fully initiated female member of the *baloba* is allowed inside the special enclosure at the foot of the tree unless invited to enter by the religious specialist in order to bathe in the sacred water. This is usually only done when a woman is trying to get pregnant. Otherwise, the *ospri* make their requests and are bathed from head to toe with the medicinal water from outside the corral by holding on to two wooden stakes located along the border. Bathing on the women's side of the sacred space, however, is actually the last step when attending the *Kasunkal*.

First, *ospri* wait for the senior female of the *baloba* to become possessed by the *irán*. This spirit proceeds to listen to each *ospri*'s request in turn through the oracle and a translator selected from among the *fidju di tera*. The *irán* of the *baloba* only speaks Nalú and therefore must be translated by a local. Afterward, the *ospri*, one by one, are led to the men's side, accompanied by their local sponsor.

The men's side of the *baloba* has two items of note. First, the clearing contains a hut with a small table and a number of natural objects such as shells containing more of the sacred water. Sitting on the table shrouded in cloth are the three wooden carvings housing the *irán* of the three families of Kassumba (see figure 7.3). Beside this hut is a large bundle of palm branches reaching over six feet in height (figure 7.4). When an *ospri* enters the male side of the *baloba*, the supplicant is asked to speak all of their desires into a new palm branch so that the *irán* can hear what is being requested (figure 7.5). Once these wishes have been clearly spoken to the palm, it is added to the bundle of other requests made throughout the year. These palm branches serve an important function in the *baloba* as conduits to the spiritual world. The Nalú can directly communicate with their family spirits; however, outsiders need the aid of their natural surroundings and the *fidju di tera*. Offerings in the form of spirits, tobacco, and small amounts of money (about U.S. $0.40) are given to both the male operator and the female *baloberu*.

If and when an *ospri*'s needs are satisfied through spiritual intervention, it is the responsibility of the *ospri* to show their appreciation and respect by providing a second offering at the *Kasunkal*, the size of which is in proportion to the wealth of the supplicant and the size of the request. This offering usually consists of a goat, several kilograms of rice (about twenty), and one or two liters of palm oil. If this offering is not forthcoming within a year of being granted a request, the *ospri* is in danger of retaliation by the *irán*.

Figure 7.4. Men's Side of the *Baloba* with the Palm Fetish. (Photo by Brandon D. Lundy)

When I attended the *baloba* in July 2007, an offering of chicken, rice, and oil was being prepared since an *ospri* had conceived a child after many years of trying. On that same day, the medicine was replaced inside the clay pots by putting new acacia bark inside them and removing the old. A car with three women also arrived in Kassumba from the capital city of Bissau. One wanted to get pregnant; another wanted her husband to return from abroad.

On August 8, 2007, I documented the arrival of thirteen more *ospri* to the *Kasunkal*. One had loaned his friend more than three million franc guineas only to have his friend visit a Muslim *moro* (mystic) to try to get him to forget about collecting the debt. His *pidi* was for his friend to return the money. Another woman wanted to get pregnant. They warned her that the medicine would only work if she remained faithful to her husband. Another man needed help obtaining cement for his new house. There was also a mother who brought her sick son who had a skin disease. Finally, another woman had arrived with a water bottle, the contents of which were discolored. She was having trouble conceiving and had previously come to the *baloba* to ask the spirits to grant her a child. Upon her first visit, the *baloberu*, Yoto of neighboring Cassebesse, instructed her to grind

Figure 7.5. Palm Branch as a Conduit to the Supernatural. (Photo by Brandon D. Lundy)

rice flour, mix it with the powerful water from the *Kasunkal*, and then eat
the mixture. She had returned to Kassumba from the capital of Bissau
because someone had defecated in the water when the woman was not at
home. She brought the bottle back to divine and punish the perpetrator.
Obviously, in this instance, someone strongly disapproved of this alternative religious tourism to a sacred grove.

Once all thirteen *ospri* had made their demands on the spirits, a large
group of young girls aged three to twelve arrived at the *Kasunkal* from the
neighboring market town of Iraque. They were preparing to begin their
finadu (initiation and circumcision) the following day. The week before,
the women of the *Kasunkal* had made strips of white cloth tied with knots,
one per initiate. They had been left draped around the clay pots in order
to transfer power to the white strips of cloth. Then these knotted strips
were tied around each of the girls' waists to offer protection during their
circumcisions. After the *ospri* and young girls had left the *Kasunkal*, the
ritual operators, both men and women who had worked in the *baloba* that
day, divided up the bottles of alcohol, tobacco, and money. They actually
shared a fourth of a bottle of alcohol with me as well as five thousand
franc guineas (about U.S. $1).

Besides foodstuffs, payment and offerings made at the *baloba* regularly
included alcohol, tobacco, and money. The use of alcohol and tobacco are
probably holdovers from before the Nalú converted to Islam. These types
of offerings, however, are still readily accepted there. Many of the Nalú
seem to compartmentalize their religious practices between the *baloba* and
the mosque, with each fulfilling separate socioreligious functions. Even
the most fundamentalist Muslims among the Nalú recognize the importance of their *Kasunkal* and respect its practitioners.

The Nalú youth of Kassumba view the role of the *Kasunkal* as important
to their cultural identity. During a focus group I ran in April 2007, these
youths expressed:

> The ocean makes Kassumba a better place to live than elsewhere. We have
> fresh air blowing off the ocean keeping the temperature lower than inland.
> Fish are plentiful and easy to catch when necessary. Since our village is small
> and isolated, whites might not like it here in Kassumba. But, our environ-
> ment provides valuable resources. The second best beach in all of Guinea-
> Bissau is located here. If this beach were in Europe, we would have hotels
> and other businesses here. Kassumba, as the primary village for all the Nalú
> of the world, allows us to take advantage of these abundant resources. The
> Nalú keep their secrets here in the *baloba*.[14] All the Nalú came to our sacred
> grove first after the war for independence to ask for forgiveness. There are
> also two other sacred places nearby, the sacred grove near Kadabu, and
> another near Mamadu's *bolanha* [rice paddy]. Whenever the Nalú need to

assemble, they do it here. Even the Nalú from Guinea Conakry come to Kassumba. Every year they perform a ceremony here. (Notes from April 4, 2007)

Kassumba's residents view their environment as particularly rich. The inhabitants regularly expressed their good fortune at having abundant access to the mangroves, ocean, oil palm trees, and rice paddies.

Besides visitors arriving over land, several large pirogues built for the open ocean from long, wooden planks occasionally passed through the local port of Kassumba as well. These vessels arrived from Cacine, Cassaka, and Guinea Conakry across the river. Often acting as motorized fishing vessels, they sometimes doubled as conveyances for people traveling between towns and crossing borders. These pirogues, which could seat more than fifty people at once, often shuttled people between Guinea-Bissau and Guinea Conakry, hauled thatch for roofs, transported large amounts of fish out of Guinea-Bissau, and, of course, served as bases of operation for fishing expeditions lasting several days. In addition, these pirogues would bring revelers to Kassumba's beach for the First of May festival each year. Many of these visitors took time away from the festivities to also pay respects at the nearby *Kasunkal*.

A final aside of note is that the Nalú's sacred groves in and around Kassumba show no signs of agricultural activity, although most of the accompanying landscape has been transformed into paddy-rice fields. These groves have great potential as arable agricultural land, and yet, they have remained pristine. As can be seen from aerial views, current and ancient rice fields are easily observable. At the same time, the sacred groves housing the spiritual protectors and granters of agricultural success remain untouched. Recognizing the need for balance, at a community-wide meeting on July 9, 2007, Inusa discussed the start of the planting season. He stated, "Since we live here in Kassumba Nalú, foreigners are always arriving to see our beach or visit our *baloba*. This is a big problem because these people need to be housed and fed. This is why we must be more successful in our rice campaign this year."

This ethnographic detail is suggestive of a complex and fluid phenomena in which the Nalú sacred grove is undergoing change. Local Nalú practioners are dwindling due to religious conversion to Islam, while the number of tourists seems to be remaining steady or possibly even increasing in part as a result of the disappearance of traditional religious spaces throughout West Africa. As the value of the service increases, will this help recruit new, younger local participants? If the men's side of the *baloba* is any indication, then the Nalú traditional religion is slowly disappearing and the economic benefits are not enticing enough to replenish interest in this cultural practice. At the same time, the burden of *hospitality* is quite high for community members who are feeding and housing tourists for upward of a week at a time when the locale is fairly isolated and it may take several days to round up enough local interest to initiate a ceremony. This added economic burden on the community may also detract from this service continuing.

CONCLUSION

Based on my 2007 and 2010 ethnographic data, Kassumba residents saw nearly two hundred *ospri* arrive in their small, semi-isolated hamlet, which exceeds the entire number of Nalú hosts. The tourists are provided beds that belong to local inhabitants with little complaint. Locals also invite these pilgrims to *bem no komé* (come and eat), offering them what meager food they have, sometimes going hungry in the process. This sense of hospitality is a strong cultural value found among groups throughout West Africa. At the same time, as the popularity of Kassumba's *Kasunkal* increases, primarily through word of mouth throughout the region, the local residents may find it harder and harder to accommodate these visitors.

I remember my host family giving me a pile of mangoes intended to be my meals during a particularly active period at the *baloba* when *ospri* were arriving on a daily basis. My host feared that she would run out of rice for her family; but instead of refusing hospitality to strangers, she instead altered her menu to discourage visitations to her household. In a similar vein, the community was working with a nongovernmental organization (NGO) from Bissau to build three small guest huts complete with zinc roofs and latrines that could be used by tourists visiting Kassumba. The slow progress of this project, however, led to the collapse of at least one hut by the start of the rainy season in 2007.

In addition, it is becoming harder to find the necessary knowledgeable locals initiated into the sacred grove since the interpretation of Islam is becoming increasingly strict in Kassumba and throughout the region. This is especially true among men. On many occasions, the women's side of the *Kasunkal* would be full with more than twenty local women and children waiting for the rituals to begin or the offerings to be made so that all could participate in commensalism. At the same time, rituals would often be postponed for several hours or even days while an initiated Nalú male able to operate in the *baloba* was found. I foresee these difficulties becoming more prevalent over the coming years as fewer initiated men are willing to serve the ancestral and nature spirits residing in the sacred grove. At the same time, women and children are not held to the same strict religious standards, which suggests to me that they will continue to be active in the *baloba* with little stigma.

This chapter has offered a case study in alternative tourism. This type of tourism is reflected in what Bissau-Guineans call *ospri*, those individuals who live temporarily (one to seven days) in local residents' homes and eat their food as community guests free of charge. In this way, the local Nalú are *obligatorily hospitable*, a position that could eventually lead to tension with visitors as their resources are stretched thin. At the same time, throughout West Africa, hospitality is a source of great pleasure for the local who is able to accommodate his or her guest. In this sense, foreigners are always welcome since they bring news and gifts from the outside. It is up to the anthropology of tourism scholars to recognize and validate these customs in West Africa as a legitimate type of alternative tourism involving spiritual knowledge, cultural identity, and, yes, livelihood.

ACKNOWLEDGEMENTS

I am thankful to all those Bissau-Guineans who opened their homes to me, especially the Kamara, Keita, and Sylla families of Kassumba. My debt to their *Kasunkal* is great. Special thanks for the editorial advice of Christian Wells and Sarah Lyon. Partial support for my 2007 dissertation research is from the Morris E. and Lucille R. Opler Dissertation Writing Fellowship, the Mark Diamond Research Fund (MDRF), the New York State/GSEU Professional Development Award, and the Anthropology Graduate Student Research Scholarship Award. A CETL Faculty Incentive Fund from Kennesaw State University supported the 2010 trip. As usual, all inconsistencies and snafus are completely my own.

NOTES

1. Luigi Scantamburlo defines a *baloba* as "a sacred space where ethnic groups practice their cults of traditional African religion: the space is made up of a hut with a single room containing family or village religious symbols. In the *baloba*, women will sit on one side of the *baloba*, men will sit on the other side" (2003:102, translation mine).

2. Scantamburlo defines the concept of *ospri* as "an individual that lives *temporarily* in other people's homes; someone who is from outside the community. In African languages and cultures, hospitality constitutes a duty and a pleasure, something sacred; therefore foreigners are always considered welcome since they bring news and gifts from the outside. Visitor; foreigner; pilgrim" (2003:456; translation and italics mine).

3. Historian Edda Fields writes that the Nalú "represent themselves and their ancestors in multiple ways: as traditional practitioners of indigenous religions, fugitives from religious warfare, occasional participants in internal and external

trade networks, recent converts to Islam, rice cultivators, rice eaters, and exploiters of floodplains and mangrove swamps" (1999:88).

4. "Places off the beaten path—the kinds of places often of most interest to anthropologists—are increasingly opening to tourism as the international economy globalizes, and as transnational networks of transportation and communication are improved" (Stronza 2001:264; see also Lanfant et al. 1995).

5. For the purpose of clarity, I will discuss *place* in terms of "context," while *space* adds the dimension of temporality.

6. I was told that the Nalú of Kassumba converted to Islam between 1910 and 1915 (interview, April 12, 2007).

7. In his description of the Catió region, Lieutenant-Colonel of Artillery António José de Mello Machado referred to the Nalú as "refugees of the forest, the Nalú inhabited the bare places hidden in the trees, removing plants in order to cultivate. In accordance with their timid temperament and knowledge of the secrets of the great bush, they were known to prepare and to use powerful poisons that resulted from their occult practices, which imbued the Nalú with strength of arms" (1972:14, translation mine).

8. After the 1980 coup, "traditional" ceremonies became public events (see, for example, Gable 2003:98, 99) and rumor had it that Vieira "had established contracts with all the powerful *irán* of the country in order to secure the presidency for life" (Temudo 2008:259).

9. First-comers "forged relationships with ancestral spirits to ensure productivity of the land and social harmony of the villages" (Fields-Black 2008:130–31).

10. The shrine piece *Rim* (*Tönköngba*) is found on the male side of the *boloba* among the Nalú. This spirit was thought to be omniscient (Lamp 2000:20–21).

11. I define "livelihood strategy" as an adaptation or complex of adaptations made to achieve a means of support or subsistence for a social unit composed of those living and working in a unique space. According to feminist social geographer Clare Madge, "An important feature of rural Africa lies in the dynamic flexibility of household livelihood strategies. Flexibility is essential, for rural African households are required to respond to environmental, economic, social and political changes both within and between years" (1995:109).

12. For example, rates—daily, weekly, seasonally, or yearly; levels—personal, household, community, cultural, national, regional, or global.

13. I define *identity* as a fluid relationship with oneself and with others. It is a product of three processes: socialization, individual thoughts and actions, and direct and indirect "politics."

14. The nature spirit of the Nalú's *boloba* in Kassumba is powerful because of the sacred groves' nearness to the ocean. The spirit is of/from the ocean. The Nalú have a deep respect for water (Fields 1999).

REFERENCES

Bax, Mart. 1992. Female Suffering, Local Power Relations, and Religious Tourism: A Case Study from Yugoslavia. *Medical Anthropology Quarterly* 6(2):114–27.

Bérenger-Féraud, L. J. B. 1973 [1879]. *Les Peuplades de la Sénégambie*. Nendeln: Kraus Reprint.

Bruner, Edward M. 1996. Tourism in Ghana: The Representation of Slavery and the Return of the Black Diaspora. *American Anthropologist* 98(2):290–304.

———. 2001. The Maasai and the Lion King: Authenticity, Nationalism, and Globalization in African Tourism. *American Ethnologist* 28(4):881–908.

Cohen, Erik. 1988. Authenticity and Commoditization in Tourism. *Annals of Tourism Research* 15:371–86.

Crick, Malcolm. 1989. Representations of International Tourism in the Social Sciences: Sun, Sex, Sights, Savings, and Servility. *Annual Review of Anthropology* 18:307–44.

Curtis, Marie Yvonne, and Ramon Sarro. 1997. The "Nimba" Headdress: Art, Ritual, and History of the Baga and Nalu Peoples of Guinea. *Art Institute of Chicago Museum Studies* 23(2):120–33, 196–97.

Eadington, W. R., and V. L. Smith, eds. 1992. *Tourism Alternatives: Potentials and Problems in the Development of Tourism*. Philadelphia: University of Pennsylvania Press.

Fields, Edda L. 1999. Identity, Rice, and Oral Traditions: Reflections from Fieldwork among Nalu, Baga Fore, and Baga Pukur-Speakers. *Mande Studies* 1:87–107.

Fields-Black, Edda L. 2008. *Deep Roots: Rice Farmers in West Africa and the African Diaspora*. Bloomington: Indiana University Press.

Gable, Eric. 2003. Manjaco Rulers after a Revolution. *Africa: Journal of the International African Institute* 73(1):88–112.

Geary, David. 2008. Destination Enlightenment: Branding Buddhism and Spiritual Tourism in Bodhgaya, Bihar. *Anthropology Today* 24(3):11–14.

Gmelch, Sharon Bohn, ed. 2010. *Tourists and Tourism: A Reader, Second Edition*. Long Grove, IL: Waveland Press.

Greenwood, Davydd J. 1989. Culture by the Pound: An Anthropological Perspective on Tourism as Cultural Commoditization. In *Hosts and Guests: The Anthropology of Tourism, Second Edition*, ed. V. L. Smith, pp. 171–85. Philadelphia: University of Pennsylvania Press.

Hanquez Passavant, Odile. 2000. Une Histoire des Nalou, XIVe–XIXe Siècle: Naissance d'un Groupe et Appropriation d'un Nom. In *Migrations Anciennes: Et Peuplement Actuel des Côtes Guinéennes*, ed. G. Gaillard, pp. 385–401. Paris: L'Harmattan.

Journet, Odile. 1987. Le Sang des Femmes et le Sacrifice: L'exemple Joola. In *Sous Le Masque De L'animal: Essais Sur Le Sacrifice En Afrique Noire*, ed. M. Cartry, pp. 241–65. Paris: P.U.F.

———. 1993. Le Harpon et le Baton (Joola-Felup, Guinée-Bissau). In *Fétiches II: Puissance des Objets Charme des Mots*, ed. Albert de Surgy, pp. 17–37. Cahier 12. Systémes de Pensée en Afrique Noire.

Lamp, Frederick. 2000. Selections from Western, Central, and Southern Africa. In *The Presence of Spirits: African Art from the National Museum of Ethnology, Lisbon*, pp. 18–20. New York: Museum for African Art.

Lanfant, M.-F., J. B. Allcock, and E. M. Bruner, eds. 1995. *International Tourism: Identity and Change*. London: Sage.

Lewis, Sara E. 2008. Ayahuasca and Spiritual Crisis: Liminality as Space for Personal Growth. *Anthropology of Consciousness* 19(2):109–33.

MacCannell, Dean. 1976. *The Tourist: A New Theory of the Leisure Class*. New York: Shocken Books.

Machado, António José de Mello. 1972. Gentes de Catió no Sul da Provincia da Guiné. *Geographica* 8(30):2–31.

Madge, Clare. 1995. The Adaptive Performance of West African Life: Continuity and Change of Collecting Activities in the Gambia. Geografiska Annaler. Series B, *Human Geography* 77(2):109–24.

Nash, Dennison. 1981. Tourism as an Anthropological Subject [and Comments and Reply]. *Current Anthropology* 22(5):461–81.

———. 1989. Tourism as a Form of Imperialism. In *Hosts and Guests: The Anthropology of Tourism, Second Edition*, ed. V. L. Smith, pp. 37–52. Philadelphia: University of Pennsylvania Press.

———. 1996. *The Anthropology of Tourism*. Oxford: Pergamon.

Robinson, Mike, and Priscilla Boniface. 1999. *Tourism and Cultural Conflicts*. New York: CAB International.

Scantamburlo, Luigi. 2003. *Dicionário do Guineense: Dicionário Guineense-Português, Disionariu Guinensi-Portuguis, Volume 2*. Bubaque, Guinea-Bissau: Edições FAS-PEBI.

Schwartz, R. 1997. *Pleasure Island: Tourism and Temptation in Cuba*. Lincoln: University of Nebraska Press.

Sharpley, Richard, and P. Sundaram. 2005. Tourism: A Sacred Journey? The Case of Ashram Tourism, India. *International Journal of Tourism Research* 7(3):161–71.

Smith, Valene, ed. 1989. *Hosts and Guests: The Anthropology of Tourism, Second Edition*. Philadelphia: University of Pennsylvania Press.

Stronza, Amanda. 2001. Anthropology of Tourism: Forging New Ground for Ecotourism and Other Alternatives. *Annual Review of Anthropology* 30:261–83.

Taussig, Michael T. 1980. *The Devil and Commodity Fetishism in South America*. Chapel Hill: University of North Carolina Press.

Temudo, Marina Padrão. 2008. From "People's Struggle" to "This War of Today": Entanglements of Peace and Conflict in Guinea-Bissau. *Africa* 78(2):245–63.

Wallace, Tim. 2005. Introduction: Tourism, Tourists, and Anthropologists at Work. *NAPA Bulletin* 23:1–26.

World Tourism Organization (UNWTO). 2010. Facts and Figures. Electronic Document, www.unwto.org/index.php, accessed November 21, 2011.

8

✝

Becoming Tongan Again

Generalized Reciprocity Meets Tourism in Tonga

Patricia L. Delaney and Paul A. Rivera

There are no nonstop flights from the United States to the Kingdom of Tonga (figure 8.1). As the passengers deplane for a stopover in Samoa or New Zealand before continuing to Nuku'alofa, the *pa'alangi* (non-Tongans) witness a curious phenomenon. A parade of Tongan women march into the restrooms only to emerge some time later, their tank tops, skirts, high heels, and makeup gone, replaced with Tongan dresses and intricately woven *kie kie* around their waists, once again truly Tongan and ready for the last leg of the journey. This phenomenon may be observed on any flight that carries back to the kingdom some of the twenty-five thousand Tongans that return each year.

Outwardly, the transformation appears complete, and though it may be questionable whether they have also thoroughly shed their foreign habits and ideas, it is clear that these Tongan tourists value Tongan traditions and *tapu* (sacred/taboo). However, their intimate knowledge of Tongan culture and direct access to the core of Tongan society does not negate the fact that these visitors *are* tourists, permanently residing elsewhere and visiting the islands for only a relatively short period of time.

This chapter primarily addresses the role of these Tongan tourists in relation to the economy and culture of the islands. Today, nearly 25 percent of native-born Tongans live outside of Tonga (mostly in Australia, New

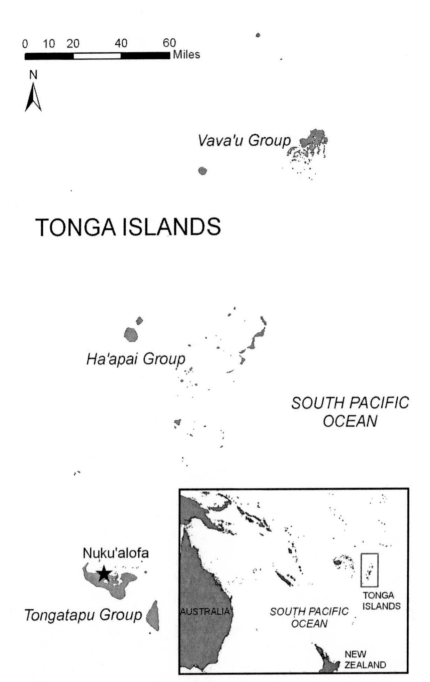

Figure 8.1. Map of Tonga. (Illustration by Kristen LaBonte)

Zealand, and the United States), and most faithfully send remittances to relatives in Tonga. Although these remittances, massive in the context of the Tongan economy, represent the fundamental driver of economic activity, the local manifestation of generalized reciprocity has been a key factor preventing the use of remittances as an engine for economic development.

Instead, we postulate that out-migration, remittances, and the return of Tongan "tourists" represent one more loop in the circle of generalized reciprocity in Tonga. It is essential to note that, while diasporic Tongans provide enormous support for their families through their remittances, the reciprocal compensation they receive is not financial. Instead, island friends and relatives reward returning Tongans with the opportunity to become Tongan again, to claim their place in Tongan society and reinvigorate their sense of identity as Tongans.

Thus, these "tourists," honored guests upon their return at lavish feasts and *kava* circles (rituals in which the root of the pepper plant is transformed into a mild drug and imbibed in a social setting), have exerted an influence far beyond the quantifiable impact of their remittances. By demanding a particular and idealized version of traditional Tongan culture, these tourists have not only perpetuated certain notions and attributes of Tongan-ness but also crowded out the opportunities for economic growth in nontraditional sectors and guided the path of Tongan cultural change.

ECONOMIC AND POLITICAL
CONTEXT FOR THE CURRENT ANALYSIS[1]

To set the stage for the current discussion of the economic realities in Tonga, in this section we draw from the extensive canon of Tongan social and economic history (see especially Sahlins 1985; Mariner 1991 [1817]; and Withey 1987), looking briefly at the historical patterns of economic and political organization.

In contrast to many of the neighboring countries in the Pacific, Tonga was never formally colonized and enjoyed comparative political autonomy for most of the twentieth century. Tonga is the only remaining monarchy in the Pacific, and traces of this structure pervade virtually all social interactions as well as the functioning of the economy.

The Kingdom of Tonga is located in the South Pacific, roughly between the island nations of Fiji and Samoa. Tongan language and culture are closely related to the other Polynesian societies in the region, including indigenous traditions of Samoa, Hawai'i, and the Maori peoples of New Zealand. Tonga is quite small, with a total population estimated at one hundred thousand in 2008. The country comprises 170 islands (of which thirty-five or so are permanently inhabited) spread out over one thousand nautical miles. The total land mass of all of these islands combined is a mere 434 square miles (World Bank 2008), or less than the total land mass of the city of Los Angeles (469 square miles) (U.S. HUD 2010). Gross domestic product was approximately U.S. $350 million in 2010, and per capita GDP was U.S. $3,400 (figure 8.2). Tonga has no significant industrial or manufacturing sectors, and the bulk of export activity takes place in the agricultural and fishing sectors. Heavy reliance on remittance income from abroad has generated both unemployment and inflation, and despite the agricultural focus of the economy, a large proportion of food for consumption is nonetheless imported to Tonga (World Bank 2008).

Like many small island states in the Pacific, Tonga experienced relative isolation from the global economy until quite recently. The traditional economy was agrarian and subsistence based, with substantial surplus production diverted to ritual feasting, production of handicrafts, and a highly ritualized system of stratified gift giving.

Tonga is traditionally classified together with other Polynesian cultural groups as a "chiefdom"-type society, in which economic stratification and political hierarchy are a major defining trait (see Kirch [1984] for a complete discussion of Polynesian chiefdoms and Earle [2002] for a comparative analysis). The three major socioeconomic groups are commoners, nobles, and royalty. Positions are ascribed at birth and are immutable. As is typical in most stratified societies in the Pacific, the divisions among the three groups are profound, comprising economic, social, political, linguis-

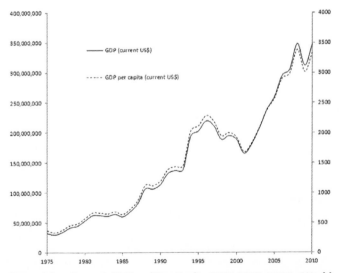

Figure 8.2. Current GDP and Per Capita GDP, 1975–2010. (World Bank 2011)

tic, and religious dimensions. The social divisions are reinforced through a series of *tapus* (taboos), cultural norms that ensure the continued functioning of a highly stratified society by providing strict rules about everything from marriage rites to foods that can and cannot be eaten by members of different social groups. Perhaps the easiest illustration of this division is found in the structure of the Tongan language, which contains three distinct forms. Only members of the royal family learn and are permitted to speak the royal language; only the nobles and the royals learn and speak the language of the nobility; all three groups learn and can speak the language of the commoners. Interestingly, although the language of instruction in schools is the language of the commoners, most government business as well as most communication between royals and commoners is conducted in English, a language free of both status and taboo.

RECIPROCITY: VERTICAL AND HORIZONTAL

On the whole, the system of economic reciprocity in Tongan society does not meet Sahlins's (1974) classic anthropological definition of "generalized reciprocity," an exchange in which there is neither a calculation of financial value of the gift nor an expectation of a specific time-bound return. Instead, as described by Campbell (1992) and Eisenstadt (1973) among others, it follows an interesting hybrid pattern as it intersects with notions of hierarchy, prestige, and the ways to maximize social prestige through ritualized giving of food, money, and other "social goods."

Generalized reciprocity can be seen to exist within social groups (for example, commoners, nobles, royalty) but differs from the intragroup interaction pattern. Villagers, fellow churchgoers, and kin groups normally engage in what anthropologists would traditionally call generalized reciprocity. They give money, food, time, and traditional goods freely, without measuring their economic value, and also receive them freely.

Between different social groups, the pattern is less well defined. Commoners are expected to give gifts (money, food, or *tapa*, an intricate and time-intensive cloth made from the bark of mulberry trees) to nobles and to the royal family. In addition to the obligations of generalized reciprocity among commoners, ritual events of significance involving nobles and the royal family (for example, funerals, weddings, coronations) require substantial contributions. Some families may save for more than a year to prepare a gift for an upcoming royal wedding. In the case of an unpredictable event, such as the funeral of a noble in the village, substantial loans may be taken out at exorbitant interest rates in order to adequately meet the social obligation. These loans are funded through both formal and informal credit channels, often using small, durable assets as collateral.

Thus, analyzing the flow of resources, a clear "trickle-up" allocation from commoners to nobles and royalty is evident and suggestive of a tributary system. However, the concept of tribute carries with it connotations of coercion that do not seem to apply to the Tongan case. Similarly, observing the great lengths to which commoners go to make gifts to those of higher rank, an economic analyst might term such allocations "onus," a burdensome requirement; however, Tongans see giving to those of higher rank and status as a privilege and make these gifts with pleasure and pride.

In either case, the intergroup gifting relationship is difficult to categorize as economic reciprocity, and from the outside perspective, the relationship appears highly extractive. However, when seen from the inside, this gifting relationship is seen not only as positive but also as essential to Tongan culture, identity, and personal fulfillment. To be sure, any rewards to commoners from this system of up-gifting are nonfinancial. When asked, Tongans express their love for those of higher social rank, their social duty to the same, and their fervent belief that nobles possess inherent superiority and that gifting is thus tied to merit. For commoners, the rewards from this elaborate system of up-gifting seem to come from the reinforcement of the system of social stratification that is such an integral component of Tongan identity. Indeed, the material gifts of commoners are reciprocated through this validation of the social contract.

An ethnographic example illustrates the point. At a Rotary Club dinner where Tongans were recognized by the organization for exemplary contributions to Tongan society, all of the recipients were commoners. After each one received their "prize" (bottle of wine, box of chocolate), they immediately turned to the Queen Regent, bowed, and offered her their prize. She would have been rude to decline. The *pa'alangis* (foreigners) were frustrated and upset by what they perceived of as a "manipulation" of the traditional system by the royal family. The awardees were honored to have been chosen, and they were even more honored that they could enhance their own status by giving such a prestigious award to their queen.

The unique cultural pattern of up-gifting draws vehement reactions from those outside the system. Typical comments about this phenomenon from our students, U.S. volunteers training in Tonga, and even anthropologists reading earlier drafts of this chapter include descriptors such as "highly extractive," "unfair," and "just wrong." In the wake of paradigms posed, for example, by Amartya Sen (2000), where social and economic development should be assessed by the extent to which people enjoy "freedoms," Tongan up-gifting seems to run counter to the core concepts that guide socioeconomic analysis.

GIFT GIVING

One of the key components in chiefdom economies is an intricate, ritualized, and culturally significant pattern of gift giving. Tongan culture places a very high value on the cultural expectations that are associated with gift giving.[2] The expression of *'ofa* (love) and *faka ápa ápa* (respect) can most often be seen through patterns of ritualized generosity, sharing, and gift giving.

In this gift-centric society, neoclassical notions of isolated individuals maximizing their own utility or consumption do not provide the most useful lens for explaining observed behavior. Most Tongans instead seek to maximize prestige (by giving away as much as possible) rather than maximizing their personal or household consumption. From an economic perspective, commoners use family- or household-level strategies within a stratified system of generalized reciprocity to ensure the sufficiency of resources for each member. Again, the concept of sufficiency—satisficing, in strict economic terms—is used deliberately and in contrast to maximizing, where the accumulation of individual or household wealth would likely hinder a gift-centric economy.[3] This economy based on gifting and extensive "borrowing" among family and community members of the same social rank ensures a broad distribution of available resources, resilience to random shocks in the availability of resources, and the continuity of social ties. Further, the achievement of social prestige enhances the ability to call on others in times of exceptional need, thus generating a sort of economic safety net.

Indeed, gift giving is central to Tongan identity. Social standing is rewarded in proportion to the magnitude of gift giving, and to be seen as stingy, gluttonous, or greedy is a major mark against you in Tongan society. The quest for social prestige within the community, achieved through these expressions of *'ofa* and *faka ápa ápa* by giving gifts to others, is thus intimately intertwined with the economic system.

Role of Food

Food is more important than money or any other component of the economy. The gift of sharing food is the single most important cultural act in Tongan society. Food is a key symbol of Tongan identity and culture, evidence of which is found in the production of food, elaborate rules about eating and feasting, as well as a myriad set of cultural taboos surrounding food. As a daily necessity, the opportunities to share food are widely available, and the sharing of food serves as a daily and highly visible mechanism to reinforce social ties. Regardless of economic standing, social obligations can be fulfilled through the sharing of food. In the absence of money, *tapa*, or other sorts of gifts, even the most economically underprivileged family can and will share food.[4]

Tongans cannot fathom why or how anyone would eat alone. During our ethnographic field school, when we would arrive back to our home stays at off-meal times, someone would always sit and eat with us, even if only a non-English-speaking grandmother. Indeed, the Tongan expression for eating alone, *kai pó*, translates as "greedy, gluttonous, disgusting, inhuman." The traditional greeting in Tongan society is "come eat." There are dozens of other expressions about eating, including "eat well," "eat happy," and "eat until you die."

Food is a shared resource. You would never fail to invite a passerby to eat if you have food in front of you. Generalized reciprocity with food is practiced among equals. For example, on Sundays, our next-door neighbors always sent over a heaping plate of traditional Tongan food from the *umu* (underground oven). They never expected anything in return, although we sometimes would send over brownies, cookies, or other treats from America. Consistent with Mauss's (1960:39–42) concept of the gift cycle, which includes both the imperative to give and reciprocate and also, importantly, the need to accept a gift, food is also rarely declined by Tongans. It would be rude to say, "No, thank you," to an offer of food from a neighbor, colleague, or friend. Indeed, it would be insulting to the person offering. Thus, the system of gifting and reciprocal obligation, and the social ties it generates, is kept alive by the acceptance of the gift of food. This gives context to what outsiders perceive as the constant offering of food and Tongans' seemingly magical ability to consume vast amounts of it.

It is worth emphasizing that generalized reciprocity is practiced among commoners, and like other economic and social goods, the rules governing the sharing of food between members of different social groups and ranks are hierarchical and elaborate.[5] Like most Polynesian societies, Tonga has a series of food *tapu* (taboos) that assign certain high-status foods to the royal family or nobility. For example, fruit bats are to be eaten exclusively by royalty. Similarly, during frequent and elaborate feasts, the most prized foods (for example, octopus, suckling pig) are reserved for honored guests, such that, even in the absence of royalty or nobility, hierarchy within the community is respected. On the other hand, while commoners take pride in their ability to gift not only within their community but also those of higher social rank, similar reciprocal gifts from nobles to commoners are rarely evident.

Ritualized feasting provides a frequent opportunity for Tongans to combine two of the most important things in their culture—eating and sharing. Feasts are organized for graduations, birthdays, visiting relatives, church conventions, holidays, or just about any other excuse. They range from one-meal events to weeklong buffets with staggering amounts of sweet potatoes, yams, raw fish, octopus, suckling pig, and, increasingly, potted spiced meat, white bread, and mutton flaps.

Role of Money

Fund-raising in Tonga is ubiquitous and seems particularly odd to outsiders who fail to understand the prominent role that giving plays in Tongan society. Tongans often borrow models of fund-raising from overseas and adapt them to the Tongan context. For example, young people frequently stand on the side of the road in the capital city of Nuku'alofa and advertise for a "car wash" using handmade signs. They collect donations from passersby in a plastic bucket. They have no soap, no brush, and no water. There is no car wash in the Western sense. Most Tongans readily give, as it would be culturally unacceptable to decline a request from a person to whom you have a social obligation. Indeed, it is often seen as rude to wait until you are asked. A good Tongan would give money before a formal request was ever made and would think it quite strange to receive something in exchange (for example, a washed car) for their contribution.

Since money is rarely stored or saved, fund-raising is necessary for school uniforms, school trips, dance costumes, food for church feasts, and so on. As social obligations prompt widespread response to every request, anyone needing something must make a similar request. To be sure, outsiders typically find the extent of fund-raising, if not the particular methods by which it occurs, both annoying and nonsensical. However, the end result is reminiscent of Lewis Hyde's (1999:11–14) concept of the "gift circle," an extension of Mauss's gift cycle, wherein the power of a gift (*hau*, in Mauss's terms) expands through constant circulation and draws together those who take part in the gift circle. Conversely, wealth accumulation effectively means taking gifts out of circulation and deliberately severing the social ties generated by the gift circle. Thus, the constant fund-raising and recirculation of wealth generates a kind of social cohesion that Tongans themselves describe as rewarding and gratifying.

Money is thus seen as a "cultural good," not as a financial investment mechanism. Money, much like any other good that could be given away, represents another vehicle to increase prestige. The concept of financial savings is thus virtually unknown, and even middle-class Tongans rarely have any cash on hand. Money is treated much like any other *koloa* (stuff, bounty, treasure). If you have it, the social expectation is that you will give it away. There are elaborate social rules about how much you give to whom (based on hierarchy), but the key component is that you give it away. For example, an observer outside the Western Union office on a Saturday morning in downtown Nuku'alofa would notice that people literally do not make it to their car without giving away some or most of the remittance money that they had just received. If you encounter nobles, teachers, preachers, or members of your community or kin network, your obligations for gift giving are clear.

Gifting and the Church

Christian and Roman Catholic missionaries who first arrived in 1747 introduced Western religion to the Kingdom of Tonga. Today, religion plays a central role in Tongan spiritual, cultural, economic, and even political life. Indeed, both the Tongan Constitution, which forbids work of any kind on Sundays, and many of the national land-use policies were written by Reverend Shirley Baker, a Wesleyan (Methodist) missionary who later served as a royal advisor. Christianity is also closely associated with the royal family, as the king is the official head of the largest denomination, the Free Wesleyan Church. The majority of Tongan high school students attend religious high schools. By most estimates, 99 percent of Tongans self-identify as churchgoers. Many major denominations are represented, including Methodist, Roman Catholic, Seventh-day Adventist, and the Church of Jesus Christ of Latter-day Saints.

Among church leaders, the expectations of "trickle up" have been used to promote a system of competitive tithing in which individuals' commitment to their religion and their church is judged by how much they contribute. Again, the way to enhance your prestige is to increase your contribution. Fund-raising happens year-round but culminates in the end-of-year *misionali* (missionary) activity, in which fund-raising totals are announced on national radio. Individual family names and fund-raising totals are read over the national airwaves. This can either be understood as a way to publicly shame those families who do not meet their obligations or as a way to reinforce cultural expectations about gift giving and its relationship to prestige and status. Throughout the year, most families hold bake sales, make *tapa*, perform dances, hold *kava* circles, and, of course, ask their overseas relatives for contributions to their *misionali*. If a family is quite poor, or if they suffer an unexpected economic shock (for example, wedding, funeral, or illness), they might very well take out a commercial loan to cover their annual church contribution.

From the perspective of economic development, the church donation system seems perverse. Although, in an absolute sense, giving to nobles affords greater prestige than giving to the church, the necessary magnitude of gifts to nobles is also substantially higher, making it difficult for poorer families (especially those without access to remittances) to achieve prestige. The end result is often that the families who are least able to afford a contribution contribute the greatest proportion of their available resources to the church. As not all members of the social community are members of the same church, there is, in effect, a smaller pool of competitors, and this affords one of the only feasible pathways for poorer families to enhance prestige. Wealthier families, while still important contributors to the church, instead more effectively enhance their prestige through large gifts to nobles. Thus, in theory, from the perspective of the church, the more you have the more you should give, but in practice, poorer families seem more motivated to give large church donations.

OVERVIEW OF MIGRATION AND REMITTANCES

Within the context of this economic and social system, the emergence of migration, remittances, and the influx of influences from the non-Tongan world provide continuing negotiation and contestation of traditional ideals of reciprocity and community. This both challenges and enhances Tongans' sense of identity and commitment to the broad-based system of generalized reciprocity.

Noticeable Tongan out-migration began in the late 1960s as college-aged students sought the educational opportunities available in New Zealand and Australia. Some chose to remain abroad, and their initial successes triggered additional waves of migration into a growing diaspora. Today, nearly 25 percent of all native-born Tongans reside abroad.[6]

Out-migration from Tonga accelerated markedly during the 1980s. As the stresses of population growth and the enactment of government

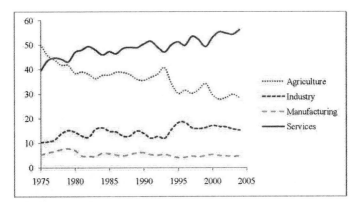

Figure 8.3. Major Economic Sectors, Percent GDP, 1975–2005. (WDI 2008)

agro-export plans became increasingly evident,[7] young Tongan men experienced difficulty securing from the nobles the bush plots to which they are entitled as per Tongan law and tradition. This limited the ability to provide sufficient subsistence crops to the household. This relative land scarcity forced greater reliance on a cash-based economy; however, the opportunities for wage labor are minimal, as Tonga has not developed a manufacturing or industrial base that would necessitate a pool of labor, and agriculture in Tonga is household based and noncommercial.

As is the case in most scenarios of substantial out-migration, the general sentiment among Tongans is that they would prefer not to have to leave Tonga in order to improve their chances to achieve status and economic success. Relative to remaining at home and keeping their families intact, out-migration has thus been a clear second-best option, but in many cases, perhaps the only genuinely feasible alternative. The cultural structures and economic realities of Tonga present substantial constraints for the average Tongan commoner, leaving a small set of feasible alternatives for economic and social advancement.

As evidenced in many other migrant-sending countries, the initial government response to the outflow of people was a façade of reluctant acquiescence caching a sense of relief. Indeed, in the absence of any other coordinated development strategy, the government provided language and vocational training that might facilitate supplicants seeking visas to other countries. Migration alleviated the immediacy of the demands on the ruling nobility and allowed the existing social and economic structures to continue largely undisturbed. Further, to the extent that migrants might be able to send remittances back to Tonga, the incidence of deep poverty might be lessened, along with the pressure on the public sector to provide greater social services. However, the shortsightedness of promoting out-migration has become obvious as Tonga now suffers from a brain drain, a shift in political values, and an unprecedented reliance on remittance income.

It can be inferred from the Tonga Department of Statistics (2010) that at least twenty-five thousand Tongans travel to Tonga each year. While the cultural impact of their continued participation in Tongan society is nuanced and complex, the economic impact is quantifiable and massive.

The remittances sent to Tonga from the diaspora make up an average of 25 percent of per capita household income. This figure vastly exceeds many other major remittance-receiving economies in which 10 to 15 percent of GDP is considered more than sufficient to transform traditional economic structures (Connell and Brown 2005:36–37). It is also worth noting that these figures do not include the value of the substantial in-kind gifts sent by relatives abroad, making any estimates of the economic impact of the Tongan diaspora on the domestic economy lower-bound estimates, at best.

REMITTANCES AND ECONOMIC TRENDS

Since 1981, per capita GDP growth in Tonga has averaged 2.37 percent (see figure 8.2), placing it in midrange status: certainly not the robust growth experienced in China, but neither lagging like much of sub-Saharan Africa. As with much of the world, Tonga experienced negative growth during the late 1980s and for a short time in the mid-1990s. Interestingly, the pattern is suggestive of a country closely linked to the global marketplace as Tonga's overall performance emulates that of scores of small countries around the world that rely on external trade and are thus subject to the highs and lows of global economic shifts. This finding is somewhat paradoxical in the case of Tonga since the economy is rather insular, and international trade in goods and services makes up a relatively small percentage of economic activity.

Ask any Tongan, however, and the link to the global economy is quickly elucidated: remittances. Income from relatives abroad—typically cash, but also in-kind—comprises approximately 25 percent of total household income in Tonga, and nearly 75 percent of all households receive remittance income. Indeed, a simple linear regression of remittance income against per capita GDP suggests that remittances explain over 75 percent of economic activity in Tonga (figure 8.4). In any remittance-receiving scenario, issues of economic dependency raise concern, but few countries approach the scope or relative scale of remittance dependency evidenced in Tonga.

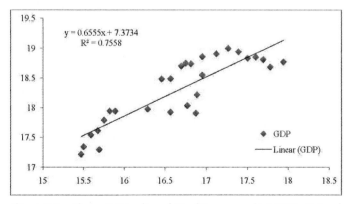

Figure 8.4. Linear Regression of Remittances against GDP, Natural Log of Current U.S. Dollars. (WDI 2008)

In conjunction with the widespread use of migration and remittances as a household economic strategy, a major shift in the composition of the Tongan economy has taken place (see figure 8.3). Thirty years ago, half of all economic activity in Tonga took place in the agricultural sector, whereas today, it makes up less than one-third. The decline in agriculture has been met with a concomitant rise in the service sector, now representing over half of all economic activity, as remittance income has fueled a growing retail cash economy.

It is difficult to overestimate the severity of this shift. In many cases, when the relative share of a sector in GDP shrinks, it may nonetheless be the case that absolute output may be rising but simply not as quickly as other sectors. However, this is not the case in Tonga: since 1975, absolute levels of agricultural production have fallen nearly 45 percent (figure 8.5). This means that Tongans today have lower food security, importing a large proportion of their food products and relying on remittance income for cash to make those purchases.

This dependence on remittance income and imported resources is perhaps most evident in the Tongan balance of trade (figure 8.6). Over the last thirty-five years, exports have fluctuated but have not shown any clear trend, while imports have grown dramatically, driven primarily by food and consumer commodities. Feasts and celebrations in Tonga today are thus as likely to involve cans of spiced ham and bottles of soda as yams and octopus.

At the household level, remittances are incorporated into the Tongan cultural and economic framework. This income provides many of the resources with which Tongans fulfill their social and economic obligations. But, further, it should not be forgotten that migration means the geographical displacement of Tongans whose desire to remain an integral

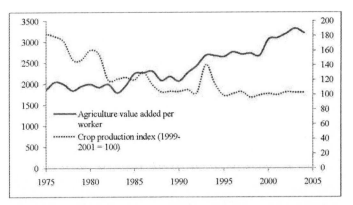

Figure 8.5. Agriculture Value Added per Worker and Crop Production Index, 1975–2005. (WDI 2008)

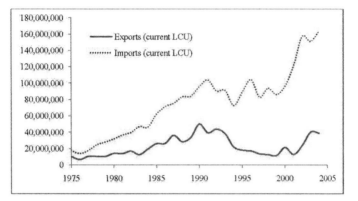

Figure 8.6. Imports and Exports, 1975–2005. (WDI 2008)

part of Tongan culture motivates extraordinary efforts to return regularly and reaffirm their Tongan identity.

BEYOND REMITTANCES: THE ECONOMIC IMPACT OF TONGAN TOURISM IN TONGA

The Tonga Department of Statistics (TDS), in its official documents and data files, summarizes the whole of the Tongan experience into the following categories: economic, social, environmental, and tourism. For a country with a population just over one hundred thousand persons, the forty thousand to fifty thousand annual visitors represent a massive influx; however, by most traditional measures, tourism seems to be a relatively small contributor to the Tongan economy.

Of the 41,208 nonresident individuals arriving by air into Tonga in 2004 (the most recent year for which data are available), 76 percent came from New Zealand, Australia, and the United States, reflecting more than anything the primary settlements of the Tongan diaspora. Further, approximately 81 percent of the individuals arriving list the purpose of their visit as either "holiday" or "visiting friends and relatives," nonexclusive categories suggesting, as per the TDS, that the actual percentage of visitors in the "visiting friends and relatives" category is likely much higher than the stated 40.3 percent. While arrivals into Tonga are relatively constant from January to November at approximately 3,200 visitors per month, that figure doubles in December as overseas Tongans return home for the Christmas holidays.

Interestingly, the above statistics are presented separately from the approximately 12,250 annual non-Tongan visitors that enter Tonga on private yachts or as cruise ship passengers or crew. These "excursionists" may only be stopping in Tonga (as opposed to visiting), and as they typically do not require housing and do not necessarily restock supplies in Tonga, their economic contribution is perceived as negligible.

The economic impact of the tourism sector in Tonga can only be assessed in a rather circuitous fashion. The industrial classification listed as "commerce, hotels and restaurants" makes up approximately 12 percent of GDP, but it is not clear what portion is attributable to spending by resident Tongans, visiting Tongans, or foreigners. Similarly, the subcategory "hotels and restaurants" constitutes 2.3 percent of GDP, but again the distribution between tourists and residents cannot be made.

What is clear is that the economic impact of Tongan tourists comes primarily not from their presence and explicit expenditures during their visits to Tonga but rather from their regular remitting behavior throughout the year. Most of the direct economic impact of their presence instead focuses on celebrations and feasts held in honor of returning friends and family.

From a cultural viewpoint, it would seem that these diasporic Tongans have the capacity to exert enormous influence on the cultural direction of the country since any ideas, customs, or habits they might bring from abroad are granted direct access to the nucleus of Tongan society.

CULTURAL IMPACT OF TONGAN TOURISM IN TONGA

For island Tongans, the restful part of the holidays begins after Christmas, after their visiting relatives have left. Starting in November, when relatives begin to arrive from abroad *en masse*, locals build *umus* (earth ovens); perform dances; hold *kava* circles; exchange *tapa*, clothing, and handicrafts; and organize feasts. The cumulative effect is draining— physically, financially, and emotionally—and locals look forward to the relative calm of January and February. During the Christmas season, it becomes abundantly clear that the plethora of overseas visitors has increased demand for the production of "traditional" Tongan culture. This kind of tourism has direct parallels to "nostalgia tourism" and notions of the relationship between the new leisure class and creativity as described by Colloredo-Mansfeld (1999).

Because most of these goods can only be produced in the islands, there is a greater obligation on resident Tongans to generate the artifacts of Tongan culture. The case of *tapa*, the highly prized cloth made from mulberry bark, serves to illustrate this point (figure 8.7). While *tapa* was once used for everyday clothing, floor mats, and even wallpaper, today it serves a largely ceremonial purpose (for example, mats for weddings and

Figure 8.7. Large *Tapa* Being Decorated and (inset) *Tapa* Detail. (Photos by Patricia L. Delaney and Paul A. Rivera)

funerals). Both the natural inputs (for example, the bark of the mulberry tree) and the materials used to process them (for example, wooden mallets, hollowed logs for drying the cloth, natural dyes for final decorations, seawater for softening the bark) are only found in Tonga and other similar Polynesian environments. The cultural knowledge and social context required to produce *tapa* is also largely unavailable outside of the islands. The production of *tapa* is a labor- and time-intensive process involving large groups of women in *tapa* circles. A group of women typically works for several weeks to complete a single large *tapa* cloth (twenty feet or more in length), which is given to a single circle member. The group then turns to the production of the next cloth for the next group member, and it may take as long as a year for the production cycle to reach every member of the *tapa* circle.

The pattern is similar with the dance, costumes, ritual foodstuffs, and the plethora of other "traditional" Tongan cultural artifacts produced predominantly or exclusively on the islands for consumption by Tongans in San Francisco, Auckland, and Sydney. Consistent with findings in the ethnographic literature on tourism,[8] this can and does lead to the commodification of these cultural processes. *Tapa*, once given at weddings and funerals as part of a system of generalized reciprocity, is increasingly seen as a high-value commodity that can be traded in the formal and lucrative market for the sale of prestigious Tongan cultural artifacts. Interestingly, Tongans abroad still give and receive *tapa* at weddings and funerals and other significant social events overseas. However, they are now disconnected from the raw materials, the cultural knowledge, and the cultural significance of the process needed to produce it. They must either acquire it from their kin who remain on the islands or purchase it.

Over time, the tremendous demand for the production and reproduction of "Tongan-ness" for Tongan tourists has led to the creation and perpetuation of an elaborate economic and social structure to support it. For example, the Tongan Cultural Center, funded largely by donations from overseas Tongans, serves both as a repository and a living museum where idealized Tongan music, dance, food, and crafts are produced. Although sometimes visited by non-Tongans, the Cultural Center is clearly a nexus of Tongan culture, holding national competitions for traditional dance, music composition, and *tapa* and basket making. Similarly, the Tongan national curriculum includes a substantial Tongan Studies component, emphasizing traditional dance, clothing, and music, in addition to the requirement that instruction take place exclusively in the Tongan language until the beginning of high school. These requirements ensure the cultural competence of all Tongans in the production of the artifacts of Tongan identity.

The influx of overseas visitors has also led to the creation of new high-profile cultural events to reinforce the "Tongan-ness" of Tongan tourists. For example, the Miss Heilala Beauty Pageant, held in December (when overseas visitors are most numerous), features contestants such as Miss Fresno, Miss LA, and Miss Auckland, and various well-funded youth group competitions and a variety of dance competitions overseas culminate in performances in Tonga. In each case, individuals or groups all compete to prove their "Tongan-ness" through the ritual performance of traditional choreography, music, and other performance. The Miss Heilala pageant, for example, contains an evening gown competition in which all the materials in the costumes must be made from traditional Tongan materials, such as *tapa*.

During the interview portion of the competition in 2004, one contestant from the United States received huge applause from the audience when she indicated that her favorite thing about returning to Tonga was the food, especially the fat and gristle dripping from mutton flaps at a Sunday meal. While no one in the audience harbored any illusion that a thin young woman from Fresno regularly, if ever, ate greasy mutton flaps, she clearly gave the answer that was expected of her: a necessary demonstration of her Tongan-ness. Such events serve both as a way for Tongan tourists to demonstrate visibly how "authentically Tongan" they are and also to project their definition of "authenticity" on the others in the audience.

This expectation of über-Tongan-ness during visits from overseas relatives perpetuates the circular flow of Tongan cultural practices. Tourism thus plays a pivotal role in the continuation of the system of reciprocity in Tonga. While abroad, Tongans send remittances not only to bolster the economic security of their families but also to maintain their relevance and position within the household and the community. When they return as tourists, it is clear that the explicit objective is for them not to feel like tourists. They come with the expectation that their remittance gifts will be reciprocated with opportunities to renew and strengthen their identities as Tongans. Their desire to reaffirm their Tongan-ness thus generates a demand for the production of Tongan culture, while their remittances fuel the mechanisms to ensure its continued production and places on resident Tongans the obligation to create it.

ECONOMIC AND CULTURAL CROWDING OUT

Between the remittance income they provide and the artifacts of Tongan culture they demand, Tongan "tourists" have essentially crowded out other options. Remittances have perpetuated the gift economy, meaning that the influx of remittance income is generally not available for saving or investment purposes. Remittances seem to have effectively neutralized the incentive to explore other development options. Further, the traditional agricultural sector has also seen itself substantially diminished as remittances promote urbanization and the importation of basic food products.

Perhaps most disturbing is the growing sentiment among younger Tongans that success should be measured in economic terms and that it can only be achieved by migrating abroad. The result has been an increasing emphasis on English language studies and the acquisition of vocational skills that might prove useful to potential migrants.

Cultural practices in Tonga also appear to have been frozen in time. The desire of diasporic Tongans to return as tourists to reassert their Tongan-ness has engaged a genre of reciprocity whereby Tongans in the kingdom are obliged to perpetuate the idealized vision of Tongan culture held by migrants. The structures and institutions created for this purpose, funded largely by remittances, have also crowded out opportunities for Tongan culture to have changed in other directions.

CONCLUSION

Viewed from a macro perspective, the pattern of migration, remittances, tourism, and the production of Tongan culture emulate the cycle of generalized reciprocity that has existed in Tonga for centuries. A system based on migration and remittances has proven to be the most effective way for Tongan commoners to enhance their prestige, as their options on the islands are limited. As we have seen, the remittances they send not only provide day-to-day support for households but also, at a macroeconomic level, fundamentally drive the Tongan economy. The contributions of overseas Tongans are huge, and it is likely that the Tongan economy would find itself in severe distress if those remittances should cease to flow.

But, in a system of generalized reciprocity, it is clear that the Tongan tourists, those overseas "givers," must, at some point and in some way, be compensated for their remittance gifts. What we postulate is that this reciprocation occurs, not in similar financial gifts, but rather in the provision of Tongan culture and the reaffirmation of Tongan identity to Tongan tourists by those who remain on the islands.

In a literal sense, Tongan tourists, while on their visits home, are welcomed with feasts and celebrations, and *kava* circles are held in their honor. But, in a metaphorical sense, the gift received is to become Tongan again, reauthenticating their legitimacy as Tongans and revalidating their place in Tongan society. From a larger perspective, then, the influence of Tongan tourists drives the perpetuation of traditional Tongan culture.

Thus, mirroring the economic reliance on remittances, the traditional idealized version of Tongan culture depends on Tongan tourists' continuing the belief in a sense of being self-grounded in Tongan cultural attributes only available on the islands.

ACKNOWLEDGMENTS

The authors wish to thank Peace Corps Tonga, the participants at the 2010 SEA Annual Meeting, and our numerous and generous Tongan informants, hosts, and guides. Support was provided by the Saint Michael's College Faculty Development Fund and the Martin V. Smith School of Business and Economics at CSU Channel Islands. The map (figure 8.1) was created by Kristen LaBonte using ESRI's ArcGIS 9.3 with data generously provided by DIVA-GIS.

NOTES

1. Data presented in this chapter stem from ethnographic research conducted by Delaney from February 2003 to March 2004 during her time working as an applied anthropologist with a U.S. voluntary agency and from subsequent economic and statistical analysis conducted by Rivera. Additional data collection and analysis were completed during an undergraduate field school in Tonga led by Delaney and Rivera in the summer of 2008.

2. See Weiner (1992) for a novel discussion of gifting.

3. As per Simon (1955), rational choice involves the pursuit of a course of action that leads to a satisfactory outcome. Traditional maximizing models instead tend to imply the insatiability of human desires, and thus, lead to a focus on the accumulation of individual wealth.

4. See Weissner and Schiefenhovel (1996) for a larger discussion of the role of food in comparative perspective.

5. While it is possible that nobles and royalty practice generalized reciprocity among themselves, our ethnographic research focused on commoners, and our access to nobles and royalty was limited.

6. Small (1997) provides rich ethnographic detail about the decision-making process and the cultural realities of both those who leave and those who stay behind.

7. See Storey and Murray (2001) for a detailed account of Tonga's unsustainable and risky attempts to become a major exporter of squash pumpkin.

8. See MacCannell (2001) for a further discussion of this process.

REFERENCES

Campbell, I. C. 1992. *Island Kingdom: Tonga, Ancient and Modern*. Canterbury: Canterbury University Press.

Colloredo-Mansfeld, Rudolf Josef. 1999. *The Native Leisure Class: Consumption and Cultural Creativity in the Andes*. Chicago: University of Chicago Press.

Connell, John, and Richard P. C. Brown. 2005. *Remittances in the Pacific: An Overview*. Manila, Philippines: Asian Development Bank.

Earle, Timothy. 2002. *Bronze Age Economics: The Beginnings of Political Economies*. Boulder, CO: Westview Press.

Eisenstadt, S. N. 1973. Post-Traditional Societies and the Continuity and Reconstruction of Tradition. *Daedalus* 102(1):1–28.

Hyde, Lewis. 1999. *The Gift: Imagination and the Erotic Life of Property*. London: Trafalgar Square.

Kirch, Patrick V. 1984. *The Evolution of the Polynesian Chiefdoms*. Cambridge: Cambridge University Press.

MacCannell, Dean. 2001. Remarks on the Commodification of Cultures. In *Hosts and Guests Revisited: Tourism Issues of the 21st Century* eds. Valene L. Smith and Maryann Brent, pp. 380–90. New York: Cognizant Communication.

Mariner, William. 1991 [1817]. *Tonga Islands: William Mariner's Account.* London: Vava'u Press Limited.

Mauss, Marcel. 1960. *The Gift.* New York: W. W. Norton.

Sahlins, Marshall. 1974. *Stone Age Economics.* London: Tavistock Publications.

———. 1985. *Islands of History.* Chicago: University of Chicago Press.

Sen, Amartya. 2000. *Development as Freedom.* New York: Anchor Books.

Simon, H. A. 1955. A Behavioral Model of Rational Choice. *Quarterly Journal of Economics* 69(1):99–118.

Small, Cathy. 1997. *Voyages: From Tongan Villages to American Suburbs.* Ithaca, NY: Cornell University Press.

Storey, Donovan, and Warwick Murray. 2001. Dilemmas of Development in Oceania: The Political Economy of the Tongan Agro-Export Sector. *Geographical Journal* 167(4):291–301.

Tonga Department of Statistics Economic Indicators. 2010. www.spc.int/prism /Country/TO/stats/Economic/eco-index.htm, accessed November 17, 2011.

U.S. Department of Housing and Urban Development (U.S. HUD). 2010. Los Angeles City MapStats. http://fedstats.gov/qf/states/06/0644000.html, accessed November 21, 2011.

Weiner, Annette. 1992. *Inalienable Possessions: The Paradox of Keeping While Giving.* Berkeley: University of California Press.

Weissner, Polly, and Wulf Schiefenhovel. 1996. *Food and the Status Quest: An Interdisciplinary Perspective.* Providence, RI: Berghahn Books.

Withey, Lynne. 1987. *Voyages of Discovery: Captain Cook and the Exploration of the Pacific.* Berkeley: University of California Press.

World Bank. 2011. *World Development Indicators 2011.* Washington, DC: The World Bank.

9

✛

Women, Entrepreneurship, and Empowerment

Black-Owned Township Tourism in Cape Town, South Africa

Katrina T. Greene

Tourism has become a growth industry for South Africa, as millions of international tourists flock to the country each year. Increases in the industry over the last fifteen to twenty years have been due to the transition of the country away from an apartheid system that advantaged a minority of South Africa's population—whites—and disadvantaged all other ethnic and racial groups in the country (Rogerson and Visser 2007a:27). The massive growth in the tourist industry has led to opportunities for many South Africans to enter the industry through a multiplicity of business activities, including the provision of transportation and accommodation services. Special interests have developed for visiting the sites of residence for the historically disadvantaged populations near the urban centers known as townships, which were often off limits to tourists during the apartheid period. Such interests have created a space for some members of the historically disadvantaged communities to emerge within the tourism industry as owners and operators, roles from which they were excluded during the apartheid era.

My research examines how various black[1] women who live in the townships outside of Cape Town, South Africa, were becoming small business entrepreneurs by turning their private residences into bed-and-breakfast establishments in order to cater to township tourists who desired to stay overnight or several days and nights in the townships. Many of these entrepreneurs believed that they had been excluded from the post-apartheid black[2] economic empowerment agenda, which commenced with a primary focus on the creation of large-scale investment opportunities and networks to redress the marginalization of blacks in the economic system. I argue that such entrepreneurs were engaged in their own grassroots or local black economic empowerment and pro-poor tourism efforts by creating bed-and-breakfast establishments, which provided a form of local economic development to their poor communities. My analysis of these entrepreneurs complements the work of Nemasetoni and Rogerson (2005:199), who suggest that since small tourism firms often impact and provide for local development among the poor in their communities that such activities may be viewed as a form of pro-poor tourism. The women entrepreneurs in my research study felt that they needed to find other avenues particular to their local contexts to empower themselves and address some of the issues of poverty and unemployment in their own communities.

My study of black women bed-and-breakfast entrepreneurs also provides a critique to some scholars who view gender as an analytical category and focus on the structural inequalities between men and women with regard to entrepreneurship opportunities. This view by some scholars characterizes women entrepreneurs as disadvantaged to male entrepreneurs (Lewis 2006:454). My research demonstrates that such a view is reductionist, as all female or women entrepreneurs are not disadvantaged due to their gendered status. In the case of the black women entrepreneurs in my study, I argue that the gender status of women did not marginalize or disadvantage them. In fact, women's culturally defined roles as caretakers of the home positioned them to emerge as bed-and-breakfast entrepreneurs in the black-owned township tourism industry.

In this chapter, I first examine the concept of black economic empowerment as it relates to changes in, and the growth of, the tourism industry. Such a discussion specifically focuses on efforts to diversify ownership patterns and to integrate those who were historically disadvantaged under apartheid as full participants in the South African economy. Second, I discuss the context for the emergence of black-owned tourism in South Africa by describing existing ownership patterns within the South African Tourism Industry and some of the financial difficulties experienced by black township entrepreneurs. Third, I present data from my ethnographic research on black women entrepreneurs who started bed-and-breakfast accommodations in several of the Cape Town townships. Such data will focus upon (1) the women's entry into the black-owned tourism accommodation subsector, (2) the community focus of their entrepreneurial efforts, and (3) their business struggles and views of black economic empowerment in South Africa. Fourth, I explore how these women were engaged in grassroots or local black economic empowerment and pro-poor tourism efforts through their entrepreneurial activities with regard to their community members. Finally, I discuss how the gendered status of women has created a space for them to enter into the accommodation subsector of the black-owned township tourism industry.

BLACK ECONOMIC EMPOWERMENT

Decades of systematic disempowerment occurred under the apartheid system in South Africa. One of the goals of the new majority-led post-apartheid government, after taking office in 1994, was to deracialize business ownership and control through black economic empowerment initiatives, as businesses were disproportionately owned and controlled by white South Africans at the end of apartheid (Department of Trade and Industry 2004:10). "Black economic empowerment" was an umbrella term used to characterize the various measures that the South African government and some private businesses pursued in order to provide blacks with greater access to the marketplace and to transition to a more equitable South African society. Many firms were encouraged to diversify the demographics of their shareholders to include disadvantaged groups in order to access government procurement contracts.

However, the new shareholders were often unable to exercise any management control over the direction of the companies. Many of these new shareholders were required to pay for their shares with future profits from the company in order for the shares to not revert back to the companies. With the Johannesburg Stock Exchange crash in 1998, many stocks lost their value, which hurt black economic empowerment investments (Harris 1999:1, 2; Turner 1999:2). Critics of the early black economic empowerment practices of the mid-1990s and early 2000s deemed black economic empowerment as "narrow-based empowerment." They saw black economic empowerment as advantaging and empowering only a small black elite and not the masses of poor South Africans who had struggled and waited so long for change and transformation of the South African economy (Sutcliffe 2006). Andreasson (2006:313) argues that black economic empowerment policies benefited those blacks who already had wealth or some access to resources or political ties to the new government and not the average poor black South African.

In 2004, the South African government passed broad-based black economic empowerment legislation to further redress the systematic inequalities in the South African economy. Such inequalities for many of the majority of South Africans were not being adequately addressed by earlier black economic empowerment initiatives. Broad-based black economic empowerment was "a tool to broaden the country's economic base and accelerate growth, job creation, and poverty eradication" (Department of Trade and Industry 2004:11). The expanded black economic empowerment focus was to encourage management- and skills-training opportunities that would enable blacks to engage in management and decision-making opportunities within enterprises. It endeavored to expand empowerment opportunities to women, workers, youth, people with disabilities, and those living in the rural areas. There was a new focus on increasing black ownership and control of existing and new enterprises and increasing the number of new black enterprises and black-empowered enterprises (Department of Trade and Industry 2004:13).

Tourism was seen as an important part of black economic empowerment (broad based and otherwise) with regard to changing ownership structures within the country. A government report in 1999 estimated that 95 percent of the tourist economy in South Africa was white owned (Rogerson 2004c:327). According to Rogerson (2004b; 2004c), there was interest by the South African government to promote tourism as a growth industry, which led to the production of numerous policy papers and other documents, including the 1996 White Paper on the Development and Promotion of Tourism, the 1998 Tourism and Growth, Employment and Redistribution (GEAR) Program, and the 2002 Tourism Growth Strategy. Each of these documents and others like them demonstrated the government's determination to focus on market-led growth and market-friendly practices to enhance the tourism industry.

Several policies and forms of government support were established to encourage and finance the growth of the small, medium, and microenterprise sector. The Department of Environmental Affairs and Tourism, for example, has financed the costs for entrepreneurs to go to international exhibitions and covered costs for the production and distribution of marketing materials. The Department of Trade and Industry has also made grants available to entrepreneurs based upon the value of the qualifying assets of the new start-ups and for some enterprise expansions. There is also the Tourism Enterprise Program, which is primarily funded by a private sector trust and works with small, medium, and microenterprises that are predominantly but not exclusively owned by previously disadvantaged individuals but does not provide direct financial support. However, according to Rogerson (2004b:225), there is still a gap that exists with regard to start-up capital for entrepreneurs who need loans in the range of R10,000 to R50,000 or R100,000, which is equivalent to U.S. $1,562.50 to U.S. $7,812.50 or U.S. $15,625.00.[3] This gap profoundly affects individuals who desire to start up businesses, including black tourism entrepreneurs.

RED DOOR IN THE WESTERN CAPE PROVINCE[4]

In 2004, the Western Cape provincial government, in support of broad-based black economic empowerment, opened its own small-business-integrated support service program called the Real Enterprise Development program, or RED Door program. The goal of the program was to assist small- and/or black-owned entrepreneurs in order to increase the survival rate of small businesses and the level of black entrepreneurship enterprises (Department of Economic Development and Tourism 2009). The first offices were located in the black township of Khayelitsha and the coloured township of Mitchell's Plain with the goal of expanding to thirty RED Doors in the province by 2007. In 2006, the RED Door launched its first mobile unit that traveled between Bellville and Wynberg in the province to take services to the disabled and others who had difficulties reaching the stationary offices.

The RED Door program was designed to capture the entrepreneurial capacities of the unemployed and the self-employed with an understanding that the small-business sector could reduce unemployment (SouthAfrica.info Reporter 2006). The RED Door offices offer assistance to entrepreneurs with regard to writing a business plan, finding access to finance, finding accountants and lawyers, finding out about government incentives, and improving business skills. In addition, they provide Internet access, small conference rooms, access to mentors, and community entrepreneurship outreach to youth, women, emerging farmers, and people with disabilities (Department of Economic Development and Tourism 2009). However, despite the existence of black economic empowerment initiatives and support services, my research demonstrated that such support was often insufficient or inadequate to the needs or desires of many of the black women bed-and-breakfast entrepreneurs in the townships of Cape Town.

THE EMERGENCE OF BLACK-OWNED TOURISM

With an increase in international tourists from 4.94 million in 1996 to 8.39 million in 2006, South African tourism has experienced an annual growth rate of 68.9 percent, which is three times the global rate (Maumbe and Van Wyk 2008:117). In 2007, it is estimated that South Africa received over nine million international tourists. The favorability of South Africa to tourists may have much to do with what some have described as the "Mandela factor," as tourists desired to visit the newly democratic country to support the transition and see sites that were before closed or unavailable to them (Rogerson and Visser 2007b:42, 43). Tourism during the apartheid period was hampered by various international sanctions against the country and continuing political violence within the country. In fact, the high levels of violence equated to the black townships being "no-go zones" for international tourists (Nemasetoni and Rogerson 2005:201). However, the cultural artifacts of apartheid and the peaceful transition to the post-apartheid period have created opportunities for the townships to emerge as popular sites for the tourism industry. Many visitors are interested in seeing the various sites of significance to the anti-apartheid struggle and gaining an understanding of how the majority of South Africans continue to live (Nemasetoni and Rogerson 2005:201; Pirie 2007:235; Rogerson 2004a:277).

According to Rogerson (2004a:277), integrated with the emergence of township tourism is the emergence of black-owned bed-and-breakfast accommodation establishments in the townships. In 2002, there were only sixty to seventy black-owned bed-and-breakfast establishments out of the approximately five thousand listed bed-and-breakfast establishments in South Africa. Such black-owned establishments were almost exclusively located in the formerly identified black areas, including the townships, and not located in the formerly white areas (Rogerson 2004a:277). The emergence of black-owned township tourism in the black townships located outside of Cape Town provides a model to examine the growth and difficulties faced by some individuals engaged or interested in engaging in tourism-related enterprises in South Africa.

Nemasetoni and Rogerson (2005:197) describe a three-tier system characterizing ownership in the South African tourism industry. At the apex is an elite group of large enterprises that represent the country's major travel and tour agencies, transportation, hotels, casinos, and conference centers. However, the next two lower levels of the triangle represent two different kinds of small, medium, and microenterprises in South Africa. In regard to the remaining two tiers, they state:

> The middle tier is formed by groups of established and almost predominately white-owned SMMEs which operate a host of different establishments from travel and touring companies, restaurants, small hotels, self-catering and resorts, game farms, bed and breakfasts, and backpackers hostels. The lowest tier or rung in the South African travel and tourist industry is represented by the emerging black-owned tourism economy which constitutes a mix of formally registered micro-enterprises as well as a mass of informal tourism enterprises. (Nemasetoni and Rogerson 2005:197)

Members of this third tier represent the focus of my research on the tourism industry. I specifically examine the accommodation subsector and focus upon the owners of black-owned township bed-and-breakfast establishments in the Cape Town townships, all of whom my research found to be women. In Rogerson's (2004a:277) research of black-owned bed-and-breakfast establishments in South Africa, he also noted that the majority of such establishments were operated by women.

Rogerson (2004b:256) argues that many black township entrepreneurs had difficulty acquiring and/or accessing adequate finance. While both white and previously disadvantaged entrepreneurs relied primarily on their own sources of finance, white entrepreneurs were still advantaged to black entrepreneurs due to the fact that they have more savings and access to capital. Most previously disadvantaged individuals who became entrepreneurs depended upon their employment retrenchment/buyout packages, their own savings, or funds from friends and relatives. Banks were often unwilling to provide such emerging entrepreneurs with loans due to their lack of collateral and a savings record (Nemasetoni and Rogerson 2005:205). With regard to larger start-up businesses and the extensions of businesses, white entrepreneurs have more "retained earnings" or returns from existing business and are also able to access funds from a commercial bank. Often the returns from their current business operations do not allow previously disadvantaged individuals to retain sufficient earning amounts for the expansion of their businesses (Rogerson 2004b:256). As my following data describes, the women entrepreneurs in my study were experiencing similar difficulties.

ETHNOGRAPHIC DATA

Ethnographic research for this project was completed in the summer of 2005 in three of the black townships of Cape Town, South Africa, and among four women, three of whom owned and operated their own bed-and-breakfast establishments at their home residences. The fourth interviewee was in the process of opening her own bed-and-breakfast establishment in a house adjacent to her property in October 2005. The involved townships included Khayelitsha (n = 1), Langa (n = 2), and Guguletu (n = 1). Such townships are located on the Cape Flats, a flat and barren area much different than the mountain, vineyard, beach, garden, and resort areas for which Cape Town is known. However, the townships continue to house the majority of black and coloured residents and have remained economically marginalized and impoverished communities in the post-apartheid period.

I also interviewed an official at the Department of Economic Development and Tourism for the Western Cape Province, which was promoting and providing indirect support services (information, training, etc.) to small-business entrepreneurs. While my research data represents a small sample, according to my contact with the Department of Economic

Development and Tourism, at the time of this research, less than eight black-owned bed-and-breakfast establishments were listed in the black African townships of Cape Town. Contact information from her as well as snowball sampling was used to access entrepreneurs. Many of the emerging entrepreneurs in the black-owned township tourism industry are familiar with one another as they frequently see each other at various tourism training courses and tourism exhibitions. Such activities, which were sponsored by the national and provincial authorities and held in Cape Town to promote black-owned township tourism businesses to tour operators and other tourism agents, often allowed the black women bed-and-breakfast entrepreneurs to share information with each other, including their goals, expectations, and struggles.

In my research study, the women who had started their bed-and-breakfast establishments were single, divorced, or widowed and had grown children or no children. One interviewee was married with younger children, but she was still in the planning stages of opening her bed-and-breakfast establishment. Each of the women had previously held or continued to hold professional positions and were engaged in their businesses on a full-time or part-time basis. The black women entrepreneurs in my study included Nazi, Ayanda, Tembi, and Zoleka.[5]

Nazi owned and operated a bed-and-breakfast establishment in Khayelitsha, which was the largest township in Cape Town and second-largest township in South Africa. Khayelitsha, located approximately twenty-five kilometers from the city center and the youngest of the Cape Town townships, was home to multiple squatter and informal settlements that attracted large numbers of tourists. Nazi had started her bed-and-breakfast establishment in 1999 after she became a registered tour guide and began to interact with various tour operators. She was in her early to mid-forties and had one adult daughter who assisted her with her business. She had worked in the community and in the rural development field in the 1990s but was currently working full-time at her business, as she ran her bed-and-breakfast establishment as well as catered luncheons and dinners at her residence. Her bed-and-breakfast establishment could accommodate a maximum of two to four guests or two couples, as she only had two guest bedrooms at her home.

Zoleka owned and operated her bed-and-breakfast on the outskirts of Guguletu, which was located approximately fifteen kilometers from the city center of Cape Town. She was fifty-seven years old and divorced with no children, although she did explain that she had a niece who consistently helped her with her business. Zoleka continued to work full-time as a nurse to supplement the income that she received from her business. Similar to Nazi, Zoleka also catered various lunches and dinners at her home for visitors. Her home could accommodate a maximum of three to six people or three couples, as she had three guest bedrooms.

Ayanda was a sixty-three-year-old widow who had retired from nursing and started her bed-and-breakfast establishment in Langa in 2002. Langa was the smallest and oldest of the Cape Town townships, and at eleven kilometers from the city center, was located the closet to the city center of Cape Town. Ayanda worked full-time running her business but did not engage in various catering service activities beyond providing breakfast for her guests. Ayanda had five adult children, including two daughters, one of whom assisted her with her business. She had three guest rooms and could accommodate a maximum of three to six people or three couples.

Tembi, my final interviewee, also lived in Langa and was in the process of starting her bed-and-breakfast establishment. She knew Ayanda, whom she called her mentor. Tembi lived on the other side of Langa from Ayanda near the Joe Slovo informal settlement, which attracted numerous tourists. She was thirty-one years old, married, and had three young children. In the past, she had owned a fish-and-chips informal business in the Johannesburg area before moving to Cape Town. Tembi worked part-time as an office administrator, which allowed her to attend seminars with Ayanda and stay in touch with the tourism board. While her husband was supportive of her efforts, she communicated to me that she was the one responsible for getting the business started and making sure that it would be successful.

Each of the women, except for Tembi, during my interview time with them provided me with professional brochures or pamphlets with pictures of their homes and information about their businesses, including their contact details, which they distributed to tour agents, operators, and guests as advertisements to promote their businesses. Two of the women had their own websites for their business and were able to confirm their own bookings with guests over the Internet, which allowed them to be less dependent on tour agents or operators for guest reservations. Nazi, for example, was quick to inform me that she did not depend solely on the Cape Town tourism board, tour agents, or tour operators for guests as she was unsure of their genuine willingness to encourage visitors to stay overnight in the townships.

I use data from my interviews with these women to explore three key areas of focus. First, I focus upon the nature of their entry into the accommodation subsector of the black-owned township tourism industry. Next, I focus upon their view of the connection between their businesses and the transformation of their communities. Finally, I focus upon the difficulties that they voiced in regard to their businesses as well as examine their understanding of their entrepreneurial activities in the context of black economic empowerment. These three foci are essential to my analysis of how these women entrepreneurs engage in pro-poor tourism activities that support members of their communities as well as how their gender roles as women advantages them in the black-owned accommodation subsector of the township tourism industry.

ENTRY INTO THE BLACK-OWNED TOURISM ACCOMMODATION SUBSECTOR

Nazi used her own savings as start-up capital for her business. She informed me that she began her bed-and-breakfast business because she became disgruntled with seeing so many tour operators and tourists visit Khayelitsha for short periods of time without engaging with members of the community or having the ability to stay overnight in the township. She stated:

> I was challenged by the fact that I was seeing lots of tour operators coming to our townships, white tour operators, with lots of visitors on their buses and they were not even giving them chances to step out of the buses and stop at any place. They were taking photos from the buses, and I said, no, that is not our job to be a spectacle. We are not animals. If people come to these townships, they have to stop over somewhere and talk with the people around them.

Nazi's statement demonstrates her desire for people in Khayelitsha not to be objectified by tourists but to be actively engaged and seen as people. She was also aware that many of the tourists, the majority of whom were international visitors from the United States, Australia, the United Kingdom, and Japan, were arriving with white tour operators who were receiving the majority of the economic remuneration from such visits to Khayelitsha.

Zoleka was a former restaurant co-owner who decided to open a bed-and-breakfast in her home in 2002 after ending a difficult partnership in order to have her own business and make her own business decisions. She used her own funds from her nursing job and savings from her former business project to start her bed-and-breakfast establishment. Ayanda also used her own funds to start her business, as she had retired early from her position as a nurse due to a health issue and used her entire pension savings to start her bed-and-breakfast establishment. She began her business because she saw an opportunity to invest her money in herself and to start something of her own. Ayanda had heard of other women starting bed-and-breakfast establishments to accommodate overnight visitors in other townships, and she thought that she could be successful with such an enterprise in Langa. While she was not in debt with her business, Ayanda was completely dependent upon it for her income.

Tembi informed me that she was starting her business because she saw the need for an additional bed-and-breakfast business in the Langa area, as it was more centrally located to the city of Cape Town than the other black townships. She had observed the number of tourists who came to Langa, especially to visit the Joe Slovo squatter camp, and felt there was need for another establishment near the camp. Tembi and her husband were combining their salaries to provide start-up capital for her business. They had already made arrangements to rent her next-door neighbor's house and planned to open the bed-and-breakfast establishment later in the year.

COMMUNITY FOCUS AND COMMITMENT

Nazi informed me that she was attracted to the tourism industry due to her work with community and rural development projects during the 1990s. She saw engagement in the tourism industry as an opportunity to advance herself and her community through a self-help activity instead of waiting for others to provide resources for the community. She was committed to her business benefiting members of her community, and she endeavored to engage them in the tourism industry. Due to the small size of her accommodations, for example, she stated that she often sent visitors whom she could not accommodate to select neighbors' homes. Such neighbors did not have a bed-and-breakfast business but had been trained by Nazi in the health and quality standards necessary to provide overnight accommodation services to guests.

Some questioned why Nazi was training her competition, but she did not see her actions in such a light. She stated:

> Many people were asking me, why are you training your competitors. Aren't you scared of competitors? I said that I would rather invest my time in assisting others in doing things correctly than having one person treated badly and having that person go out and say, those women in Khayelitsha, they do not know what they are doing. It would be all over, and no one would want to come back.

Nazi understood the fact that she could not accommodate all of the visitors that desired to stay overnight at her home. Instead of sending the guests back to the city center or to another bed-and-breakfast establishment elsewhere in Khayelitsha or another township, she engaged in a practice that would help her immediate community as well as maintain a good reputation of her establishment and a positive township experience for guests. Zoleka also stated that she often sent overflow guests from her bed-and-breakfast establishment to the homes of her neighbors as a way to generate income for some of her neighbors, although they did not operate bed-and-breakfast establishments.

Each of the women entrepreneurs in my study sought to provide an "authentic setting" for their guests by displaying traditional arts and crafts in their homes as well as by wearing traditional clothes during their guests' stays. In addition, they served a traditional-style breakfast to guests, which consisted of hot porridge, cooked vegetables or beans, fruits, and yogurts. However, toast and preserves, milk, cold cereals, scones, juice, tea, and coffee were also available to guests. The entrepreneurs all hired people from the community to assist them with the cleaning and/or cooking required at their establishments. Therefore, their businesses provided multiple-income generation opportunities for individuals. Zoleka, for example, often contracted with other women in her community to make scones or other food items that she did not have time to prepare.

Guests, with the encouragement of the bed-and-breakfast owners, often hired community residents to escort them on township walks as pseudo tour guides as well as due to safety and security concerns. Various other individuals in the community who were members of local bands or dance troupes also received funds from their provision of entertainment to guests at the bed-and-breakfast establishments. Still others were able to sell arts and crafts to many of the tourists who visited the township and stayed overnight at the bed-and-breakfast establishments. Nazi stated that she always took her guests to a nearby community center and market where they could purchase arts and craftwork from local venders. Ayanda took her guests to visit area *shebeens*,[6] local restaurants, the Langa cultural center, train station, and other township sites.

Ayanda informed me that she intentionally involved members of her community in the decision-making process of whether to open a bed-and-breakfast establishment before she opened her business. It was important for her to have members of her community actively engaged and supportive of her endeavors, which she believed would also benefit the community. Ayanda stated:

Just before I opened my business, I went to my community, the people around me. I told people that I was going to open a business and with this business I am not going to spoil children by selling liquor or doing whatever makes their children get into trouble. When I launched my business, I gathered my community to talk about my business, and I called in the tour guides to talk about the business. The people in the community talked about me being here all these years. This was good for me because the community is also watching the tourists when they come down.

Due to the respect that Ayanda had in the community and her desire to engage in a positive activity in and for the community, she received support and encouragement from her fellow community members. Such support included members of the community "keeping a watch" for the security of visitors to ensure that they had a positive experience on their visit. This support from her community was extremely helpful to Ayanda.

Tembi was also committed to having her future business help members of her surrounding community. In addition to opening a bed-and-breakfast establishment, she informed me that she also planned to use her yard as a coffee stop for tourists who would visit the Joe Slovo informal settlement. Her participation in the black-owned tourism industry as an entrepreneur would facilitate income-generating activities for multiple members of the community who would work as waitresses or sell arts and crafts to the tourists. Tembi desired to empower people through tourism, as she believed that the provision of jobs could lower the crime rate as it would give a few of the unemployed something productive in which to participate.

BUSINESS STRUGGLES AND VIEWS
OF BLACK ECONOMIC EMPOWERMENT

Nazi received some free marketing through publicity that she garnered when she was featured in various newspapers domestically and overseas. Her reputation for service and quality also traveled by word of mouth. However, while marketing was not a central concern for her, she did express the fact that she faced one major hurdle with her business: her inability to acquire adequate financing to expand her business. Nazi desired to buy her neighbor's house and/or expand her business by building a second floor or upstairs to her current home, but she did not have the funds to expand her business. She was skeptical of her ability to access a loan from a bank and even compared the act to "committing suicide" due to the past difficulties that she believed other black entrepreneurs had faced in approaching banks. However, she mentioned that she was aware of some assistance that she could receive from the Department of Trade and Industry and stated that she planned to approach the government agency for assistance.

Zoleka had brochures of her business, but at the time of this interview, she did not have a website and was unable to take bookings over the Internet. She felt that her business was being hampered by the fact that she did not have a website and could therefore not market herself online to potential guests. Instead, she was dependent on indirect access to tourists through the white tour operators to bring her customers as well as word of mouth to publicize her business. However, she was enrolled in a computer class that would teach her the skills that she needed to use online technology to promote and support her business. She had not received any direct financial help from the national or provincial government. However, she had received forms from the Department of Trade and Industry but had yet to review them. Zoleka applied to the municipal government for a permit to build three more rooms at the back of her house, but she was still waiting for approval before going forward with the project. Despite her building plans, she also identified funding as a major factor that hampered her business. She commented to me that she had a mortgage and an unpredictable business due to the seasonal nature of the tourism industry and her dependence on various tour operators. Zoleka stated that after the completion of her building project and when she could attain a profit of at least R2,500 or U.S. $391 per month (see note 3) from her business, she would consider leaving nursing or only engage in nursing on a part-time basis, as her financial needs would be met by her business and nursing would no longer need to supplement her business income.

Ayanda, like Nazi, did have her own website and checked her email each day in order to answer inquiries and to confirm bookings. However, she also cited finances as a major constraint, as she would like to paint her home as well as build a second level. She also did not desire to access a loan from a bank, nor did she feel that she would qualify for such a loan. She stated:

> About six months ago, I thought of going to a bank to get a loan. But I said to myself, if I go to the bank and borrow money there, how will I be able to pay that amount back because I am a pensioner [retired person]. I do not have money. I do not have money in the bank. How will I be able to pay this money with interest? So, I said to myself, no, I can wait.

Ayanda commented to me that she would rather access a grant than a loan, as she was uncertain about the stability of her income from her business and was fearful of being unable to qualify or repay a loan.

Tembi also identified finances as a major issue of concern as she still needed additional funds to buy the furniture for the house that she would rent for her bed-and-breakfast establishment as well as money to paint the house. She was married with young children and indicated that it had been difficult to save the funds for her business as well as raise a family. She informed me that she would welcome investors to her business but that she did not feel confident in her ability to qualify for a loan from a commercial bank.

> I need funds to do x, y, and z according to my business plan. That is always the problem. They will send you to a bank. The bank will want collateral

or security. I have only just started working. I am young. Where do I get security for a loan? The house that I live in is mortgaged. I basically owe everything. What do you call your assets that can act as a security? I am not really looking for a grant because I do not want something for free. I would not mind holding someone's hand who would invest in me and would have confidence in what we are doing and who would get paid back. The loans [from the banks] have ridiculous interest rates which doesn't help you.

Tembi would rather have a partner than access a commercial loan. She viewed her lack of collateral, young age, and the existence of her current home mortgage as barriers to being seen as a serious entrepreneur by banks. She also expressed dismay at the high-interest rates of such loans.

With regard to black economic empowerment initiatives and their role in such an empowerment process, most of my interviewees were ambivalent or even negative regarding the assistance that they had or had not received from the national and provincial authorities. Nazi, for example, had an unfavorable opinion of black economic empowerment and stated that it had not helped her. In fact, she was quick to state that she was advancing on her own initiative without government loans or other support. When specifically asked about the RED Door program, which began a year earlier (2004) in the Western Cape and had an office in Khayelitsha, the site of her home and business, Nazi stated that she had heard of the program but that she thought that it only targeted new entrepreneurs who were struggling. She did not see the program as applying to her or her business, which had been in existence for six years.

Zoleka, Ayanda, and Tembi commented that the national and provincial government were quite helpful in connecting them with tour operators and with the production of marketing materials but had not provided them much other direct financial support. They had not received any additional funds or access to loan guarantees from the government. However, Zoleka did believe that she was a part of black economic empowerment in her community at the local level. Ayanda stated that while she was grateful for the various courses that she has been able to access through various government initiatives, she needed access to money and more financial support. In fact, she seemed frustrated at the lack of direct financial support for entrepreneurs that she had experienced. Her view of black economic empowerment was that she was a part of it but that she had not benefited as much as others from such initiatives. She desired to see more change in her community, and while she had heard of the RED Door program through Tembi, she had no contact with the organization and seemed to be unaware of all the services that she could access through the program.

Tembi used the services of the RED Door to assist her in creating a business plan for her bed-and-breakfast establishment. She stated that various programs were helpful in terms of being a support system with regard to information but not as a financial support system. She suggested that black economic empowerment needed to reach more people at the grass-roots level and should be more focused upon those who lived in the communities and among the poor. Tembi suggested that many people were uninformed about the assistance that was available to them with regard to starting a business and that more information was needed to increase awareness of the assistance available to emerging entrepreneurs. She commented that she was the one who informed Ayanda about the RED Door program and that as an established entrepreneur, Ayanda should have already known about the program.

PRO-POOR TOURISM AND ENTREPRENEURSHIP

Often in low- and middle-income countries, women are motivated by necessity to join the entrepreneurial world (Hanson 2009:254–55). However, this was not the case for the women entrepreneurs in my study. Each of these black women was engaged in opportunistic entrepreneurial activities and taking advantage of an opportunity that emerged with the end of apartheid and the growth of township tourism. As similarly shown by Nemasetoni and Rogerson (2005:213) with regard to their study of black tour operators in the Gauteng Province, financing was a major difficulty for all the women who had or were opening bed-and-breakfast establishments. These women used creative ways to finance their businesses, including engaging in another employment activity and using their retirement funds to provide start-up capital for their businesses. All of the women in my research study were skeptical about their ability to access a conventional loan from a commercial bank due to their lack of collateral and/or an established credit track record as well as expressed uncertainty about their ability to repay such loans even if they were able to qualify for them.

Unlike Rogerson's (2004a:279) study of bed-and-breakfast establishments, my research did not find that there were any problems with neighbors objecting to these establishments. In fact, I found that the entrepreneurs had entered into strategic partnerships with various members of the community to ensure the safety of tourists and the profitability of their enterprises for themselves and various other members of the community, many of whom were poor. As Ashley and Roe (2002:78) discuss, it is important to understand that small earnings are a survival strategy for the poor and can often reduce the vulnerability of such individuals. Each of the entrepreneurs described their efforts to use their businesses as ways to enhance the economic status of others in their communities. Their entrepreneurial activities provided employment and other financial benefits to reduce poverty in their communities and demonstrate a form of pro-poor tourism.

Pro-poor tourism and local economic development structures refer to those initiatives in the tourism sector that involve partnerships with key actors, such as the private sector, government, and civil society and community members that create opportunities for tourism to alleviate or reduce poverty (Ashley and Roe 2002:77; Rogerson 2006:39–42). Many of these interventions engage poor communities in the search for new markets and tourism products. The combination of tourism growth with the empowerment of formerly disadvantaged South Africans has even been called empo-tourism or empowerment tourism (Ashley and Roe 2002:62–63). The entrepreneurs of my study were not partnered with the private sector or community-based organizations. However, they were engaged in activities that provided economic opportunities to some of their fellow community members. They were contributing to their communities and seeking to empower others around them through their entrepreneurial efforts. Hanson (2009:247) argues that women are using entrepreneurship not only to change their lives by generating profits or income but also "to change the places where they live." Therefore, it is valuable to connect the black township entrepreneurs in my study to their gendered status as women.

GENDER AND ENTREPRENEURSHIP

Lewis (2006:456) argues that a gender emphasis must be a focal point for an understanding of entrepreneurship. She identifies two ways in which gender is viewed with regard to the research involving gender and entrepreneurship. The first view of gender is as "an intervening variable" to which challenges to entrepreneurship are explored and if found efforts are made to reduce those challenges. A second view of gender is as an "analytical category" related to structures, institutional and cultural practices and discourses that distinguish men and women and relate to considerations of advantage and disadvantage. Lewis (2006:454) argues that masculinity is normally associated with the category of an entrepreneur and that the use of the term *female* or *women* in front of the term *entrepreneur* singles out women as being different from other entrepreneurs, who are male and who are often seen as the growers of the economy. Women business owners may also challenge the stereotypical understandings of what it means to be a successful entrepreneur due to their "commitment to small and stable businesses," and for this reason, they may not be seen as serious business people (Lewis 2006:456).

While I, too, acknowledge that it is important to understand that there are still gender barriers and inequalities with regard to many types of entrepreneurial activities, I believe that scholars must be mindful not to see the usage of terms like *female entrepreneurs* or *women entrepreneurs* as reinforcing the oppression of women as a gendered category. Such arguments may lead to a form of reductionism that characterizes all female entrepreneurs as disadvantaged due to their gendered status. In the case of the black women entrepreneurs in my study, their gender did not marginalize or disadvantage them. The culturally defined gender roles of women positioned them to emerge as bed-and-breakfast entrepreneurs in the black-owned township tourism industry. As discussed by Chitsike (2000:74), the occupations in which women engage are often based upon their skills; available resources, including time; and their caring role for the family as well as cultural expectations. The women entrepreneurs in my study were using the skills taught to them as girls with regard to their role as homemakers to establish and maintain bed-and-breakfast establishments. They were intersecting their gendered roles as caretakers of the domestic sphere with the emerging opportunities to engage in the growing tourist industry that allowed them not only to work at home but also to actually make home their work.

Each of the women who currently owned and operated a black-owned bed-and-breakfast establishment had another special status that was also vital to their participation in their entrepreneurial activities. The fact that they were never married, divorced, or widowed as well as had adult children or no children created the context for them to have the ability to focus on their businesses as well as make their own decisions about their business operations and practices. Tembi, for example, the only woman who was married with young children among my interviewees, was continuing to struggle to open her business and mentioned that care and support for her young children and family was hampering her ability to save the resources necessary to open her business.

CONCLUSION

The emergence of black-owned tourism as well as the growth of the tourism industry as a whole in South Africa is reflective of the reintegration of South Africa into the global tourism industry since the end of apartheid. In addition to white-owned tour operators, blacks also have begun to enter the tourism industry. However, many of these blacks, while having access and knowledge of the areas of interest to tourists in the townships, struggled to acquire the finances to start and then expand their businesses despite the existence of black economic empowerment initiatives. These entrepreneurs were interested in their businesses benefiting their larger community through job creation and a range of direct and indirect income-generation opportunities. While my research demonstrates the entrepreneurs had either a negative or neutral view of national and provincial efforts to promote black economic empowerment, these emerging entrepreneurs felt that they were engaged in black economic empowerment and pro-poor tourism efforts at a grassroots or local level as they navigated through various ways to alleviate poverty and transform their communities through their entrepreneurial activities.

The fact that the entrepreneurs who opened bed-and-breakfast establishments were women continues to highlight how women were investing their skills in a myriad of activities to empower themselves. In the case of these women entrepreneurs, their gender status enabled them to influence the structure of opportunity in favor of themselves and not men with regard to the accommodation subsector of the black-owned township tourism industry. They were able to generate income from opening their homes to the public for overnight and short stays that not only allowed them to care for visitors but also enabled them to care for their community by providing employment and other income-generating opportunities for others. This chapter demonstrates that these women entrepreneurs started their businesses with great hopes and expectations for themselves, their families, and their communities. They acted as primary examples of the value of grassroots or local black economic empowerment as they opportunistically engaged in the black-owned township tourism industry to empower themselves and their communities. In the process, they were indeed contributing to the development of a new South Africa.

NOTES

1. My research focused on women who would have been considered members of the indigenous groups referred to as Africans under the Population Registration Act of 1950. My research did not focus upon individuals formerly known as Coloureds (mixed-race people) and Indians/Asians. Therefore, my use of the term *black* in this chapter to describe the women entrepreneurs upon which my study focused exemplifies a much more exclusive and narrow use of the term when compared with its use by the post-apartheid South African government (see note 2 for more information).

2. *Black* is used by the post-apartheid South African government as an inclusive term that includes black Africans, Coloureds, and Indians/Asians (Department of Trade and Industry 2004:12). Therefore, members of all of the formerly historically advantaged groups, including Coloureds and Indians/Asians in South Africa, could use black economic empowerment policies and initiatives, although these latter groups did not experience the same level of discrimination as other black South Africans.

3. In 2005, the average currency exchange rate was U.S. $1 to R6.4.

4. Cape Town is located in the Western Cape Province.

5. All names used in this chapter have been changed to ensure the privacy of the informants.

6. *Shebeens* are small local taverns located in the black townships.

REFERENCES

Andreasson, Stefan. 2006. The African National Congress and Its Critics: "Predatory Liberalism," Black Empowerment and Intra-Alliance Tensions in Post-Apartheid South Africa. *Democratization* 13(2):303–22.

Ashley, Caroline, and Dilys Roe. 2002. Making Tourism Work for the Poor: Strategies and Challenges in Southern Africa. *Development Southern Africa* 19(1):61–82.

Chitsike, Colletah. 2000. Culture as a Barrier to Rural Women's Entrepreneurship: Experience from Zimbabwe. *Gender and Development* 8(1):71–77.

Department of Economic Development and Tourism. 2009. RED Door Small Business Advice Centers: Overview. Provincial Government of the Western Cape. www.capegateway.gov.za/eng/your_gov/13464, accessed November 21, 2011.

Department of Trade and Industry. 2004. South Africa's Economic Transformation: A Strategy for Broad-Based Black Economic Empowerment. www.kznhealth.gov.za/TED/strategy.pdf, accessed November 21, 2011.

Hanson, Susan. 2009. Changing Places through Women's Entrepreneurship. *Economic Geography* 85(3):245–67.

Harris, Shaun. 1999. Black Chip Shares Hold Promise. *Daily Mail & Guardian*, September 10, 1999:1–2.

Lewis, Patricia. 2006. The Quest for Invisibility: Female Entrepreneurs and the Masculine Norm of Entrepreneurship. *Gender, Work, and Organization* 13(5):453–69.

Maumbe, Kudzayi Chitiyo, and Laeticia J. Van Wyk. 2008. Employment in Cape Town's Lodging Sector: Opportunities, Skills Requirements, Employee Aspirations and Transformation. *GeoJournal* 73(2):117–32.

Nemasetoni, Irene, and Christian M. Rogerson. 2005. Developing Small Firms in Township Tourism: Emerging Tour Operators in Gauteng, South Africa. *Urban Forum* 16(2–3):196–213.

Pirie, Gordon. 2007. Urban Tourism in Cape Town. In *Urban Tourism in the Developing World*, eds. C. M. Rogerson and G. Visser, pp. 223–44. New Brunswick, NJ: Transaction.

Rogerson, Christian M. 2004a. Transforming the South African Tourism Industry: The Emerging Black-Owned Bed and Breakfast Economy. *GeoJournal* 60(3):273–81.

———. 2004b. Financing Tourism SMMEs in South Africa: A Supply-Side Analysis. In *Tourism and Development Issues in Contemporary South Africa*, eds. C. M. Rogerson and G. Visser, pp. 222–67. Pretoria: Africa Institute of South Africa.

———. 2004c. Black Economic Empowerment in South African Tourism. In *Tourism and Development Issues in Contemporary South Africa*, eds. C. M. Rogerson and G. Visser, pp. 321–34. Pretoria: Africa Institute of South Africa.

———. 2006. Pro-Poor Local Economic Development in South Africa: The Role of Pro-Poor Tourism. *Local Environment* 11(1):37–60.

Rogerson, Christian M., and Gustav Visser. 2007a. Tourism Research and Urban Africa: The South African Experience. In *Urban Tourism in the Developing World*, eds. C. M. Rogerson and G. Visser, pp. 13–40. New Brunswick, NJ: Transaction.

———. 2007b. International Tourism Flows and Urban Tourism in South Africa. In *Urban Tourism in the Developing World*, eds. C. M. Rogerson and G. Visser, pp. 41–56. New Brunswick, NJ: Transaction.

SouthAfrica.info Reporter. 2006. RED Door Opens for Small Business. www.southafrica.info/business/trends/newbusiness/reddoor.htm, accessed November 21, 2011.

Sutcliffe, Jim. 2006. BEE Fuelling Economic Revolution. *Financial Times*, May 2, 2006.

Turner, Chris. 1999. Black Economic Empowerment in South Africa and the Implication for U.S Firms. *International Market Insight*, June 25, 1999.

III

REDEFINING
TOURISM'S "IMPACT"

10

✝

Sacrificing Cultural Capital for Sustainability

Identity, Class, and the Swedish Staycation

Cindy Isenhour

Aside from mistaken references to chocolate or the Alps, the most common response I get when I mention my research in Sweden is a story about meeting a Swede, often in the strangest of places. I have heard stories about a Swede on a train in Italy, at a youth hostel in New Zealand, in an African refugee camp, on an Indian reservation in the American Great Plains, and in a herding camp in the middle of the Mongolian steppe. While this might seem surprising given that there are only about nine million people living in Sweden, according to the World Tourism Organization, on a per capita basis Swedes are among the most well-traveled people in the world (WTO 2010). Further, given the Scandinavian affinity for nature tourism and Sweden's investment and involvement in international development efforts, Swedes can be found not only in the typical tourist destinations but also often in less-visited communities from the Himalayas to the Amazon Basin and Saharan Africa.

My research centers on ecological risk perception and economic response in wealthy postindustrial urban societies. As such, I never anticipated that tourism would become a significant theme in my work. Yet during my fieldwork I quickly realized the importance placed on international travel in Sweden—where knowledge of world affairs and cosmopolitan identities are highly valued (Dahl 2007). Stockholm subways and dailies are littered with uncountable advertisements for low-cost trips to Malaysia, Thailand, and Fiji. And during the dark of winter, when the sun only shines for a few hours a day, many privileged Stockholmers escape for a week to Spain or Florida. Swedes also clearly like to speak about their travels. Not only were these experiences mentioned frequently in interviews but I also often overheard stories about trips to Machu Picchu or Budapest on crowded buses, on trains, or at sidewalk cafés.

Despite the cultural import of travel in Sweden, some environmentally concerned Swedes are increasingly conflicted about flying as the ecological impacts of air travel are made strikingly clear. In Sweden, a nation well known for its strong and proactive stance toward the environment, environmentalists and many not previously concerned with such issues have recently mobilized around concerns about climate change. The Stern Review (2007), Al Gore's movie *An Inconvenient Truth* (Guggenheim 2006), and the 2007 Intergovernmental Panel on Climate Change (IPCC) Fourth Assessment Report all acted to raise awareness of climate issues in Sweden so that by 2007, when I began my fieldwork, coverage of environmental issues in daily newspapers had more than doubled 2005 levels (Jagers and Martinsson 2007). In this context many Swedes spoke of a significant, almost palpable, momentum for the sustainability movement—centered on climate change. Today there is a strong political and scientific consensus about anthropogenic climate change in Sweden, particularly relative to other nations.[1] According to the Swedish Environmental Protection Agency's most recent study on public attitudes toward climate change, 89 percent of Swedes consider themselves climate conscious and 84 percent said they have taken at least one measure to reduce their climate impact in the last two years (Naturvårdsverket 2009).

During fourteen months of fieldwork in and around Stockholm, I spoke with seventy-two Swedish citizen-consumers who, in response to concerns about climate change, the environment, and human health, were trying to modify their lifestyles and consumer behaviors[2]—many of them by limiting their travel. Although the call for research participants was cast wide for this study, the sample was composed exclusively of members of Sweden's middle class[3]—mirroring research from many international contexts that suggests that a concern for sustainable consumerism is found disproportionately among the middle class (for example, CNAD 2005; Ferrer and Fraile 2006; Micheletti and Stolle 2004).

To understand these middle-class views on sustainability and corresponding actions,[4] I also explored the context of sustainability in Sweden via policy reviews and interviews with thirty-one representatives of twenty-four governmental, nongovernmental, and research organizations working on issues related to sustainability. In this chapter I draw upon a small segment of that research to explore how Swedes concerned about sustainability attempt to resolve the conflicts that exist between their desire to travel and their concerns for the environment. I explore tourist motivation among Sweden's environmentally concerned middle class and suggest that for those trying to make a smaller environmental impact, international travel is one of the hardest things to give up. This difficulty, I argue, is linked not only to a desire to see the world but also to Sweden's egalitarian ethos, which works to downplay class differences at the same time that a hierarchical social structure elevates the importance of differentiation. In this context international travel provides a clear means to accumulate cultural capital and differentiate oneself without breaching cultural taboos that discourage more explicit displays of difference and privilege. Despite travel's clear association with the performance of middle-class status in Sweden, many research participants are limiting their air travel or are no longer flying. I argue here that, given the number of international development and biological conservation programs that have placed their hopes for the future in ecotourism development, the case of the conflicted Swedish tourist may prove to be increasingly relevant.

TO FLY OR NOT TO FLY

I begin with the story of Ingrid and Johan, retirees living in a southern suburb of Stockholm. Ingrid subscribes to a consumer advocacy newsletter that often includes information related to social and environmental sustainability. In the winter of 2008 Ingrid received an email about my study from the newsletter's director. Soon after, she contacted me to participate, suggesting we meet in the cafeteria at Åhléns City, a large department store in the heart of central Stockholm. It was just a few days before Christmas, and she still had some shopping to finish up. After finding my way through the massive department store, I met Ingrid for coffee in the cafeteria overlooking Sergelstorg, a large square in the center of the city's shopping district. As we began to talk, it quickly became clear that Ingrid was deeply concerned about the impacts of industrial chemicals on human health. As such, when I asked her to free list all the things that an individual could do to live a more sustainable life, she focused on things like buying organic foods, natural home cleaners, chemical-free shampoos, and natural medicines rather than actions that resulted in lifestyle changes or reduced consumption levels. While Ingrid was not unconcerned about things like resource depletion, energy use, or climate change, it appeared she was not engaged with these issues. When we finished talking about everything from the sociality of consumption to her views on nature and environmental governance, I invited Ingrid, like all research participants, to volunteer for more in-depth research.

Ingrid accepted the invitation, and her household was one of twelve that took part in a series of iterative interviews, income- and budget-tracking surveys, carbon footprint calculations, and consumption inventories the following spring.[5]

A few months after our original meeting, I visited Ingrid and her husband, Johan, in their home to go over their consumption inventories and the carbon calculators they'd recently completed. Ingrid greeted me at the door. After the obligatory greetings and exchanges I noticed an odd look growing on Ingrid's face. Before I had the chance to inquire, Ingrid said, "Cindy, I'm so embarrassed. I've just finished my carbon calculator and it is horrible!" I assured her that she wasn't the only research participant shocked by the calculator, as she led me to the kitchen table where we would have coffee and look over the paperwork she had completed. As we began to look at the forms, Johan came in the back door, saying, "You will not be impressed with us, we emit nearly eight times the amount of carbon that we should!" Ingrid and Johan were both clearly surprised by the calculations and were, apparently, feeling guilty about it. While the average Swede emits approximately eight to ten tons of CO_2 per year (Naturvårdsverket 2010), according to the Swedish Environmental Research Institute, the scientific consensus places the sustainable level somewhere between .7 and 1.5 tons of CO_2 per person annually (Svenska Miljöinstitutet 2010). Ingrid was shocked to discover that she emitted 8.9 tons of CO_2 in 2007, and Johan was even worse with 10.2 tons. "It was really from the flying," said Ingrid. "We put in our flights to Australia . . . I knew that flying wasn't good but I did not understand!"

There does, in fact, seem to be ample evidence to suggest that flying has an extraordinary impact on carbon emissions. One flight from Stockholm to Thailand—named Sweden's "top tourist destination" for eight consecutive years between 2002 and 2010 (Tourism Authority of Thailand 2010)—emits more carbon per person than driving a gas-powered Volvo V70 twenty kilometers to work and back for two years (Åkerman 2008). Further, according to the IPCC (2001), because jets release gases at altitude, the impact of their emissions is roughly 2.7 times greater than the effect of the carbon alone due to a "radiative forcing effect." The Swedish government has also recognized the environmental impact of flying, writing in a recent report,

> Long-haul flights, for example to Asia, have a significant climate impact. In these cases there are no alternative modes of transport that result in lower emissions. If one wishes to reduce one's emissions, it is necessary to either choose less far-away destinations or to travel a little more rarely and perhaps stay away longer when a journey is made. (Naturvårdsverket 2010:48)

Unlike Ingrid and Johan, many other research participants were already keenly aware of the impact of flying. A total of 44 percent of the sample, in fact, mentioned "flying less" when free listing all of the things an individual could do to live more sustainably. Even more listed related actions like "take the train" or "use public transport," which are highly feasible options in Sweden and Europe where rail travel is relatively accessible and often markedly more sustainable than flying. Sweden's national rail company, SJ, runs its trains on electricity generated solely from renewable sources, both hydro and wind. The trains are certified as a "good environmental choice" by the Swedish Society for Nature Conservation and are aggressively marketed for their environmental benefits. The company's website, in fact, says, "Did you know, going between Stockholm and Gothenburg, an average car gives off an average of 44.5 kilos of carbon dioxide into the air. An entire SJ train with up to 300 passengers gives off four hectos"[6] (SJ 2010). Even outside of Sweden it is estimated that traveling by rail is, on average, between three and ten times less CO_2 intensive as driving or flying (OECD 2009).

In order to avoid the conflict between the desire to travel and environmental concerns, research participants used a wide variety of strategies. Ida and her teenage son, for example, were planning a journey to China and back on the train. While she recognized how long traveling by rail would take, they had planned stops along the way and were excited about the ride as part of their experience together. Others were signing up for a new service offered by Svierge's Resor, a charter tour company that had recently started offering more environmentally friendly options, including rail travel to southern Europe for those concerned about flying. Others insisted that impoverished people would suffer without tourism dollars and were exploring the World Wildlife Fund's ecotours and planning to offset the carbon generated by their flights by donating to reforestation efforts in the Brazilian Amazon. Some were simply trying to wait it out, hoping that new technologies would make air travel more sustainable in the future. Research continues, but it seems as though there are currently no viable alternatives for kerosene jet fuel, and while the new Airbus A380 is reported to burn less than three liters of jet fuel per person per one hundred kilometers, commercial passenger jets typically remain in service for up to thirty years, meaning that the transition to more efficient jets will likely take significant time (Hickman 2006). Further, while the airline industry is aggressively promoting carbon offsets, many environmental activists argue that no program can make the same impact as simply removing planes and the carbon they emit from the skies.

TRAVEL ALTERNATIVES AND THE SWEDISH *HEMESTER*

Erik and Carolin, one of the families most committed to sustainable living in the sample, had recently declined a holiday in Thailand—deciding instead to plan a *hemester*, the Swedish equivalent of a staycation. Erik explained the situation one day as his son played on the living room rug between us:

> I have two brothers and their families—my mother would like to pay for all of us to go to Thailand. So she asked one week ago and of course we said no. Of course because of the airplane thing. Going with the plane . . . it is not okay if you think about the carbon dioxide. It was not a hard decision for me and my wife . . . but it was hard thinking about what my brothers and my mother think about that . . . and me. I don't know if they are that aware of why we say no . . . no one should travel that far. And, my carbon dioxide that I have and my family's[7] . . . I would like to use it for smaller travel, maybe to England or something like that in three or four years, but "thank you anyway." And of course . . . we are going to go by train to some other place in Sweden and it will be extreme luxury because if you are going to use that amount of money going to Thailand you can do whatever you want in Sweden.

The concept of vacationing close to home is certainly nothing new. People have long spent their holidays at home, particularly during periods of economic recession. Indeed, there is a strong precedent for domestic tourism in Sweden, where there is a fascination with nature-based vacations, particularly during the summer when the sun only sets for a few hours each night. Both the east and the west coast of Sweden are excellent sailing destinations, and the far north is attractive for hiking and camping, while many throughout the country spend their summers on biking holidays or at their ancestral country homes. The Swedish government has a long history of encouraging domestic tourism. Orvar Löfgren (2001) has described how the state helped to create Sweden's contemporary fascination with camping, biking, and hiking vacations in the early twentieth century with their "Know Your Country" campaign. Designed to build patriotism and keep Swedish tourist dollars in Sweden, the campaign solidified nature tourism as a mass movement in Sweden by emphasizing that the country's natural landscapes provided equal access to all.

Yet despite this history, the portmanteau *hemester*, combining *hem* for "home" and *semester* for "vacation," is a new word that has recently become popular among Swedes concerned about the environmental impact of flying. And while the economic downturn had only begun to be felt in Sweden when I left the field in September of 2008, the concept was quickly gaining steam. While there is no good data to indicate the number of Swedes who have given up international vacations in favor of a *hemester*, the most recent climate attitude survey conducted by the Swedish Environmental Protection Agency indicates that two out of three Swedes have changed their travel habits and one out of three have changed their vacation plans due to their concerns about the climate (Naturvårdsverket 2009). Further, 2008 data from the Swedish Agency for Regional and Economic Growth reveals that approximately 7 percent of total household spending is linked to domestic tourism and that these expenditures—by Swedish households in Sweden—were up nearly 7 percent over 2007 and by more than 65 percent since 1995 (NUTEK 2008). While the growth since 1995 is, in part, attributable to an economy that also grew over this time period and the growth since 2007 may reflect a hesitancy to travel internationally given the hints of a coming recession, my research suggests that concerns about the environmental impacts of air travel and tourism were also a contributing factor.

Because of Sweden's strong environmental policies and low population densities, there are many places for nature tourism, and many environmentally concerned Swedes see this as an attractive alternative to international travel. Olaf, for example, was excited about the possibility of further developing Sweden's domestic tourism potential. It had been several years since he'd flown, but with a young family he was looking for a new way to travel close by, to get reconnected to nature:

> I have lots of thoughts about how we could use the nature in the region to get this vacation. Do you know Härjarö on the west side of the city, there is the big lake Mälaren? They have taken a piece of dirty land and turned it into a wonderful place of nature. And I can see how you do those kinds of things, for animals to get back to the land and people also . . . I can see how we could develop our way of getting connected to the landscape and this needs fulfilled really.

And Olaf was not alone. During my stay I heard several other men and women talk about the need for expanded local opportunities. Sweden's ecotourism association has made significant progress in this regard, organizing everything from dogsled rides near the Arctic Circle to birdwatching trips in Skåne, Sweden's southernmost province. Their certification system, "Nature's Best," has earned "good international acceptance and respect" and seems to be drawing a good number of tourists, both foreign and domestic (OECD 2010). Staycations are also becoming increasingly popular in the United States, where they were recently included on a list of things that are "in" by *Entertainment Weekly* (Ozols 2009). Like Wilk and Wilhite's study of energy consumption in the United States (1985), these observations suggest that political activism and environmentalism can make a serious impact on consumption decisions—including those concerning tourism and travel.

BARRIERS TO ALTERNATIVE TRAVEL

Although lots of people participating in this study recognized that flying less or vacationing closer to home would help to make their lives more sustainable—those that listed flying less in their list of sustainable actions also reported that they weren't very good at doing it themselves. I asked each person to look at the list of sustainable actions they had listed and to tell me how good they were at doing each of them. I sat with Ingrid as she went through her list. She pointed just below where she'd written "buy natural foods," then slid her finger across the boxes to the right. "Really good, good, okay, bad, really bad," she mumbled as she considered her choices. "I think I'm really good at that," she said as she placed an oversized X in the "really good" box. Ingrid moved down her list, checking mostly "good" or "really good" as she went. But when she came to "fly less," she moved her pen to the far right and made a small X in the box that said "really bad." She grimaced as she looked up at me and said:

> I know I'm really bad at that, but I lived in Australia for over twenty years and my daughter still lives there with my grandchildren. There is no way that I could stay here because it is important for me to see my grandchildren.

Throughout the course of the research I heard many similar stories. While most found it extremely easy to complete the sustainable actions they listed such as buy organic foods, take the public transport system in Stockholm, turn out lights, or take shorter showers, the twenty-eight people who listed flying less said, on average, they were just "okay" at actually doing it. The reasons are not difficult to understand. Like Erik, many others had also been invited on all-expenses-paid trips by parents or other family members. Yet most did not find it quite as easy to pass up as Erik had. Sam and his family, for example, had recently been invited to Turkey by his parents. He said, "That was so nice of them. I thought about it and decided that you can't make every change you want to. And I didn't want to make them disappointed so, we went." Similarly, Hans and his family were invited to his mother-in-law's seventieth birthday trip to Bulgaria. "There was no way we weren't going, ten days with everyone in the family on the beach," said Hans. He continued:

> So we said okay we'll go by train and meet you there but it ended up being impossible because the hotel was packaged with the airfare so we would have to pay for both. So we gave up and are going with air. We cannot be totally clean all the time. Sometimes there is a conflict, either with them to say we are not going or with my own feelings going on the trip.

These stories of the social pressures associated with flying for family vacations were common, but others also mentioned barriers concerned with price. For those that hope to fly less by taking the train, the process often proves both overwhelming and prohibitively expensive. After lamenting that he'd be going to Bulgaria via plane, Hans mentioned that he always takes the train when he's traveling in Sweden, but complained:

> Now it is cheaper to take a plane to London than the X2000 [an SJ fast train] to Gavle [a town about one hour north of Stockholm], so as long as it is like that, then idealism is not enough even for people like me and even less for people who are not concerned about it. We must support this by taxes and investment in public transport. I like these lifestyle things, I really promote making lifestyle changes but sometimes politicians say, "It is not up to me, it is up to every one of you. . . . Why don't you take the train?" And so, that I don't like. But also the other way around . . . some people in Sweden say I don't do anything until the politicians do something. I also don't like that.

Like Hans, many of the environmentally concerned men and women participating in this study wish the government would take a more active role in regulating travel and encouraging more sustainable options. Sweden has a CO_2 tax that has been credited with significant reductions in CO_2 emissions and a rapid conversion to biomass since its passage in 1991. Further, Stockholm has implemented one of the world's first congestion tax schemes for car commuters in Stockholm. These programs have helped Sweden to reduce their carbon emissions by almost 12 percent since 1990 (Miljödepartmentet 2010). Nonetheless, many research participants felt the state was not going far enough. Jacob, for example, thought the messages from politicians were inconsistent:

> There are a lot of differences between what is being said in this country and what is being done. They say don't go by plane, go by train. But they say to the [state-run] train company that they must break even or make a profit. But if they really want people to take the train then they could very well put some money in it. If they really wanted people not to go by car they could try for a year or two to put some money into it to make it free instead of building this *förbifart* [the highly contentious Stockholm bypass]. They ask people to do their share and I think that is right but they don't always do their share. The other day I checked the trains and the cheapest thing I could find was 14,000 SEK [about U.S. $2,300[8] for a family of five] to get the family down to Lund. It was a lot cheaper to fly, so we flew.

These stories demonstrate that even those who are aware, interested, and actively engaged in trying to curb their impact frequently run in to barriers beyond their control (Isenhour 2010). These are often attributable to much more than a lack of awareness—for example, availability, price, quality, or, as many research participants pointed out, concerns about sociality and belonging (see Douglas 2004).

SACRIFICING CULTURAL CAPITAL
IN SWEDEN'S MIDDLE-CLASS SOCIETY

While there was a sharp drop in international flights going out of Sweden in 2009 (OECD), it is extremely difficult to distinguish the effects of the recession and those related to a growing concern about sustainability. While the popularity of staycations is undoubtedly on the rise among a small but growing group of people—the long-term trend seems to suggest that the aviation industry is growing. According to the IPCC, aviation is currently responsible for approximately 12 percent of global transportation-related CO_2 but is the fastest-growing source of emissions. Further, demand for flights is increasing internationally—in Europe by about 5 percent a year but by as much as 14 percent in China and 15 percent in India (Hickman 2006). According to the Swedish Agency for Regional and Economic Growth (2010), Swedes took 12.7 million international trips with overnight stays in 2007, and air travel was the most common means of transport, constituting nearly 84 percent of business trips and 60 percent of leisure trips.

Scholars of tourism have long suggested that privileged international tourists "scavenge" the earth looking for authentic people and landscapes, those untouched by modernity (Crick 1989; MacCannell 1976). Cohen (1988) argues that this is driven by the tourist's desire to escape the alienation and superficiality of modernity in search of the pristine, the primitive, and the natural—that which is rare in postindustrial urban societies. Yet while many Swedes attribute their decision to fly with their passion for travel and desire to see and experience new things, giving up air travel may be difficult because of more than simply these desires or the barriers previously discussed. My research suggests that international travel is perhaps most difficult to give up in Sweden because it is a key marker of cultural capital in a so-called classless society that valorizes cosmopolitan identities and foreign experiences.

Sweden has long been regarded as an international leader in social democracy (Rowe and Fudge 2003). With a welfare system that considers an adequate income, health, and education to be the political right of all citizens, Sweden has taken progressive steps to redistribute wealth on a more egalitarian basis. These interventionist and redistributive policies have led many to argue that class inequalities have been significantly reduced, particularly at the low end of the economic spectrum (Bihagen 2000; Gullestad 1984; Löfgren 1987). In their place, strong nationalist ideologies of solidarity and equality have emerged over the last several generations. While these ideologies have recently been challenged by growing anti-immigration sentiment among some Swedes, Erickson (1997) has argued that, at least in rhetoric, Swedish policies have worked to advocate the worth and dignity of every human being and foster a sense of compassionate solidarity.[9] Tied then to nationalism, identity, patriotism, and a culturally constructed sense of morality, the egalitarian ethos in Sweden has produced the ideology of a "classless" society. In this context objective class dissimilarities are "muted" (Löfgren 1987), "played down," and purposefully "undercommunicated" (Gullestad 1984)—particularly in interpersonal exchanges. While class consciousness is strong in Sweden, in part due to the continued strength and relevance of labor unions, there are many social logics, both spoken and implied, which discourage Swedes from explicit displays of privilege and inequalities.

Yet, while the economic bases of class difference have been somewhat diminished by the long history of social democratic policy and accompanying discourse of equality and solidarity, it is important to reconsider the multifaceted understandings of class associated with Max Weber (1958) and Pierre Bourdieu (1977, 1990) to understand how existing class differences play out in unique ways. In Sweden's "classless" society, Bourdieu's notion of cultural capital takes on special significance. While members of Sweden's middle class rarely speak explicitly about their economic privilege, it is not uncommon to hear marking discourses centered on education and cultural experiences. Löfgren (1987) argues that the contemporary ideology of classlessness in Sweden has, in reality, resulted in subtle yet powerful class conflicts. He writes, "The ideology of classlessness can be contrasted with an everyday obsession with rituals of social distinction and boundary markers . . . in the age of consumerism, taste and tastelessness became a new cultural arena of muted class conflict" (1987:81). Later Löfgren wrote that the consumption histories of Sweden's educated middle class reveal an "obsession with distinction and taste" and "a recurrent need to distance oneself from other consumers, to stress one's role as a critical observer of the consumption habits of the others" (1994:55).

However, there is not—as is often assumed—a clear correlation between the desire to differentiate oneself and the accumulation of material goods. Many middle-class Swedes, rather than focusing on the accumulation of material goods, are more concerned with "quality," "designer," and "experiential" consumerism. Similarly, Douglas Holt argues in his study of American consumers that in the context of pervasive materialism the only way for cultural elites to differentiate themselves is "structurally speaking . . . to develop a set of tastes in opposition to materialism: consuming which emphasizes the metaphysical over the material. Thus

materialism is associated with 'showy,' 'ostentatious,' 'gaudy,' or 'unre-
fined'" (2000:247).

Maureen O'Dougherty has also observed, in her study of middle-
class Brazilians, that the construction, maintenance, and performance
of middle-class identity is not only found in the consumption of goods
and services but is also equally salient in discourses about education
and cultural experiences (2002). In the context of middle-class Sao Paolo,
a particularly salient cultural experience is a trip to Disneyland. For
Swedes international travel experiences, particularly to exotic and unique
locations, become part of a class commentary on taste, distinction, and
cosmopolitanism. Crick (1989), Urry (1990), and Nash (1996) are only a
sampling of authors who have written about tourism as a form of conspicuous consumption, one in which international experiences help to
build the status of the tourist, despite often negative environmental and
sociocultural consequences for the host community.

One afternoon on the way home from having completed an interview,
I heard two young people talking on the *tunnelbana*, Stockholm's subway
system. They were sitting just behind me. Guessing from their voices and
the content of their conversation, they were fairly young, maybe in their
late twenties or early thirties. The two of them, a man and a woman, were
listing all of the foreign countries they'd been to. She had taken some time
off after university and had traveled extensively in South Asia one summer. She'd also been to Africa as a young girl on safari with her grandpar-
ents. While he seemed impressed by her experiences, he countered with
a description of a hiking trip in Iceland and the week he spent traveling
in the United States while visiting a friend. For these young people, both
seemingly proud of their international experiences, the meaning attached
to travel experience is clearly positive.

The men and women who participated in my research were all highly
educated,[10] middle-class Swedes who placed great value on knowledge
of global affairs. Yet for many research participants, like Sara, it was difficult to maintain this identity without international travel experience:

The difficult thing is that everyone is always talking about where they have
been on holiday, the interesting people they met, the different food, the music and the nature. And you get the feeling they are trying to make you feel
bad because you have not also been there—or maybe more they feel good
they have been there and I haven't. But for me, I can't say anything to them.
They don't understand that I would like to go there too to experience those
things, but I cannot do it. When people tell me stories like that—all I can
think about is how many of those places, those people, that food will soon
be underwater . . . because people keep flying there.

Sara, like so many other Swedes, compared her moral and more responsible tourism to the vulgar consumption behaviors of Sweden's upper class. This might seem to go against much of the received wisdom in consumption theory, which posits that the consumption behaviors of the working class are typically the subject of scrutiny (Bourdieu 1984; Veblen 1994). However, it makes sense in the Swedish context, where middle-class values of solidarity and equality have been strengthened by the Lutheran church and a history of ethnic homogeneity and social democracy (Isenhour 2010). Yet Sara, like many others, was clearly saddened and angered by the flying habits of Sweden's wealthier citizens, who she believes know about the negative environmental impacts of flying but do it anyway. Sara's words echoed George Monbiot, who recently wrote in the *Guardian* that for those that understand the impact of flying and do it anyway, "the moral dissonance is deafening" (2006:1).

Yet in Sweden, where a culture of conformity is apparent to ethnographers and citizens alike, there is a strong pressure to consume to socially mandated levels—in terms of not only furnishings, clothing, or the latest mobile phone but also international travel. These experiences help middle- and upper-class Swedish consumers to accumulate cultural capital, signaling their class status in a society that discourages recognition of objective material difference. Without the ability to travel without a bad conscience, many middle-class, highly educated Swedes feel deeply conflicted. And while they say this is because they also wish to see the world, ethnographic observation reveals that in this highly conformist culture obsessed with markers of cultural capital, international travel is also hard to give up because people don't want to be seen as narrow minded, inexperienced, uneducated, immoral, or acting in bad taste.

THE CONFLICTED SWEDE
AND THE IMPLICATIONS FOR ECOTOURISM

So while it might be difficult for many Swedes to sacrifice a key means through which they can build cultural capital—many are doing it nonetheless. Yet this trend raises several important questions. First, as I spoke with research participants about their concerns for sustainability, I learned that many Swedes attribute changes in their worldview, lifestyle, and priorities to their experiences abroad. Stina, for example, explained that she was deeply affected by a trip to the Philippines as a young girl:

It goes back to when I was eleven—I attended a course in the Philippines . . . about children all over the world in need. So I went there for a month with other eleven year old children and for the first time in my life I saw very, very rich people. They had chauffeurs and a lot of people working for them—but I also saw a lot of poor people with children in the streets. And I hadn't seen that before either . . . so it was a big contrast between the rich and poor. So I am now interested in aid and street children—or child labor and these kinds of things. And then I also have a big interest in traveling in other parts of the world and the environment.[11]

Similarly, Gudrun attributed her interest in sustainable living to her experiences traveling around the world:

I think that . . . the reason I really started to think about it [sustainability] is because I have been traveling a lot. I've been in South America and have done a minor field study in Kenya . . . so I've got to see all the problems that our western lifestyles causes in those countries. That is why I have really started to feel a lot.

Perhaps it is precisely because so many Swedes have international experiences that the citizenry has, relative to other nations, been so responsive to sustainability initiatives. While movements intended to create more sustainable societies are growing internationally, Swedes have been particularly responsive to alternative forms of consumerism. In 2004 Sweden ranked first among European nations in the number of its citizens who boycott (33 percent) and report purchasing products for political, ethical, or environmental reasons (55 percent) (Micheletti and Stolle 2004). In a 2006 study 60 percent of Swedes said that they had buycotted or boycotted certain products or companies, compared with an average of 34 percent for the rest of Western Europe (Ferrer and Fraile 2006). My broader research illustrates that despite the common assumption that these men and women are motivated by reflexive modernization and the perception of direct environmental risk, concerns for impoverished communities and future generations (perhaps fostered by Sweden's long-term emphasis on equality or significant international travel experience) were much more salient factors in the Swedish context (Isenhour 2010).

If this awareness is, in part, linked to international awareness and knowledge of the conditions of life in less developed countries, could a decline in international tourism actually be detrimental? Ulf, for one, argues that his experiences working in Africa had a drastic impact on his life and his contemporary concern for sustainable living. He said, "I worked in Tanzania . . . in the 60s and saw quite a lot of the spin-off effects of big agriculture and development aid that introduced things that did not belong there and caused serious problems." Ulf went on to explain how people were often given incentives to start growing cash crops for export. According to Ulf, these projects often destroyed local food production, leaving people food insecure and dependent on aid.

Stories like Ulf's certainly suggest that international experience is beneficial for some. However, as Crick (1989) and later Stronza (2001) have already pointed out, while there is a significant amount of data on the effects of tourism on host communities, we know very little about how tourists are affected by their experiences. It is certainly possible that anthropology has avoided such questions because, as Crick says, "Tourists appear in some respects to be our own distant relatives" (1989:311) or because we have a disciplinary bias toward what Trouillot calls the "savage slot" (2003). Yet I would like to suggest, following MacCannell (1976), that we can better understand the world by following the footsteps of tourists, even if their path is short—for instance, from Stockholm to a small cottage in the Swedish countryside.

Further, there is a significant need to move beyond speculation to understand tourist motivation and experiences. Crick writes that tourists "are poor cultural carriers" and that tourism "involves more hedonism and conspicuous consumption than learning or understanding," thus often resulting in the perpetuation of stereotypes and misunderstanding (1989:328). He writes, "No matter how often international tourism is represented as a force for understanding, the empirical evidence suggests that with increasing numbers individual perceptions are replaced by stereotypes" (1989:329). Yet with a more recent focus on alternative (for example, green, eco, cultural, or responsible) tourism, some have suggested that if done properly tourists can walk away with a better understanding of both the local people and their environment (Orams 1997).

Certainly there are many different forms of tourism, and some are much more educational and sustainable than others, making a greater impact on their visitors. Gudrun's and Ulf's experiences working and studying in developing nations are certainly much different than the experiences of those Swedes who spend a week at all-inclusive gated resorts in Cancun or Koh Samui. As Stronza (2001) notes, over the past few decades there has been a significant shift in the tourism industry toward sustainable travel that is designed to foster international understanding and contribute to local development without harming the ecosystem. Many scholars, activists, and local communities alike are currently focused on ecotourism as a strategy for sustainable development, one that can help people to preserve their natural resources while still earning a decent living. They are targeting tourists in search of sustainable options, those men and women concerned about the environment and interested in seeing beautiful natural landscapes, wild animals, and authentic human communities.

Unfortunately, however, this strategy targets many of the same people that are concerned about the carbon impact of flying. As the case of the conflicted Swede reminds us, this strategy could be as precarious as the coffee, rubber, or palm oil schemes that were once seen as the path out of poverty. Grist.com commentator Umbra Frisk has written about American carbon policy:

> If the government does somehow establish a functioning cap and trade program that brings our emissions down 83 percent in the next 40 years, flying life as we currently know it will have ended. The days of cheap fuel will be, and should be, over. Flying will become cost-prohibitive. (2009)

Further, Swedish consumers concerned about sustainability are increasingly turning inward, toward local production and consumption. Yet development agencies continue to herald the benefits of ecotourism in developing economies. But given the ambivalence of northern consumers, is it wise to subject impoverished peoples to the whims of northern tourists, advising them to continue to put all their eggs in the proverbial basket of coffee, rubber, palm oil, or the hottest new ecotourism project? While these projects may certainly bring money in the short term, development efforts must help vulnerable communities to maintain an ability to be resilient and resistant to the whims of the market and the ambivalence of northern consumers with multiple priorities. Crick calls this strategy "naïve," writing, "In short, to opt for tourism as a growth strategy is to ask for continued control by overseas forces" (1989:321), while Nash goes even further, referring to tourism as the vanguard of neocolonialism (1989).

Anthropology has long contributed to our understandings of how host communities are drawn into globalized markets and production regimes, often at extreme disadvantage and with disastrous consequences. However, the discipline has, in many ways, neglected an examination of how these processes are affected by communities, everyday real people, at the other end of the commodity chain—the wealthy northern consumers upon whose tourist dollars so many have come to depend. Yet, given the growing number of ecologically concerned Swedes willing to sacrifice their cultural capital in the interest of sustainability, it seems a study of the conflicted Swedish tourist is increasingly relevant.

NOTES

1. I have not been in the field since "climate gate," when critics accused climate scientists of data manipulation based on emails leaked from the University of East Anglia in late 2009. Nor have I been in Sweden since the IPCC acknowledged some mistakes in its 2007 assessment report. However, I have spoken with several

research participants, and while they acknowledge that these stories have cast some doubt, the general consensus about anthropogenic climate change remains relatively strong in Sweden.

2. Because the population of sustainability-minded consumers in Sweden was unknown, I drew upon Harraway's (1991) concept of affinities to identify five organizations working on issues related to sustainability. A call for research participants was sent to each group's subscribers or members, and nine to fourteen volunteers from each group participated in a semistructured interview, for a total of fifty-eight. Twelve of these participants and fourteen of their family members also participated in case-study household research, which included a review of household expenditures, consumption inventories, and a series of iterative interviews.

3. These were defined not only by income but also by education, occupation, discourse, and cultural performance (see O'Dougherty 2002).

4. I recognize and acknowledge significant diversity in the middle class and that essentializing terms like the *middle class* can obscure inequalities (see Patillo-McCoy 2002; O'Dougherty 2002). I focus here on similarities in order to understand larger shared cultural logics that help script for the reproduction of class inequalities.

5. Twelve families, a subset of the original sample, were chosen for participation based on a quota sample controlling for household income, age, group membership, and the sex of the original respondent.

6. This trip, from Sweden's east to west coast, is approximately 480 kilometers or 300 miles.

7. Here Erik illustrates the concept of a "fair share of environmental space," a philosophy and proposed solution increasingly common among Swedes concerned about sustainability. The idea is that each global citizen is entitled to a fair share of his or her environmental space, including the right to emit. From this perspective, wealthy citizens, like those in Sweden, must drastically restrict their current emissions in order to ensure that humans in less privileged locations have an equal capacity to use environmental resources and create emissions.

8. Calculated using the average exchange rate for April 2008.

9. Economic redistribution policies and the welfare state have been challenged in recent years for several reasons beyond the scope of this chapter. First, the economic downturn and high unemployment in the 1990s helped to usher in political support for a reduced tax burden. Further, an influx in the arrival of immigrants from the Middle East, primarily Islamic in faith and Arab in ethnicity, has increasingly challenged Sweden's welfare state and the associated ideology of equality within the nation. In fact, the nationalist party, Sverigedemokraterna, although still very small, is one of the fastest-growing parties in Sweden. It is centered on a rejection of multiculturalism and stands in opposition to the extension of Sweden's generous social services to refugees and immigrants. These movements have also created, in many instances, Islamophobic discourse, reflecting Sweden's struggle with an internal Islamic Other (Bunzl 2005) and challenging the long-standing emphasis on solidarity and internal equality.

10. Ninety percent of the fifty-eight citizen-consumers who participated in the research had a postsecondary degree.

11. Stina's response in many ways reflects Sweden's long-term emphasis on social democracy and efforts to support the creation of a large middle class through the leveling of significant income disparities.

REFERENCES

Åkerman, Jonas. 2008. Klimatepåverkan fran Utrikes Resor. *Swedish Royal Institute of Technology TRITA INFRA-FMS* 2008:7.

Bihagen, Erik. 2000. *The Significance of Class: Studies of Class Inequalities, Consumption and Social Circulation in Contemporary Sweden.* Doctoral Thesis, Department of Sociology, Umeå: Universitets tryckeriet, Umeå.

Bourdieu, Pierre. 1977. *Outline of a Theory of Practice.* Cambridge: Cambridge University Press.

———. 1984. *Distinction: A Social Critique of the Judgment of Taste.* London: Routledge.

———. 1990. *The Logic of Practice.* Cambridge: Polity.

Bunzl, Matti. 2005. Between Anti-Semitism and Islamophobia: Some Thoughts on the New Europe. *American Ethnologist* 32(4):499–508.

Center for the New American Dream (CNAD). 2005. New American Dream Public Opinion Poll. www.newdream.org, accessed November 21, 2011.

Cohen, Erik. 1988. Authenticity and Commoditization in Tourism. *Annals of Tourism Research* 15(3):371–86.

Crick, Malcolm. 1989. Representations of International Tourism in the Social Sciences: Sun, Sex, Sights, Savings and Servility. *Annual Review of Anthropology* 18(1):307–44.

Dahl, Ulrika. 2007. Progressive Women, Traditional Men: Globalization, Migration and Equality in the Northern Periphery of the European Union. In *The Gender of Globalization: Women Navigating Cultural and Economic Marginalities,* eds. Nandini Gunewardena and Ann Kingsolver, pp. 105–25. Santa Fe: School for Advanced Research.

Douglas, Mary. 2004. Consumers Revolt. In *The Consumption Reader,* eds. David B. Clarke, Marcus A. Doel, and Kate M. L. Housiaux, pp. 144–49. New York: Routledge.

Erickson, Rita J. 1997. *Paper or Plastic: Energy, Environment and Consumerism in Sweden and America.* Westport, CT: Praeger.

Ferrer, Mariona and Marta Fraile. 2006. *Exploring the Social Determinants of Political Consumerism in Western Europe.* Working Papers Online Series 57/2006. http://portal.uam.es/portal/page/portal/UAM_ORGANIZATIVO/Departamentos/CienciaPoliticaRelacionesInternacionales/publicaciones%20en%20red/working_papers/archivos/Working-paper-UAM-2006.%20Marta%20fraile.pdf, accessed November 21, 2011.

Frisk, Umbra. 2009. Ask Umbra on Flying Less. www.grist.org/article/2009-08-13-ask-umbra-flying-less, accessed November 21, 2011.

Guggenheim, Davis, dir. 2006. *An Inconvenient Truth: A Global Warning.* 100 min. Paramount Pictures.

Gullestad, M. 1984. *Kitchen-Table Society: A Case Study of the Family Life and Friendships of Young Working Class Mothers in Urban Norway.* Oslo: Universitetsforlaget.
Harraway, Donna. 1991. *Simians, Cyborgs and Women: The Reinvention of Nature.* New York: Routledge.
Hickman, Leo. 2006. Is It Okay to Fly? *Guardian,* Saturday May 20, 2006:P4.
Holt, Douglas B. 2000. Does Cultural Capital Structure American Consumption? In *The Consumer Society Reader,* eds. Juliet Schor and Douglas B. Holt, pp. 212–52. New York: New York Press.
Intergovernmental Panel on Climate Change (IPCC). 2001. Aviation and the Global Atmosphere. www.grida.no/climate/ipcc/aviation/064.htm, accessed November 21, 2011.
———. 2007. *Climate Change 2007: The Physical Science Basis. Fourth Assessment Report of the IPCC.* Cambridge: Cambridge University Press.
Isenhour, Cindy. 2010. Building Sustainable Societies: A Swedish Case Study on the Limits of Reflexive Modernization. *American Ethnologist* 37(3):511–25.
Jagers, Sverker, and Johan Martinsson. 2007. *Svensk Opinion i Klimat- och Havsmiljofagor: Nya Siffor fran SOM-Institutet.* Goteborgs Universitet, SOM Institutet.
Löfgren, Orvar. 1987. Deconstructing Swedishness: Culture and Class in Modern Sweden. In *Anthropology at Home,* ed. A. Jackson, pp. 74–93. London: Tavistock.
———. 1994. Consuming Interests. In *Consumption and Identity,* ed. Jonathan Freidman, pp. 47–70. Amsterdam: Harwood.
———. 2001. Know Your Country: A Comparative Perspective on Tourism and Nation Building in Sweden. In *Being Elsewhere: Tourism, Consumer Culture, and Identity in Modern Europe and North America,* eds. Shelley Osmun Baranowski and Ellen Furlough, pp. 137–54. Ann Arbor: University of Michigan Press.
MacCannell, Dean. 1976. *The Tourist: A New Theory of the Leisure Class.* New York: Shocken Books.
Micheletti, Michele, and Dietlind Stolle. 2004. Swedish Political Consumers: Who Are They and Why They Use the Market as an Arena for Politics. In *Political Consumerism: Motivations, Power and Conditions in the Nordic Countries and Elsewhere,* eds. Magnus Boström, Andreas Föllesdal, Mikael Klintman, Michele Micheletti, and Mads P. Sörensen, pp. 145–64. Oslo: Nordisk Ministerråd, TemaNord.
Miljödepartmentet. 2010. Swedish Greenhouse Gas Emissions at Record Lows in 2008. www.sweden.gov.se/sb/d/11459/a/137113, accessed November 21, 2011.
Monbiot, George. 2006. We Are All Killers. *Guardian,* February 28, 2006.
Nash, Dennison. 1989. Tourism as a Form of Imperialism. In *Hosts and Guests: The Anthropology of Tourism,* ed. Valene Smith, pp. 171–85. Philadelphia: University of Pennsylvania Press.
———. 1996. *Anthropology of Tourism.* Kidlington: Pergamon.
Naturvårdsverket. 2009. *Allmänheten och klimatförändringen 2009, Rapport 6311.* Stockholm, Sweden.
———. 2010. *The Climate Impact of Swedish Consumption, Report 5992.* Stockholm, Sweden.
NUTEK. 2008. *Tourism and the Travel and Tourism Industry in Sweden.* Stockholm: Swedish Agency for Economic and Regional Growth.

O'Dougherty, Maureen. 2002. *Consumption Intensified: The Politics of Middle-Class Daily Life in Brazil*. Durham: Duke University Press.

Orams, Marc B. 1997. The Effectiveness of Environmental Education: Can We Turn Tourists into "Greenies"? *Progress in Tourism and Hospitality Research* 3:295–306.

Organization for Economic Cooperation and Development (OECD). 2009. *International Transport Forum*. Paris: OECD.

———. 2010. *Tourism Trends and Policies 2010*. Paris: OECD.

Ozols, Victor. 2009. Staycation Story Trend Saves Travel Journalism. www .jaunted.com/story/2009/3/29/12409/3189/travel/Staycation+Story+Trend+ Saves+Travel+Journalism, accessed November 21, 2011.

Patillo-McCoy, Mary. 1999. *Black Picket Fences: Privilege and Peril among the Black Middle Class*. Chicago: University of Chicago Press.

Rowe, Janet, and Colin Fudge. 2003. Linking National Sustainable Development Strategy and Local Implementation: A Case Study in Sweden. *Local Environment* 8(2):120–48.

SJ. 2010. The Environment. www.sj.se, accessed November 21, 2011.

Stern, Nicholas. 2007. *The Stern Review on the Economics of Climate Change*. London: HM Treasury.

Stronza, Amanda. 2001. Anthropology of Tourism: Forging New Ground for Ecotourism and Other Alternatives. *Annual Review of Anthropology* 30(1):21–83.

Svenska Miljöinstitutet. 2010. Testa din Klimatpåverkan. www.climate.ivl.se, accessed November 21, 2011.

Swedish Agency for Economic and Regional Growth. 2010. Fakta Om Svensk Turism. www.tillvaxtverket.se/huvudmeny/faktaochstatistik/omturism.4.21099e 4211fdba8c87b800017331.html, accessed December 1, 2011.

Tourism Authority of Thailand. 2010. Thailand Wins the Prestigious Swedish Grand Travel Award for the Best Tourist Country 2010. www.tatnews.org/ AWARDS_WON_BY_THAILAND/5301.asp, accessed November 21, 2011.

Trouillot, Michel-Rolph. 2003. *Global Transformations*. New York: Palgrave.

Urry, John. 1990. *The Tourist Gaze: Leisure and Travel in Contemporary Societies*. London: Sage.

Veblen, Thorstein. 1994. *The Theory of the Leisure Class*. New York: Dover.

Weber, Max. 1958. *Essays in Sociology*. H. H. Gerth and C. Wright Mills, eds. New York: Oxford University Press.

Wilk, Richarch, and Harold Wilhite. 1985. Household Energy Decision Making in Santa Cruz County, California. In *Families and Energy: Coping with Uncertainty*, eds. Willett Kempton and Bonnie Maas Morrison, pp. 449–59. Lansing: Michigan State University Press.

World Tourism Organization (WTO). 2010. Factbook and Database. www .wtoelibrary.org/home/main.mpx, accessed April 4, 2010.

11

✝

Reproductive Tourism

Health Care Crisis Reifies
Global Stratified Reproduction

Amy Speier

M edical tourism, "the practice of patients seeking lower cost health
care procedures abroad, often packaged with travel and sightseeing excursions" (Senate Committee on Aging 2006:1), is a vastly expanding industry that reveals new healthcare-seeking practices. Health care
costs in North America have been the primary motivating factors for
people seeking care outside of the United States (Connell 2006; McLean
and McLean 2007; Turner 2007). Medical tourism reflects the "global
networks" (Scheper-Hughes 2000:192–93) of late capitalism, in which
markets tend to reduce everything, including body parts, to commodities
(Scheper-Hughes 2002:3).

Some scholars have argued that rather than use the term *reproductive
tourism*, which connotes pleasurable travel, the term *reproductive exile* better
reflects the pain associated with infertility and the fact that couples must
evade regulations or high costs that prevent them from accessing treatment
at home (Inhorn and Patrizio 2009; Matorras 2005). While to some extent
cost exiles North American reproductive patients, they still have the freedom to travel to whatever region they choose, and in some cases they travel
back to their "roots." In this way, exile would be a misnomer. The widely
accepted term *cross-border reproductive travel* (Pennings 2005) will be used
in this chapter. It must be maintained that the extent to which reproductive

travelers do participate in sightseeing and touristic experiences does vary tremendously. Throughout the chapter, the term "patient traveler" will also be used to connote the tension that exists between the leisure of travel and the seriousness of medical treatment being sought.

Spending on average sixty billion dollars annually, one hundred million patients seek health treatment abroad each year (Jones and Keith 2006). While people have always traveled on a "quest for therapy" (Janzen 1978), the speed and scale of travel has dramatically increased over the past twenty years. Furthermore, the ways in which patients make the decision to travel abroad for health care reflects global, neoliberal models of consumer health care (Scheper-Hughes 2002). As American patients are acting as consumers with respect to their health care, we must view this consumption of treatment and body parts as meaningful practice (Becker 2000:10).

This chapter will examine the complex reasons Americans "choose" to travel to the Czech Republic for reproductive care, most often seeking in vitro fertilization (IVF) treatment combined with egg donation. Reproductive travel has grown as one of the main forms of medical tourism, and people who want more affordable or less regulated fertility treatments seek it out. Reproductive travelers may be couples, traditional or nontraditional, or single women. Americans are especially interested in more affordable treatments, since fertility treatment in the United States is generally considered "elective," and each attempt could cost upward of ten thousand dollars.[1] For patient travelers traveling to the Czech Republic, treatment for IVF is roughly U.S. $5,600, and for an egg donor cycle the cost is U.S. $8,000, compared with anything ranging from U.S. $10,000 to U.S. $40,000 in the United States. A couple can make the trip to the Czech Republic for egg donation and stay within a U.S. $10,000 budget.

Reproductive travelers criticize the commodification of fertility treatment in the United States yet fail to extend this critique to the foreign markets serving them. In the Czech Republic, the market of reproductive technologies is rendered invisible, as they are cloaked in the lower prices and altruism of Czech doctors and donors. In this chapter, I frame the politics of reproductive medicine within an international market, exploring the ethical issues surrounding the "choice" of patient travelers and egg donors. Finally, the economic relationship between Czech egg donors and American patient travelers will be explored, ending with a consideration of how to understand the international market of gametes.

METHODS

My informants include company representatives and clients of a medical tourism broker company, which assists couples by arranging fertility care in the Czech Republic. This company, which I will call IVF Holidays, provides ground transportation, travel tips, suggestions for accommodations, local representatives in the country, transfer of medical records, and the negotiation of rates for service—as do similar medical tourism companies (Turner 2007). Tom and Hana, who also have the help of family in the Czech Republic, own the company. In the summer of 2008, I traveled to their home-based company in the Midwest, where I conducted informal and semistructured interviews with both owners of the company. This company is one of two North American consulting firms that work exclusively with their respective reproductive clinics in the Czech Republic. At the time of this research, their company provided roughly 25 percent of the clientele to the *Klinika Reprodukční Medicíny a gynekologie*—or the Clinic of Reproductive Medicine and Gynecology in Zlín. In addition, 90 percent of IVF Holidays' clientele is American, but they have provided service to Canadians, Australians, Nigerians, and some Europeans as well. Finally, phone and email interviews were conducted with three former clients of this company, after obtaining informed consent from both the owners and the clients. Pseudonyms have been used for all informants. However, the difficulty of maintaining anonymity when working with public businesses must be acknowledged.

Other scholars (Inhorn 2004; Whittaker and Speier 2010) have noted the difficulty of identifying and recruiting patient travelers. Anthropologists must rely on clinics or such intermediary companies like IVF Holidays to access patients. Some women or couples did not want to participate in interviews because they maintain secrecy about their fertility problems and their attempts at IVF, here or abroad. One patient traveler told me, "In general, I don't share my fertility problems with anyone." One of the IVF Holidays owners, Hana, suggested that some women do not want to talk about the trip they took at all, wanting to forget that it ever occurred. She said, "Some people when they get pregnant or they deliver the baby, they are doing like they've never been on the trip and they never want to talk about it." This suggests perceived stigma and secrecy attached to infertility and the use of new reproductive technologies, particularly when they are pursued overseas. It may also indicate denial on the part of those who use Czech egg donors.

COMMODIFIED TECHNOLOGY, GAMETES, AND HOPE

Scholars have argued that reproductive medicine typifies a consumer model of health care. Becker writes, "The coalescence of business and medicine is nowhere near so obvious to consumers of reproductive medicine" (2000:245). This is compounded by the fact that these procedures are not fully covered by insurance. Reproductive medicine has been complicit with the commodification of health care, since it is a booming, profitable "baby business" (Spar 2006). Kimbrell (1993:73) has referred to this business as "the human body shop," whereby elements of reproduction are sold. As is the case with biomedicine in general, reproductive medicine reifies body parts, making them into objects, and subsequently commodities (Scheper-Hughes 2002). Kimbrell (1993:73) argues that reproductive medicine "represents the invasion of the market into our most intimate selves."

Reproductive technologies exist fully within the private sector, whereby technologies, gametes, and hope are bought and sold (see also Bonaccorso 2005). Sperm and eggs are bought and sold, often to be used with assisted reproductive technologies. Hence, technology and gametes are in the process commodified. Lock claims, "In order for body parts to be made freely available for exchange they must be first conceptualized as thing-like, as non-self and as detachable from the body without causing irreparable loss or damage to the individual person" (2001:71). In this case, gametes become commodities. It seems that egg and sperm donors distinguish clearly between the gametes they donate and the potential future development of that gamete. A coordinator at the clinic said, "I don't think they think it through."

When Americans come to the Czech Republic for egg donation they are seeking an anonymous donor. They have no desire for contact with their egg donor, and they indicate preferred education level and phenotypes that resemble their own. If Americans are traveling for egg donation, the personal qualities of these "gifts" are denied (Mauss 1922). In addition, Mauss has been criticized for assuming equality between giver and receiver in gift exchange (Lock 2001), which does not exist in the case of Americans coming to Czech clinics for egg donation. Taussig (1987) has written about the differential value attributed to bodies, which do not have universal value. In the case of the reproductive medicine industry, Czech eggs are valued at a much lower price.

For patient travelers, eggs and sperm are fetishized commodities because they promise possible life (Scheper-Hughes 2002). Appadurai (1996) has written about the social meaning and significance of commodities, whereby nothing is fixed or stable about commodities. In the case of global reproductive medicine, there is a clear demand for gametes and reproductive technology, and assisted reproductive technologies may be inciting further demand.

POLITICS OF REPRODUCTIVE MEDICINE

Feminists have shown how new reproductive technologies must be considered "hope" technologies. Hope is closely associated with American notions of individualism and responsibility for health, and it has become embedded within the process of commodification (Becker 2000:117). Clinical statistics often skew the success rates of reproductive technologies in order to garner business. At the same time, as new medical advances are made, couples inevitably feel "compelled to try" any way possible to have a baby (Sandelowski 1991). Women find themselves continually trying new procedures to get pregnant (Becker 2000; Franklin 1997; Sandelowski 1991). Sandelowski (1991:33) considers how new reproductive technologies exacerbate the extent to which "women feel compelled by their doctors and male partners to undergo medical treatments for infertility because of the strong cultural pressure for married couples to have children and to demonstrate their normality in reproducing." The American Society for Reproductive Medicine has raised concerns about the exploitation of infertility patients.

I argue that reproductive travel further complicates the "hope" embedded in reproductive technologies, since now patients can travel across the globe in pursuit of reproductive technologies. I asked one patient, Anita, whether she had any misgivings about traveling abroad for treatment, since this constituted her first trip abroad. She said, "I said I was going to do it. I mean, it's worth a try. 'Cause what happens if you don't try and you're always going to have in the back of your mind 'what if'?" Hana said of the patients:

> They're very excited about the possibility of saving a lot of money, having a vacation, and doing the program. You know, after learning how much the prices are in the United States, many people give up their hope. Or like us, say we will have to save for three or four years before we can actually afford this. When they learn, for example, the donor egg cycle is the third of the price that they will be paying in the United States, they are excited.

Aptly, the front cover of the brochure for the clinic reads, "Where hope is turned into happiness . . ."

Bioethics support the "choice" of the consumer, here a "new class" of the medical traveler (Scheper-Hughes 2002:45). Bioethicists tend to argue in favor of the purchasing power of patient travelers, supporting their power to purchase medical treatments where they are available. In the context of reproductive travel, bioethicists support the "choice" of patient travelers to travel for health care. In talking to Tom and Hana, they both said separately in response to my question as to whether they had any restrictions on the type of client they help, "We do not play God." At first, I thought this a fair statement: they were inclusive of couples, women of all ages, and sexual orientation. However, in looking back, I realized that when I asked if there were age limits for those whose travel they would arrange, Hana said that they do not try to stop women from first trying IVF using their own eggs, if that is what they want to pay for. She said,

"That's . . . their decision if they want to spend money." Thus, choice is couched within a consumer framework. Since most American clinics refuse to treat women over the age of forty or forty-five, I think it necessary to reconsider how liberating or empowering this purchasing power may be for the patient traveler in tandem with feminist analysis of patients feeling compelled to try reproductive technologies across the globe. If the women have very little chance of having a healthy pregnancy result in IVF using their own eggs, and if the technologies keep inciting further attempts with little success rate, how positive is this "choice" their money allows them? The reproductive travel industry seems to further extend the promise of cheaper, hence possibly more, chances to conceive. Arguments made by Tom and Hana in favor of the spending power of the patient traveler have been "thoroughly disciplined and brought into alignment with the needs and desires of consumer-oriented globalization" (Scheper-Hughes 2002:31). However, it must be stated that patient travelers are consuming not only reproductive technologies but also a vacation abroad.

THE TOURISTIC EXPERIENCE

There are many parallels between reproductive and adoptive travel, but there are important distinctions to be made as well. While the general flow of travelers from the West for adoption or the use of gametes is the same and touristic elements are roughly the same, the element of disclosure to future children remains a vital distinction. Usually, adoptive parents must tell their children that they were adopted, while some reproductive travelers hope to pretend they never went for treatment using donated egg or sperm or embryos. While adoptive parents travel to particular regions intending to adopt, they are ultimately responsible for their child's memories. Thus, while abroad, they participate in heritage tourism to learn about their child's national heritage (personal communication, Frayda Cohen, June 23, 2010). This element of travel may be missing from reproductive travel.

Another parallel between reproductive travel and adoptive travel is that both groups of travelers are limited in mobility once they are abroad; they tend to stay near the clinic or children's home when they visit particular regions. Thus, reproductive travelers coming to the Czech Republic stay in a small Moravian town, Zlín, which is three hours away from the bustling tourist hot spot that is Prague. The clinic in Zlín does set up its clients' schedules so they have long weekends to travel to nearby cities, including Budapest, Prague, or Vienna. However, while they are in Zlín, they are visiting the Czech clinic daily or every other day. Joan, another client of IVF Holidays, described her visit to the Czech Republic for fertility treatment. She and her husband were picked up at the Prague airport by IVF Holidays and taken to their hotel. Their first appointment was with the clinic at 9 a.m. Tom and Hana picked them up at their hotel at 8:30, helped them fill out all the paperwork, and walked them through everything. They were told that their donor had been there a day early, and at that point her husband was told to go to the "happy room." They waited five days for a transfer, during which time they traveled to Vienna and Prague. Joan summarized the perks of the trip for me: "I had a ten-day vacation and a donor."

The website of IVF Holidays has a page devoted to sightseeing excursions. It reads:

> Within your 21 day visit, you will have plenty of time to see exactly what you want and leave with wonderful experiences. We will organize two day trips, one to Prague, the capital of Czech Republic, and the other to Vienna, the capital of Austria. The beauty of these two cities is that everything is within walking distance. There is lots to see . . . and to taste. Some couples even had time to go see Budapest, Krakow, Venice. Feel free to ask us about directions, train schedules and tips from past clients. All of these locations are within several hours away and everybody had such a wonderful time on their trips.

The actual amount that patients travel varies with respect to their budget. Some patient travelers maintain a tight budget and limit themselves to trips to the local zoo and the shopping mall. Others, however, do take advantage of the long weekend to venture further out to nearby Eastern European capitals. The patient travelers receive from IVF Holidays a map of Zlín, a brochure on Moravia, and a list of nearby sights to visit while staying for treatment. Possible day trips range from nearby towns to forests, cemeteries, spas, cathedrals, and zoological gardens.

PATIENT TRAVELERS

When I asked if there was a general socioeconomic status of their clients, Tom said:

> It's been weird, it's been rather bizarre, we've actually had several doctors that have gone. We've had lawyers, nurses, and I was amazed at the amount of people in the medical field that have gone. A lot of teachers. So I would say better than half of our clients are higher educated. When we started doing this, we were thinking people like ourselves, who had money but not a whole lot. That most of the people who have gone seem to have more money than we do. . . . They've traveled more, they know more. So they know the medical situations around the world a little bit, they're a little more research oriented, so they do the research and plan out.

As mentioned, the main reason to travel abroad for fertility treatment is the lower prices, at least for Americans. Tom said, "The main reason would be the money. It doesn't matter how much you make, if you can save fifteen thousand dollars on a procedure and feel confident that it's going to be done in the same manner," then you will do it. But, he adds, "There are a lot of other little reasons that go into that, but I would say the main reason is money."

In 2004, more than one million Americans underwent some form of fertility treatment, participating in what had become a nearly U.S. $3 billion industry (Spar 2006:3). Tom and Hana spoke about how expensive reproductive care is in the United States, as did their clients. Tom said regarding America, "It is most expensive here. Insurance doesn't cover much of anything. I mean, some do, some don't. We've had women that their meds are covered, or partial IVF, little bits and pieces. The ones that have the flex plans have got it good." In addition to the sheer expense, Tom characterized the general experience with American infertility treatment as one that entails endless consumption. He paints a scenario:

> The bottom line is they knew going in, more than likely, is you're going to need IVF. But they end up nickel and diming you with these surgeries. They go to IUIs and all these little things that nickel and dime you and you don't have any money. And oh, fifteen thousand dollars, you've got to do IVF, that's the only way. Say you scrape the money and you do IVF. Well, now you're 38, 39 years old, it doesn't work. Well, you know what, you're getting kind of up there, your egg quality is not quite what it should be. Thirty thousand dollars, egg donor, and it's almost like they're in sales. Out of pure economics, the sky's the limit on that.

Unfortunately, according to Tom, there is no incentive for biomedical clinics in the United States to lower the cost of treatment:

> There are a lot of people out there that can't afford it. . . . Better than half the country. It is still out of their price range for that kind of money. You know as long as they've got 45,000 people that are getting it done and paying them fifteen to thirty thousand dollars, they're going to keep charging them. Even with the people going overseas, I don't think we're stealing patients from them. They're just getting the ones that would never even dream of going abroad. If money dictates whether you can conceive or not, or you spend so much money to conceive that now the kid's born and you lose your house because you've got nothing left. That's problematic.

The harsh economic reality of reproductive medicine in the United States, it seems, exiles many women and couples to seek treatment abroad.

The reproductive travelers who go to the Czech Republic have tried minimal procedures in the United States before traveling abroad. Kay, a client of IVF Holidays, said that she spent U.S. $28,000 in two years' time doing several different treatments for her infertility in the United States before she decided to go abroad. She and her husband had insurance, but it didn't cover infertility. For her, the main reason she traveled was cost. She said, in comparing the price of the United States and the Czech Republic, "Three failed cycles in Zlín have cost us roughly U.S. $18,000, while one failed cycle in St. Louis would have cost more than twice that amount." Joan, another client, said that her insurance would not cover any more after one trigger shot. She told me at that point they went right to the donor egg option. "Here [the United States], reproductive medicine is a business," she explained.

Tom and Hana can also be considered reproductive exiles (Matorras 2005), since they found the cost of fertility treatments to be prohibitive. They first went through fertility treatment in the Czech Republic. Hana is Czech, and Tom is American. As they were seeking treatment, they both had the idea of helping other couples. As I talked to them, they described how wonderful their personal relationships were with their clients. Their words minimized the entrepreneurial aspect of their company. Hana talked about their first time going through treatment, as they also hosted their first two clients. She said, "Once you see them over there, you just become more like a friend than a formal client, you know, business relationship." Tom said, "A lot of us share a lot of our personal information about ourselves, you know. So people feel more comfortable. We wanted to make it a little more personal, we didn't want it to be the big professional, because we want people to realize that we were just like they are." Tom and Hana avoid advertising their own cases of successful IVF treatment by having television networks like CNN and Fox interview their clients. At the top of their website, they write, "See the latest interview of one of our clients and their babies on CNN.com," and they provide a direct link to several news clips, ranging from MSNBC to mommy blogs that recount successful trips to the Czech Republic that resulted in babies. Those patient travelers who are willing to talk tend to share the details of their experiences continuously on the IVF Holidays website, on blogs, and with the media, as well as with the anthropologist. Thus, their stories are continuously recirculated.

In my conversations with Tom and Hana, as well as with the patient travelers, they often contrasted their experiences at the Clinic of Reproductive Medicine in Zlín to their experiences in the United States. Czech doctors were characterized as kind, patient, and not looking for money. Tom said the Czech doctors are "stunned that they can charge so much money in the United States for what they're doing, because it's minimally invasive. It's just stunning. I mean . . . 30,000 dollars for a donor cycle?" Despite the dismay of Czech doctors at the amounts of money American doctors make, Czech doctors are profiting from American patient travelers coming to their private clinics.

The patient travelers with whom I spoke viewed American medical practice as a business profiting from their hopes; their views of medicine shifted as they began to see themselves as consumers rather than patients (Becker 2000:129). In the case of patient travelers in the Czech Republic, they seemed to criticize the American medical system as commodified but praised the Czech system as gratuitous. However, the clinic in Zlín is still profiting from their business; they are simply keeping costs down because they can pay egg donors U.S. $800 as opposed to U.S. $5,000 to U.S. $10,000, the amount they receive in the United States.[2]

Czech doctors give patient travelers attentive care, and thus their emotions seem more authentic in contrast to the bureaucratic nature of medical treatment in the United States. One patient traveler, Kay, said about her care in the United States, "I never felt like a patient, just a checkbook. The treatment was never discussed with me, I was just told what to do and when that didn't work, there was no discussion of why, [I was] just told to write another check and come back for cycle day 2 monitoring." She said of the Czech doctor that he was "warm, friendly and truly interested in getting his patients pregnant." I argue the individualized, more affordable care that patient travelers receive directly from Czech doctors, and not just nurses, is interpreted as compassion.

TRANSLOCAL REPRODUCTIVE CLINICS

The Czech Republic has a large medical travel industry worth over U.S. $182,000,000 in 2006 (Warner 2009). The services of a number of reproductive clinics, counting twenty-three centers[3] (Donovan 2006), are advertised in Prague and surrounding provinces. Czech clinics seem to market especially for those who are seeking ova donation. Clinic websites advertise in English, German, Italian, and Russian, stressing the ready availability of student ova donors with only a three-month waiting period. The profitability of the Czech clinic is from the ready supply of Czech eggs for patient traveler consumption. The clinic has five hundred women on the books who are egg donors, according to the coordinator at the clinic, Lenka. Most of the egg donors are university students, while some are younger local women who have already had their own children. Patient travelers seek, as they do in the United States, relatively well-educated, blonde-haired, and blue-eyed donors, as well as women who have proven fertile by conceiving their own child. Tom and Hana work with a clinic in Zlín; however, they do not have a contract with the clinic. They repeatedly told me that they work for the patient traveler.

The clinic in Zlín is a manifestation of global biomedical technoculture, with similar clinical procedures and routines, roles, and technology as those found in the United States. The clinic is the same one Tom and Hana used when they went for fertility treatments, since it is close to Hana's natal home. The destination sites for fertility treatment usually have evolved through a combination of sophisticated medical infrastructure and expertise, particular regulatory frameworks (or the lack of them) that enable certain procedures, and lower-wage structures that allow reproductive technologies to be performed at competitive lower costs than in other countries. Good traveler infrastructures, such as hotels, government policies supportive of medical travel in general, the common use of English among medical providers, the availability of translators, religious affiliations, and ease of travel and visa requirements, all play important roles in determining which countries are popular destinations. Many point to the fact that, unlike its Catholic neighbors Slovakia and Poland, the Czech Republic is predominantly atheist, which allows loose regulatory frameworks regarding assisted reproductive technologies. The Czech government is quite liberal in terms of regulations, allowing egg, sperm, and embryo donation, all anonymous by law, and preimplantation genetic diagnosis (PGD) (Slepičková and Fučík 2009).

The advent of a market oriented toward relatively wealthy foreign patient travelers has encouraged the development of clinics with access to the latest technology and procedures and has created an incentive for IVF specialists to remain in these countries. However, it does encourage the brain drain from public hospitals into private clinics. The clinic in Zlín treats both Czech and foreign patients—who have separate schedules at the clinic—and the enforcement of regulatory standards seems to shift just slightly depending on the patient and the situation.[4] For Czechs, the tests to determine infertility are fully covered by national Czech health insurance (www.sanitoriumhelios.cz). It is estimated that 15 percent of Czech couples suffer infertility (Slepičková and Fučík 2009), and 7 to 10 percent of Czech babies are born via assisted reproduction. Three treatments of egg removal from ovaries, fertilized in a lab and transplanted back to the uterus, are all covered by Czech insurance, and a woman may receive up to three cycles if she is under the age of thirty-nine.

The clinic in Zlín has assisted couples in having over a thousand babies in the nine years since it opened in 2001. According to Tom, Americans who are even older than Czech patients have a higher success rate. Some attribute this to the way patient travelers are on "vacation" and are more relaxed. Tom said, "They do our patients a little differently than they do the Czech patients. People are flying halfway around the world to come over here, they're spending all this money, we need to do what we can to get their successes as best we can." Thus, even if Americans are saving money by traveling to the Czech Republic, their money privileges them above Czech patients who are receiving treatment covered by insurance. Their economic status becomes tied to personal rates of success.

Becker states that "new reproductive technologies are a global phenomenon characterized by hierarchical relations and power constellations" (Becker 2000:21). Medical travel intensifies the global stratification of reproduction (Ginsburg and Rapp 1995). Inequalities empower certain categories of people to reproduce and nurture but disempower others. In this case it may privilege the reproduction of elites across wealth and nations. Cross-border reproductive trade parallels the international divisions of hosts and guests within the travel trade.

The globalization of reproductive biotechnologies has created even newer tastes and desires, inciting desire for the bodies of "others" (though their difference is suppressed) (Cohen 2002). These inequalities are most intensely illustrated in a consideration of the marketing of bioavailability—the trade in poor women's bodies for ova donation (Heng 2006, 2007). Even the reproductive body parts—ova, sperm, and embryos—are stratified, marketed according to place of origin, the characteristics of their donors, and gender. The IVF Holidays website claims, "The doctors who interview the donors accept only intelligent and attractive donors." Patient travelers traveling to the Czech Republic are, according to Hana, seeking "white" babies from Czech egg or sperm donors. Hana characterized their general client: "Most clients are in need of donor eggs. I would say 85 percent of our clients are interested in the donor egg option. Most of the women are over 40, most of the women are looking for a blue-eyed, blonde-haired donor."

In terms of other reasons patients want to travel to the Czech Republic, as mentioned previously, egg and sperm donation are anonymous. Many patient travelers want to maintain anonymity. Tom said:

> Donor wise, women are happy that it's an anonymous donor. You don't want to have to worry about someone knocking on your door. They can feel comfortable being in the no-tell camp, knowing that the donor doesn't even know if there is a birth, and the only thing she knows about them is that they exist. They don't know where you're from, they don't know how old you are, you exist. There's a woman out there who wants your eggs, and that's all they know and that's all they ever know.

Sacrifice of the egg donor is invisible with anonymity. Services of reproductive clinics cater to buyers' desire to choose (Spar 2006:46). The fertility trade functions like medical trade in general; the people do not see themselves as participating in a commercial relationship, while fertility is emphatically a for-profit endeavor (Spar 2006:49).

DONOR EGGS

There is a class structure in the reproductive industry, in which individuals are ranked and considered appropriate for different reproductive tasks (Heng 2006, 2007; Tober 2002:157). The regional and global circulation of reproductive gametes (ova, sperm) brings stratification into sharp relief. Countries such as the Czech Republic trade on their ready supply of a bioavailable population of ova and gamete donors. Czech donors are "available for the selective disaggregation of one's cells or tissues and their reincorporation into another body" (Cohen 2005:83).

In June 2006, the Czech Republic passed Legislative Act No. 227/2006 Col., which governs sperm and egg donation. Under this legislation, donation is legal but must be voluntary, gratuitous, and anonymous. Donors cannot be paid, but are offered attractive "compensatory payments" for the discomfort involved in ovarian stimulation and egg retrieval. In a region where the average monthly salary is U.S. $1,085, these young women receive U.S. $800 per egg donation. So we return to the question: Is the egg a gift, a commodity, a scarce commodity, or a commodity of last resort? Scholars and lay people have wondered if it is ethical for a woman to be paid for her eggs. Those who claim that a woman should not be paid for her eggs are attempting to frame egg donation in altruistic terms. However, Almeling (2007) writes that egg and sperm donation is not as altruistic as blood or organ donation because the donors do receive financial compensation.

While bioethicists wholeheartedly support the purchasing power and consumer choice of reproductive travelers, the question remains: How much individual autonomy and choice do the egg donors have? Tom anticipated a common response when I asked how much Czech donors are paid: "People say that is just not that much and they get so much here. Well, when you consider the fact that if you're working in a shop, like a grocery, you're going to make 250 or 300 dollars a month. So it's roughly three months' wages for a girl." Lenka said that none of the donors talked about it as a gift; they were only interested in the money. While critics tend to denounce financial motivations of egg donors, students tend to have a bit more leeway when they are financially motivated (Almeling 2006:153). As is the case with sperm donation, the clinic advertises for egg donors in Zlín, with many recruited from the local university. Tom claims:

> A lot of these girls get accepted into college, they get married, they get pregnant, and then while they're going to school, grandma watches the kids [because they all live in an extended family]. She can go to school to better her life still, school is free, she's getting paid, so she can concentrate on her

studies, and then she donates eggs on the side. She's an approved donor because she has a healthy child, she can donate up to three times . . . I mean, that's nine months' salary just for doing egg donation while she's going to school for extra money. Plus, insurance is free.

He fails to problematize their class position within an international travel framework. Is selling their eggs a mode of empowerment, or is it a sacrifice disguised by the language of altruism? The language of gift disguises the sacrifice of egg donors, rendered even more invisible with the anonymity of gamete donation. The dichotomy between gift and commodity is collapsed when discussing sperm and egg donation (Tober 2002). Scheper-Hughes (2000:192) writes that the global market for organs, similar to the global market for gametes, blends altruism and choice, magic and science, gift and barter.

If we consider the market of eggs, the clinic in Zlín has many more donors than it needs. Lenka claims that they categorize donors as A, B, or C, and, "A is perfect, pass, more than average, B is average, and C is not very good . . . and because we have so many donors, we really do not have a need. They are in the database. We have some C's, but I do not have a need to call her because I still have enough A's and B's." She has donors calling all the time to see if they can be used. As in the case of North America, there is an "oversupply of women willing to be egg donors . . . far outstripping recipient demand. Despite this abundance, egg donor fees hold steady and are often calibrated by staff perceptions of a woman's characteristics and a recipient's wealth" (Almeling 2007:336).

Another way to frame egg donation is to ask how similar and dissimilar it is to sperm donation. Tober (2002) claims sperm donors are sex workers, in a sense, while I find this to be a stretch. I prefer Almeling's (2007:324) label of "reproductive service workers." Eggs are more controversial than sperm, there is greater complication in finding donors, and the long-term implications for donors are not known (Spar 2006:41–43). Since eggs are a limited supply and it is more difficult to donate eggs, we can say, "Eggs are a scarce resource compared to sperm, and thus women's donation of eggs will be more highly valued than men's donation of sperm" (Almeling 2007:323). Furthermore, since it is a riskier endeavor, egg donors are compensated with more money than sperm donors. "Egg donation has features that make it more exploitative than sperm donation . . . at U.S. $2,000 per donation, ova donors are more subject to outright economic coercion than are sperm donors" (Kimbrell 1993:86–87). The market of eggs obviously parallels the market of sperm (Almeling 2007:320). However, Almeling (2007:320) shows how eggs are also more highly valued because of "economic definitions of scarcity and gendered cultural norms of motherhood and fatherhood." Almeling (2007:328) writes, "Women are perceived as more closely connected to their eggs than men are to their sperm." According to Almeling, gametes are gendered, and eggs are more highly valued since they contribute to the motherhood project.

We also see an international market structure that determines different valuations depending on the regional context of the reproductive medical industry. Thus, we must complicate the issue of "choice" of Czech egg donors, as we did for reproductive travelers. Although egg donors are university students, not living in below-poverty conditions, their "choice" is not unproblematic. They are embedded within socioeconomic and political constraints of the international market. The valuation of their eggs reflects the stratification of reproduction reflecting global inequalities when it comes to differential values of body parts.

We need to problematize the commodification of health care and body parts on a global scale, as we complicate the consumer and seller choices made by patient travelers and egg donors. Although Czech egg donors may not legally be monetarily compensated, they are given money for their "time," blurring the distinction between profit and altruistic motivation. Egg donors are seeking the financial rewards of egg donation. Lenka bluntly said to me, "I never met a donor who would do that from my point of view from just altruistic reasons. It is all about money, and they are not as sensitive as I should say they should be . . . they just ask when they get the money and that's why I don't think that they really realize what they are doing."

CONCLUSION

The expansion of the market in reproductive services in the Czech Republic has provided opportunities for many international couples to access treatments and produce families—opportunities often denied to them by the costly treatment options in the United States. The challenge as anthropologists is to study the advent of global reproductive travel with compassion and respect, while casting a critical eye over the political economy of the trade and the relations of power it entails. This research reveals how medical travel complicates the "compulsion" to try for couples or women regarding their infertility, rather than simply democratizing access to treatment.

The expansion of reproductive travel possibilities has created new demands and invented needs for the reproductive capacities and genetic body products of women and men from these sites. Unable to acquire treatment in their home countries, patients use the health systems and trained medical staff of less developed countries to do so. Throughout these transactions is the division between those able to reproduce and

Amy Speier

those who cannot, and those who have the money to reproduce and those who do not. Divisions based on race, "whiteness," class, and wealth are the culture medium supporting the growth of global in-vitro babies. Even choices of clinic, ova, and sperm donors and embryos carry considerations of race, "whiteness," sex, class, and eugenic potential as market forces cull undesirable qualities.

NOTES

1. Insurance coverage for fertility treatment varies state by state. Five states are mandated, in that insurance companies must provide coverage for IVF cycles. All states have at least one company that has some form of coverage. However, it varies greatly.

2. The Society for Assisted Reproductive Technologies has stated that egg donors may be paid $5,000 to $10,000, but any amount more than $5,000 must be explained, and sums over $10,000 are not appropriate (Egg Donation, Inc. 2011).

3. Since the time of conducting this research, at the time of writing this chapter, there are now thirty centers of assisted reproduction in the Czech Republic. This reveals the extent to which a country with a population of ten million has a fiercely competitive field of reproductive medicine, increasingly vying for foreign patients.

4. Surrogacy is a shady topic, since it involves egg donation. Czech law stipulates that the woman who gives birth is the mother, and then the intended parent must adopt the child. The clinic in Zlín is beginning to help Czech couples with surrogacy but will not help foreign patients, although I think there may be some room to negotiate.

REFERENCES

Almeling, Rene. 2006. Why Do You Want to Be a Donor? Gender and Production of Altruism in Egg and Sperm Donation. *New Genetics and Society* 25(2):143–57.
———. 2007. Selling Genes, Selling Gender: Egg Agencies, Sperm Banks, and the Medical Market in Genetic Materials. *American Sociological Review* 72(3):319–40.
Appadurai, Arjun. 1996. *Modernity at Large: Cultural Dimensions of Globalization.* Minneapolis: University of Minnesota Press.
Becker, Gay. 2000. *Elusive Embryo: How Women and Men Approach NRTs.* Berkeley: University of California Press.
Bonaccorso, Mona. 2005. Programmes of Gamete Donation: Strategies in (Private) Clinics of Assisted Conception. In *Reproductive Agency, Medicine and the State: Cultural Transformations in Childbearing*, ed. Maya Unnithan-Kumar, pp. 83–102. New York: Berghahn Books.
Cohen, Lawrence. 2002. The Other Kidney: Biopolitics beyond Recognition. In *Commodifying Bodies*, eds. Nancy Scheper-Hughes and Loic J. D. Wacant, pp. 9–30. London: Sage.

————. 2005. Operability, Bioavailability, and Exception. In *Global Assemblages: Technology, Politics, and Ethics as Anthropological Problems*, eds. Aihwa Ong and Stephen Collier, pp. 79–90. Malden, MA: Blackwell.

Connell, John. 2006. Medical Tourism: Sea, Sun, Sand and . . . Surgery. *Tourism Management* 27(6):1093–1100.

Donovan, Jana. 2006. Childless Couples Flock to CR for help. www.praguepost .com/articles/2006/12/20/childless-couples-flock-to-cr-for-help.php, accessed November 21, 2011.

Egg Donation, Inc. 2011. Recipient: Frequently Asked Questions. www.eggdonor .com/?section=recipient&page=rfaq, accessed November 21, 2011.

Franklin, Sarah. 1997. *Embodied Progress: A Cultural Account of Assisted Conception*. London: Routledge.

Ginsburg, Faye, and Rayna Rapp. 1995. Introduction. In *Conceiving the New World Order: The Global Politics of Reproduction*, eds. Faye Ginsburg and Rayna Rapp, pp. 1–17. Berkeley: University of California Press.

Heng, Boon Chin. 2006. "Reproductive Tourism": Should Locally Registered Fertility Doctors Be Held Accountable for Channeling Patients to Foreign Medical Establishments? *Human Reproduction* 21(3):840–42.

————. 2007. Regulatory Safeguards Needed for the Traveling Foreign Egg Donor. *Human Reproduction* 22(8):2350–52.

Inhorn, Marcia. 2004. Privacy, Privatization, and the Politics of Patronage: Ethnographic Challenges to Penetrating the Secret World of Middle Eastern, Hospital-Based In Vitro Fertilization. *Social Science and Medicine* 59(10):2095–2108.

Inhorn, Marcia C., and Pasquale Patrizio. 2009. Rethinking Reproductive "Tourism" as Reproductive "Exile." *Fertility and Sterility* 92(3):904–6.

Janzen, John M. 1978. *The Quest for Therapy: Medical Pluralism in Lower Zaire*. Berkeley: University of California Press.

Jones, C. A., and L. G. Keith. 2006. Medical Tourism and Reproductive Outsourcing: The Dawning of a New Paradigm for Healthcare. *International Journal of Fertility and Women's Medicine* 51(6):251–55.

Kimbrell, Andrew. 1993. *The Human Body Shop: The Engineering and Marketing of Life*. San Francisco: Harper.

Lock, Margaret. 2001. The Alienation of Body Tissue and the Biopolitics of Immortalized Cell Lines. *Body and Society* 7(2–3):63–91.

Matorras, Roberto. 2005. Reproductive Exile versus Reproductive Tourism. *Human Reproduction* 20(12):3571.

Mauss, Marcel. 1922. *The Gift: Forms and Functions of Exchange in Archaic Societies*. London: Routledge.

McLean, Thomas, and Patrick McLean. 2007. Is a Black Market in Telemedicine on the Horizon? *International Journal of Medical Robotics and Computer Assisted Surgery* 3(4):291–96.

Pennings, Guido. 2005. Reply: Reproductive Exile versus Reproductive Tourism. *Human Reproduction* 20(12):3571–72.

Sandelowski, Margarete. 1991. Compelled to Try: The Never Enough Quality of Conceptive Technology. *Medical Anthropology Quarterly* 5(1):29–47.

Scheper-Hughes, Nancy. 2000. The Global Trafficking in Human Organs. *Current Anthropology* 41(2):191–210.

———. 2002. Bodies for Sale—Whole or in Parts. In *Commodifying Bodies*, eds. Nancy Scheper-Hughes and J. D. Wacquant, pp. 1–8. London: Sage.

Senate Committee on Aging. 2006. *The Globalization of Health Care: Can Medical Tourism Reduce Health Care Costs?* Washington, DC: U.S. Government Printing Office.

Slepičková, Lenka, and Petr Fučík. 2009. The Social Context of Attitudes toward Various Infertility Strategies. *Czech Sociological Review* 45(2):267–91.

Spar, Debora L. 2006. *The Baby Business: How Money, Science, and Politics Drive the Commerce of Conception.* Boston: Harvard Business School Press.

Taussig, Michael. 1987. *Shamanism, Colonialism and the Wild Man: A Study in Terror and Healing.* Chicago: University of Chicago Press.

Tober, Diane. 2002. Semen as Gifts, Semen as Goods. In *Commodifying Bodies*, eds. Nancy Scheper-Hughes and J. D. Wacquant, pp. 137–60. London: Sage.

Turner, Leigh. 2007. Medical Tourism: Family Medicine and International Health-Related Travel. *Canadian Family Physician* 53(10):1639–41.

Warner, David. 2009. *Trends and Drivers of Trade in Health Services.* Paper presented at the WHO Workshop on the Movement of Patients across International Borders: Emerging Challenges and Opportunities for Health Care Systems, Kobe, Japan, February 24–25.

Whittaker, Andrea, and Amy Speier. 2010. "Cycling Overseas": Care, Commodification, and Stratification in Cross-Border Reproductive Travel. *Medical Anthropology* 29(4):363–83.

12

+

The Uses of Ecotourism

Articulating Conservation and
Development Agendas in Belize

Laurie Kroshus Medina

The concept of ecotourism has shouldered a heavy burden of expectations since its emergence. Within the field of tourism studies, ecotourism has been hailed as a form of development that sustains the natural resource base upon which it depends, a means of increasing social justice and economic equality across the globe, and a tool for inciting and enabling conservation commitments in both tourists and tourees. Much of the literature on ecotourism has focused on normative arguments about how to define the concept and prescriptive arguments about how to implement it. Extensive literatures in the specialized *Journal of Ecotourism* and *Journal of Sustainable Development* and the broader *Annals of Tourism Research* diagnose the relative success or failure of ecotourism projects in meeting environmental, economic, or social objectives; some studies identify best practices, while others identify problems that complicate earlier prescriptions for ecotourism and offer refinements to those prescriptions. In addition, scholars have focused on preventing the appropriation of the ecotourism concept for "greenwashing" through the refinement of certification procedures and programs that entail the validation and enforcement of particular definitions of ecotourism (Font and Buckley 2001; Font and Harris 2004; Honey 2002; Jamal et al. 2006; Medina 2005). Beyond the academy, organizations such as The Ecotourism Society were established precisely for the purpose of shaping the definition and implementation of ecotourism according to principles of environmental and social justice and sustainability.

Definitions of ecotourism emerged in large numbers in the early 1990s, becoming more rigorous and more oriented toward environmental and social justice principles as the decade progressed (Fennell 2005; see also Bjork 2007; Diamantis 1999). By 2007, in an assessment of the state of the field, Weaver and Lawton suggested that scholars had reached "near-consensus" on three core criteria for ecotourism: (1) attractions should be nature-based, (2) visitor experiences should focus on learning or education, and (3) products should be sustainable in ecological, sociocultural, and economic terms (Weaver and Lawton 2007:1170; see also Blamey 1997, 2001). However, Weaver and Lawton note that "each criterion . . . leaves ample room for interpretation, giving rise to ongoing deliberations about the appropriate parameters of each"; thus, despite the emergence of "something resembling a consensus" on criteria for ecotourism, scholars have not settled on a single definition (Weaver and Lawton 2007:1170). Hunt and Stronza (2009) express concern that this lack of agreement regarding a definition for ecotourism may limit the impact of the field of ecotourism studies on the practice of ecotourism.

Efforts to strengthen the academic field of ecotourism studies in order to shape the practice of ecotourism constitute a particular problematic of ecotourism that structures the questions asked and the knowledge produced regarding ecotourism. Within this problematic, principles and definitions generate guidelines for practice; in turn, the practice of ecotourism becomes the target of assessment, which often leads to refinements of definitions and principles (figure 12.1).[1] As Ferguson notes, a dominant problematic is often only challenged in its own terms; the object at the center of the problematic is measured against its own standards (Ferguson 1994:xiv). Thus, for example, challenges to or critiques of specific definitions or practices of ecotourism have not led scholars in the field to jettison the concept; instead, such critiques have prompted efforts to refine both knowledge and technique to further specify the content and delimit the boundaries of what should legitimately count as ecotourism.

In this chapter, rather than working within the ecotourism problematic to advocate for, critique, or refine a particular definition of ecotourism, I step outside that problematic to explore how efforts to generate and impose universally shared norms and definitions for ecotourism become articulated with the pursuit of other agendas.[2] I examine how groups of social actors in Belize have deployed particular definitions of ecotourism to advance particular—socially and historically situated—agendas, and whether or how these definitions of ecotourism have worked for them. In asking how particular definitions of ecotourism have "worked," I refer

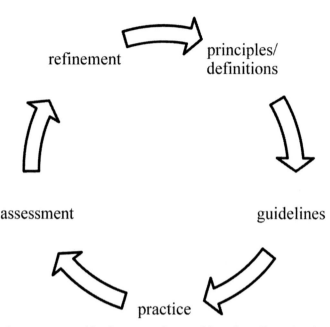

Figure 12.1. Inside the Ecotourism Problematic. (Illustration by Laurie Kroshus Medina)

not to the goals set by scholars and NGOs who seek to shape its definition and implementation, the goals at the center of the ecotourism problematic, but rather to the ways actors have used the concept to secure their own, perhaps quite divergent, objectives. In his analysis of "development" as a problematic, Ferguson notes that, while development interventions may fail to deliver what they have promised, they "nonetheless have regular effects"; "What is most important about a 'development' project," he argues, "is not so much what it fails to do but what it does do" (Ferguson 1994:xv, 254). Applying this logic (see also Foucault 1979), I explore the effects produced through actors' deployment of the concept of ecotourism in Belize. What definitions of ecotourism have been advanced by those who use the term in Belize? What did these actors seek to accomplish by invoking particular definitions of ecotourism? How have these definitions been articulated with other agendas? What outcomes have been enabled by the use of this concept?

In addition to distinguishing between scholarly work performed within and outside of the ecotourism problematic, this chapter engages a related tension in scholarly analysis between efforts to secure recognition for concepts and definitions as "universals" and the context-specific contingencies through which such concepts are deployed and through which they produce effects. Tsing reminds us that claims to universality are only *claims*; purported universals can only be put into play through "sticky engagements" in specific locales (Tsing 2004:6). "In overcoming the parochialism of the case study," Tsing warns, theory may "overreach" by depicting each local situation as "nothing more than" an exemplification of larger processes, of universals (Tsing 2004:206). Though much of the power of theory derives from its ability to discern the larger processes at work in specific cases, the danger inherent in portraying any case as an instantiation of larger processes is that the particularity of the conjuncture is not fully realized (Mitchell 2002). Thus, I interrogate the "contingent articulations" (Tsing 2004:77) through which particular versions of ecotourism are brought into being by particular social actors at particular historical conjunctures in this study of Belize. In so doing, this study reveals that these local articulations do intersect in important ways with debates taking place within the ecotourism problematic at a global scale. Local struggles around conservation, development, and indigenous community empowerment shape and are shaped by the ecotourism problematic, though they are in no way determined by emerging points of consensus among ecotourism scholars and advocates.

This chapter draws from research conducted between 1997 and 2009, which involved both archival research and interviews with staff from departments and ministries of the Belizean state with responsibilities for facilitating tourism development or managing natural resources, personnel from Belizean and transnational conservation NGOs engaged in implementing conservation and ecotourism initiatives, and residents of three Maya communities in southern Belize involved in three different ecotourism initiatives.[3]

ECOTOURISM IN THE AGENDAS OF CONSERVATION NGOS

Conservation NGOs, both Belizean and transnational, were early and enthusiastic promoters of ecotourism in Belize. Their interest in ecotourism derived from their prioritization of biodiversity conservation through the creation of protected areas. Leaders of the nation's oldest and largest conservation NGO, the Belize Audubon Society (BAS), had lobbied the Belizean state to designate parks and protected areas in critical wildlife habitats and locations with special scenic value since the 1960s. As the concept of ecotourism emerged during the latter 1980s, the Belize Audubon Society and its transnational NGO allies embraced the concept as a means to persuade the government to designate the protected areas they sought.

Ecotourism emerged to play this role at a time when habitat destruction and species extinctions were accelerating at an alarming rate (Takacs 1996), and scientists were sounding alarms about global climate change. Escalating threats to biodiversity stimulated environmentalists' efforts to expand the network of protected areas around the world; indeed, more protected areas were created during the period from 1985 to 1995 than at any other time in history (Brockington et al. 2008:1, 38). Tropical forests of the global South attracted the concern of environmentalists from across the world for their significant biodiversity and their capacity as carbon sinks (Slater 2003). As concern for the global environment grew, leaders seeking to reconcile development aspirations with environmental concerns advocated for "sustainable development." Ecotourism emerged at this juncture as a form of integrated conservation and development project. If ecotourism was cast as a form of environmentally sustainable development, it was also promoted as a means of making conservation economically sustainable. For during this same time period, neoliberal political-economic reforms were being imposed on indebted states across the global South through structural adjustment packages, which decreased the ability of those states to regulate nature or pay for environmental protection (Medina 2010; Brockington et al. 2008). Tropical forests came under increased pressure, as debt-ridden countries sought to convert forests to agriculture in order to maximize economic returns. At this confluence of extinction and debt crises, environmentalists embraced ecotourism as a means to fund biodiversity conservation by tapping markets for nature rather than state coffers. If states could not pay for protected areas' management, entrance fees paid by ecotourists who visited those protected areas would cover the costs of their management. Ecotourism advocates also emphasized the potential of ecotourism to generate economic development and earn foreign exchange, addressing two issues of great significance to governments of developing countries confronting debt crises.

As the BAS and its transnational allies—including the Wildlife Conservation Society, the World Wildlife Fund, and several U.S. Audubon chapters—lobbied the Belizean government to declare protected areas in habitats critical to biodiversity conservation, they emphasized the tourism potential of such protected areas. Designating protected areas in Belize's tropical forests, wetlands, and barrier reef, they argued, would effectively position Belize to tap rapidly expanding markets for tropical nature in the global North. Thus, conservation NGOs defined ecotourism specifically as travel to protected areas, driven by tourists' appreciation for and desire to see rare or endangered species and ecosystems. Conservationists argued that the designation of protected areas would highlight for potential tourists both the quality of Belizean nature and the nation's commitment to safeguarding its natural heritage.

ECOTOURISM IN STATE AGENDAS

When Belizean nationalists attained self-government in 1964, they took control of a national territory in which only 5 percent of the lands with high agricultural potential were under cultivation; the remainder was forested (Dobson 1973:273).[4] Prioritizing economic development, the new Belizean government pursued a development strategy based on the production of agricultural exports. The government distributed state-owned forested lands to investors who would convert those lands to agricultural production; it also acquired forested lands from foreign owners and distributed them to farmers for the production of export crops (Bolland and Shoman 1977). Sugar became the country's dominant agricultural export and foreign-exchange earner. In addition, a fishing industry exported lobster, and a tiny tourism sector emerged, based almost exclusively on the country's largest caye and its proximity to the Belizean barrier reef, the second longest in the world. Tourism had developed with virtually no government support, either in the form of promotion or the provision of infrastructure, as the government was wary of the neocolonial potential of tourism (Barry 1995:52).

However, in the early 1980s, just as Belize achieved full independence, international sugar prices slumped. Foreign exchange earnings plummeted, and the Belizean state confronted a debt crisis. In exchange for assistance, the IMF imposed a structural adjustment package—demanding a reduction in state budgets, diversification of the Belizean economy, and efforts to increase the country's foreign exchange earnings—required to pay its debts. In response, the state encouraged the expansion of nonsugar agricultural exports, again providing state land to small- and large-scale farmers who would clear its forest cover to produce citrus and bananas. Consequently, forest clearance in Belize doubled or tripled during the 1980s (King et al. 1993).

Despite the state's previous disregard for tourism, the debt crisis also prompted the state to reconsider tourism as an option for diversifying and expanding the national economy. Warming to tourism, in 1982 the government created the Belize Tourism Board (BTB) and assigned to it two tasks: to expand the industry geographically beyond the largest caye in order to provide development opportunities and income to other regions of the country and to develop a Belizean "brand" to market the country as a destination (Government Information Service 1982). As the government weighed the prospects for tourism development in Belize, the emerging concept of ecotourism proved attractive on several grounds. Despite the acceleration of forest-to-agriculture conversion during the 1980s, the Forestry Department estimated that 70 percent of Belizean lands remained under forest cover (Jacobs and Castañeda 1998:v).[5] These lands comprised part of the largest contiguous forested area north of the Amazon Basin, stretching across the boundaries of Belize, Guatemala, and Mexico (Wildlife Conservation Society 2011). Though for two decades the Belizean state had promoted the conversion of forested lands to export agriculture as its primary development strategy, conservation NGOs argued that the creation of protected areas in Belizean forests and wetlands could prove more lucrative than their conversion to agriculture. Protected areas would attract a rapidly expanding market for tropical nature and rare species in the global North. Drawing on knowledge produced by scholars and advocates of ecotourism as well as their own experiences, conservationists portrayed ecotourists as a growing, high-value market segment comprising discerning consumers committed to conservation and ethical consumption. The new ecotourists were highly educated urban professionals, relatively more affluent than mass tourists and willing to stay longer and pay more than mass tourists for high-quality experiences (for an overview of these arguments, see Wight 2001). Thus, conservationists asserted that protecting forests and wetlands could dramatically increase tourist numbers and tourism revenues, expand and diversify the national economy, and increase foreign-exchange earnings. Ecotourism to inland protected areas in forests and wetlands would also accomplish the government's goals of extending the benefits of tourism more widely across the country. At the same time, terrestrial protected areas would differentiate the Belizean ecotourism product from the tourism products of more established competitors in the Caribbean: while promoting tourism to its cayes and coral reef would place Belize in direct competition with the rest of the Caribbean, combining these assets with inland rain forests and wetlands would set Belize apart as a uniquely rich and diverse destination (Government Information Service 1973). Ecotourism would also require less expenditure on infrastructure than mass tourism. Though the Belizean government lacked funds to launch a project similar to the Mexican state's creation of Cancun, the predicted growth of ecotourists as a market segment raised the possibility that the extremely rudimentary condition of Belize's tourism infrastructure could become an asset rather than a liability, an indicator of Belizean commitment to low-impact, sustainable tourism. Perhaps Belize could be promoted as the anti-Cancun.

By the early 1990s, the expansion of the tourism sector became an even more attractive option. Belizean agricultural exports had all benefitted from the provision of preferential access to protected markets in the United States and Europe, on the basis of Cold War geopolitical calculations (Medina 2004). Aggressive trade liberalization following the end of the Cold War eroded Belizean trade preferences, and Belizean agro-export production was revealed to be relatively inefficient and uncompetitive (Medina 1998). Uncertain how far trade liberalization would go or how long Belizean agro-exports would remain viable, the Belizean state sought to identify and promote products that Belize could produce competitively. Conservationists asserted that tropical nature was such a product.

In order to tap what conservationists and ecotourism advocates described as an expanding ecotourism market, the state worked to "brand" Belize as a place endowed with—and committed to the protection of—abundant biodiversity and natural beauty. Responding to the arguments of conservation NGOs, the state made the official designation of protected areas central to the Belizean brand, extending protected status to more than one-third of the country's total territory, declaring several marine reserves, and winning recognition for the Belizean barrier reef as a UNESCO World Heritage Site. Marketing efforts by the BTB and the new private-sector Belize Tourism Industry Association (BTIA) emphasized this extensive protected areas network. Casting Belize as "Mother Nature's Best-Kept Secret," they represented the country as an ecotourism destination that was "green" in every sense of the word, from its spectacular natural endowments, to the state's active protection of those endowments, to the "rustic and simple" condition of Belize's tourism infrastructure—"perhaps lacking in sophistication but certainly not in charm" (Belize Tourism Board 1993:46). Clearly influenced by conservationists, the Belizean state deployed a definition of ecotourism that focused primarily on travel to protected areas and secondarily emphasized its small scale and low environmental impact, as evidence of authenticity and sustainability for a market segment said to value these qualities.

These marketing efforts largely achieved state goals. During the 1960s, tourist arrivals averaged around eleven thousand annually, rising to an annual average of thirty thousand during the 1970s, and reaching sixty-four thousand by 1980 (Barry 1992:50). But tourist arrivals climbed sharply once the BTB launched its first marketing campaign, more than doubling between 1985 and 1990, when tourist arrivals exceeded 207,000 (King et al. 1993:87–88). Tourism became the largest contributor to gross domestic product (GDP), accounting for nearly 16 percent of GDP in 2005. Between 2006 and 2008, overnight tourist arrivals consistently surpassed 230,000 (Belize Tourism Board 2008; Richardson 2007:27). Thus, ecotourism had enabled the government to meet its goals of diversifying and expanding the national economy, generating foreign exchange, and incorporating new regions of the country into the Belizean tourism product and the development opportunities therein.

However, despite placing such a significant amount of its land and sea territory under state protection, the debt-burdened Belizean state was unable to enforce the restrictions on farming, hunting, fishing, and collecting that accompanied protected areas conservation. The state allocated most management responsibilities for protected areas to the BAS or newer Belizean conservation NGOs; however, these conservation NGOs also lacked resources to manage the protected areas. Northern conservation NGOs provided grants to Belizean NGOs to fund the start-up costs of ecotourism, including building tourism infrastructure (trails, visitor centers, and accommodations) and hiring and training park staff (Medina 2010). Subsequently, protected area entrance fees and a conservation tax levied on tourists were projected to fund the long-term management of protected areas.

During the time period in which it established protected areas and began to market Belize as an ecotourism destination, the state's overriding priorities were to expand and diversify the national economy and increase foreign exchange earnings. The primary goal of conservation NGOs from within and outside Belize was biodiversity conservation, through the creation of protected areas. By presenting ecotourism as a means to accomplish the state's primary goals, conservation NGOs persuaded government policymakers that ecotourism provided a promising market niche for a country with so much forest and so little infrastructure. Further, by defining ecotourism specifically in terms of travel to protected areas, conservationists positioned protected areas as the foundation for a competitive ecotourism product. However, the state had only to designate protected areas; subsequently, northern NGOs would fund ecotourism infrastructure in the parks, and international markets for nature would generate revenues to manage and maintain them. If wildlife sanctuaries and marine reserves were required to attract the rapidly expanding market segment represented by ecotourists, the state was persuaded to create such protected areas and market itself accordingly. Thus, the definition of ecotourism as tourism to protected areas enabled the articulation of conservation agendas as state development goals, even in the context of a debt crisis and structural adjustment, and the creation of terrestrial and marine-protected areas became a crucial element of the state's branding of Belize as an ecotourism destination.

However, highlighting the state's prioritization of economic diversification and expansion, not sustainable tourism per se, the state also began to court cruise lines, attempting to tap into another segment of the tourism market. Significantly, this segment could also be tapped with relatively little state expenditure on infrastructure because cruise lines themselves, in partnership with local entrepreneurs, were willing to pay for the development of infrastructure such as port facilities to accommodate cruise passengers, as long as they could control access to that infrastructure. Cruise tourism grew from 0.2 percent of total tourism in 1988 to account for 72 percent of total tourist arrivals in 2008 (Belize Tourism Board 1998, 2008). The tensions between a strategy based on ecotourism and one based on cruise tourism are obvious and unresolved. The state's decision to pursue both types of tourism underlines the priority of its economic goals and suggests that protected areas must generate tourism revenues in order to maintain government support.

ASPIRATIONS FOR ECOTOURISM IN THREE RURAL COMMUNITIES

Residents of the three communities included in this study shared fundamental priorities: meeting their subsistence needs and generating cash income to invest in education for their children and access to health care and consumer goods. Two of the communities sought to use ecotourism to generate cash incomes that would augment their subsistence production, while one sought cash incomes to replace subsistence production, which had been curtailed by the imposition of a protected area.

Maya Centre

Lobbying by allied Belizean and U.S. conservation NGOs persuaded the state to establish the Cockscomb Basin Wildlife Sanctuary (CBWS) in 1986 in order to protect the significant jaguar population that roamed the forests of the Cockscomb Basin in southern Belize (Rabinowitz 2000). Residents of Quam Bank, a largely Mopan Maya village of 112 people located within the Cockscomb Basin, were expelled at the reserve's creation (Medina n.d.). Many relocated to Maya Centre, one of several villages located near the eastern perimeter of the sanctuary, doubling that community's population. Though other villages around the sanctuary's perimeter also lost some access to resources, Quam Bank and Maya Centre were the communities most affected by the imposition of the sanctuary. Maya Centre, a predominantly Mopan Maya community, is hemmed in by citrus and banana plantations on the uplands to its north, west, and south. Prior to creation of the sanctuary, village residents had depended upon the Cockscomb Basin, which lay to the west of these plantations, for hunting, collecting housing materials, and access to well-drained soils on which to cultivate subsistence crops. Though the village was granted land to the east on the coastal plain, this land was too poorly drained for the production of subsistence crops. Thus, the imposition of the CBWS prevented villagers from practicing subsistence activities such as the cultivation of staple crops, hunting, fishing, and the collection of foods and construction materials from the forest. Not surprisingly, villagers in Maya Centre opposed the CBWS, and some advocated for reclaiming the Cockscomb Basin for subsistence purposes.

The BTB's marketing campaign transformed the CBWS into the country's flagship inland park, the only jaguar sanctuary in the world. Within a decade, many small upscale resorts, most owned by North American expatriates, sprang up on the coast nearby. These resorts offered reef and rain forest packages, as conservation NGOs had predicted, with the jaguar reserve representing the rain forest portion of their packages. As tourism to the southern coast of Belize grew, so did tourist traffic to the reserve, increasing from 256 visitors in 1986 to more than four thousand per year by the 1990s and as many as nine or ten thousand per year between 2003 and 2007 (Belize Tourism Board 2006; Emmons et al. 1996:24).

Maya Centre villagers struggled to insert themselves into the CBWS ecotourism product (Medina n.d.), alternately challenging and cooperating with the Belize Audubon Society, which had been assigned responsibility for managing the sanctuary by the Belizean state. Villagers' activism on their own behalf coincided in time with global conversations among conservation NGOs regarding "people and parks," which generated revised approaches to protected areas management that explicitly sought to increase local support for protected areas (Brandon 1993; Wells and Brandon 1992; West and Brechin 1991; Western and Wright 1994). As a result, social justice dimensions of ecotourism definitions, emphasizing the provision of benefits to local communities, gained increasing acceptance between the early and mid-1990s (Fennel 2005). Indeed, the community of Maya Centre was the subject of a 1993 study sponsored by the World Wildlife Fund, which formed part of that global conversation. Study results demonstrated that economic benefits from ecotourism had increased community support for the protected area; income for members of the women's craft cooperative averaged U.S. $1,168 per family for the year ending in March 1993. The study points out that this number "compares favorably" with the average per capita GDP in Belize of U.S. $1,562, "especially as this is a rural area with otherwise below average income-generating opportunities" (Lindberg and Enriquez 1994:63). The World Wildlife Fund used the study results to shape international criteria for ecotourism, bolstering arguments that ecotourism should serve as a tool to enable communities near protected areas to benefit from the creation of protected areas in order to win their support for conservation. Residents of Maya Centre used the study results to press the BAS to agree to strategies to increase the economic benefits they derived from tourism by deepening their integration into upscale ecotourism in southern Belize, in order to sustain or increase their support for the reserve (Medina n.d.). Maya Centre residents thus came to deploy definitions of ecotourism that emphasized the need for local communities to benefit from conservation-

related tourism as a form of compensation for the loss of access to resources caused by the creation of protected areas.

Though the BAS had not initially envisioned ecotourism in those terms,
the NGO arrived at a revised version of ecotourism as a result of its negotiations with Maya Centre residents and its participation in debates
within the ecotourism problematic itself regarding how to resolve the
tensions between rural communities and protected areas. BAS staff attended international conferences, where they listened to presentations by
other conservation organizations regarding the importance of enabling
protected areas to generate benefits for rural people whose lives and live-
lihoods were disrupted by their creation. They incorporated these ideas
into their own dealings with Maya villages in Belize and later contributed
their own stories and strategies to subsequent international conferences
that debated how the relationships between protected areas and rural
communities should be structured. Thus, both Maya Centre residents and
the BAS participated in the global debates that legitimized social justice
dimensions of ecotourism. The resulting refinements to definitions of ecotourism, which featured the participation of communities near protected
areas in the tourism product and the accrual of economic benefits to these
communities, enabled villagers and the BAS to articulate their development and conservation agendas locally.

Eventually, all households in Maya Centre came to earn income
through tourism, though in different amounts according to the resources
they were able to invest and their members' relative facility with English.
Families with more economic resources and greater English language facility launched guesthouse, taxi, or tour-guiding businesses, while those
with fewer economic or linguistic resources produced crafts for sale,
worked as porters for tourists on longer treks into the reserve, or sought
jobs at the upscale ecotourism lodges on the coast. Most tourists to the
CBWS did not stay in the village or use local taxi services or guiding;
instead, they arrived on day trips from upscale coastal lodges. However,
through negotiation with the BAS, the women's craft cooperative gained
responsibility for the CBWS guest register and the collection of entrance
fees. This required every tourist to the CBWS to enter the women's group
gift shop, which increased the group's sales. The group also retained
10 percent of the proceeds from entrance fees, a sum that amounted to
U.S. $4,500 to U.S. $5,000 per year between 2003 and 2007. The women's
group donated a portion of these funds to the local primary school each
year. The group's guaranteed access to all tourists visiting the sanctuary
provided incentive for village residents to belong to the women's group,
which claimed a membership of over 90 percent of the village's women
in 2002. Although women's individual incomes varied according to the
amount of crafts they were able to produce and the flow of tourists,

women reported earning anywhere from U.S. $10 to U.S. $200 to $300 per month.[6] Interviews conducted in 2002 revealed that all of the twenty-eight households in Maya Centre earned income directly or indirectly from tourism to the CBWS and that income from ecotourism had won villagers' support for the protected area. This success resulted from the efficacy of marketing efforts to attract large numbers of tourists to the CBWS and the villagers' ability to access and derive income from each one of them.

Red Bank

The village of Red Bank (population 657, distributed across 116 households) is also located on the perimeter of the CBWS, but at a distance of approximately ten miles. Whereas Maya Centre is surrounded by large-scale plantations on three sides, residents of Red Bank have access to upland soils for subsistence cultivation at the edge of the village. They also have easy access to employment on nearby banana plantations, where many perform field labor on a daily basis or work banana shipments three to four days a week. Thus, Red Bank residents are able to combine subsistence farming with wage labor, and the imposition of the CBWS had less of an impact—positive or negative—on this community than on Maya Centre. In 2002, 86 percent of village households engaged in subsistence cultivation, and 86 percent engaged in wage labor.

However, the community became involved in a separate conservation and tourism initiative in 1997, when Belizean conservationists received word that Red Bank residents had killed a large number of scarlet macaws. Staff from the Belize Audubon Society and a more recently formed conservation NGO, Programme for Belize (PfB), investigated these reports and discovered that large flocks of scarlet macaws migrate annually from their nesting grounds in western Belize to the forested hills directly behind Red Bank to feed on varieties of fruit available in the area between January and March. Since the birds appeared in large numbers, villagers did not imagine them as endangered, and some villagers hunted them for meat. Conservationists also became concerned that villagers were chopping down the trees whose fruit drew the birds to this area. "Something had to be worked out for villagers to be convinced to protect the area and the scarlet macaws," explained one NGO staff member. "We came up with tourism as an opportunity." Conservation NGO staff made Red Bank residents aware that this species of bird was endangered and should not be killed. They predicted that, if villagers were to protect the birds, tourists from Belize and abroad would travel to Red Bank to view the huge flocks of macaws that gathered there, enabling villagers to earn income through the sale of guiding services, food, accommodations, and crafts. Indeed, the months of the macaws' annual return to the forested hills behind the village coincided with the high season for tourism in Belize.

Thus, in Red Bank, conservation NGOs emphasized ecotourism as a means to generate income for rural communities from the outset, in order to raise support for protecting macaws. After a decade of publications and international conferences that addressed issues involving "people and parks" and a decade of experience working with rural communities near protected areas in Belize, the NGOs were prepared from the initiation of these conversations to articulate how protecting scarlet macaws could—and should—generate income for Red Bank residents through ecotourism. If ecotourism had served earlier as a tool to win state support for protected areas conservation by diversifying and expanding the national economy, it now served conservationists as a tool for convincing villagers that efforts to conserve biodiversity through the creation of protected areas would generate income for village households as well.

This vision of ecotourism was embraced by at least some residents of Red Bank, who saw engaging in ecotourism within their community as an attractive means to generate cash income to supplement their subsistence farming. Fourteen families formed the Scarlet Macaw Group, which petitioned the government to establish a protected area for macaws on twenty acres of hills behind the village. With assistance from PfB, the group accessed small grants from transnational conservation donors to purchase building materials, and Scarlet Macaw Group members invested their labor in the construction of a guesthouse, kitchen, and resource center, where entrance fees to the protected area would be collected and crafts offered for sale. Group members also invested labor in tour guide training and in cutting trails along which to guide tourists. PfB helped the group publicize its scarlet macaw population via Belizean television and print media and outside of Belize through birding magazines and the *Rough Guide* book series. At the urging of conservation NGOs, the Scarlet Macaw Group also created a community fund into which they deposited a portion of their profits each year to be used for projects that would benefit the whole community. The "best practices" that had been identified in the literatures on ecotourism and conservation were implemented in this project: NGOs assisted a community-based organization to establish its own protected area to conserve an endangered and charismatic species; the revenues to be generated by tourists who came to see the birds would be distributed among group members and shared more broadly through a community fund. Conservationists asserted that Red Bank villagers "really grasped" the value of these endangered birds; "they started feeling pride" in the macaws.

However, reality did not match expectations. Very few tourists visited the community, and those who did visit seldom opted to stay overnight in the village's guesthouse. In 2001, considered a good year in retrospect, only fifteen tourists stayed in the guesthouse. More frequently, tourists came on day trips from upscale coastal resorts to view the macaws, perhaps purchasing lunch or guiding services in the village. Members of the Scarlet Macaw Group decided that visitors were too few and income too low to warrant staffing the resource center. The group earned approximately U.S. $1,500 in 2000 (an average of U.S. $214 per family) and U.S. $1,850 in 2001 (an average of U.S. $263 per family). However, the group's income dropped to an estimated U.S. $250 during 2002 (only U.S. $35 per family), after a hurricane in late 2001 blew the fruits sought by scarlet macaws off the trees, making both macaws and tourists scarce.

Compared with the case of Maya Centre, the costs of protecting the hillsides where the macaws congregated were relatively low for most village residents. Since they did not farm these steep hills, the major way that protecting scarlet macaws altered the community's resource use involved increased travel to collect firewood. If the costs were lower, however, so were the benefits villagers derived. A survey conducted in 2002 of a 25 percent random sample of households in Red Bank revealed that only 10 percent derived income from tourism. Further, despite the Scarlet Macaw Group's donation of U.S. $100 to the village primary school in 2001 (a small sum, though it represented 5 percent of the group's income), the survey demonstrated that villagers who did not belong to the Scarlet Macaw Group did not perceive themselves as gaining any advantage from the protection of macaws.

For households that did participate in ecotourism, the costs were high relative to benefits. Tour guiding was the most lucrative dimension of participation in ecotourism, but in order to be available to guide tourists, who often arrived with little or no advance notice, men had to forgo opportunities for wage labor on the nearby banana plantations, which would take them out of the village. Further, individuals and families were required to invest labor in maintaining the trails and guesthouse on the chance that tourists might arrive. Since tourists often did not arrive, the returns from tourism were smaller and less secure than those derived from wage labor on nearby plantations. The high labor and opportunity costs of participation in the Scarlet Macaw Group led many to drop out, and by 2002 its membership was down to seven families, half the number that had started four years earlier. When international markets failed to deliver the predicted numbers of ecotourists or income, support for ecotourism and conservation in Red Bank narrowed.

Toledo Ecotourism Association

In 1990, Mopan and Kekchi Maya from five villages in the Toledo District of far southern Belize initiated the Toledo Ecotourism Association (TEA). Their definition of ecotourism was quite distinct from other initiatives in Belize, emphasizing social justice and taking a different approach to human-nature relationships. The TEA's project did not involve travel to a protected area; instead, the TEA offered the opportunity to experience and learn about "the Maya way of life." An early TEA brochure asserted: Although "the high priests and princes of the Classic Maya period are no longer with us" and "the temples and ball courts are deserted," the wisdom of the ancient Maya "lives on in native medicine, philosophy, food, housing and implements." Emphasizing the Mayas' "profound understanding of the balance of nature" and "affinity with the rain forest environment," the brochure extends this invitation: "We offer an experience close to the Earth. Come feel its pulse in our daily lives" (Toledo Ecotourism Association n.d.). Thus, the TEA portrayed its member communities as living sustainably with or in nature, as they farmed, fished, and collected plant materials, in contrast with Maya Centre and Red Bank, communities that lived next to nature, cast in the form of "wilderness" that must be protected from use by people (see Cronon 1996).

Families that joined together to organize a TEA group in their village sought tourism income to supplement subsistence production or to augment earnings from cash crop production or wage labor, the latter being less available in the Toledo District than in Red Bank. In each village TEA group, member households took turns servicing the guesthouse, providing meals to tourists in their homes, performing Maya music or dances, or guiding tourists through the village or nearby forests, farms, caves, or ruins. Just as they rotated responsibilities and income within villages, the TEA also used a rotation system among villages, with groups in different villages taking turns receiving tourists. This system aimed to disperse the income generated by tourism as broadly and evenly as possible and minimize tourism's potential negative impacts.

The TEA deployed a definition of ecotourism that reflected its members' goals, focused on income generation as a facet of larger efforts toward social justice. The TEA emphasized the empowerment of indigenous community-based organizations and the significance of indigenous cultures that bound people and nature together sustainably. The TEA's version of ecotourism could not easily be articulated with the goals of conservation NGOs, and neither local nor transnational conservation NGOs engaged the TEA. Instead, the TEA found support from transnational NGOs that focused on alternative development and social justice. The association won international acclaim as an ecotourism project in

1996, when it received the To Do! Prize for Socially Responsible Tourism from the German Institute for Tourism and Development. The Institute, concerned by a trend toward the prioritization of environmentally responsible tourism over socially responsible tourism, had initiated this award to promote the latter (Studienkreis fur Tourismus und Entwicklung 2010). Thus the TEA, like Maya Centre, itself became a participant in global-scale contests over the definition of ecotourism, and the TEA publicized its receipt of this award to promote and legitimize the version of ecotourism it embraced.

Though the organization drew only small numbers of tourists, within a few years the association expanded to accommodate participation by six more villages. As a result, tourists were distributed too broadly across villages to provide the levels of income desired by many participating families: while in 1994 some 380 tourists were shared among five village groups, in 1997 some 330 guests were dispersed across eleven communities (McClintock 2000:38). Research conducted in one of the TEA villages in 2004 (population 310) revealed that only nine of approximately forty households in the village belonged to the TEA group and earned income from tourism and that the income they derived from tourism was insufficient to meet the cash needs of several participating households. According to the chairman of the association, TEA leaders estimated that each village would need to host 1,248 overnight visitor stays per year in order for participating families to meet their income goals. The TEA group in the study village hosted seventy-one visitors for a total of ninety-three visitor nights during 2002 and 2003, which amounts to only 7.5 percent of that goal. Thus, many households depend on wage labor outside the community to augment their subsistence production and their tourism income. Envisioning ecotourism as a means to achieve the priorities of income generation and social equity, TEA members won support and praise from international organizations that also prioritized social justice. However, this version of ecotourism has not generated the levels of income its participants had hoped for. Continuation of the initiative may be attributed in part to the lack of other opportunities for income generation in far southern Belize.

DEFINING ECOTOURISM AND ARTICULATING AGENDAS

In this chapter, I proposed to step outside of the ecotourism problematic to explore how, and with what effects, particular definitions of ecotourism have been deployed by actors in Belize. Data from Belize reveal that actors embraced and promoted particular definitions of ecotourism based on the degree to which those definitions enabled them to pursue their highest priority goals, although these goals were unrelated to increasing the sustainability of tourism. None sought to implement ecotourism in a "pure" form. Nor was ecotourism an end in itself. Rather, ecotourism served as a means to diverse ends: conservationists sought the creation of protected areas; the government sought economic expansion and foreign exchange; rural communities sought cash incomes and social justice.

Further, many Belizean actors selectively drew upon specific definitions of ecotourism in order to articulate otherwise divergent agendas to integrate their own priorities into the agendas of other actors. The concept of ecotourism enabled conservation NGOs to articulate their conservation agendas to development agendas at widely divergent scales, from government officials' priorities for expanding and diversifying the national economy to villagers' aspirations for cash incomes to replace or augment subsistence production. Some versions of ecotourism made it possible for conservationists, state officials, and some rural residents to imagine forms of development that built on conservation as a foundation. These examples from Belize suggest that the achievement of consensus among ecotourism scholars regarding a definition of ecotourism may not extend the impact of the field on practice as far or as effectively as scholars might hope, since actors who deploy and implement something they call ecotourism may use particular definitions precisely because those definitions most closely represent—or enable—their own goals, which fall outside the ecotourism problematic.

However, if Belizeans deployed particular definitions of ecotourism in the service of higher-priority goals not directly tied to the goals set for ecotourism by advocates and scholars, they also engaged in conversations and debates within the ecotourism problematic. As they proposed and contested definitions of and criteria for ecotourism that would advance their own agendas in Belize, they operated both inside and outside of the ecotourism problematic. Conservation NGOs saw their definitions of ecotourism legitimized, but also reoriented, through engagements with global conversations occurring within the ecotourism problematic itself. While one conservation NGO used Maya Centre as a case study to reshape definitions and criteria for ecotourism, the community itself used this study to reshape the local implementation of ecotourism. Similarly, the TEA was awarded a prize for socially responsible tourism by an organization that sought to promote this dimension of ecotourism. In turn, the association used this award to promote its own product and its own vision for ecotourism. The broad range of actors engaged in contesting definitions of ecotourism demonstrates the mutual relationships among experts in the field of ecotourism studies, those who implement ecotourism, and even those who experience the impact of ecotourism implementation. Thus, the production of knowledge regarding ecotourism turns out to be a complicated enterprise in which experts use communities as case studies, but those communities also speak and act as self-advocates. The boundary between the inside of the ecotourism problematic and the outside is revealed to be porous.

It is also important to note that, in these Belizean examples, only actors enabled by ecotourism to attain their primary goals continued to support the concept; where ecotourism did not deliver the anticipated results, support for ecotourism waned. These outcomes are linked to the market-based nature of ecotourism: as a market-based strategy, the success of ecotourism depends on the creation of ecotourism products desired by consumers and the ability of the producers of ecotourism products and the consumers who desire those products to identify and locate one another and transact an exchange. Scholars and ecotourism advocates portrayed ecotourists as a rapidly growing, high-value market segment. Following the advice of consultants, the Belize Tourism Board and the Belize Tourism Industry Association targeted this market segment and succeeded, according to the metrics applied by the Belizean government at a national scale. However, data from the villages suggest that the tourists targeted by BTB and BTIA marketing do not desire the kinds of products offered by village entrepreneurs or community-based organizations. McKercher suggests that advocates who believe ecotourism is capable of optimizing the social, cultural, and ecological benefits of tourism understand ecotourism to be "so morally, ecologically, and ethically sound" that "a mass market *must* exist for such activities" (McKercher 2001:565). But Maya Centre residents benefited from the BTB's marketing campaign only because they were able to establish mechanisms that enabled them to access all visitors to the CBWS, even though most of those visitors chose not to stay in the village. The other two villages have benefited little from this marketing strategy, though it is not clear whether there is insufficient consumer demand for their products or whether they have simply not managed to connect with the market segment of tourists that desires their product. Ultimately, no version of ecotourism can successfully meet the goals of the actors who wield it—regardless of whether those goals originate within or outside of the ecotourism problematic—without consumer demand. Thus, efforts to shape the preferences of tourists, to produce ecotour*ists*, will be as critical as efforts to shape the definition and implementation of ecotour*ism*.

NOTES

1. This relies on Foucault's (1980) conceptualization of a spiraling relationship between power and knowledge, in which expertise seeks to shape practice.

2. Several critiques of ecotourism also position themselves outside of the ecotourism problematic, suggesting that the practice of ecotourism can never attain the objectives imagined for it. For example, critics point out that the reliance on transnational travel by the majority of ecotourism projects in the global south makes the whole enterprise environmentally unsustainable over the long term. Since transnational travel exacerbates processes of climate change, ecotourism that depends on transnational travel challenges the very possibility of biodiversity conservation at smaller scales: it may well destroy the conditions that sustain the ecosystems proponents seek to protect (Becken 2002; Becken and Schellhorn 2007; Gossling 2000; Hall 2007). Scholars have also critiqued ecotourism in terms of its aspirations for social justice, interrogating the ways that ecotourism—as ideal (Cater 2006) or as practice (West and Carrier 2004)—reproduces social inequities across and within nations.

3. I gratefully acknowledge the Research and Writing Grant from the John A. and Catherine T. MacArthur Foundation, which funded the bulk of this research. An All-University Research Initiation Grant from Michigan State University and funds from the Dean of International Studies and Programs also funded initial and follow-up research, respectively.

4. Only 38 percent of Belizean lands were deemed to have high agricultural potential, with the rest having less or no agricultural potential (Dobson 1973:273).

5. This figure includes broadleaf forest, pine forest, and mangrove swamps (Barry 1992:130). The official data on forest cover have been criticized as inaccurate and inflated by environmental consultants (Hartshorn et al. 1984); however, state land assessments that use new techniques to increase accuracy continue to assert similar numbers (Jacobs and Castañeda 1998:v).

6. According to the 2000 census, the mean income for Belize in 2000 was U.S. $417 (Central Statistical Office 2001).

REFERENCES

Barry, Tom. 1992. *Belize*. Albuquerque: The Inter-Hemispheric Education Resource Center.
———. 1995. *Inside Belize*. Albuquerque: The Inter-Hemispheric Education Resource Center.
Becken, Susanne. 2002. Analysing International Tourist Flows to Estimate Energy Use Associated with Air Travel. *Journal of Sustainable Tourism* 10(2):114–31.
Becken, Susanne, and Matthias Schellhorn. 2007. Ecotourism, Energy Use, and the Global Climate. In *Critical Issues in Ecotourism*, ed. James E. S. Higham, pp. 86–101. Oxford: Elsevier.
Belize Tourism Board. 1993. *Tourism towards 2000*. Belize City: Belize Tourism Board.
———. 1998. *Travel and Tourism Statistics*. Belize City: Belize Tourism Board.
———. 2006. *Travel and Tourism Statistics*. Belize City: Belize Tourism Board.
———. 2008. *Travel and Tourism Statistics*. Belize City: Belize Tourism Board.
Bjork, Peter. 2007. Definition Paradoxes. In *Critical Issues in Ecotourism*, ed. James E. S. Higham, pp. 23–45. Oxford: Elsevier.

Blamey, R. 1997. Ecotourism: The Search for an Operational Definition. *Journal of Sustainable Tourism* 5(2):109–30.

———. 2001. Principles of Ecotourism. In *Encyclopedia of Ecotourism*, ed. D. Weaver, pp. 5–22. Wallingford, UK: CABI.

Bolland, O. Nigel, and Assad Shoman. 1977. *Land in Belize 1765–1871*. Kingston: Institute for Social and Economic Research, UWI.

Brandon, Katrina. 1993. Basic Steps toward Encouraging Local Participation in Nature Tourism Projects. In *Ecotourism: A Guide for Planners and Managers*, eds. Kreg Lindberg and Donald Hawkins, pp. 134–51. North Bennington, VT: The Ecotourism Society.

Brockington, Dan, Rosaleen Duffy, and Jim Igoe. 2008. *Nature Unbound*. London: Earthscan Press.

Cater, Erlet. 2006. Ecotourism as a Western Construct. *Journal of Ecotourism* 5(1-2):23–39.

Central Statistical Office. 2001. *Belize 2000 Census: Major Findings*. Belmopan, Belize: Central Statistical Office.

Cronon, William. 1996. The Trouble with Wilderness. In *Uncommon Ground*, ed. William Cronon, pp. 69–90. New York: W. W. Norton.

Diamantis, Dimitrios. 1999. The Concept of Ecotourism: Evolution and Trends. *Current Issues in Tourism* 2(2–3):93–122.

Dobson, Narda. 1973. *A History of Belize*. Kingston: Longman Caribbean.

Emmons, Katherine, Robert H. Horwich, James Kamstra, Ernesto Saqui, James Beveridge, Timothy McCarthy, Jan Meerman, Fred Koontz, Emiliano Pop, Ignacio Pop, Hermelindo Saqui, Scott C. Silver, Linde Ostro, Dorothy Beveridge, and Judy Lumb. 1996. *Cockscomb Basin Wildlife Sanctuary: Its History, Flora and Fauna for Visitors, Teachers and Scientists*. Caye Caulker, Belize: Producciones de la Hamaca.

Fennell, David. 2005. A Content Analysis of Ecotourism Definitions. *Current Issues in Tourism* 4(5):403–21.

Ferguson, James. 1994. *The Anti-Politics Machine*. Minneapolis: University of Minnesota Press.

Font, Xavier, and Ralf Buckley, eds. 2001. *Tourism Ecolabelling*. Oxon: CABI.

Font, Xavier, and Catherine Harris. 2004. Rethinking Standards from Green to Sustainable. *Annals of Tourism Research* 31(4):986–1007.

Foucault, Michel. 1979. *Discipline and Punish*. New York: Vintage Books.

———. 1980. *Power/Knowledge*. New York: Pantheon.

Gossling, Stefan. 2000. Sustainable Tourism Development in Developing Countries: Some Aspects of Energy Use. *Journal of Sustainable Tourism* 8(5):410–25.

Government Information Service. 1973. Visit to Proposed Reserve at Crooked Tree Lagoon. *New Belize*, June.

———. 1982. New Thrust for Tourism. *New Belize* 16(8).

Hall, Michael. 2007. Scaling Ecotourism. In *Critical Issues in Ecotourism*, ed. James E. S. Higham, pp. 243–55. Oxford: Elsevier.

Hartshorn, Gary, Lou Nicolait, Lynne Hartshorn, George Bevier, Richard Brightman, Jeronimo Cal, Agripino Cawich, William Davidson, Random DuBois, Charles Dyer, Janet Gibson, William Hawley, Jeffrey Leonard, Robert Nicolait,

Dora Weyer, Hayward White, and Charles Wright. 1984. *Belize: Country Environmental Profile*. Belize City: Robert Nicolait and Associates.

Honey, Martha, ed. 2002. *Ecotourism and Certification*. Washington, DC: Island Press.

Hunt, Carter, and Amanda Stronza. 2009. Bringing Ecotourism into Focus. *Journal of Ecotourism* 8(1):1–17.

Jacobs, Noel D., and Anselmo Castañeda, eds. 1998. *Belize National Biodiversity Strategy*. Belmopan, Belize: National Biodiversity Committee, Ministry of Natural Resources and the Environment.

Jamal, Tazim, Marcos Borges, and Amanda Stronza. 2006. The Institutionalization of Ecotourism. *Journal of Ecotourism* 5(3):145–75.

King, R. B., J. H. Prat, M. P. Warner, and S. A. Zisman. 1993. *Agricultural Development Prospects in Belize*. Natural Resources Institute Bulletin 48. Chatham, UK: Natural Resources Institute.

Lindberg, Kreg, and Jeremy Enriquez. 1994. *An Analysis of Ecotourism's Contribution to Conservation and Development in Belize. Volume 2: Comprehensive Report*. Belmopan, Belize: World Wildlife Fund (US), Ministry of Tourism and the Environment and USAID.

McClintock, Edith. 2000. *Conservation and Ecotourism in Southern Belize*. MA Thesis, Department of Environmental Studies, Florida International University.

McKercher, Bob. 2001. The Business of Ecotourism. In *The Encyclopedia of Ecotourism*, ed. David B. Weaver, pp. 565–77. New York: CABI.

Medina, Laurie. 1998. The Impact of Free Trade Initiatives on the Caribbean Basin. *Latin American Perspectives* 25(5):27–49.

———. 2004. *Negotiating Economic Development*. Tucson: University of Arizona Press.

———. 2005. Ecotourism and Certification. *Journal of Sustainable Tourism* 13(3):281–95.

———. 2010. When Government Targets "the State." *Political and Legal Anthropology Review* 33(2):245–63.

———. n.d. *Imposing Possibilities*. Unpublished manuscript.

Mitchell, Timothy. 2002. *Rule of Experts*. Berkeley: University of California Press.

Rabinowitz, Alan. 2000. *Jaguar*. Washington, DC: Island Press.

Richardson, Robert. 2007. Economic Development in Belize. In *Taking Stock: Belize at 25 Years of Independence*, eds. Barbara Balboni and Joseph O. Palacio, pp. 21–45. Benque, Belize: Cubola Press.

Slater, Candace. 2003. In Search of the Rain Forest. In *In Search of the Rain Forest*, ed. Candace Slater, pp. 3–37. Durham, NC: Duke University Press.

Studienkreis fur Tourismus und Entwicklung (Institute for Tourism and Development). 2010. TO DO! Contest. www.todo-contest.org/objectives.html, accessed November 21, 2011.

Takacs, David. 1996. *The Idea of Biodiversity*. Baltimore: Johns Hopkins University Press.

Toledo Ecotourism Association. n.d. *Promotional Brochure*.

Tsing, Anna. 2004. *Friction*. Princeton, NJ: Princeton University Press.

Weaver, David, and Laura Lawton. 2007. Twenty Years On: The State of Contemporary Ecotourism Research. *Tourism Management* 28(5):1168–79.

Wells, Michael, and Katrina Brandon, with Lee Hannah. 1992. *People and Parks.* Washington, DC: The World Bank, the World Wildlife Fund, and USAID.

West, Paige, and James Carrier. 2004. Ecotourism and Authenticity. *Current Anthropology* 45(4):483–98.

West, Patrick, and Steven Brechin, eds. 1991. *Resident Peoples and National Parks.* Tucson: University of Arizona Press.

Western, David, and R. Michael Wright, eds. 1994. *Natural Connections.* Washington, DC: Island Press.

Wight, Pam. 2001. Ecotourists: Not a Homogenous Market Segment. In *The Encyclopedia of Ecotourism*, ed. D. B. Weaver, pp. 37–62. New York: CABI.

Wildlife Conservation Society. 2011. WCS Belize (electronic document). www.wcs.org/where-we-work/latin-america/belize.aspx, accessed November 28, 2011.

13

✛

Who Owns Ecotourism?

The Ecoturismo Seri Case

Diana Luque, Beatriz Camarena, Patricia L. Salido,
Moisés Rivera, Eduwiges Gomez, María Cabral,
and Rubén Lechuga

"We turned poor when the money arrived."

Davíd Morales, young Comcáac politician, 2005

This chapter examines an initiative by a group of residents of the
Comcáac indigenous community—inhabitants of the central coast of
the Sonoran Desert in the Sonora state of Mexico and the central portion
of the Gulf of California.[1] The group, supported by researchers from the
Centro de Investigación en Alimentación y Desarrollo (CIAD) and other
public and private institutions, developed an ecotourism project, titled
Ecoturismo Seri, as a community sustainable development alternative
from 2005 to 2009. This chapter considers the experience of Ecoturismo
Seri from the perspective of political ecology and biocultural diversity, presenting the ecotourism debate within the larger context of the
indigenous-environmental problematic. The factors that determined the
design of Ecoturismo Seri as a commercial product are presented within
a framework that reflects the biocultural diversity of the region, the
Comcáac people, the regional market, and the environmental features of
the sites to be visited within the Comcáac territory. A description of the
marketing process, which was accompanied by a survey, is also analyzed
and discussed. The analysis is guided by a qualitative methodological

framework, including participatory action research and participant observation from 2005 to 2009, which was accompanied by two quantitative instruments: a regional market survey applied to Kino Bay (state of Sonora) visitors in 2006, and a quality control survey applied to Ecoturismo Seri visitors in 2008.

Critical reflection on the current indigenous problematic, questioning the benefits generated by ecotourism, highlights some of the basic dilemmas that must be dealt with if tourism is to be useful for economic development. Most of all, the dilemmas we pose in this chapter can clarify the decision-making processes faced by indigenous peoples in touristic contexts. Even though this project was designed in terms of community sustainable development, the Comcáac characteristics, the political and economic context, and the limited government support make this effort a vulnerable one, which will come to rely on entrepreneurs in the tourism industry who will likely take higher profits compared to those of the Comcáac group. Therefore, the question of "Who owns ecotourism?" finally arises.

TRENDS IN ECOTOURISM

Officially, since 1994, Mexico has had a National Ecotourism Strategy that proposes to help indigenous communities and peoples improve their socioeconomic condition by enabling them to reappropriate and use natural resources in the territories in which they are settled.[2] Unfortunately, this strategy has not been fully implemented. Many of the projects are impeded by a series of organizational, financial, technical, and marketing problems; thus many of the projects are not operational. These failures are greatly, although not exclusively, due to the concentration of resources on infrastructure while neglecting the development of a tourism culture involving education, interpretation, and the provisioning of services in the local communities (López Pardo and Palomino Villavicencio 2008:44–48).

Involving indigenous communities in the start-up of ecotourism projects within their territories gives rise to what the World Tourism Organization (WTO) defines as ethnic tourism: that which brings about visits to places of one's own ancestral or millenary origin, settled in the rural space (of a human settlement) and which besides is administrated under the principles of environmental sustainability. As a result of the deregulation of the Mexican economy during the 1990s, ecotourism and thus ethnic tourism have been fundamentally linked to the private sector because, unlike most native communities, only private enterprise has sufficient capital to start up projects in many indigenous territories. The attractiveness of these spaces lies in their indisputable biocultural wealth. However, most of the activities developed by tour operators focus on "adventure tourism," particularly mountain biking, rappelling, and river running, which are activities that may not always fully respect the fragile natural and cultural environments in which they take place.[3]

The role of private enterprise in ecotourism has been strongly criticized as a new way of exploitation of indigenous territories, sustained by a neo-liberal scheme that markets nature and culture. One of the main criticisms is that indigenous peoples can be denigrated by being shown as objects of tourism rather than as peoples capable of reaping the actual benefits of tourism, thereby stimulating a "boutique-type tourism" or "tourism of poverty" (Leff 2008:149). Indigenous communities in San Juan Chamula in Chiapas, Mexico, for example, have prevented the construction of a tourist site in their territory (Henríquez 2008). Nonetheless, it is important not to forget that some indigenous communities have also organized to market their territories and culture, using the same activities some criti-cize as denigrating to their culture and territory: ecotourism.

It is clear the coherent integration of communities and projects is vital for their good operation; that is, the way in which any ecotourism project interacts with the region's inhabitants and the natural environment is of crucial importance to its success. It is therefore critical to incorporate into the tourism program indigenous knowledge, culture, and practices that have interacted with local environments for long periods. Not con-sidering the identity of communities implies not considering the region's environment, and destroying the communities' identity implies destroy-ing the keys to a sound interaction with the respective natural enclaves (Blount 2001:514; Keene et al. 2001:64).

Political ecology is understood as the conceptualization of relations be-tween political economy and nature (Paulson et al. 2003:206). Ecotourism and its branch, ethnic tourism, are the objects of debate in which forms of exploitation of indigenous territories and participating stakeholders com-prise the topics of discussion. For the purposes of this chapter, it is im-portant to emphasize that globalization processes, such as those involved in the increase in ethnic tourism, do not necessarily imply the destruction of the identity of local groups (García Canclini 2000:30–31). Therefore, it should be remembered that, although ecotourism is a well-defined global concept, the actual implementation varies widely in response to local factors. Nevertheless, beyond concerns regarding cultural traditions, the central dilemma of ecotourism in indigenous communities is this: Does it actually benefit the community? That is, who owns ecotourism?

BIOCULTURAL DIVERSITY AS A CONTEXT FOR REFLECTION

Generally speaking, the term *biocultural diversity* refers to a concern about the deterioration of ecosystems and its relation to indigenous groups that still inhabit parts of their ancestral territories. That is, biocultural diversity acknowledges the existence of a complex relationship among biodiversity, cultural diversity, indigenous knowledge, and language. As such, indigenous territories are seen as reservoirs of traditional values and ancestral knowledge in the management of natural resources. This perspective has implications for the progress of biotechnology in the production of foods, pharmaceuticals, and biofuels.

The concept of "environmental services" has fertilized the subject of sustainable development, in which the conservation of natural resources is being reevaluated in economic terms. Within this context, environmental services of indigenous territories are acknowledged as strategic for national economic development. Hence, it is already possible to propose the existence of "biocultural services," whose implications should be to reorient the environmental as well as developmental policies of the indigenous peoples (Boege Schmidt 2008; Luque and Doode 2010; Maffi 2001).

Other foci, such as the anthropology of nature, nourish bioculturality by focusing on the culture-nature complex within the context of the environmental crisis, not only as a confrontation at the epistemological level (between local knowledge and Western science) but also at the cognitive level, to confront local and/or indigenous worldviews within the dispute over access to and usufruct of nature (Descola and Pálsson 2001). Yet, Leff (2008) interprets the contemporary environmental problematic as a crisis of Western civilization, a problem of knowledge. He traces its roots to positivist epistemology by arguing that cultural diversity will contribute to the construction of an environmental epistemology sustained on the dialogue of knowledge (scientific knowledge and local knowledge), which is transcendental for the new environmental rationality. This view of biocultural diversity is the context that forms the basis of the Ecoturismo Seri project's mission, which is "to promote the sustainable use of natural resources in the Comcáac territory, based on the universal rights of indigenous peoples, on traditional uses and customs and on the self-government of the territory."

BACKGROUND OF ECOTURISMO SERI

The Comcáac traditional system of subsistence was based on a nomadic territoriality (central coast of the Sonoran Desert and the Gulf of California), a nonhierarchical political organization, a social organization in territorial subgroups on the basis of kinship, and gathering marine and desert flora and fauna for self-subsistence (mainly food of marine origin and desert plants as herbs) founded on collective access. The Comcáac, like most of the indigenous peoples of Mexico, are economically and politically marginalized. The processes of cultural hybridization have advanced rapidly with particular characteristics: (1) belonging to a nomad (sea and desert) gatherer culture, but strongly geared to using marine resources; and (2) maintaining a strong cultural identity through their mother language—*cmiique iitom*—their collective history, artistic traditions, and the traditional management of their territory, which includes collective access to its natural resources.

The integrity and health of the territory is the Comcáac's main priority. It is composed of an island and a continental portion that is less than 10 percent of its original pre-Hispanic size. Tiburón Island, with a legal agrarian status of communal property, belongs to the Seri Indian community (Comcáac people) and is part of the Biosphere Reserve of the Gulf of California Islands within the National System of Natural Protected Areas. In front is the continental portion, named *Ejido de Desemboque y su anexo Punta Chueca*, which is another type of legal communal property. The territory has no serious land invasion problems. Furthermore, the Comcáac possess a legal Exclusive Fishing Area, the Infiernillo Channel, with well-conserved native biodiversity in relation to the regional environmental status (figure 13.1).

It could be asserted that under conditions of historical marginalization, they have resisted pressures to sell or lease their territory as well as problems resulting from their relation with the national state and the advancement of an ideology of development within a scheme of global market economy and private appropriation of the territory. Currently, the Comcáac have become sedentary, and the almost one thousand inhabitants have settled in two localities, Desemboque and Punta Chueca. Their food and morbidity patterns have changed dramatically, which has had repercussions, including a growing dependence on commercial exchange involving money (Luque and Robles Torres 2006).

Their current economy is a mixed system composed of regional market productive relations, in which self-consumption community relations still persist. Their primary activities, fishing and the production of artisan goods, continue to reflect long-standing traditions. Although commercial in nature, those traditions are carried out in their desert and sea territories and are regulated through traditional political and community forms of organization (Luque and Robles Torres 2006). Tourism is a very recent economic activity, with practically no impact on the Comcáac way of living.

Even though there are no specific scientific data that show their low-income level in quantitative terms, there is qualitative evidence based on participant observation that describes the current dynamics of poverty (Luque 2008). Also, they represent themselves as a poor people, and in social welfare public institutions they are considered a priority sector. Traditional relations within the productive system and natural resource regulations are weakening quickly but still buffer the impact of poverty.

—·—·— Present Comcáac Territory

— — — Comcáac Territory Prior to Colonization
(This is the border proposed by E. Moser).

░░░ Zone of Comcáac Territory (according to oral tradition)

Figure 13.1. The Comcáac Territory. (after Luque and Robles Torres 2006:12)

Despite the strong constraints resulting from the dynamics of poverty, this community has little out-migration, little malnutrition as a community health problem, and their subsistence is not subject to processes of proletarianization.

The Comcáac are searching for economic alternatives and development strategies as a result of the growing intrusion of national culture into their daily lives, as reflected in a breakdown of traditional subsistence strategies: the adoption of values of the national society, a greater dependence on money, a greater fishing specialization for the regional market, and growing environmental deterioration through overexploitation of fishing resources in the Gulf of California. Therefore, the Comcáac are greatly interested in proposals for community-sustainable development.

One example of such a proposal is the acceptance of environmental certification for their territory, which has introduced a series of educational and training initiatives. Tiburón Island is part of the Biosphere Reserve of the Gulf of California Islands within the National System of Natural Protected Areas. In 2009, the Infiernillo Channel (Exclusive Fishing Area) was registered as a Ramsar Site, since it is a coastal wetlands complex. Tiburón Island and the continental portion are registered before Semarnat as a UMA (unit of sustainable natural resources management), which is the platform for sustainable hunting known as synergistic management.

The Comcáac community maintains several Comcáac groups who monitor diverse environmental issues, the so-called *paraecologos* in charge of the synergistic organization: *tortugueros* and *pajareras*, who monitor marine turtles and birds, respectively; and the Ecoturismo Seri group, who monitor mangroves and estuaries. In general, such efforts are supported by American and Mexican academic institutions and financed by public funds or resources from national and international private institutions.

The first stage of the Ecoturismo Seri project, which resulted in a product of the same name, came about with the support of local institutions, including the Council of Elders and *Ctam Coyai*, A.C., and academic institutions such as CIAD, which coordinates INE (Instituto Nacional de Ecología [National Ecology Institute]), FMCN (Fondo Mexicano para la Conservación de la Naturaleza [Mexican Fund for Nature Conservancy]), GGF (Global Green-grant Fund), and Cofetur (Comisión para el Fomento del Turismo de Sonora [Sonora State Tourism Committee]). Presently, the project is in its second phase and, since ecotourism is a relatively new activity for the Comcáac, as well as for the region, CIAD continues to provide support in the areas of community organization, marketing, and environmental monitoring.[4]

ECOTOURISM PRODUCT DESIGN

Ecoturismo Seri, geared to the regional market, was launched in 2006 by a group of Comcáac supported by a CIAD group of researchers. When it was designed, three issues were considered: characteristics of the Comcáac, characteristics of the regional market, and characteristics of the environment. Each of these is described below.

Characteristics of the Comcáac

At the turn of the century when a public agency[5] evaluated the tourism potential of Tiburón Island, an attempt was made to further ecotourism in Comcáac territory. The promoters of this effort considered the project a failure, because "the Seri people did not comply," and they lacked institutional support and sufficient funds to expand the "trial and error" period required for their implementation and follow-up process.

Years later, a Comcáac group interested in finding alternative income sources to fishing encouraged a commercial strategy referred to as Ecoturismo Seri. This project was intended to be subject to and take into account the ambitions of the indigenous community, including its worldview, sociopolitical organization, economic organization, and local capacities. Nonetheless, several problems arose, among which the most important was the constant between communal organization and the logic of a private company created for individual economic profit.

This effort concentrated on extended families, which are the basis of the productive organization and include men and women ages ten to eighty years old. Other interested parties received an explanation about the few possibilities of incorporation into the project in light of market limitations. Although these measures conflicted with their policies of "collective access to natural resources," the Comcáac themselves have recognized that presently they have had to organize into workgroups with differentiated rights and duties.

Another critical issue linked to the Comcáac's culture is related to respect for their territory, particularly Tiburón Island. As an ancestral land, it represents the struggles for territory and the transmission of knowledge revealed in specific sacred sites (Luque and Robles Torres 2006). Consequently, they do not look favorably on the entry of outsiders into their territory, and even less so for recreational purposes. To minimize such confrontation, the Ecoturismo Seri workgroup decided not to allow tourists to enter into the heart of the island, to solely visit its coasts, not to build fixed infrastructure, and to provide correct and constant information on the activities to the community's traditional government. Two members of the Council of Elders and their family members were included in the workgroup.

The local capabilities were important considerations in the design of the project. The Comcáac do not have a tradition of taking care of outsiders, and even repudiate doing so in the case of foreigners. They are accustomed to short and nondaily work schedules, and their experience in promoting and marketing any productive activity is nil; therefore it is difficult for them to reach agreements with persons outside the family environment. Furthermore, the available infrastructure is minimal, and all public facilities and services (potable water, sewer, telephone service, roads, medical services, food and lodging services) are deficient. It may not sound like the ideal place for a tourism project, but since the Comcáac are trying desperately for new ways of economic development that do not destroy their natural resources—and knowing the beauty of their territory—ecotourism seems the best alternative.

Characteristics of the Regional Market

The tourist industry is among the most important economic activities in Sonora. In 2009, it accounted for 8 percent of the state's gross domestic product. International tourism as a source of foreign exchange in Sonora registered a noticeable growth during the first five years of this decade, growing from 4,224.1 billion pesos in 2000 to 7,632 billion in 2005. This trend is due not only to the significant increase in foreign tourists but also to the increase in average daily expenditures by tourists (Salido 2007).

Over 1,200 kilometers of coastline, an ocean considered one of the world's most beautiful, significant biodiversity, and a 580-kilometer-long border with the wealthiest market in the world are some of the factors that have guided the course of tourism in Sonora. Beach resorts, such as Puerto Peñasco and San Carlos, have been favored not only by the preference of visitors but particularly by those interested in developing tourist infrastructure. In such sites, tourism is relatively well consolidated in terms of an increasing provision of services and facilities and a regular flux of visitors. Still, it is already reaching the limits of massive expansion in which the main challenge is searching for ways that may enable a sustainable tourist development while at the same time responding to a more demanding and active tourism (Salido 2007).

The estuaries and the cultural heritage of the Comcáac, highlighted in the Ecoturismo Seri project, constitute a unique experience in the region, with a tremendous potential for attracting tourists. According to the results of a visitor survey conducted in 2006 (Luque 2006), the potential market is mainly tourists visiting Kino Bay, the tourist area closest to the

Comcáac-Seri territory. Nearly 90 percent of these tourists are domestic. In both types of tourism, the geographic closeness of the region and their places of origin is a decisive factor in the number of visitors. Spring and summer bring the highest numbers of tourists, almost all of whom come from other parts of the state and the country (76 percent). Most of the visitors coming in fall and winter are foreigners.

An analysis of the market potential for the Ecoturismo Seri project highlights an ever-growing interest among visitors and investors in the development of eco- and adventure tourism, as well as noticeably increased interest in exotic destinations. There is also a specialized tourism sector that seeks to know more about different cultures directly in their own environment. Despite the fact that Sonora has a tremendous potential for these tourist modalities, there are few projects that offer their products in an organized and safe way.

Characteristics of the Environment

The Infiernillo Channel (Xepe Cossot) is a coastal wetland complex of marine grass, reefs, and nine estuaries with a mangrove forest. Wetlands are considered an international conservation priority (Ramsar Convention) because they enable critical processes for hydrographic basins and for the reproduction of land and coastal life. In the analysis of the social-environmental situation of the Comcáac, the Infiernillo Channel was identified as the area of greatest environmental vulnerability. Despite its recognized high biological productivity, it is heavily fished, since the community's subsistence still is based on fishing (Luque 2008; Luque and Robles Torres 2006).

Besides its relevance for the current subsistence of the Comcáac, the Infiernillo Channel is considered sacred: "It is like a father or a mother," "It has been sprinkled with the blood of the Hantxmocat [ancestors]," and it is "like a university. Knowledge is revealed there" (Don Antonio Robles, personal communication, 2003). Furthermore, young Comcáac say that Taheöjc (Tiburón Island) is "our body," while Xepe Cossot (Infiernillo Channel) "is our heart" and "the blood that runs through our veins" (Luque and Robles Torres 2006).

The cultural and subsistence relevance of the Infiernillo Channel for the Comcáac is reflected in the native names given to locations, the *cmique iitom*.[6] During the preparation of the Map of Comcáac Sites of Cultural Value, conducted with the Council of Elders from 2003 to 2004, 290 traditional cultural properties with their respective names in *cmique iitom* were recorded, seventy-one of which are in the ocean in the Infiernillo Channel and one hundred of which are on the eastern coast of Tiburón Island that faces the channel.

The channel's nine estuaries were classified as *Ihizitim*, which is a portion of territory assigned to an extensive family where the exploitation and control of natural resources is under its guardianship. For such purposes, some of the *Hant icaheme* or ancient camps of Comcáac ancestors, who in their nomadic life migrated for their subsistence, were made on the *Ihizitim*. In these places, they built their ephemeral housing units, the *haaco haemza*, a group of which formed the *Hant icaheme* that was abandoned in the seasonal migrations following natural resources.

Some of the names of the estuaries refer to the *Hant icaheme*, others tell the history of extermination of the Comcáac, and still others are homes of their heroes, such as the legendary Coyote Iguana in the *Xtáasi it* estuary. The *Ihizitim* as well as the *Hant icaheme* are archeological sites and major referents for collective history, as well as the sources of the current cultural identity and cohesion. These environmental, cultural, and historical factors made it difficult for the community to select sites that would be accessible for the ecotourism project since the extermination war made by the Mexican government in the nineteenth century is still alive among elders and there were systematic conflicts with the regional society in the twentieth century.

THE ECOTURISMO SERI PROJECT

As described, the Ecoturismo Seri project was based on an analysis of the Comcáac social-environmental context, their characteristics as indigenous people, the regional market, and the territory's environmental and scenic quality. The project underwent a participatory action research process, as well as a systematization of the traditional knowledge in the management of estuaries, a market survey, training of the Comcáac team, and the acquisition of equipment.

Ecoturismo Seri has been rolled out in stages. The first phase featured a simple tour, accessible to the regional market, which is easily managed by the Comcáac. It consists of a twelve-hour package for groups of fifteen persons leaving the city of Hermosillo, Sonora. Tourists travel to Kino Bay on the Gulf of California. From there, they enter Comcáac territory until reaching the Punta Chueca settlement. By then, the group has received information on the safety of the ecotour, the background of the Comcáac and the territory, a list of ecotourism rules of behavior taken from international quality codes (adapted to local reality and approved by the Comcáac team), and a brochure with information on the cultural and environmental value of the estuaries. Once the visitors have arrived at Punta Chueca, they are taken to one of the estuaries facing the Infiernillo Channel on an ecotourism boat.

On a beach adjacent to the estuary, ecotourists are received by the Com-cáac Ecoturismo Seri team guides. As mentioned previously, the team is composed of men and women, elders, adults, and children, belonging to three Comcáac extended families. These guides will have already set up the campsite referred to as *Hant icaheme* to honor Comcáac ancestors. At this point, tourists can engage in several activities: guided walks to admire the landscape and biodiversity as well as its traditional uses; bird watching; snorkeling; kayaking (only kayaks can go into the estu-ary, and no motor boats are allowed); swimming; coexistence with the Comcáac; traditional games, dances, and songs; traditional face painting; storytelling by the elders; purchase of arts and crafts; and, if requested in advance, eating delicious, fresh seafood. Once these activities have ended (approximately six hours), ecotourists return to Punta Chueca by boat, where they can purchase arts, crafts, and fresh seafood so that the families of the indigenous community can obtain further benefits. Then ecotourists once again board the vehicle that will take them back to Kino Bay and Hermosillo.

The Comcáac guides take down the campsite and leave the site fully clean. As has been described, this system of ephemeral and rotational occupation is based on the nomadic tradition of the Comcáac. It is con-sidered pertinent for the sustainable use of estuaries and has been easily appropriated by the group of Comcáac guides.

To date, it is the only ecotourism product managed by a group of Com-cáac families that guarantees quality care, safety, and comfort. In contrast to other projects of this type, participating Comcáac people have train-ing, organization, and own the equipment for providing the services. In other cases, local groups are the last link of external tour operators, which does not generate community appropriation, organization, and training processes. However, the final income is not enough to be considered a viable economic alternative since it depends on many factors that will be described in the next section.

Marketing Process

By the time of the pilot Ecoturismo Seri tour in October 2006, it was evident that the Comcáac would not be able to market the product by themselves due to lack of training and low educational level. Another portion of this project that could not be handled by the Comcáac was the transport of ecotourists from the city of Hermosillo to their territory. This is due to the logistics and the prejudice of urbanites against indigenous people whom they do not trust in addition to the growing danger result-ing from drug trafficking in the region. Thus, the group from CIAD negotiated further financing with the Christensen Fund (from 2007 to 2008) to develop marketing and environmental monitoring of the estuaries.

The result was the following marketing strategy: (1) the development of an attractive name (Ecoturismo Seri), definition of mission and vision, as well as a business plan; (2) hiring a project promoter and guide (this person was certified by the National Interpretation Association, thus enabling her to fine-tune the ecotour to the audience); (3) negotiations for financing from the FMCN for an "Environmental Education through Ecotourism" project geared to middle- and higher-education-level students and teachers in Sonora to promote the value of biocultural and coastal wetland diversity (Camarena et al. 2008); (4) support was requested from Comisión Nacional Forestal (CONAFOR) for the acquisition of equipment and biocultural signage for the estuaries and from Secretaría de Desarrollo Social (SEDESOL) for a van that could safely transport ecotourists; (5) design of a logo and promotional material, such as posters, brochures, flyers, and educational CDs, as well as a Web page (no longer in use, since it could not be afforded); (6) diffusion through several of the local media outlets (newspapers, radio, TV) and also electronically; (7) participation in tourist fairs and academic events; and (8) design of a tool for evaluating what ecotourists learned as a result of their participation (the results show a positive proenvironmental change in their attitude; see Camarena et al. 2008).

Service Quality Evaluation

From November 2008 to November 2009, twenty-eight groups bought the Ecotourism Seri estuaries product. Eighteen of these groups were independent, mostly coming from local schools, bringing a total of 228 visitors. Different means of promotion were used (brochures, flyers, and a Web page) to promote Ecoturismo Seri. The majority of the participants were student and teachers groups (preschool, elementary, junior and senior high school), who participated as a result of the personalized steps taken by the promoter hired specifically for this project. The remaining ten groups were 120 local teachers invited by the "Environmental Education through Ecotourism Project" (a program supported by FMCN), which brought a total of 348 ecotourists (Camarena et al. 2008; Luque 2008).

To evaluate the marketing of the project, an optional survey was given to all visitors (n = 228), with a return rate of 128. The survey did not include the teacher ecotourists from the environmental education project. Tourists visiting Ecoturismo Seri were most likely to be Mexican nationals (98 percent) and female (70 percent). Of the 95 percent who provided their age, 80 percent were under twenty-five years of age. Nearly 97 percent of visitors were students, with most of the rest representing educators or academics. Of the 75 percent of respondents who disclosed their region of residence, 91 percent are from the state of Sonora's capital city, Hermosillo; 2 percent are from outside Mexico; 3 percent are from outside Sonora; and 4 percent are from elsewhere in Sonora.

Of the 48 percent of visitors that responded to whether they purchased any product in the indigenous town, a little over half (56 percent) answered "Seri arts and crafts product," and 6 percent bought "another product besides arts and crafts" (for example, food, sodas, and/or seafood), while the rest did not make any purchases. The average amount spent by those who purchased items was less than U.S. $20. These data show that throughout the Ecoturismo Seri project other Seri people, aside from the guides, were benefiting from the experience, but in a very small way.

Visitors gave very high marks for their experience (Likert scale: excellent, good, OK, bad), specifically giving excellent or good marks to transportation (92 percent), information (98 percent), activities (98 percent), food and beverage hygiene (93 percent), cleanliness (94 percent), security (97 percent), service by the indigenous community (99 percent), guides (98 percent), and price (96 percent). The high marks for guides also indicate that Comcáac guides have been open to receiving the "yori" ecotourists.

To conclude the survey, tourists were asked, "Would you recommend this ecotourism tour?," to which 87 percent answered "definitively yes" and 13 percent "probably yes." Finally, ecotourists were requested to answer a question defining the overall experience (56 percent answered the question): 22 percent stated that it was fun and unbelievable; 14 percent suggested that it would be wonderful to have more frequent trips, highlighting the beauty of the place; and 9 to 11 percent suggested a greater variety of activities, wanting to repeat the tour, as it was an excellent project. Respondents also remarked on their desire to establish contact with the rest of the community, to become better acquainted with the local ecosystem, to promote the project more widely, and to encourage better care of the cleanliness and organization of the Punta Chueca Seri settlement.

Environmental Education Evaluation

One of the main goals of ecotourism is to change attitudes toward the environment and different cultures. The data obtained in the "Environmental Education through Ecotourism Project" survey indicated a certain level of success. This survey indicated a positive change in attitude among a group of teachers from the city of Hermosillo toward the value of biocultural diversity, wetlands, the Gulf of California, and the Comcáac culture (Camarena et al. 2008). However, there are limitations to these types of visitor surveys and the data they provide. The survey does demonstrate that, at the time of their visit, the ecotourists thought positively about ecological protection and cultural diversity as an enriching social factor, but it does not prove that they went home and made any changes in their own lives. It is necessary to apply subsequent research instruments in order to evaluate this possibility.

Community Impact Evaluation

The most important evaluation about the Ecoturismo Seri project emphasizes its impact on the Comcáac community. As stated, the project belonged to three extended families, but not all of their members participated; only twenty-two persons were involved. It is difficult to calculate the final earnings per Comcáac guide, since it was established as an internal policy that money will be distributed equally among those guides who worked during the day of the trip and that the guides would rotate since there were so many. In general, an average of eight Comcáac guides worked on every trip. Also, the cost of each trip varied depending on the number of visitors and if they had their own transportation. The average cost per person was $350 pesos (around U.S. $35). The total average amount paid during the year was estimated in $121,800 pesos (approximately U.S. $12,000). Taking into account the average costs of production (car rental, fuel, and other expenses, which make up around 30 percent), every guide received an average income of $11,000 pesos (U.S. $1,100) per year. It must be added that a single family could have two or three members as guides per trip and that they could sell some handicrafts as well. Because of the weather, the trips were concentrated during the spring and autumn seasons, so during these months the ecotourism project brought about certain economic release to those families.

Perhaps one of the main achievements of the project is that the Comcáac guides often commented that they "liked it very much" and had "lots of fun" working on this new commercial activity, despite the fact that they were afraid of having foreigners in their own territory because of their past history of engagement with them. In addition, the guides were trained as environmental monitors of mangroves and estuaries, based on the elders' traditional knowledge. In the summer of 2008, a traditional-foreign gastronomy event was organized, resulting in a new set of recipes for the community and for tourists. These factors induced a greater respect for their ecosystems and culture. However, those family members that did not want to be involved in the project at the beginning became jealous of its success and started trouble in the project's operation, claiming rights on the equipment property. Nowadays, these families desire more ecotourists.

In 2006, most of the community members were sure that the ecotourism project would not work out because of previous failures. By 2009, the project had gained the community's respect because it attracted tourists to their town, offered the community an opportunity to sell handicrafts, and did not register environmental impact; therefore, they allowed the project to continue. At the same time, since most families were not directly involved in the project, they claimed that the project benefited only a few families, despite having been told that this was only an introductory project and that they would have to wait until the market grew.

Ecoturismo Seri Perspective

Despite the gratifying scenario presented in the evaluations, by 2009 external support for promotion, organization, and transportation was limited. Support was weakened by the global financial crisis, which contracted the regional market; the lack of safety resulting from the war on drugs and drug trafficking; the threat of the swine flu virus; and the extreme climate of the region—the cold from December to February and high temperatures from June to September—which limits the flow of tourists and decreases the availability of school tours to a few months during the year. The year 2009 evidenced the high vulnerability of the Ecoturismo Seri project and many ecotourism projects in general. It is clear that such projects stimulate the conservation of ecosystems, the reappropriation of traditional knowledge, and the appreciation and value by ecotourists and teachers. Most importantly, the Seri community sees the Ecoturismo Seri project as a potential alternative for income. The circumstances that put the permanence of such programs at risk need to be analyzed.

REFLECTIONS FROM A POLITICAL ECOLOGY PERSPECTIVE

"I need a job."

Don Antonio Robles, seventy-eight, chairman of the Council of
Elders and leader of the Ecoturismo Seri project, 1999

In general terms, it can be concluded that any ecotourism project that must comply with the logic of markets—strategies to define the product, diagnosis of local capacities, market studies, business plan, marketing strategies, and evaluation tools—is critical in order to negotiate for funds for marketing and in product development. Nonetheless, the specific problems posed for indigenous communities—economic and political marginalization, ethnic discrimination, educational lags, inefficient infrastructure and public services, and, most of all, the dilemmas stemming from community transformation in the encounter of different cultural rationalities—imply that the analysis of an experience of this type includes many intersecting issues.

"I need a job." This statement, expressed recurrently by an elder of the Comcáac community who is in charge of the promotion and conservation of traditions, is emblematic of the transition of these indigenous peoples from a system of self-subsistence and nomadism to capitalist monetization and sedentary life. This declaration acquires further poignancy because it is shared by all adult and young Comcáac, letting us know that the life of the ancestors is in the past.

The Comcáac have undergone deep cultural hybridization, which has resulted in the local process of dissolution of the traditional social and environmental community and has deepened the capitalization process of nature and labor proletarianization. Hence, the current problem should be placed on a terrain in which there is a simultaneous debate of different cultural dynamics where confrontation, negotiation, struggle, and agreements converge; that is, an encounter of what is related to the community and the private appropriation of capital. Ethical-philosophical dilemmas, up to practical everyday issues going through the productive and political organization, underlie such processes.

Thus, the question is this: How can a communal tradition introduce an ecotourist activity whose objective is private gain in the short term—even more so when such activity has an evident impact on its territorial organization, since it continues to be the source of identity, subsistence, and community organization? In other words, the dilemma of the community becomes the center of critical analysis.

A key institution of a community subsistence pattern based on nomadism is the collective access to natural resources, which has been regulated by a series of traditional laws. This is an institution that has been challenged by the integration of productive activities of a mercantile nature, such as fishing, arts and crafts, and, most of all, the synergistic management of the territory, where the usufruct of these activities generates internal corruption and social inequality, and therefore political conflicts. Usufruct of ecotourism, although negligible and not constant, is subject to the immediate complaint of the rest of the group, since it is a project that does not benefit all, despite the recognition that there are productive workgroups and that it is respected by the community.

The traditional community organization has been the source of resistance to migration and the inertia of proletarianization in a poverty state, resulting from monetization processes of self-subsistence. Nevertheless, in view of the difficulties of promoting and organizing certain portions of the productive process of ecotourism, doubts arise as to whether it will be possible to maintain this resistance. In this context, ecotourism has brought about the dilemmas that stem from the commodification of respected collective traditions: the discomfort of the spirits of the ancestors due to the entry of so many "foreign people" to Tiburón Island; traditional dances and songs that have been kept as part of the collective heritage; and the tradition of face paintings, which acquire a new internal significance since they were prohibited by Christians at one time and are used only during festivities and as part of the activities provided to ecotourists and which Comcáac guides feel deserve a higher price due to their ancestral value. Another significant tradition is community distribution of food. During the first ecotourism tours, the Comcáac expected ecotourists to share their food with them, and any refusal to do so was hard for the Comcáac to accept. In fact, the community distribution of food is revealed in a series of traditions, such as distributing surplus fish. However, regional market specialization, which, besides the fact that they are expensive, has propitiated a decrease in the diversity of fish species and has weakened this tradition.

In other words, the impact of marketing on Comcáac subsistence, to which ecotourism has been added, has generated contradictory processes. On the one hand, the financial income enables them to guarantee certain levels of health and community security. On the other hand, the revenue has exacerbated internal political conflicts resulting from the inequitable distribution of the commercial usufruct of the territory's natural resources. In the field of the biocultural relations complex (culture, biodiversity, knowledge, and language), ecotourism has stimulated the systematization of traditional knowledge in the management of estuaries and has opened new channels for its transmission between generations through the Dialogue of Knowledge-Based Monitoring System. However, it is deepening the mercantile resignificance of traditional practices, depriving them of their ancestral symbolic content, which has been a factor of community cohesion and identity.

The dilemmas can be seen clearly. Can the community survive under the conditions of poverty generated by an inequitable political and economic relationship with the national society? If the community has been the source of endurance and a buffer against greater pauperization, how can productive activities that tend to dissolve the community be introduced? As stated previously, if the community is a fundamental institution of the biocultural complex, then how can biodiversity be conserved without the community? Or, perhaps, are we facing a process that will provide a new significance to community?

Due to all the listed reasons, it may concluded that the Comcáac team is currently incapable of being in charge of commercialization and administration processes of the Ecoturismo Seri project, allowing local tourist entrepreneurs to take advantage of this situation. Taking into account the collective request, "Please, make ecotourism work, because we need to work," the question remains: Who owns ecotourism?

ACKNOWLEDGEMENTS

The Ecoturismo Seri Project has received the support of the following institutions: Comcáac Elders Council, Comcáac Traditional Government, CIAD, FMCN (Fondo Mexicano para la Conservación de la Naturaleza [Mexican Fund for Nature Conservancy]), TCF (The Christensen Fund), Cofetur (Comisión de Fomento al Turismo-Gobierno del Estado de Sonora [Tourist Development Commission—Government of the State of Sonora]), SEDESOL (Secretaría de Desarrollo Social [Department of Social Development]), and CONAFOR (Comisión Nacional Forestal [National Forestry Commission]). We also wish to thank the Instituto de Investigaciones sobre Desarrollo Sustentable y Equidad Social de la Universidad Iberoamericana (Sustainable Development and Social Equity Research Institute of the Ibero-American University) for the support provided to continue furthering Ecoturismo Seri and for making this chapter possible.

NOTES

1. The Comcáac community is better known in Mexico as the Seri community. However, they refer to themselves as Comcáac, which, in their language, means "the people." This indigenous group is undergoing a transitional process from oral to written traditions. Therefore, a consensus regarding the way to write their language, the *cmiique iitom*, is still missing. For example, several ways of writing "Comcáac" include Kunkaak, Concaac, Comcáac, Conca'ac, and Cunca'ac. In this chapter, Comcáac will be used, which is the version accepted by Lorenzo Thompson, a native of the group, who has been acknowledged for having studied the way in which to write the language for over twenty years. In addition, this is the version accepted by the Seri Dictionary "Comcáac quih Yaza quih Hant Ihíip hac" (Moser and Marlett 2005). Furthermore, on occasion, the term *Comcáac community* is used, not because they present the typical features of an indigenous community, but rather because it is the noun with which they represent themselves (Luque and Robles Torres 2006:10).

2. The first experiences with ecotourism projects among Indian communities occurred in 1989 with the furtherance of the Indian Peoples, Ecology, and Production for Sustainable Development Project of the former National Indigenous Institute. By 2007, there were 404 ecotourism projects in twenty-four states in the country involving 50,137 Indians.

3. The WTO considers "adventure tourism" as one of the variables linked to ecotourism.

4. This project has received support from SEDESOL (Secretaria de Desarrollo Social del Gobierno Federal [Department of Social Development of the Federal Government]), CONAFOR (Comisión Nacional Forestal [National Forestry Commission]), and SEMARNAT (Secretaria de Medio Ambiente y Recursos Naturales del Gobierno Federal [Department of the Environment and Natural Resources—Federal Government]), as well as of the FMCN (2008) to foster an environmental education program focused on promoting the value of wetlands and biocultural diversity among secondary school students and teachers in Sonora.

5. This includes IMADES (Instituto del Medio Ambiente y Desarrollo Sustentable de Sonora [Institute of the Environment and Sustainable Development of Sonora]) and Cofetur (Comisión para e Fomento al Turismo de Sonora [Commission for the Development of Tourism of the Government of the State of Sonora]).

6. The *cmique iitom* is the mother tongue of the Comcáac.

REFERENCES

Blount, Ben G. 2001. Indigenous Peoples and the Uses and Abuses of Ecotourism. In *On Biocultural Diversity: Linking Language, Knowledge, and the Environment*, ed. Luisa Maffi, pp. 503–16. Washington, DC: Smithsonian Institution Press.

Boege Schmidt, Eckart. 2008. *El Patrimonio Biocultural de los Pueblos Indígenas de México: Hacia la Conservación in situ de la Biodiversidad y la Agrodiversidad de los Territorios Indígenas*. México: Instituto Nacional de Antropología e Historia.

Camarena, Beatriz, Diana Luque, and Delisahe Velarde. 2008. *Educación Ambiental a Través del Ecoturismo: Diversidad Biocultural y Humedales Costeros del Canal del Infiernillo en Territorio Comcáac (Seri), Golfo de California*. Paper presented at the 1st Biennial Conference of the Program of Marine Ecological Regulation of the Gulf of California.

Descola, Philippe, and Gisli Pálsson, eds. 2001. *Naturaleza y Sociedad: Perspectivas Antropológicas*. México: Editorial Siglo XXI.

Fondo Mexicano para la Conservación de la Naturaleza (FMCN). 2008. *Informe anual*. Fondo Mexicano para la Conservación de la Naturaleza, México, DF.

García Canclini, Nestor. 2000. *La Globalización Imaginada*. Buenos Aires: Paidos.

Henríquez, Elio. 2008. Zanjan Conflicto Católicos y Evangélicos de Comunidad de San Juan Chamula. *La Jornada*, November 9, 2008.

Keene Meltzoff, Sarah, Michael Lemons, and Yair G. Lichtensztajn. 2001. Voices of a Natural Prison: Tourism Development and Fisheries Management among the Political Ghosts of Pisagua, Chile. *Journal of Political Ecology* 8(1):45–80.

Leff, Enrique. 2008. *Discursos Sustentables*. México: Editorial Siglo XXI.

López Pardo, Gustavo, and Bertha Palomino Villavicencio. 2008. Políticas Públicas y Ecoturismo en Comunidades Indígenas de México. *Teoría y Praxis* 5:33–50.

Luque, Diana, ed. 2006. *Xtáasi Hant Comcáac: Ecoturismo, Cultura y Naturaleza*. Report submitted to the Mexican Fund for the Conservation of Nature. Hermosillo, México: Centro de Investigación en Alimentación y Desarrollo.

———. 2008. *Comercialización del Ecoturismo Seri*. Report submitted to The Christensen Fund. Hermosillo, México: Centro de Investigación en Alimentación y Desarrollo.

Luque, Diana, and Shoko Doode Matsumoto. 2010. Los Comcáac (Seri): Hacia una Diversidad Biocultural del Golfo de California y Estado de Sonora, México. *Estudios Sociales* 17:274–300.

Luque, Diana, and Antonio Robles Torres. 2006. *Naturalezas, Saberes y Territorios Comcáac (Seri): Diversidad Cultural y Sustentabilidad Ambiental.* México, DF: Instituto Nacional de Ecología.

Maffi, L., ed. 2001. *On Biocultural Diversity: Linking Language, Knowledge, and the Environment.* Washington, DC: Smithsonian Institution Press.

Moser, Mary Beck, and Stephen A. Marlett. 2005. Comcáac quih Yaza quih Hant Ihíip Hac: Cmiique iitom—cocsar iitom—maricáana itom = Diccionario Seri—Español—Inglés: Con índices Español—Seri, Inglés—Seri. Hermosillo, México: Editorial Uni Son and Plaza y Valdés Editores.

Paulson, Susan, Susan Gerzon, and Michael Watts. 2003. Locating the Political in Political Ecology: An Introduction. *Human Organization* 62(3):205–17.

Salido, Patricia L., ed. 2007. *Plan Rector Para el Desarrollo Turístico Sustentable de la Ruta del Río Sonora.* Report submitted to the Tourist Development Commission, Centro de Investigación en Alimentación y Desarrollo. Hermosillo, México: Centro de Investigación en Alimentación y Desarrollo.

14

+

The Effects of Tourism and Western Consumption on the Gendered Production and Distribution of Bogolan

Development Initiatives and Malian Women as Agents for Change

Sarah Lockridge

"When many women have the idea to make a group there are [fewer] barriers. If they have the help of NGOs that are being born everywhere now, it is obvious that there are more organizations than ever before to help women."

Urban NGO Coordinator for Women in Mali

Urban women of Mali are playing an active role in the Malian bogolan tourist market. Bogolan is a textile characterized by complex black-and-white patterns made with mud. The commoditization of this Malian cloth has caused major shifts in the traditional production and distribution of the textile, creating a whole new group of urban producers and distributers comprised of both women and men. Bogolan is a commercialized version of a more traditional cloth referred to as *bogolanfini* that was formerly controlled by women.

Feminists are concerned with issues of oppression, exploitation, and subordination of women within society and attempt to change or transform them through social action (Parpart et al. 2000:203–9). Borrowing from Marxist feminist theory, this chapter investigates the marginalization of Malian women's traditional socioeconomic status once their craft products are integrated into tourist and international markets, as well as social action taken to combat their subordination. Historically, the knowledge of bogolanfini production was a highly secret task guarded from outsiders and performed exclusively by rural women who learned from female kin passing the knowledge from generation to generation. In Bamanakan, *bogo* means "mud," *lan* means "with or by means of," and *fini* means "cloth." The mud cloth was produced for significant social events in Bamana women's lives, such as weddings and excisions. Newly married women wore the cloth during their wedding ceremonies. During excision, young girls wore it as a protection from spiritual powers that might become dangerous and cause them sickness or fatality. Finally, in death, women were wrapped in the cloth for burial. Today, Malian men and women, who know little of its religious significance and social origins, produce the cloth for tourist and international markets, creating a whole new form of the textile now commonly referred to as *bogolan*. Yet, while women sell fewer bogolan products than do men, numerous studies suggest that tourism often gives women access to new economic opportunities, and the women of the study illustrate this trend (Chambers 2000:59–63).

Tourism in Mali generates approximately $155 million a year in revenues. Most foreign tourists are from Europe, predominantly France. There are also visitors from the USA, Japan, Middle East, and other West African nations (Europa World Year Book 2009). Tourists often visit Mali to experience its diversified cultures, view the architecture, buy arts and crafts, and hear the music of internationally acclaimed musicians. Popular destinations from south to north include Ségou, Djenné, Mopti, Dogon Country, and Timbuktu.

Ségou, where this study takes place, is one of the largest towns in the country, with a population of approximately ninety thousand; the majority are the Bamana people. It is a historic town, located in south-central Mali along the Niger River and was a center for the French colonial economy. Ségou *Koro* (Old Ségou), the location of the precolonial Bamana kingdom during the seventeenth and eighteenth centuries, is nearby. Ségou has two architectural styles of interest to tourists—French colonial and Sudano-Sahelian. Popular items made by the Bamana and purchased by tourists include bogolan, pottery, and traditional weavings in the form of blankets. The town also sponsors the Festival on the Niger (*Le Festival Sur le Niger*), the largest cultural festival in Mali, best known for its music featuring top Malian musicians.

Anthony Giddens (1979:88) defines agency as the "transformative capacity" of agents to use their power to reshape the world through acts. International and national development trends are encouraging Malian women to compete with men in the bogolan mud cloth market. Men have greater political, economic, and social advantages, which give them an edge. For instance, men are more likely to be educated as professional artists, providing an unfair advantage in innovation and design. The focus here is on the actions taken by members of urban women's arts and crafts associations organized around income-generating activities to empower themselves economically. Although the odds are seemingly against them, by working in collaboration with nongovernmental (NGO) and governmental organizations (GOs) women increase their presence in the market.

The following research questions guide this chapter: How have tourism and Western consumption of Malian bogolan affected the gendered production and distribution of the cloth? What strategies do Malian women use to overcome gendered barriers in the marketplace? Anthropological research methods such as semistructured interviews, life stories, and participant observation were used to collect data. The methodology included interviews conducted from 2000 to 2003 with twenty-two female members from two different arts and crafts associations as well as collaborating NGOs, GOs, boutique owners, and two prominent male mud cloth producers. To protect their privacy, pseudonyms have been used for naming the women's organizations.

The situation of female members of arts and crafts associations illustrates the complexity of the affects of tourism and Western consumption on women's socioeconomic status. While rural Malian women have lost their total control over the cloth's production and distribution and the traditional social and economic power it afforded them, commoditization of the cloth has now provided new options for urban women.

THE ORIGINS OF BOGOLANFINI: A CLOTH OF SOCIAL SIGNIFICANCE AND FEMALE CONTROL

Bogolanfini refers to the rural and traditional origins of the textile first produced by the Bamana people. The Bamana consider themselves Muslims but also practice indigenous religions associated with initiation societies and a strong belief in wilderness spirits (Rovine 2008:16). Bogolanfini is a ritual cloth produced only by women to mark major life transitions, particularly for females (Aherne 1992; Brett-Smith 1982). The knowledge of bogolanfini design and production has been a secret that women have until recently guarded from outsiders, especially men. The cloth motifs are generally composed of geometric forms such as dots, circles, crosses, triangles, and zigzags. The motifs represent objects such as drums, and locations such as towns, animals, and historical events (Rovine 2008:22). According to Sarah Brett-Smith, "Medicinal knowledge, historical facts, and moral precepts for correct behavior are all encoded into *bogolan fini* designs" (1984:142).

Knowledge for the Bamana is a highly valued commodity, perceived as a powerful and hard-earned resource for women who possess it. Producers must know the codes and how to identify, collect, and prepare various plant ingredients necessary to create the sacred cloth. It is not uncommon for women to have their own secret concoctions using a different species of leaf to achieve darker colors (Aherne 1992:9). Through the exclusive rights to producing bogolanfini, Bamana women who have historically been constrained by patriarchal society possess the power of secret knowledge that gives them a certain amount of prestige in Bamana culture.

Brett-Smith (1984) divides the cloth into three color categories: red, black, and white, each with symbolic meaning. Bogolanfini in the red category is associated with blood and transformation, black with fertility and productivity, and white with death and purity (Rovine 2008:16). In some Bamana areas the cloth is an important element of female dress and ritualistic practice. Young women must wear the red cloths during excision and during the subsequent period of isolation. Red wraps are believed to heal the wound while simultaneously protecting the wearer from *nyama*, a spiritual power in Bamana religion, released at such moments, which is potentially dangerous if not controlled. In fact, wearing the cloth is so critical to the practice that some women believe "excision began with the creation of *bogolanfini*" (Aherne 1992:8).

A newly married woman wears a white cloth during her wedding ceremony and when leaving her natal village to live in her husband's village (Aherne 1992). In death, the white cloth is used to wrap her corpse before burial (Brett-Smith 1982:251).

Traditionally the only men who wear the cloth are the hunters who commonly wear red bogolanfini to protect them from evil powers that may lurk during hunting expeditions (Rovine 2008:25). The Bamana believe hunters possess considerable powers necessary for confronting both physical and supernatural dangers on hunting expeditions: "Bamana mythology and history is rife with stories of hunters as leaders, heroes, and adventurers" (Rovine 2008:25).

The process for making bogolanfini is long and complicated and follows a strict gendered division of labor, like other activities in Malian culture. In the household, for example, women collect firewood and fetch water while men kill animals and prepare the meat for women to cook. In the fields, men are responsible for growing millet crops, but women winnow the grain to prepare it for storage. In relation to textile production, men traditionally weave cloth and tailor garments. Tailoring is a specialized occupation performed by only a few men.

Bogolanfini production begins with the "cleaning, carding, and spinning" of cotton on wooden hand spindles—a task performed by older women (Rovine 2008:17). Men weave the thread into cloth strips on foot looms, then sew them together to form a *tafe*, or in French *pagne*, about thirty-six inches wide. Women place the cloth in a dye bath made of leaves that have been mashed, boiled, or soaked. Mud used for creating the designs is collected from the center of large ponds, then placed in a clay pot, covered with water, and left to sit for an entire year (Imperato and Shamir 1970:38). The fermented mud is used to paint the cloths—usually with an iron spatula or stick carefully outlining the linear designs. This is a time-consuming process: "Bamana women must paint the mud dye onto the thick cloth stroke by stroke if they are not to smudge the clear line between the dark, mud dyed background and the negatives spaces of the white motifs" (Brett-Smith 1984:131). The intricate and symbolic patterns differentiate bogolanfini from other Malian cloth.

Bogolanfini production has provided women the power to secure an economic livelihood for centuries. Historically, the making of the cloth provided financial benefits to rural women and their families. Because most Bamana are farmers and often suffer from lack of capital during drought-stricken years, women who make the cloth are able to bring in a supplemental income (Aherne 1992:13). However, this income is often unpredictable and modest (Short 1996:40). Rural women's lives are filled with reproductive responsibilities and domestic responsibilities. Bogolanfini is generally produced during the dry season when farming responsibilities are decreased. Older women beyond childbearing years leave domestic responsibilities to their daughters and daughters-in-law, giving them more time to engage in bogolanfini production (Rovine 2008:17). They are often helped by extended kin during the cloth-making process. Entire households sometimes engage in the dyeing and painting process. In contemporary contexts, this may include both males and females of varying ages (Short 1996:40).

The distribution of the cloth within local perimeters is seldom purely economic. When a female bogolanfini producer sets a price for the cloth she often considers the individual debts she may owe her client, her client's political position, and, above all else, her personal or family relationship with the client. Until recently, no traditional bogolanfini producer would paint a cloth for a client she disliked (Brett-Smith 1982:6). For rural women, cloth production has both social and economic benefits.

In the late nineteenth century and early twentieth century almost every young Bamana girl learned to produce bogolanfini as apprentices to their mothers (Brett-Smith 1982:56). A producer calculated that during her childhood, twenty-seven women in her extended family were regularly occupied with the production (Brett-Smith 1982:56). Girls commonly begin learning the craft by the age of seven or eight, or sometimes even earlier (Aherne 1992:15).

The number of young, rural girls interested in learning how to make bogolanfini has declined. Tavy Aherne (1992:15) speculates this is because they have more economic opportunities than their mothers. However, the decrease of bogolanfini production by rural women is countered by a rapid increase in the making of bogolan by urban women. This shift to urban centers is linked to the commodization of the cloth and is accompanied by a gender shift in production and distribution.

THE REVITALIZATION OF BOGOLAN: A BROAD CHRONOLOGICAL ACCOUNT OF EVENTS

Bogolan, or the commoditized version of the textile, has become a national and international phenomenon. Diversified and simplified patterns of bogolanfini appear in modern versions of the textile distributed in a number of different venues simultaneously—mainly fine art, fashion, international markets, and Malian tourist markets. The spectacular rise in the textile's popularity is primarily due to the cloth's (1) position as a symbol of Malian national pride, (2) changing designs and uses introduced by Malian males for the male-dominated fine art and fashion design milieus, and (3) becoming a source of African identity for African Americans.

Remarkably, until recently, the traditional form of the cloth, bogolanfini, was devalued by Malian urban populations largely due to Islamic and French colonial influence. Because bogolanfini garments were used in rural Bamana rituals, urban populations preferred robes associated with Islamic practices (Duponchel 1995:36). Under French colonial rule (1885–1960) assimilationist policies drove many of Mali's indigenous cultural practices underground, particularly those related to spirituality. The French enforced the adoption of "French language, governance, and mores" to strengthen their political and economic dominance. Aggressive devaluing of a precolonial Malian way of life and the general Malian sense of cultural pride included stigmatizing the use of bogolanfini as a "backward practice" (Grace 2003:12).

After independence in 1960, a rejuvenation of indigenous cultural pride began. Under the socialist rule of Modibo Keita, Malians held "cultural weeks," organized regionally. Women, as the traditional producers of the textile, were commissioned to paint bogolanfini for costumes worn by government-sponsored dance troupes. By the end of the 1960s, the textile had two roles: one still rooted in the traditions of Bamana rituals and village social life, and the other as a government-supported symbol of national pride conveyed through theatrical performances staged in Bamako, the capital city of Mali, by people from different regions (Duponchel 1995:36). In these early days of the cloth's revival, rural women's role in the cloth's production still dominated. However, removing the textile from its local context and transforming it into a national symbol marked the beginning of bogolanfini's road to international notoriety and the end of women's control over the production of the cloth.

In the 1970s, new adaptations of the cloth, using innovative techniques and designs, were appearing in the male-dominated fine art scene. Kandioura Coulibaly, a young Malian male artist graduating from the National Institute of Art (*Institut National des Arts*) located in Bamako, was an early innovator who dared to use, for artistic purposes only, the technique that had been the secret domain of Bamana women for centuries. Coulibaly and fellow artist Lamine Sidibe expanded their influence by organizing workshops teaching bogolan production techniques for dyeing cloth with vegetable dyes rather than the traditional use of mud (Duponchel 1995:35).

Currently, the Groupe Bogolan Kasobane, an organization comprised of four men (Kandioura Coulibaly, Kletigui Dembele, Souleyman Goro, Boubacar Doumbia) and one woman (Nene Thiam), are internationally acclaimed for their bogolan pieces. All were educated at the National Institute of Art in the 1970s and did much to popularize the textile's use as a fine-art medium. They collaborate in the creation of bogolan paintings depicting Malian subjects such as masks, mosques, drummers, and dancers. Their bogolan has been exhibited all over the world, including a solo exhibition at the Museum of African and Oceania Art (*Musée des Arts Africains et Océaniens*) in Paris (Rovine 2008:69–72). Since the international market for fine-art bogolan is small, some of the members also sell their work in Malian tourist markets. In fact, one of the members has opened a bogolan boutique strategically located near the most frequented tourist hotel in Ségou, and he successfully attracts tourists.

African fashion designers also played a central role in the revitalization of the textile. In 1979, the cloth debuted as a fashion piece when Malian Seydou Nourou Doumbia, alias Chris Seydou, a man considered Africa's first African designer with Western appeal, incorporated bogolan in a draped scarf and headdress for his winter collection (Duponchel 1995:36). In 1981, after many successful years in the Paris fashion scene, Chris Seydou returned to Bamako to have direct access to the weavers and dyers who were the sources of his craft. He continued to place emphasis on bogolan by using it for his high-fashion creations in the hope that a designer of his reputation would increase the quality of the bogolan products available in the capital's market (Rovine 2008:112). Although Chris Seydou died tragically of AIDS in the 1990s, during his short career he enhanced the status of traditional textiles of West Africa generally, and bogolan in particular, both within Africa and abroad (Duponchel 1995:36).

WESTERN CONSUMPTION OF BOGOLAN

Western consumption of the cloth has also played a significant role in expanding the popularity of bogolan. Since the 1990s modern versions of the cloth have reached many destinations abroad, primarily across the industrialized West, so that familiarity with the cloth at home piques the interest of tourists visiting Mali.

Bogolan products found abroad are either handmade (generally produced in Mali) or are bogolan-inspired items such as bedsheets, wrapping paper, and travel mugs that are industrially manufactured in the West.[1] In the USA, as in Mali's tourist bogolan markets, designs are simplified and barely resemble the motifs of "traditional" bogolanfini. Rovine notes that "the cloth's abstract designs and its black and white hues are often its sole defining features" (Rovine 2008:132). The designs are assigned new African names such as "Totem Elephant" and "Zanzibar" (Rovine 2008). When advertized in American catalogues, Western views of Africa as a "primitive," "exotic," dark continent still steeped in tribal practices and a preindustrial way of life are often conveyed. A Bloomingdale's advertisement for a bogolan style of bedding called "Sahara" illustrates the links: "A beguiling study in black and tan and recalls the tribal beauty of Africa. Our Sahara duvet cover . . . creates a smooth, soft covering; add accents of midnight black and tan motifs, reminiscent of ancient drawings and symbols" (Rovine 2008:134–35).

These items carry broad cultural associations throughout the African diaspora, where bogolan products are often used as an expression of black cultural identity. For African Americans in the United States, however, the cloth is not necessarily associated with the "exotic" but rather becomes a positive symbol of pride in African heritage (Rovine 2008:136).

GOVERNMENT POLICIES AND TRADE IN BOGOLAN ABROAD

Malian government policies have also facilitated the spread of bogolan. Since Mali's new democracy was established in 1991, the government has made a number of regulatory and institutional reforms to encourage Mali's role in Western markets. These reforms were significant considering the more restrictive role in trade played by the state until 1968 under President Modibo Keita's socialist economic platform. The military dictatorship that followed, led by Moussa Traore, kept aspects of socialism by keeping a centralized and command economy (Koenig et al. 1998:73). By the early 1980s, due to structural-adjustment pressures from the World Bank and aid donors, the government moved away from central control toward economic liberalization (Koenig et al. 1998:75). However, market liberalization efforts were discouraged by the government's problems with mass corruption and embezzlement. When Moussa was overthrown in 1991, Mali became a democratic state. The continued pressures under structural adjustment remained high, and under president Alpha Toumany Toure the government moved slowly in the direction of relying increasingly upon trade and the free market. With liberalization of the market, many individual traders in Mali moved into private commerce (Warms 1994:99).

Democracy in Mali increased trade flows between Mali and the United States, which meant that Malian bogolan traders could expand more readily their distribution networks to other countries as well. A boutique owner in Washington, DC, who sells African textiles, commented that he had never seen bogolan on American markets until 1992, and shortly thereafter the American markets were "completely saturated with it."[2]

MALE DOMINATION IN BOGOLAN MARKETS AND BARRIERS TO WOMEN'S EMPOWERMENT

The revitalization of bogolan is also linked to changes in the gendered production and distribution of the cloth. Although women do play a pivotal role in the bogolan tourist market, men have greater political, economic, educational, and social advantages in Mali, which gives them dominance.

Political and economic factors in the masculinization of the cloth's production and distribution include the changing situation of Bamako's largely male university students. Until the mid to late 1980s, Mali's students received scholarships for their living expenses and after graduation were expected to find employment in the Malian government bureaucracy. Increased implementations of structural adjustment programs led to significant cutbacks in government spending, reducing the availability of both scholarships and employment positions within the government. As a result, some desperate male graduates seeking alternate ways to gain revenue decided to get involved in bogolan markets (Rovine 2008:46).

As noted, many of the young, male producers are former students from the National Institute of Art, the only formal institute for fine art education in Mali. Few female students attend the art institute. For example, when art historian Victoria Rovine (2008:151) visited the institute, she discovered a class was comprised of one female and thirty-three males. With less formal artistic training, women often lack the confidence to engage in the cloth's production. When confident, they may lack the artistic ability necessary to compete with men who have been trained in art composition.

Although Rovine (2008) focuses on men in the bogolan tourist market, there are all-women arts and crafts associations visibly active in Ségou and throughout the country. In Ségou, the women's associations produce and distribute mainly for tourists rather than international markets. However, the quality of their pieces is rarely as good as those created by their main male Ségouvian competitor, Boubacar Doumbia, a member of the famous team of bogolan artists Groupe Bogolan Kasobane. Tourists, expatriates, and local hotels in Ségou typically purchase bogolan pictures, housewares (bedcovers, curtains, pillowcases), and accessories such as scarves from Doumbia, whose main boutique is strategically located across from the most popular hotel for tourists in the center of town, while the women's association's boutiques are nowhere near it. Doumbia also sells bogolan pieces from his production center located on the periphery of Ségou next door to a women's arts and crafts association. Tourists drawn by his international reputation flock to him, largely ignoring the women's boutique. Additional attractions are the bogolan workshops Doumbia offers for organized groups of tourists.

In Bamako, it is men who manage the shops and stalls and work as "runners" who find potential bogolan customers. In 1997, in Artisanat, one of Bamako's major markets for tourist art, out of one hundred stalls there was only one female stall owner (Rovine 2008:46). Malian women are deterred from entrepreneurial positions due to patriarchal social sanctions that often confine them to small, petty trading of cloth and food produce. As entrepreneurs, men selling the same cloth and food items realize greater profits. Rovine suggests male bureaucrats who "object in principle to women in business" are largely responsible for this discrimination (Rovine 2008:47). Lalla Tangara Toure, a struggling boutique owner, reported problems negotiating with the merchant bureaucracy, which discouraged her from applying for loans, securing grants, and obtaining shop rentals (Rovine 2008).

Men producing the cloth for entrepreneurs are typically hired workers organized in male-headed production facilities. The owner of these shops makes larger profits than a female who is making single items for sale as a member of an association. Jane Turrittin (1989:68) reasons that this is because Malian men also have greater access to formal education than women. As literate entrepreneurs, men have a competitive advantage. Development literacy efforts in Mali, until recently, have been aimed at male and not female youth (Turrittin 1989:6). Education facilitates greater access to foreign donors, foreign buyers, and foreign tourists, not to mention Malian elites working for development agencies.

Because women in most developing countries work long hours each day engaged in domestic and reproductive chores, men have more time than women to devote themselves to entrepreneurial efforts. A woman from a Ségou arts and crafts association complains:

> The men who make *bogolan* do not have the same problems as women do. These men do not have many duties. While I'm here many other problems are waiting for me in the family. This is not the case with men. Men's work is more profitable for them than ours is for us. They have much more time to commit themselves to one thing and to get a lot of money for what they do.[3]

The Bamana practice patrilineal descent and patrilocal residence, whereby brides marry into male-dominated households where the patriarch, or eldest brother, often makes final decisions. Through the institution of marriage, the husband's household gains rights to a woman's field and domestic labor and frequently her income and other resources as well. If a married woman wants to engage in activities outside the household, she must get permission from her husband. If a widow, she must appeal to other males in the household. Women who are engaged in bogolan production as members of women's associations generally have support from male family members.

Even when participation is male authorized, women will sometimes confront negativity from men in the household who believe women are neglecting their domestic duties. For example, though some female members have servants who cook in their absence, men often refuse to eat dishes prepared by servants (Institut des Sciences Humaines 1988:35). If a wife does not cook for her husband, she is not only neglecting both her domestic and cultural duty but also showing her husband disrespect.

GROUP MEMBERSHIP AND WOMEN AS AGENTS FOR CHANGE

Despite political, economic, educational, and social barriers to women's economic empowerment, members of women's arts and crafts associations strategize to overcome barriers via external development efforts and internal group organization. Most members are not educated enough to find work in the formal sector and, prior to membership, struggled to gain income as petty traders in Mali's informal sector. A collective of organized women has greater power to overcome gendered barriers because they have access to a broad network of development organizations that are formed to ensure economic success.

Since the democratization of Mali, there has been a dramatic increase in the number of women participating in a variety of associations, including political groups, unions, literacy programs, income-generation projects, and credit associations (De Jorio 1997:195–216). An NGO coordinator

responsible for urban women's issues explains why women are experiencing an increase in hope and freedom:

> Women are better informed now. They are better educated, and they com-
> municate better now than in the past. We can say that the poor woman, who
> formerly had to stay in her little corner, knowing nothing else but cooking
> and taking care of the children and the other needs of the family is chang-
> ing. So are those men who were also reticent to some forms of freedom for
> women. With all these fights, all this information and education, with all this
> communication from one level of the society to another, this all opened the
> spirit of women and helped them to say, "instead of remaining in my corner,
> I have the right to meet other women and form organizations. My husband
> could not understand before, but now he understands." When many women
> have the idea to make a group there are [fewer] barriers. If they have the
> help of NGOs that are being born everywhere now, it is obvious that there
> are more organizations than ever before to help women.[4]

This optimism is supported by development structures recognizing the
tremendous economic role women play in societal progress. For example,
the Malian government has implemented a rigorous development program with multiple areas identified for change. There are two long-term
development goals: (1) raising the literacy level of Malian women; and
(2) diversifying the income-generating activities—petty trading and domestic servitude—which women traditionally dominate (Diakité 1995).
Many NGOs focus on providing women access to markets currently
dominated by men, such as bogolan production and tailoring.

Perhaps the NGO most involved in the production and marketing of bogolan for Malian women's associations is the National Federation of Malian
Artisans (*La Fédération Nationale des Artisans du Mali*), or FNAM, founded in
1987. FNAM establishes connections between bogolan-producing women's
groups and other organizations to ensure success in the market. These
organizations, such as NGOs and GOs, offer workshops to teach technical
skills, expand bogolan markets to venues such as crafts fairs held in Mali
and neighboring countries, and also provide access to credit necessary for
the production of large bogolan orders. FNAM (2001) has regional locations
in each major town throughout the country to meet the needs of arts and
crafts associations' members more effectively.

FNAM works closely with Swisscontact, an NGO established in 1989
to provide urban development programs in Bamako, Sikasso, Koutiala,
Ségou, and Mopti with the goal of creating more opportunities for crafts-
people working in the informal sector. Swisscontact promotes professional technical training activities to increase skill levels and to support
microenterprise development. The technical programs targeted are auto

repair, electricity, metal construction, carpentry, air conditioning, electronics, and tailoring (Sissoko 2000:20).

Initial program designs did not consider issues of gender discrimination, however, and over time it was men who benefited from their programs and not women. This occurred in part because men dominate in all of the craft domains Swisscontact chose (Sissoko 2000). As noted, even sewing is primarily associated with men in Mali who have learned the trade via apprenticeship to male tailors. Men also learn bogolan as apprentices to already qualified craftsmen.

By 1995, the women of Mali had already begun organizing and forming multifunctional associations that include technical skills, literacy, and social education classes in tandem with income-generation opportunities. In 1998, determined to reverse both the cultural practice of male apprenticeship and discrimination of women in their training programs, Swisscontact, in collaboration with the GO, Fund to Support Professional Training and Apprenticeship (*Fonds D'Appui à La Formation Professionnelle et à L'Apprentissage*), or FAFPA, initiated a series of sewing programs for women (Sissoko 2000). With this new skill, women have expanded their repertoire of bogolan products from pagnes and pictures to include a variety of items such as housewares and accessories.

Women's arts and crafts groups often begin mud cloth production in two different ways: (1) they have contacts with development agents and/ or expatriates who are aware of the cloth's monetary value and recommend the group engage in the activity; or (2) they have group members who convince the others to get involved, and the association is subsequently supported by development partners.

In 1995, the Work of Women (*Muso Baraw*), a women's association in Ségou town, was initially organized around knitting and batik. In 1996, the Work of Women established a working partnership with a Peace Corps extension agent in small-enterprise development. The volunteer suggested the group take advantage of their location as a prime tourist destination because of Ségou's rich history and French and Sudano-Sahelian architecture and produce bogolan for tourists.

Everything Is Good (*Kow Kanyi*) is a women's group in Ségou town whose main activity is tailoring clothes for local Malians. Although bogolan is not their focus, an informant reports center members began making the cloth because they had heard of the Work of Women's success in the market and decided to compete.

The women's associations have a variety of ways to market their work. The NGO Action for Enterprise, AFE, is a USAID-sponsored project that gives classes in bogolan skills, thereby enhancing opportunities for connections with export wholesale markets. Items deemed worthy are selected by the director of AFE, who places them on commission in the NGO's gallery in Bamako, where international buyers visit.

There are also some private wholesalers in Mali who act as intermediaries to help women's mud-cloth groups reach international and tourist markets by capitalizing on a Western desire to help alleviate poverty for Malian women. The Internet is used to reach international buyers, and brochures are placed in hotels to interest tourists. The following excerpt is from a brochure made by a Ségou wholesaler interested in promoting local women's groups:

> Bogolan is a Bamana tradition made with the earth and uses an ancient dying technique of natural colors on bands of cotton tissue. African (*Farafina*) is a local boutique offering a new initiative in Ségou, with the goal of promoting local textiles. Representing two Ségouvian women's centers: [The Work of Women (*Muso Baraw*)] and [Everything Is Good (*Kow Kanyi*)], we hope to market their work on international and tourist markets. (Farafina Boutique 2001)

The boutique African was established by a woman, the former director of the urban NGO Free Association for the Promotion of the Habitat and Housing (*Association Libre Pour la Promotion de l'Habitat et du Logement*), or ALPHALOG. In her new role in the commercial market, the former director hopes to continue her advocacy for some of the women's associations she worked with. Her German nationality can facilitate business liaisons with buyers from Germany and other European countries.

The center Working Women sells its pieces to a Malian African arts and crafts boutique owner catering to tourists in the Mopti region, who also exports products to many American destinations. Peace Corps headquarters in Bamako holds annual Malian arts and crafts fairs on their premises where women's groups can sell their items.

Mere access to markets is not a perfect solution. Female informants complain bitterly about the way they are often exploited by predominantly male intermediaries who sell their work on tourist and international markets and profit two to three times more than they do and describe attempts to bypass these by marketing their products through their own group initiatives. All arts and crafts groups in Ségou have established boutiques on their premises.[5] In addition, the women market their work inside of tourist hotel boutiques, and sometimes set up stalls in the regional weekly markets held in Ségou town.

French is the language of the Malian bureaucracy, so to ensure access to bureaucratic structures, women's groups in urban centers select one of the few female members who are highly educated and fluent in French to act on behalf of the association and create partnerships with development organizations. She is officially referred to as the "secretary of external relations."

Even to participate in an association, however, women must strategize to find ways to diminish their household responsibilities. Many associations have secured grants provided by NGOs to build kindergartens on their premises. These are accessible to all the children in the community, but center members receive a discount. A few members have servants to help with domestic tasks, usually young girls from the countryside who are paid low wages. Sometimes female kin are willing to offer aid, and co-wives are willing to rotate responsibilities.

As noted, membership is possible only with permission from the family patriarch. Urban men are often open to their wives' participation in income-generating groups because it might increase their capacity to contribute to household needs. Urban households are more dependent than their rural counterparts on a cash-based economy. NGOs hold consciousness-raising sessions with husbands of potential members to gain their support.

THE BOGOLAN MARKET: THE ROLE MEN AND WOMEN PLAY

Despite multiple variations in visual and physical forms, bogolan always resembles traditional bogolanfini in some way. Producers seek to retain strong similarities between the two forms because tourists traveling in Mali are interested in the cloth's links with rural, indigenous Malian culture. When buying bogolan, tourists are buying a piece of "traditional Mali" (Rovine 2008:41).

Bogolan producers, whether they cater to the fine art, fashion, or tourist markets, have created a broad spectrum of colors that enrich the visual possibilities of the cloth. Rather than using deep black with striking white, as in traditional bogolanfini, contemporary producers experiment with off-whites, grays, and tawny ochres. Unconventional plant- and mineral-based dyes have introduced reds, lemons, yellows, oranges, and a whole range of indigo blues. Instead of traditional lightening agents to create the white portions of the designs, laundry detergent or bleach are applied to achieve brighter whites and increase contrast (Grace 2003:14).

The secret knowledge, once guarded by rural women for finding raw materials necessary for bogolanfini production, is now common knowledge. The women's groups in Ségou, for example, place orders with rural farmers who make deliveries to the centers. Most contemporary Malian producers of bogolan have little or no knowledge of bogolanfini motifs and their symbolic meanings. If used in their work, the old symbols are mixed in with newly created motifs. Art students taking bogolan courses today focus on making figurative designs depicting Malian culture such as dancers, drummers, female figures, and masks (Rovine 2008:66). In contrast, the pioneers of the revitalization of bogolan, such as Groupe Bogolan Kasobane, have significant knowledge of the traditional motifs and incorporate them intentionally in their work (Rovine 2008:70).

In order to streamline bogolanfini's time-consuming production, producers of bogolan will use homemade stencils to mark designs on the cloth. Stencils are made from plastic or metal. A variety of tools are used to apply the color to the cloth; instead of the traditional paintbrush, producers may use European-style paintbrushes, toothbrushes, or recycled squeeze bottles fabricated for lubricating oil (Grace 2003:14). Stencils create a more geometrically consistent pattern on the cloth.

Female informants in Ségou report hand-painted pieces have greater appeal for Western consumers because they are more closely associated with traditional or "primitive" bogolanfini practices. The women's associations primarily produce hand-painted bogolan pagnes containing new geometric motifs selling them either as pagnes or transforming them into other tourist products like toy animals. In contrast, the men in Ségou tend to used more innovative techniques and designs such as a combination of stenciling and hand-painted figurative drawings as their niche in the tourist market. In a culture where labor in a broader context is divided strictly between men and women, it is not surprising that in a radically changing textile form, men and women have differing stylistic approaches.

Although there are some gendered differences in technique and the types of products made, both males and females make accessories such as scarves and housewares such as pillowcases, bedcovers, and curtains for tourists and international markets. As noted, cloth for these items is typically woven locally by men on narrow, single-heddle looms; this is to make the cloth recognizable as traditional and not industrially produced, adding authenticity to the pieces by linking them to traditional bogolanfini (Rovine 2008:37).

Defying traditional gendered roles, which formally would have denied them access to tailoring skills, women are now able to transform the cloth into desired items using the sewing abilities they acquire through the arts and crafts associations. In contrast, because male bogolan producers do not know how to sew, they must rely on male tailors, incurring added cost.

The quality of bogolan products varies. When stencils are used, the amount of time required to produce the cloth is reduced significantly. The mostly male apprentices involved in this type of mass-produced bogolan often have little skill and produce low-quality products with visual mistakes such as stray marks where the mud was accidentally placed on the white parts of the design (Rovine 2008:38–41).

At the other extreme, the fine art–trained entrepreneurs generally produce the highest quality of bogolan. Their figurative drawings and use of design are the most sophisticated. Stray marks are rare. Quality control is high in this context because a person with a formal education in art design is in charge of what is produced, and his apprentices are forced to pay particular attention.

Products produced by women vary as well, with the majority located somewhere between the two extremes of low and high technical skill. Among the women's associations of Ségou, quality varies not only between members but also between the associations themselves. Although individual artistic ability plays a role, in general associations with the greatest number of mud cloth courses offered have the highest overall quality. To compete with trained male artist entrepreneurs like Boubacar Doumbia and his apprentices, however, a woman's group in Ségou will charge lower rates for their products: Work of Women asks U.S. $30 (15,000 CFA) for their bedspreads, while Doumbia's cost U.S. $60 (30,000 CFA).[6] One male artist complains that "women in groups are ruining our market because they charge too little for their work."

The first women's association in the Ségou region involved in bogolanfini production for Western consumers is located approximately thirty kilometers north of Ségou in the town of Markala along the Niger River. In 1975, the women of Markala, with the help of a former schoolteacher Mariam Thiam, started a women's association to provide members with a source of income. The group worked with the American Field Service, a Quaker development organization, and catered to a small demand by expatriates in Bamako interested in bogolanfini cloth. Elderly producers from rural villages on the periphery of Markala were their teachers. Today, while most members of the Markala group produce bogolan pieces, original members still make authentic bogolanfini cloth. Their textiles are put on commission in a shop called The Peasant (*La Paysanne*), which is a major source for bogolan products catering to expatriates in Bamako.

In contrast, the Ségou women's associations involved in bogolan production since the 1990s were taught by men and women predominantly familiar with contemporary bogolan techniques. Sometimes a master male artist is invited to teach a workshop over a short period of time. Associations also invite local urban women who are considered adept in mud cloth techniques but do not belong to an association. These women have learned bogolan skills from family members rather than the art institute. For example, an association in the study invited an older, widowed woman who built her reputation by selling bogolan to Malians in the same neighborhood as the center. She learned the craft from her deceased husband's older brother, who lives in San.[7]

Despite some success in competing with men in the tourist market, males disproportionately dominate international markets, especially the high-end markets where Western consumers often demand high-quality

products. The director for AFE claimed she had serious difficulties finding international buyers for women's bogolan products because "they
aren't as good as what is out there made by men trained in fine art." This
becomes clear when women's work is displayed in their Bamako ware-
house alongside those produced by such artists as Boubacar Doumbia of
Groupe Bogolan Kasobane.

The FNAM may help facilitate access to tourists via craft fairs in Mali,
but when it comes to international markets an informant working for
FNAM reports Western-buyer contacts made via the Internet prefer the
bogolan of male artists they represent more than items produced by
women's groups.

The problem faced by women's arts and crafts associations with boutiques is their dependence on fluctuations in the tourist market and subsequent variations in income generation. European and American tourists
travel to Mali in large numbers during Mali's cold season (approximately
four months long) to escape winter. A successful female producer can
make as much as U.S. $461 (230,000 CFA) a month during the height of
the tourist season, but profit as little as U.S. $30 (15,000 CFA) during the
off season. Such variations in income make it difficult for members to rely
on bogolan sales to meet household necessities.

URBAN WOMEN DOMINATE BOGOLAN PRODUCTION

Urban women dominate bogolan production over rural women due to
two significant factors: (1) development efforts for rural women place
little emphasis upon arts and crafts production; and (2) rural women
confront more barriers such as greater distances from potential tourist
markets and lower levels of literacy.

Development efforts to increase rural women's revenue focus on farming activities—livestock, fowl cultivation, gardening, tree plantations, rice
growing—transforming some of these into goods for sale. Some groups
produce and market fruit tree products (mangos and bananas) and traditional soaps. Household obligations are different as well since rural
women work more hours than their urban counterparts. Development
projects have endorsed machines that grind millet as an alternative to
the traditional and more labor-intensive practice of pounding. Groups of
women are often organized around the maintenance, management, and
marketing of the millet machine (Ministère de la Promotion de la Femme,
de l'Enfant et de la Famille 1995:27).

Wire-fence production is traditionally men's work, but there is a project for teaching rural women this skill in the Ségou region. The urban
Markala women's arts and crafts association is instructing neighboring

rural women's groups in fencing techniques. One member explains that wire fences are in high demand because they keep animals out of gardens. The Markala group is not interested in teaching their rural sisters mud-cloth production because "the market for *bogolan* is too limited. We don't need to create more competition for ourselves."

Some rural women's groups attempt to produce mud cloth despite difficulties reaching potential tourists. When rural women's groups exist they are often located near tourist towns such as Ségou, where they have direct access to foreign buyers. For example, a group of women producing bogolan across the river from Ségou town had numerous problems distributing their cloth. They were dependent on boats that crossed the river only once a week to transport patrons to the weekly regional market, a venue sometimes frequented by tourists who want to experience a traditional African market. These rural women sometimes commissioned the sale of their bogolan pieces by placing them with women's arts and crafts associations in Ségou already constrained by fluctuations in the tourist market. The combined problems caused the group across the river to disband.

Because most Malian women do not speak French, both urban and rural women experience difficulties collaborating with development organizations and communicating with tourists. The problem is exacerbated in rural areas where even fewer women are literate. While many NGOs have representatives who are open to negotiating with rural women's groups, and the success of the group often depends on these partnerships, members are frequently reluctant to make contact because they believe bureaucrats can be condescending. Urban women who speak French are hesitant to request collaboration but feel empowered by membership in women's organizations. As an urban woman who speaks fluent French remarked, "I used to be scared to enter into those places. Since I became a member of the association I have to go there. The glass which was there has been broken."[8]

CONCLUSION

Tourism in Mali and Western consumption of bogolan in international markets has caused major gendered shifts in the production and distribution of a popular African textile. Before commoditization, rural Bamana women were the exclusive manufacturers of the traditional form of the cloth called bogolanfini. The traditional cloth was imbued with symbolic meaning used to protect Bamana women who wore it during significant social events such as weddings and excisions. In contrast, bogolan is made predominantly by urban women and men in search of income, who know little of the cloth's origins and symbolic significance.

Malian men dominate the production and distribution of bogolan because of the social, economic, and political advantages they possess as the more powerful gender in a patriarchal culture. Although the odds are seemingly against them, Malian urban women organized in exclusively all-female arts and crafts associations strategize to empower themselves as agents for change. Members work in collaboration with NGOs and GOs to build their role in the mud-cloth market. As individuals, members must negotiate domestic responsibilities in order to participate in bogolan-group activities. Women in the arts and crafts associations of Ségou attempt to compete with men, particularly in tourist bogolan markets because their products are of good quality and are less expensive than those produced by male artists. They advertise their work to tourists and expatriates in boutiques on their premises and commission their pieces to privately owned stores. Active participation in national craft fairs also aids women in their marketing endeavors.

The situation of female members of arts and crafts associations illustrates the complexity of the effects of tourism and Western consumption on women's socioeconomic status. While rural Malian women have lost their total control over the cloth's production and distribution and the traditional social and economic power it afforded them, commoditization of the cloth has now provided new options for urban women to empower themselves economically.

NOTES

1. The literature on bogolan fails to mention that due to the cloth's appeal, people of neighboring African countries, such as Burkina Faso, have started to make the cloth to cater to their tourist markets and may export to Western destinations as well. Also, Malians immigrating to the United States are producing the cloth with Western materials, then selling it as traditionally African. Some African artifact mail-order catalogues even offer mud-cloth-making kits to American consumers.

2. African textile boutique owner, interview, March 8, 1998.

3. Female member of arts and crafts association, interview, December 8, 2001.

4. Urban NGO coordinator for Women in Ségou, interview, August 15, 2001.

5. Some women's groups have more success than others attracting potential buyers to their boutiques because the boutiques are advantageously located on major roads readily traveled by tourists. In addition, their boutiques are not enclosed within high-walled compounds that obstruct their visibility from potential foreign clients.

6. The exchange rate is based on U.S. $1 as equal to 499 CFA in 2010.

7. San is a town north of Ségou that has become a major center for tourist bogolan production.

8. Female member of arts and crafts association, interview, May 3, 2003.

REFERENCES

Aherne, Tavy. 1992. *Nakunte Diarra: Bogolanfini Artist of the Beledougou*. Blooming-ton: Indiana University Art Museum.

Brett-Smith, Sarah. 1982. *Iron Skin: The Symbolism of Bamana Mud Cloth*. PhD dis-sertation, Department of Art History, Yale University.

———. 1984. Speech Made Visible: Irregular as a System of Meaning. *Empirical Studies of the Arts* 2(2):127–47.

Chambers, Erve. 2000. *Native Tours: The Anthropology of Travel and Tourism*. Long Grove, IL: Waveland Press.

De Jorio, Rosa. 1997. *Female Elites, Women's Formal Associations, and Political Practices in Urban Mali (West Africa)*. PhD dissertation, University of Illinois at Urbana-Champaign.

Diakité, Fatoumata N'Diaye. 1995. *Projet Appui à La Promotion Feminine et Ren-forcement Institutionnel du Commissariat à la Promotion des Femmes*. MLI/95/P06. Bamako, Mali: Commissariat à la Promotion des Femmes.

Duponchel, Pauline. 1995. Bogolan: From Symbolic Material to National Emblem. In *The Art of African Textiles: Technology, Tradition, and Lurex*, ed. John Picton, pp. 36–39. London: Barbican Art Gallery.

Europa World Year Book. 2009. Mali: Statistical Survey. In *The Europa World Year Book vol.* 2:3027–36. London: Routledge.

Farafina Boutique. 2001. *Farafina Boutique Brochure*. Segou, Mali.

FNAM (Fédération Nationale des Artisans du Mali). 2001. *Présentation de la Fé-dération Nationale des Artisans du Mali*. Bamako, Mali: Fédération Nationale des Artisans du Mali.

Giddens, Anthony. 1979. *Central Problems in Social Theory: Action, Structure and Contradiction in Social Analysis*. Berkeley: University of California Press.

Grace, Claire. 2003. *Intersections Dankun: Contemporary Mudcloth of Mali*. Provi-dence, RI: International Gallery for Heritage and Culture.

Imperato, Pascal James, and Marli Shamir. 1970. Bokolanfini: Mudcloth of the Bamana of Mali. *African Arts* 3(4):32–42.

Institut des Sciences Humaines. 1988. *Exode des Femmes au Mali*. Bamako, Mali: Institut des Sciences Humaines.

Koenig, Dolores, Tieman Diarra, and Moussa Sow. 1998. *Innovation and Individu-ality in African Development: Changing Production Strategies in Rural Mali*. Ann Arbor: University of Michigan Press.

Ministère de la Promotion de la Femme, de l'Enfant et de la Famille. 1995. *Rapport National sur la Situation des Femmes au Mali. IViéme Conférence Mondiale*. Bamako, Mali: Ministère de la Promotion de la Femme, de l'Enfant et de la Famille.

Parpart, Jane L., Patricia M. Connelly, and Eudine V. Barriteau. 2000. Appendix. In *Theoretical Perspectives on Gender and Development*, eds. Jane L. Parpart, Pa-tricia M. Connelly, and Eudine V. Barriteau, pp. 203–9. Ottawa: International Development Research Center.

Rovine, Victoria. 2008. *Bogolan: Shaping Culture through Cloth in Contemporary Mali*. Bloomington: Indiana University Press.

Short, Julianne. 1996. *Musokorobaya: Practice, Embodiment, Transition, and Agency in the Lives of Senior Bamana Women of Mali*. PhD dissertation, University of Indiana.

Sissoko, Youssouf. 2000. Swiss contact Etend l'Offre de ses Opportunités aux Artisans Maliennes. *Amina: Le Magazine de la Femme* 6:20.

Turrittin, Jane. 1989. Integrated Literacy. *Comparative Education Review* 33(1):59–76.

Warms, Richard. 1994. Commerce and Community: Paths to Success for Malian Merchants. *African Studies Review* 37(2):97–120.

Index

About the Editors and Contributors

María Cabral is an ecotourism consultant and a lawyer who works to promote alternative secondary education in Hermosillo, Sonora, México.

Beatriz Camarena is a researcher in the Program for Political Ecology and Sustainable Development at the Centro de Investigación en Alimentación y Desarrollo A.C. in Hermosillo, Sonora, México. She obtained her PhD in environmental education from the Universidad de Salamanca, Spain, with additional degrees in methodology of science from the Instituto Politécnico Nacional (México) and in economics from the Universidad de Sonora (México). Her research interests include environmental issues and educational processes, modernization, and cultural and environmental sustainability.

Patricia L. Delaney is an associate professor of anthropology and gender studies at Saint Michael's College, a small liberal arts college in Vermont. She is an applied social anthropologist, with substantial research and field experience in Tonga, East Timor, and Brazil. Her work typically is located at the intersection of academic and applied inquiries. In the Kingdom of Tonga, she conducted applied research during and after her appointment as the associate director of the Peace Corps. Her current ethnographic and applied work in East Timor on gender and the transition to development has appeared in *Practicing Anthropology*. Her major research interests include gender and international development and the role of culture and identity in the midst of sociocultural change. She holds a PhD in anthropology from the University of California, Los Angeles, and a BS in foreign service from Georgetown University.

Alejandro J. Figueroa is a PhD student in anthropology at Southern Methodist University. He received his BA in anthropology from Saint Lawrence University and an MA in applied anthropology from the University of South Florida. His research interests include the archaeology of Mesoamerica and upper Central America, cultural heritage management and policy, and spatial analytical technologies (especially Geographic Information Systems). His current research evaluates how cultural patrimony and archaeological remains on the island of Roatán, Honduras, have been impacted by recent economic development, mass tourism, and urban growth.

Eduwiges Gomez is a community sustainable development consultant who works with the indigenous people of Sonora, México. She holds the MSc degree in regional development from the Centro de Investigación en Alimentación y Desarrollo A.C. in Hermosillo, Sonora, México.

Whitney A. Goodwin is a PhD student in anthropology at Southern Methodist University. She received her BA in archaeology and anthropology from the College of Wooster and an MA in applied anthropology from the University of South Florida. Her research interests include the archaeology of Mesoamerica and upper Central America, ethnoarchaeology, household archaeology, and pre-Hispanic cultural affiliations. Her current research focuses on the cultural affiliations of native Bay Islanders of Honduras as well as the implications of such affiliations for the representation of indigenous groups and heritage tourism in the Bay Islands.

Katrina T. Greene is associate professor of anthropology and intercultural studies at Biola University. Since 1997, she has conducted periodic fieldwork in the townships of Cape Town, South Africa, including her dissertation work (1999–2000) as a Fulbright Scholar, in which she examined the transformation of indigenous savings and credit practices among women for housing development and long-term investment projects in the new South Africa. Her recent work, "Is It Possible to Overcome the 'Tragedy of *Ubuntu*'? The Journey of a Black Women's Economic Empowerment Group in South Africa," is included in the Society for Economic Anthropology volume *Cooperation in Economic and Social Life* (2010). Her current research interests focus on examining local forms of economic empowerment as they relate to the gendered realities of black women in the Cape Town townships.

Jenny Huberman is an assistant professor of anthropology at the University of Missouri–Kansas City. She received her PhD in anthropology from the University of Chicago in 2006. Her research focuses on tourism, childhood, and consumption. She is currently working on a book manuscript titled *Ambivalent Encounters: Children, Tourists and Locals on the Riverfront of Banaras.*

Cindy Isenhour recently completed her PhD in the department of anthropology at the University of Kentucky. Her work centers on an examination of sustainability policy and practice in wealthy, postindustrial urban contexts. Most recently, she conducted fourteen months of research in Sweden with the support of the Wenner-Gren Foundation for Anthropological Research, the American Scandinavian Foundation, the University of Kentucky Graduate School, and the Fulbright Program. Her work has been published in *American Ethnologist* and in several edited collections. Isenhour is currently teaching at the University of Kentucky and at Transylvania University in Lexington, Kentucky.

Rubén Lechuga is a researcher at the Instituto Nacional de Antropología e Historia, México, whose work focuses on the political economy of local sustainable development. He holds a PhD in social anthropology from the Universidad Iberoamericana, México, DF.

Sarah Lockridge teaches in the Women and Gender Studies Program at the University of Southern Maine. She received her PhD in cultural anthropology from American University in Washington, DC, in 2006. As a Peace Corps volunteer, she lived in the Ségou region of Mali from 1992 to 1994 and worked on forestry and agricultural projects. She returned to Mali to conduct her dissertation research, which focused on urban women's arts and crafts associations. Her scholarly interests include development—specifically emic ways of measuring empowerment—economic anthropology, and gender. As an applied anthropologist, she has helped promote more gender-sensitive approaches toward positive change for poor Malian women and has presented her findings to nongovernmental organizations (NGOs) working in Mali.

Brandon D. Lundy is assistant professor of anthropology in the Geography and Anthropology Department at Kennesaw State University, Georgia. He received his PhD from SUNY at Buffalo in 2009. This work was based on ethnographic research examining the intersections of household livelihood strategies, cultural identity, and globalization in a remote village in southwestern Guinea-Bissau, West Africa. He also holds a PhD from Université des Sciences et Technologies de Lille, France. From 1999 to 2001, he served as a U.S. Peace Corps community development volunteer, teaching computer skills in the rural farming town of São Domingos in the West African island nation of Cape Verde. He has authored a number of articles and national and international conference papers, including a "Field Notes" feature in the *Anthropology News*.

Diana Luque is a researcher in the Program for Political Ecology and Sustainable Development and a professor in the MSc program in regional development at the Centro de Investigación en Alimentación y Desarrollo A.C. in Hermosillo, Sonora, México. She obtained her PhD in social and political sciences at the Universidad Nacional Autónoma de México. She is an environmental activist whose research focuses on political ecology, biocultural diversity, and community sustainable development. In 2007, she received the Ecology National Prize, awarded by the government of México.

Sarah Lyon is assistant professor of anthropology at the University of Kentucky. Her research examines the nexus of tourism, consumption, agriculture, and the global economy. She is the author of *Coffee and Community: Maya Farmers and Fair Trade Markets* (2010) and coeditor of *Fair Trade and Social Justice: Global Ethnographies* (2010).

Keely Maxwell is assistant professor of environmental studies at Franklin and Marshall College. She is an environmental anthropologist and has conducted interdisciplinary ethnographic, ecological, and historical research in the Peruvian Andes for over a decade. Her research interests in Machu Picchu include forest-society relations, tourism and development, rural livelihood strategies, and the cultural politics of heritage conservation. She has published on fuelwood politics and household labor in *Human Ecology* and *Human Organization*. Another research project examines *vicuña* conservation and commodification. She recently spent a year as an Agrarian Studies Fellow at Yale University.

Laurie Kroshus Medina is associate professor of anthropology at Michigan State University. From the mid-1980s to the early 1990s, she conducted research on agricultural development in Belize, exploring the ways farmers, plantation laborers, processing companies, and government officials mobilized around collective identities to shape the trajectory of Belizean development. This work culminated in the book *Negotiat-*

ing Economic Development: Identity Formation and Collective Action in Belize. From the late 1990s to the present, she has been studying the ways that economic development and conservation agendas intersect in ecotourism, examining collaborations and conflicts among Belizean and transnational conservation nongovernmental organizations (NGOs), Belizean government officials, upscale ecotourism investors, and Maya communities involved in implementing ecotourism in southern Belize. This research also explores how the development and conservation agendas pursued through ecotourism intersect with struggles by Maya people of southern Belize to obtain secure tenure over the lands they traditionally use.

Moisés Rivera is a researcher in the Regional Development Division at the Centro de Investigación en Alimentación y Desarrollo A.C. in Hermosillo, Sonora, México. His background is in ecology, and he studied at the Centro de Estudios Superiores del Estado de Sonora, México. His main research interests are related to the conservation and sustainable management of natural resources in indigenous territories. For the past several years, he has studied biological monitoring in the indigenous community Comcáac (Seri) and is currently working on an environmental characterization of the Quitovac (Papago).

Paul A. Rivera is associate professor of economics in the Martin V. Smith School of Business and Economics at California State University, Channel Islands. He received a BA in economics from Texas A&M University; an MA in economics from California State University, Long Beach; and a PhD in economics from the University of Southern California. As a specialist in development economics, Rivera's work has addressed a broad array of topics, including educational reform in Taiwan, banking reform in Venezuela, migration and remittances in El Salvador, and the historical development of property rights in Brazil. His current projects focus on the determinants of decline and recovery from the Great Depression in Latin America.

Noel B. Salazar obtained his PhD from the Department of Anthropology at the University of Pennsylvania. He is currently a senior researcher and lecturer at the Faculty of Social Sciences, University of Leuven (Belgium), and visiting research associate at the Centre for Tourism and Cultural Change, Leeds Metropolitan University (UK). His research interests include anthropologies of mobility and travel, the local-to-global nexus, discourses and imaginaries of Otherness, cultural brokering, and cosmopolitanism. He has published widely on these topics, in various languages, and is the author of *Envisioning Eden: Mobilizing Imaginaries in Tourism and Beyond* (2010). He is on the editorial boards of *Social Anthropology, Annals* *of Tourism Research, International Journal of Tourism Anthropology, Mondes du Tourisme,* and *AIBR—Revista de Antropología Iberoamericana,* as well as on UNWTO's and UNESCO's official roster of consultants.

Patricia L. Salido is a researcher and teaching staff member in the MSc program in regional development at the Centro de Investigación en Alimentación y Desarrollo A.C. in Hermosillo, Sonora, México. She is an economist (with degrees from the Universidad de Sonora and the University College London) whose main research interests center on regional specialization processes, particularly in the services sector. Over the last decade, she has conducted several studies on tourism, including health tourism and sustainable tourism planning.

Robert Shepherd is assistant professor of anthropology and international affairs at The George Washington University in Washington, DC. His work on tourism and heritage issues has appeared in *Consumption, Markets, and Culture; Tourist Studies; Heritage Management;* and the *Journal of Contemporary Asia,* among other publications. He has also written an ethnographic study of Washington's Eastern Market, a weekend street fair (*When Culture Goes to Market,* 2007). His research interests are Chinese culture and society, the moral framework of marketplace behavior, and the politics of cultural heritage. Before becoming an academic, he served as a Peace Corps volunteer in Nepal and worked with the United Nations in China and Indonesia. He is currently engaged on a joint field project analyzing the impact of World Heritage status on local residents of Mount Wutai, China.

Amy Speier is an assistant professor of anthropology at Eckerd College. She earned her PhD from the University of Pittsburgh with her dissertation, "Czech Balneotherapy: From Public Health to Health Tourism." This research focused on the transformation of balneotherapy, a traditional Czech healing technique that involves complex drinking and bathing therapies, as it was increasingly being incorporated into the development of a Czech health tourism industry. Over the last few years, she has been conducting ethnographic research with patients and owners of Web-based companies that facilitate travel for North Americans to visit the Czech Republic for in vitro fertilization. She is focusing her attention on the ways in which patient travelers are making decisions to travel abroad for care, the networks that are established between North American patient travelers, and their experiences in Czech clinics.

E. Christian Wells is associate professor of anthropology, director of the Office of Sustainability, and deputy director of the Patel School of Global

Sustainability at the University of South Florida. He received his BA from Oberlin College and his MA and PhD in anthropology from Arizona State University. He is an environmental archaeologist whose research seeks new directions in sustainable tourism by examining the influence of environmental worldviews on economic decision-making. He has undertaken field research in Honduras, Guatemala, Belize, and Mexico. His current work focuses on the fate of heritage tourism and cultural patrimony in postcoup Honduras. He has written or edited six books and journal issues, including *Dimensions of Ritual Economy* (with P. A. McAnany) and *Mesoamerican Ritual Economy* (with K. L. Davis-Salazar), as well as more than eighty-five articles, chapters, and reviews.